STUDIES IN IMPERIALISM

general editor John M. MacKenzie

When the 'Studies in Imperialism' series was founded more than twenty years ago, emphasis was laid upon the conviction that 'imperialism as a cultural phenomenon had as significant an effect on the dominant as on the subordinate societies'. With more than fifty books published, this remains the prime concern of the series. Cross-disciplinary work has indeed appeared covering the full spectrum of cultural phenomena, as well as examining aspects of gender and sex, frontiers and law, science and the environment, language and literature, migration and patriotic societies, and much else. Moreover, the series has always wished to present comparative work on European and American imperialism, and particularly welcomes the submission of books in these areas. The fascination with imperialism, in all its aspects, shows no sign of abating, and this series will continue to lead the way in encouraging the widest possible range of studies in the field. 'Studies in Imperialism' is fully organic in its development, always seeking to be at the cutting edge, responding to the latest interests of scholars and the needs of this ever-expanding area of scholarship.

Imperial citizenship

MANCHESTER
1824

Manchester University Press

Imperial citizenship

EMPIRE AND THE QUESTION OF BELONGING

Daniel Gorman

MANCHESTER UNIVERSITY PRESS
Manchester and New York

distributed exclusively in the USA by
PALGRAVE

Copyright © Daniel Gorman 2006

The right of Daniel Gorman to be identified as the author of this work has been asserted by him in accordance with the Copyright, Designs and Patents Act 1988.

Published by Manchester University Press
Oxford Road, Manchester M13 9NR, UK
and Room 400, 175 Fifth Avenue, New York, NY 10010, USA
www.manchesteruniversitypress.co.uk

Distributed in the United States exclusively by
Palgrave Macmillan, 175 Fifth Avenue,
New York, NY 10010, USA

Distributed in Canada exclusively by
UBC Press, University of British Columbia, 2029 West Mall,
Vancouver, BC, Canada V6T 1Z2

British Library Cataloguing-in-Publication Data is available

Library of Congress Cataloging-in-Publication Data is available

ISBN 978 0 7190 8214 6 paperback

First published by Manchester University Press in hardback 2006

This paperback edition first published 2010

Printed by Lightning Source

For Jo

CONTENTS

Acknowledgements—page ix
General editor's introduction—xi
List of abbreviations—xiii

1 Imperial citizenship — page 1

Part I Theories of imperial citizenship

2 Lionel Curtis: imperial citizenship as a prelude to world government — 40

3 John Buchan, romantic imperialism, and the question of who belongs — 77

4 The imperial garden: Arnold White and the parochial view of imperial citizenship — 115

Part II Experiments in imperial citizenship

5 Richard Jebb, intra-imperial immigration, and the practical problems of imperial citizenship — 146

6 'Practical imperialism': Thomas Sedgwick and imperial emigration — 178

7 The failure of imperial citizenship — 205

Appendices—217
Bibliography—226
Index—239

ACKNOWLEDGEMENTS

I have benefited from the help of many people in the research for and the preparation of this book. Research funding was generously provided by the Social Sciences and Humanities Research Council of Canada, the Ontario Government, Trent University, and the Fuller Scholarship at McMaster University. The staff at the following archives gave both their time and their expertise: the Bodleian Library; the Institute of Commonwealth Studies at the University of London; Mills Library at McMaster University; the National Archives (Kew); the National Archives of Canada (Ottawa); the National Maritime Museum; Queen's University; Rhodes House, Oxford; and the Royal Commonwealth Society Library at Cambridge University.

Richard Rempel has been an inspirational and supportive mentor. I have profited immensely from discussions with David Barrett, Stephen Brooke, Jim Greenlee, Stephen Heathorn, Peter Henshaw, David Leeson, Greg Stott, and John Weaver; from the comments of the anonymous readers; and from the work of the many scholars on which I have drawn. My thanks go also to everyone at Manchester University Press for their hard work in preparing the book. My parents, Barry and Linda, have supported me from the beginning, and as modest repayment I offer this addition to their shelves. Finally, as with everything else, Jo has made this book much better than it would have been without her.

GENERAL EDITOR'S INTRODUCTION

The Edwardian Age is a paradoxical period in the history of both Britain and the British Empire. Often described as the climax of the 'long nineteenth century,' as a final 'Indian summer' of the social mores and political tone of the Victorian era, it has also been seen as a time of considerable change, which stimulated much apprehension and uncertainty. The bourgeoisie had come to occupy key positions in political, commercial, and intellectual life. For the working classes, standards of living were rising while emigration opportunities still beckoned. The territories of settlement of the Empire, the 'dominions', were emerging as significant new entities with Australia and, from 1910, South Africa joining Canada and New Zealand as federated or united states. The cities of these colonies, together with their cultural, religious and intellectual institutions – schools, universities, museums, theatres, societies, churches, cathedrals – had come to rival those of the so-called 'mother country' while their economies clearly exhibited independently strong and multilateral relationships. Yet the 'dominions' still lacked full control over their foreign or defence policies. Many legal and constitutional, as well as cultural, links to the imperial metropole remained in place.

It was, in other words, a transitional era in which characteristics of the past survived into a time of palpable change. The First World War would emphasise this yet further. The War appeared to confirm imperial loyalties in all sorts of ways (once the pro-German Boer revolt in South Africa had been suppressed), but by the war's end it was clear that it had been a tremendous catalyst of dominions' nationalism, as well as a stimulant to independence movements in India and elsewhere. The war had appeared to become a joint imperial project, even to the extent of the creation of an imperial War Cabinet, but fragmentation was inherent in the activities and ambitions of the politicians and the sense of separate nationalism engendered in its participants. The foundation of the League of Nations emphasized this, not least because the mandates system, in effect, turned New Zealand, Australia, and South Africa into minor, regional, imperial powers in their own right.

We can now see that what was happening was simply the historical working-out of the whole series of transformations resulting from the previous war, the Anglo-Boer War of 1899–1902. Canadian, Australian, and New Zealand contingents had also been involved in that war, but its effects had been to point up weakness rather than strength. Industrialism and the social conditions of British cities had appeared to produce the degeneration of the so-called British 'race,' leading some to believe that its only hope lay in the new climatic and environmental conditions of those very dominions. The imperial power was also isolated, driving it first into an alliance with Japan, the supposed Britain of the Far East, and then *ententes* with France and Russia. Many social and military reforms were put in place, together with a

GENERAL EDITOR'S INTRODUCTION

significant rethinking of naval policy. It was consequently a time when a ferment of ideas, based upon often exaggerated fears, was characteristic of British and imperial life. The emergence of a new, and potentially highly dangerous, enemy in the shape of Germany (what J. A. Cramb in 1913 called 'our enemy of enemies,' the equivalent of France in the eighteenth century and Spain in the sixteenth) sharpened and hurried the character and pace of reform.

In the light of all of this, it is perhaps not surprising that it was also a time of intensive thinking about the imperial relationship, particularly as it involved what were perceived as transplanted British communities overseas. Daniel Gorman's book provides an exceptionally valuable comparative study of many of the ideas circulating in this period, particularly those relating to notions of imperial citizenship. These appeared to offer a variety of heady solutions to contemporary problems of cooperation and unity, all of which turned out to be, in one way or another, chimerical. Gorman usefully examines these through the thinking of five key figures, Lionel Curtis, John Buchan, Arnold White, Richard Jebb, and Thomas Sedgwick. Their approaches were different, though inter-related or complementary. And all connected, more or less, to the concluding gestures in the direction of forms of imperial federation, concepts of national efficiency, ideas that have been dubbed 'social imperialism', emigration schemes, and many scientific and pseudo-scientific ideas connected with germ theory, micro-biology, eugenics, and much else. It was an era in which many societies (including women's organizations) were founded to promote such programmes, when the literature of such figures as H. G. Wells, Arthur Conan Doyle, and Buchan himself reflected both the anxieties and the perceived solutions.

Gorman's book will do much to explain the welter of imperial ideas circulating in the period.

John M. MacKenzie

LIST OF ABBREVIATIONS

CAB	Cabinet Office
CJH	*Canadian Journal of History*
CG	Correspondence General
CO	Colonial Office
CUB	Central Unemployment Body
EHR	*English Historical Review*
EIO	Emigrants' Information Office
FO	Foreign Office
HO	Home Office
JBH	*Journal of British History*
JICH	*Journal of Imperial and Commonwealth History*
JRSA	*Journal of the Royal Society of Arts*
LRCS	Library of the Royal Commonwealth Society
MHTD	*Memory Hold The Door*
MSS	manuscript series
NAC	National Archives of Canada
NMM	National Maritime Museum
OHBE	*Oxford History of the British Empire*
OSC	Over-Seas Club
PRCI	*Proceedings of the Royal Colonial Institute*
QUA	Queen's University Archives, Kingston
RCI	Royal Colonial Institute
RG	record group
RSSG	Royal Society of St George
RTPLC	Round Table Papers of Lionel Curtis
TNA PRO	The National Archives (Public Record Office), Kew

CHAPTER ONE

Imperial citizenship

> So the tribune came and said to him, 'Tell me, are you a Roman citizen?'
> And he said, 'Yes.' The tribune answered, 'I bought this citizenship for a large sum.'
> Paul said, 'But I was born a citizen.' So those who were about to examine him withdrew from him instantly; and the tribune also was afraid, for he realized that Paul was a Roman citizen and that he had bound him.
> (Act 22: 27–9)

As all early twentieth-century British schoolchildren knew, Great Britain presided over an Empire upon which the sun never set. Yet the Empire itself was not a unified state, the solid red on imperial maps belying the dizzying array of political identities which existed under the Union Jack. Some Britons believed this diversity spoke to the legitimacy of the nation's imperial rule, and saw Empire as a vehicle of peace and progress. Others feared the loss of an Anglo-European cultural identity, and sought to reassert British values at the expense of indigenous local identities. Adherents of each view saw in the idea and the institution of citizenship the means through which to pursue their goals. They sought to create an imperial citizenship, an idea which consisted of two interconnected parts: the desire to foster a greater sense of a shared imperial identity and the effort to codify this shared identity in law. This book examines how imperial ideologues used the language of imperial citizenship as part of broader discourses concerning the purpose, the constitution, and the future of Empire in the late nineteenth and early twentieth centuries.

Citizenship is a primary means through which societies assert, construct, and consecrate their sense of identity. It is about who belongs to the nation, who does not, and why. Citizenship thus connotes a sense of civic belonging, comprising both social and legal–political identities. Debates about imperial citizenship expanded these questions of belonging to the Empire, and thus help us assess how Britons conceived of the Empire: was it an extension of the nation state, a separate entity in itself, or a type of 'world state'? What was the relation of individual members of the Empire to the broader collective? Efforts to create an imperial citizenship were thus efforts to integrate cultural, social, and political identities within a broader *imperial* identity. The institution of citizenship provides a practical window through which to view the political ideology of Empire and how it was modified in the face of growing colonial autonomy. The concept of citizenship was much on the lips of British imperial thinkers and activists in the late-Victorian and Edwardian eras, the result of both an increased sense of international military and economic competition and domestic pressures for greater social, economic, and political equality.[1] Defining the 'national identity' became an urgent collective task. Debates about imperial citizenship were debates about the place of Empire in British society, its importance to the national identity, and the degree to which imperial subjects were or were not seen as 'fellow Britons.' The imperial ideologues who participated in these debates, in the main conservatives but also including liberal imperialists, saw in the idea of imperial citizenship a means of fostering imperial unity and cementing Britain's status as the leading imperial power in an increasingly competitive geopolitical world. In seeking to create an imperial citizenship, however, they faced the challenge of developing political and cultural bonds under the aegis of an Empire which was not, in and of itself, a state.

The Empire constituted part of the mental infrastructure of men and women in the late nineteenth and early twentieth centuries, as unquestionably permanent and benign, if not indeed benevolent, as were the Thames or the Lowlands of Scotland. Neither ardent imperialists, such as the Round Table's co-founder Lionel Curtis and the writer and politician John Buchan, nor critics of Empire, such as the liberal writer and economist J. A. Hobson, saw the British imperium as *wrong* in any absolute sense. Their differences were in degree, not in kind. Indeed, one would be hard-pressed to find in late-Victorian or Edwardian Britain any audible voice calling for the dismantling of Empire. Criticism of Empire in the pre-1920 era was, on the whole, reminiscent of the 'Little Englandism' of Richard Cobden and the Manchester School, rather than a denunciation of Empire in and of itself. J. A. Hobson and E. D. Morel, for instance, criticized the economic exploitation they believed imperialism made possible; the pro-Boers opposed war (or, perhaps more accurately, its excesses) in South Africa; and the Independent Labour Party (ILP) position on Empire was framed in pacifist, anti-militarist language.[2] What did exist were many competing commentaries on how imperialism ought to be managed. Even that most famous of tracts on Empire, Joseph Conrad's *Heart of Darkness*, is not so much the work of an anti-imperialist, but rather a morality play which at its core asserted that we, the British, really were much more humane at this sort of thing than were the debased Belgians. As such, the debate was not whether imperialism was 'just,' or 'fair,' or 'right,' but rather how was it to be constituted? Who belonged? Did all under the British flag have equal rights and responsibilities, or did there exist a scale of difference? If so, why? And how, finally, were such issues to be weighed? These are the questions with which this book is concerned.

By the late nineteenth century, many imperialists viewed the Empire as a means of advancing Britain's national interest and maintaining its political and cultural influence abroad. Alfred, Lord Milner, Pro-Consul in South Africa and later a member of Lloyd George's War Cabinet, epitomized this position. Milner argued that the task of imperial decision-makers at the century's end was now one of consolidation, the strengthening of bonds between the existing components of the imperial family, rather than further aggrandizement. Indeed, Milner had been drawn to the conservative rather than liberal fold because of his conviction that the 'nation,' rather than the individual, must be the basic building-block of society.[3] To preserve, to maintain, to solidify, to perpetuate – these were the stated goals of imperial actors of the late-Victorian and Edwardian periods, many of whom shared Milner's view of society as an organic whole. It is precisely through an understanding of these impulses that the historian can come to grasp the 'imperial mind', that particular set of individuals, assumptions, perceptions, prejudices, and hopes which influenced the geopolitical shape of Empire. Such an understanding is not focused on a study of the 'official mind,' that amorphous body of decision-makers which some historians have identified as responsible for the shape and thrust of British imperialism in the long nineteenth century, especially in the era of the 'new imperialism.'[4] Neither, though, is the present project one in the model of the *Annales* school, an attempt to capture in its totality the imperial *ethos* or *mentalité*. The British Empire still awaits its Braudel, and given the immensity of the Empire, both physically and metaphysically, such a project may be, if not impossible, highly improbable. The Empire defies a 'definitive' explanation, a truth demonstrated by the many 'definitive' or general explanations that have been offered from numerous separate and mutually exclusive perspectives.

What this book *does* present is an exegesis of one distinct strand of the imperial thought-web – the idea of imperial citizenship in the late-Victorian and Edwardian periods. The institution of citizenship, the basis of any discussion of imperial unity or cooperation, deserves closer scrutiny. The notion of imperial citizenship can provide historians with a partial map of the imperial mind of the pre-Great War period, offering insight into the political development of Empire, as well as the vast discrepancies in the benefits and the status of different classes of *citizens*.

The purpose of this book is thus to examine the development of ideals of a common imperial citizenship as derived and propagated by British imperial ideologues between 1895 and 1920. Debates over imperial citizenship took place within the relatively small circle of Britons drawn from the educated and aristocratic elites who constituted what Stefan Collini has termed the 'upper ten thousand.' Many of these individuals, most of them men, were Oxbridge educated. As such, a small number of interconnected, and often interrelated, individuals wielded an inordinate degree of influence in both the political and intellectual worlds of late-Victorian and Edwardian Britain. These same individuals were in turn selected for key imperial positions abroad, and as such constituted a nexus of imperial influence binding the Empire to the metropole.[5]

Who were the 'British imperial ideologues' who advanced arguments of imperial citizenship? Though Disraeli had tried in the 1870s to capture Empire as the political preserve of the Conservative Party, by the late nineteenth century imperialism had become increasingly bi-partisan. On the Left, leading Fabians such as Beatrice and Sidney Webb and G. B. Shaw supported Empire as a means of more quickly spreading the democratic socialist reforms the society advocated, though other members of the society disagreed. The British trade union movement was also concerned with its counterparts in the colonies, and sent representatives to guide the colonials in tactics and strategy. This concern became more overtly paternalistic in the interwar period, when British labour leaders criticized the political and sometimes violent nature of colonial worker unrest. The Trades Union Congress even worked directly with the Colonial Office to train moderate labour leaders in the colonies.[6] The Liberal Party also turned increasingly to pro-imperial policies after Gladstone's death. Liberal imperialists such as Grey, Asquith, and especially Rosebery, identified themselves with imperial policies in an effort to shed the party's 'Little Englander' image.[7] Imperialism's broad appeal was also evident in the increasingly popular ceremonial celebrations of Empire, publicly casting the national identity in imperial hues.[8] Queen Victoria's Diamond Jubilee (1897), the imperial *durbars* of Edward VII (1903) and George V (1911), both in Delhi, and the introduction in 1904 of an annual Empire Day all speak to the public nature of Empire in the late nineteenth and early twentieth centuries.[9] It was within conservative circles, however, that the most fervent discussions of imperial citizenship were to be found. There were several reasons for this situation: many of the imperial organizations and discussion forums of the period, such as the Navy League, the Tariff Reform League, and the Royal Colonial Institute, were conservative bodies;[10] many Edwardian imperial ideologues had been either directly or indirectly influenced by Milner; and the Tories themselves sought to shed their image as the party of 'the classes' in favour of a re-branding as the representatives of the 'patriotic public.'[11]

British conservatism was never a collective body, united in pedigree and pronouncement. Indeed, the late Victorian and Edwardian periods bore witness to great cleavages among conservatives. The tariff controversy split the party itself into contrary factions,[12] a dispute which ultimately cost Arthur Balfour[13] the party leadership in 1911. In terms of political philosophy, British conservatives since the Reform Act of 1867 had been caught between the Scylla of electoral reform, and its attendant intensification of mass politics, and the Charybdis of maintaining their political base within 'the upper ten thousand.' Their response, predictably, was to defend the status quo, a position pursued with great success by that most practical of prime ministers, Lord Salisbury: 'The perils of change are so great, the promise of the most hopeful theories is so often deceptive, that is it frequently the wiser part to uphold the existing state of things, if it can be done, even though, in point of argument, it should be utterly indefensible.'[14] The 'existing state of things' in terms of Empire was fortuitously favourable to conservatives for much of the pre-1920 generation.[15] The Empire was at its apex, despite the claims of historians such as Max Beloff that it contained the seeds of its own imminent destruction.[16] Historians have mistaken the triumphalism thus expressed by conservative voices for unanimity. However, the differences apparent in domestic conservative politics were also apparent tactically and ideologically regarding Empire. Most significant for a study of imperial citizenship is the division between those who advocated a parochial, *nationalist*, imperial citizenship and those who supported a nascent, *cosmopolitan*, imperial citizenship.

E. H. H. Green's description of the Conservative Party as 'if not the "stupid party" then an institution lacking a deep interest in ideas'[17] expresses the orthodox view. In contrast to the Edwardian Left, wellspring of both British socialism and the 'New Liberalism', the Tories have been identified with no emergent, or indeed coherent, ideas at all. Green disputes this notion by reference to the study of political economy in which, he argues, conservatives were profitably engaged.[18] Imperialism itself is a second area where conservatives were intellectually active.[19]

However, because many of their ideas concerning Empire proved ultimately unsuccessful, at least in their original form, conservative imperialism has usually been portrayed as reactionary, the dying embers of Victorian expansionism. Salisbury, Balfour, and Bonar Law, Unionist leaders from 1895–1923, were each practitioners of *realpolitik*, carefully balancing the concerns of policy, party unity, and the polls in search of political equilibrium. Beneath this search for stability was a concern for Empire both as political position and as idea. The two dominant conservative political positions during this era, tariff reform and opposition to Home Rule, were not solely national issues. Domestic debates over 'the Big Loaf' and Ulster were also debates about Empire, and it was the issue of Empire which the Unionists sought to make their own, for better and worse, in the Edwardian era.[20]

Conservative imperialism was dominated above all by the anxiety of perceived national decline.[21] Salisbury's Government[22] feared national isolation, and looked to Empire as the means of maintaining Britain's status as a Great Power in the face of growing economic and political competition from Germany, the United States, France, and Russia. Britain's victory in the South African War (1899–1902), the most significant imperial event of the period, had two important consequences. One was to tarnish Milner as an illiberal expansionist, charges which played a role in the Unionists' disastrous defeat in the election of 1906. The other was to initiate the age of 'efficiency.' 'National efficiency'[23] became a byword for reform – reform of the army, of the navy, of public health, of education, and of imperial organization itself. Even tariff reform, which split the party in the wake of Chamberlain's inaugural speech in favour of protection on May 15, 1903, in Birmingham, can be seen as part of the broader 'national efficiency' debate.

This anxiety of decline paradoxically pushed imperialists to support more liberal reforms as means of preserving imperial unity and securing Britain's strategic interests. Indeed, something of a minor constitutional revolution transpired in these years. Joseph Chamberlain signalled the growing political importance of Empire by choosing the Colonial Office in Salisbury's 1895 Cabinet,[24] and the party interpreted its victory in the 'Khaki' election of 1900 as a mandate for imperial change.[25] The Colonial and Imperial Conferences, the 1907 decision to formally describe the self-governing colonies as 'dominions,' and the Union of South Africa Act and the Morley-Minto Reforms (both in 1909) each reflected imperial influences within Asquith's Liberal Government.

The conservative-dominated National Government under Lloyd George created the Imperial War Cabinet in 1917 and passed the Government of India Act (1919). All these measures were important constitutional markers in the evolution of a more decentralized Empire.[26]

Domestic and imperial concerns and ideas were thus fused in the conservative mind in a manner which was less pronounced in the Liberal and nascent Labour camps. Out of this environment emerged a generation of men who became conservatives, rather than liberals or socialists, because they believed in organic stability, collective rather than individual action, the importance of imperial tradition, and the intellectual fallibility of man. They were sceptical of man's ability to govern himself through moral and rational self-awareness and self-improvement, and sought instead collective solutions to governance, both public and private. In Empire, they found an institution perfectly suited to these tasks.

Studying ideas

Rather than present the late Victorian and Edwardian debate concerning imperial citizenship *in toto*, or examine imperial pressure groups,[27] I present a series of intellectual biographies, biographies which should be envisioned as beads on a thread, part of a linked public discussion on imperial governance and the identity of the imperial citizen. Instead of treating their ideas in a teleological manner – viewing Adam Smith as the founder of the market or August Comte in terms of the creation of sociology – I aim to treat them within their historical context. The book thus borrows from the pattern of intellectual history advanced by historians such as Stefan Collini and John Burrow, who have positioned intellectual history as the historical recovery of 'the thought of the past in its complexity.'[28]

Individuals, not amorphous social forces, it is argued here, are the kinetic elements of history. Intellectual biography provides an ideal method by which to measure and to reconstruct such thought and context. What is of significance for the intellectual historian are the ideas which contemporaries recorded, argued, and propagated. Of less importance are the quotidian details of individual's lives, excepting when these impinged upon their thoughts and ideas. For these reasons, the intellectual historian must tread warily in attributing hidden or unconscious motives to his or her subjects. The written record rarely betrays clear evidence of such motives. What does emerge from the study of actions is *intent* or *purpose*, which may be differentiated from motive in that actions do not incorporate psychic reasoning.[29] Thus, historians can interrogate their subjects, but should be wary of, as has become fashionable among writers of creative non-fiction, 'imagin[ing] their way into their subject's experiences.'[30]

In focusing on imperial ideas, there are related issues of importance which can be addressed here only in tangential fashion: specifically, the role played in the definition of imperial citizenship by gender dynamics,[31] the perennial problem of Ireland,[32] education,[33] and psephology[34] are accorded little attention. There are also geopolitical limitations, though these reflect the concerns of contemporaries themselves. While bearing in mind the importance to Empire of the dependencies, especially India,[35] the historical focus of the present argument is Great Britain and its relationship with the white-settlement colonies, known after 1907 as 'the dominions.' Frederick Cooper and Ann Stoler have called attention to the need to integrate the study of the metropole and that of the colonies. While they had in mind work on the dependent colonies, their point also hold for studies of Britain and the settlement colonies, as Simon Potter has noted.[36] Contemporary imperialists devoted most of their attention and energies to relations with the dominions. This devotion reflected the sense of community built through emigration, the shared experience of the South African War, and economic investment. Though interest in the dependencies was of course not absent, Britons by and large did not feel for them the sense of shared identity they found with the dominions.

This myopia concerning the dependent Empire was largely due to imperial ideologues' blinkered views on race. Benedict Anderson has written that 'no one in their right mind would deny' the racist nature of the British Empire.[37] 'Race', however, is a notoriously slippery term, and one which contemporaries used in many different ways. As Douglas Lorimer has observed, late Victorian racial discourse was fluid, marked by discontinuities rather than any essential character.[38] If the language of race was pervasive in the social and political climate of the time, contemporaries nonetheless held disparate and often contradictory ideas about what race actually meant.[39] Some, such as the Victorian Charles Lamb, averred that class, not race, was the primary categorical descriptive: 'The human species, according to the best theory I can form of it, is composed of two distinct races, the men who borrow, and the men who lend.'[40] The liberal humanist Gilbert Murray, meanwhile, believed that

> there is in the world a hierarchy of races. The bounds of it are not, of course, absolute and rigid, but on the whole, it seems that those nations which eat more, claim more, and get higher wages, will direct and rule the others, and the lower work will ... be done by the lower breeds of man.[41]

Others, such as the anatomist Robert Knox and the writer and civil servant Benjamin Kidd, took up the language of social Darwinism, evincing biological and anthropological racism in asserting the superiority of British rule. The waters were further muddied by the common conflation of 'race' and 'culture.' These various racial discourses helped shape Britons' perceptions of the non-white members of the Empire; and they had become increasingly strident in the half-century after the Indian Mutiny. The Empire was thus constructed along racial lines, as evidenced by the attitude of white settlers toward the Maori in New Zealand, the Asians in Australia, and the indigenous peoples in South Africa, to give but three examples. It is less clear whether Britons pursued Empire because they held racialist ideas or whether they held racialist ideas because they pursued Empire.[42] Whichever was the case, proponents of imperial citizenship certainly drew upon ideas of race in multiple and often contradictory ways,[43] as will be made clear in the following chapters.

Citizenship and imperial history

Imperial historians have not in the main concerned themselves with the study of citizenship.[44] Several factors account for this lacuna, foremost among which is the consideration that no individual was ever legally a *citizen* of the Empire. Citizenship, after all, is technically a republican notion. In British law the unifying legal structure is the crown: all individuals living under the crown are subject to its sovereignty, and thus are *subjects* rather than citizens. Historians' attention has consequently been drawn to the construction of the sovereign State, and the dissemination of this political model throughout the Empire.[45]

Second, historians have tended to focus on citizenship in primarily domestic terms. Much important work has been done explaining the integration, or lack thereof, of immigrants into British society.[46] Work in this field is concentrated on the late and the post-imperial era, when immigration from the Empire became a political issue in Britain. Others have used citizenship as a rubric to assess, in Pat Thane's words, the 'important ways, through welfare and other measures, [in which] the British state helped shape the identities of inhabitants of Britain and Empire.'[47] Such studies have helped immensely in illustrating how 'Britishness' was constructed along class and gender lines, but, while they also incorporate imperial themes, they tend to do so in a centrifugal manner. In both of these cases, citizenship is understood as primarily a political identity, centered around the expansion of political rights, especially the franchise. As I hope to show, the language of citizenship in the late Victorian and Edwardian eras combined such political discourse with a broader social identity of 'Britishness' which held that an attachment to and a participation in civic life were necessary precursors to formal citizenship. In short, the language of imperial citizenship also functioned as the consecration of cultural connection. Just as Christian confirmation is achieved only once an individual has shown herself committed to the Church community, conversant in its beliefs, so citizenship was seen as the acknowledgement of a demonstrated commitment to the socio-political community.

Finally, and most importantly, the study of citizenship has often been lost among broader concerns. Until the late 1970s, imperial historians cast their gaze primarily upon politico-military, economic, or social imperial explanations of empire.[48] The place of the individual was often lost among such macro-historical concerns. This imbalance has been addressed in recent decades by historians interested in how imperialism shaped British culture. Despite claims to the contrary, the critical mass of cultural studies of imperialism show it had a strong, if not always consistent, resonance for Britons, particularly in the late nineteenth and twentieth centuries.[49] Post-colonial scholars have also been interested in issues of imperialism and identity, though their focus is mainly on race and class rather than citizenship itself. This has been both post-colonialism's strength and its weakness: drawing critical attention to the heretofore neglected or assumed power structures of Empire, while simultaneously deflecting attention from an assessment of Britain's (and Britons') imperial ideologies and identities. While scholars have recently begun to correct this imbalance, such as in the engaging work of Catherine Hall,[50] more needs to be done. If post-colonialism has a unifying principle, it is that, as in war, the first casualty of imperialism is the truth: 'Conquest entailed not only mastery of peoples and ecologies, but also the conquest of truth itself.' To overcome the privileged version of the truth offered by the colonizer, post-colonialism seeks to provide a hermeneutical procedure aimed at dislodging and exposing the master narratives of race, class and gender which both dominated European thought and underpinned imperialism.[51] The main shortcoming of such work is that it sometimes conceives of the imperial power, and of imperialism itself, as a *deus ex machina*, obscuring any nuanced understanding of dynamics at the metropole, and conflating disparate individuals and time periods. As Rhonda Cobham has argued, studies of the colonial world, particularly those contributing to 'the Black Nationalist project,' often obscure the multi-valenced fluidity of colonial discourse by contrasting either a 'monolithic' imperial power with a marginalized and dispersed colonial other or a debased imperial power and a heroic colonial resistance.[52]

Post-colonial work has also under-examined the idea of citizenship because it conceptualizes individuals as 'histories', as an accumulation of experiences in relation to the accumulation of experiences of others. This has led some critics to lament what they see as an over-reliance on theory at the expense of an empirical base,[53] though there is evidence to counter this claim.[54] More specifically, by conceiving of past individuals as always provisionary, post-colonial studies can rob them of their objective outline, of their context. They cease, in effect, to have a present. While our spatial and geographical lives may be important, they are always dependent on our temporal existence. Human beings *are*: they are active, not passive, beings. They are not subjects in and of themselves – they are subjects only in the minds of others. If discourse and experiential relations dictate human existence, then an individual alone would and could not exist. As Defoe's Robinson Crusoe illustrates, man has an objective, as well as a subjective, essence.[55]

By analyzing both my subjects' thought on the issue of imperial citizenship and how that thought created and reinforced new discourses of imperialism, I am attempting to unite the objective and subjective identities of late Victorian and Edwardian imperialists. I am aware of the criticism that such a project risks appropriating Empire as a canvass upon which an essentially nationalist history is painted.[56] I would argue, however, that to properly understand how the intrinsically unbalanced power relationships constitutive of Empire were constructed, it is essential to examine the ideologies employed by the dominant power: in this instance, the British. This is not to apologize for Empire, a trap into which Niall Ferguson's *Empire* falls, but rather to explain imperial ideas and policies in their historical specificity.[57] To explain is not to condone. Here I would distance myself from post-colonialism's presentist political underpinnings.[58] Post-colonialism itself is an inherently teleological undertaking. It seeks to understand the progress and process of the emancipation of various under-represented groups (whether self-identified, ascribed by the colonial power, or identified *ex post facto*) in the broadly defined 'colonial' and 'post-colonial' historical period. The shortcoming of post-colonialism is not, then, that it paints Britons in a negative light, as some more reductionist critics lament (other historiographies, after all, have their heroes and villains – workers and industrialists for Marxists, constitution builders and 'regressive' nationalists for Whigs); rather, the attention it gives to discourse in an effort to rebalance or rediscover the historical lives of colonial subjects tends to occlude the motivations of the dominant imperial power. I seek to contribute a better understanding of Britain's role in the construction of imperial discourses by reassembling, in the mode of an intellectual archaeologist, the fragments of ideas left by imperial ideologues, contextualizing them with both our narrative of Empire and the various colonial discourses scholars have drawn to our attention. Such a reconstitution of the imperial mental world is particularly important for the late Victorian and Edwardian periods, for it was then that the intersection of exterior concerns (increased foreign economic and military competition, the rise of colonial nationalism) and interior concerns (the national efficiency movement, class and suffragette unrest) shattered the complacent superiority that had marked most of the Victorian age and led imperial ideologues to rethink Empire. One of the means through which they sought to re-imagine Empire was the rubric of imperial citizenship.

Each of the three preceding historical themes – the status of Britons as *subjects* rather than *citizens*, domestic attitudes to immigration, and post-colonialism – sheds some light on the evolution of citizenship in British political culture. Yet each perpetuates a conceptual gap between the imperial metropole and the imperial periphery that has plagued imperial studies from its foundation as a sub-discipline in the early twentieth century.[59] By defining 'Britain' and 'the Empire' in isolation, historians have implied that the two entities were mutually exclusive. Such an approach obfuscates the interdependence of the relationship between Britain and its Empire. The roots of this division stretch back to the beginnings of decolonization itself.

In the main, two contrasting arguments have characterized imperial historiography since the retreat of the British Empire after 1945. One view holds that the nature and development of Empire were shaped by events in Great Britain, the imperial metropole. Notions of British racial and cultural hegemony, the capitalist concerns of the City, and the dictates of Great Power diplomacy are here given explanatory weight.[60] In contrast, proponents of the periphery argument hold that it was events in the extra-European world, not the home country, which largely propelled imperial activity. First given shape by Ronald Robinson and John Gallagher, and later developed by David Fieldhouse and others, the periphery argument sees Empire as having evolved, if not quite in a fit of absence of mind, then certainly without a single guiding influence.[61] Analogous to this debate over the development of Empire are national histories of the dominions, which read imperial events within the frame of the birth of a nation, and consequently under-emphasize imperial connections. This theme is particularly notable in Canadian history. Even those national works which have treated the imperial theme seriously, notably Carl Berger's *Sense of Power*,[62] have usually cast colonial imperialism as a manifestation of English nationalism. More recent contributions to the field of

Britain–dominion relations, including those whose subject is Canada,[63] have extended empirical knowledge of the field, but have remained faithful to the idea of nationalism as the most significant theme governing dominion–Britain relations.

While this book is intended as a contribution to these discussions, it adds a broader imperial perspective to these explanatory constructs in fitting with recent work coalescing around the idea of the *British world*, a global British culture transmitted mainly through the sinews of Empire.[64] In focusing on relationships, among both individuals and governments, within the Empire itself, this is a study of how Empire worked. In concentrating on imperial citizenship, the intent is to contribute an *imperial* history, if from the vantage point of Britain. Citizenship, though, is a contested notion, both politically and historically, and one which is by nature contextual. Before discussing the nature of imperial citizenship in the late Victorian and Edwardian eras, then, it is necessary to consider the historical and political models of citizenship that contemporaries drew upon to formulate their positions, models whose roots stretch to ancient Greece and Rome.

Students of citizenship have often looked to Athenian democracy as the ideal polity, a community where man's highest function was the political, and where citizenship was a privilege that held both rights and responsibilities. In the words of Aristotle, a good citizen 'must possess the knowledge and the capacity requisite for ruling as well as for being ruled.'[65] The Greek model, born of the city–state, stressed civic values and ethics, and bequeathed an exclusive and inward-looking citizenship.[66] The Greek city–state model, however, was supported by a slave hinterland – citizenship thus applied to some but not to others. The Roman model, based not on the city but on the idea of a commonwealth, was outward-looking.[67] The British Empire, as illustrated by commentators as varied as the civil servant C. P. Lucas and the diplomat and legal historian James Bryce[68], had a greater affinity to the Roman model. From the mid-Victorian period, the two Empires were consciously and consistently compared, epitomized by Disraeli's 1876 initiative to name Victoria 'Empress' of India, a title with no pedigree in post-Settlement Britain. The two exceptional characteristics which Britons believed their Empire shared with that of their Roman predecessors were liberty and peace. *Imperium et Liberatas* became a rallying cry among imperial voices in Britain. Liberty would be developed and maintained through the imperial endeavour because the institution valued peace over conflict by binding people together rather than casting them apart. Central to this idea of Empire as a leavening institution was the principle of British citizenship. To be a subject of the British crown meant to share a common identity with all fellow-subjects. Thus a favourite analogy of Victorian imperialists, made famous by Palmerston in the Don Pacifico affair of 1850, was of St Paul's invocation of Roman citizenship to protect himself from persecution by the authorities after his conversion to Christianity.[69] Like the apostle, the 'citizen' of Britain was perforce a free citizen of the world.

Not all late Victorian and Edwardian minds found such comparisons to the good. In *Patriotism and Empire* (1905), the liberal writer J. M. Robertson put forward the argument that it was Empire itself which corrupted, and that the true significance of the Roman Empire lay in its decline. Edward Gibbon Wakefield's *Decline and Fall of the Roman Empire* also gained in popularity among British intellectuals at the *fin de siècle*.[70] However, it was the sense of ecumenicalism and duty with which Roman imperial citizenship was imbued that remained most influential. Earlier Victorians admired the symbolism of Edward Poynter's *Faithful unto Death* (1865), which portrayed a petrified Roman sentry at Pompeii, still on guard.[71] If an identification with the Roman model of citizenship held sway in the mid-Victorian period, the Greek model, a Platonic conception of citizenship whereby the citizen strives to attain the ideal, began to gain favour by the turn of the century, as concerns of national efficiency came to the fore.

The association of the classical and the current did not necessarily betray an ahistorical sensibility on the part of contemporaries. Ideas of citizenship had remained relatively unchanged from the classical period through to the eighteenth century. In medieval Europe, citizenship had been conceived of largely as a familial relationship between sovereign and citizen. Citizenship in medieval England implied that the burgher and later residents of a city possessed a municipal, and thus local, identity. This identity was based upon the possession of property, thus establishing a link between citizenship and residence.[72] Early modern European notions of citizenship were tied to the city–state. Leaders of Italian city–states and Renaissance writers such as the Frenchman Jean Bodin, in his *Six Books of the Commonwealth* (1576), held to the notion that such a relationship would provide a bulwark against internecine religious conflict.[73] In post-1648 Europe, the Westphalian nation–state replaced the city–state as the polity of significance. Despite the subsequent 150-year era of absolutism, the emergence of the nation–state signalled a transfer of sovereignty from God and his earthly delegates, whether cleric or crown, to – in Hobbes's language – 'the Commonweal.' It was the Enlightenment which ultimately sparked change. Aided by the growth of the nation–state, emerging Enlightenment notions of rational thought, materialism, individualism, and internationalism led directly to the political upheavals of the French Revolution. It was the seminal events of 1789–93 which produced an alternative citizenship model to the classical one – a new republican model which privileged the individual over the state and autonomous thought over tradition and religion.

The republican model has proved the framework for modern citizenship. As we will see, however, the imperial citizenship conceived of by British thinkers in the late Victorian and Edwardian eras did not, and indeed could not, adopt this republican model holus-bolus, but rather piecemeal, in the tradition of Britain's historical reaction to the Revolution itself.[74] Before addressing the British hybrid citizenship model, though, it is necessary to first provide a picture of how historians have tracked the progress of this second republican citizenship model since its birth, and to note its impact upon the study of British imperial citizenship.

Two works merit mention here: the abstract citizenship model of T. H. Marshall and the socio-historical model of Charles Tilly. Marshall, the mid-twentieth century political sociologist, further developed the nineteenth-century notion of dutiful citizenship by incorporating, in step with the extension of civil rights in European nations after the Second World War, the notion of individual rights. Marshall posited that post-Enlightenment British citizenship had developed in three distinct stages:[75]

1 the nineteenth-century model of civil citizenship, based upon civil rights fully realized in the 1832 Reform Act;
2 political citizenship, which emerged fully in the Reform Act of 1918, and was based upon political equality in theory, if not always in practice; and
3 social (or egalitarian) citizenship, wherein all citizens were assumed to enjoy certain social rights, an ideal which emerged in step with the intensification of capitalism and became possible once the Poor Law, which recognized the social rights of some (workers) but not others (paupers), was abolished through the reorganization of local government in 1928–29.

Marshall's abstract concept of citizenship stressed the developing moral basis upon which it is increasingly constructed:

> Citizenship is a status bestowed on those who are full members of a community. All who possess the status are equal with respect to the rights and duties with which the status is endowed. There is no universal principle that determines what those rights and duties should be, but societies in which citizenship is a developing institution create an image of an ideal citizenship against which achievement can be measured and towards which aspiration can be directed.[76]

Political and social citizenship, Marshall contended, arose in tandem to replace the older *civil* notion of citizenship.[77] British imperial ideologues' efforts to create an imperial citizenship existed, using Marshall's theory, in the space between the nineteenth-century civil citizenship ideal and the emerging notions of political and social citizenship. Their ideas conformed with Marshall's argument that societies, in this case the supra-state of Empire, which lack a coherent notion of citizenship seek to create such a citizenship first as an abstract ideal, and only subsequently, if at all, as a legal or political reality.[78]

Charles Tilly has proffered a practical model of citizenship. His premiss is that citizenship is a relational phenomenon,

> a continuing series of transactions between persons and agents of a given state in which each has enforceable rights and obligations uniquely by virtue of (1) the person's membership in an exclusive category, the native-born plus the naturalized, and (2) the agent's relation to the state rather than any other authority the agent may enjoy.[79]

Tilly's definition of citizenship stresses the relationship between individual and state, employing the concrete term *transaction*.[80] This relationship can be *thin*, where it entails few rights or responsibilities, or *thick*, where it accounts for most of the activities individuals engage in.[81] This model also acknowledges that much negotiation occurs within the boundaries of citizenship, the more important being between notions of *jus sanguinis* (principle of descent) and *jus soli* (principle of residence), and between ties of gender, ethnicity, and military service.[82]

Using Tilly's model, British citizenship for much of the nineteenth century was generally *thin* until the final thirty or so years, when a new dynamic – nationalism – altered the status quo.[83] Class consciousness is a horizontal category, whereas nationalism is a vertical category.[84] An exclusive notion, nationalism forces minority groups within the nationalist polity either to assimilate or to create a nationalism of their own.[85] While the Enlightenment had created an alternative model of citizenship to the classical, one which gave space to 'the informed citizen,'[86] the development of this new ideal often led to the veneration of the nation–state in essentialist terms. Here the political influence of the romantic reaction to the rationalism of the Enlightenment was of decisive significance. The language of essentialist nationalism was patriotic, militarist, pseudo-scientific, racialist, and finally imperialist. Such an intense and often emotional construct accounted for the European rush to embrace the 'new imperialism' of the 1880s and 1890s.

Such popular imperial expressions were ironic. The proponents of Enlightenment citizenship, such as the political pamphleteer Thomas

Paine, claimed that their new creed was international and humanist in its ambition. Yet this internationalist scope was itself a horizontal, rather than a vertical, category: it incorporated Europeans, but left little room for non-Europeans. This paradox between international pretensions pursued through national means was clearly evident in British imperial rule. While the British often claimed to be pursuing internationalist and liberal intentions, they nonetheless held firmly to the belief that such intentions were part of a *national* mission.

Indeed, nationalism has been viewed by some commentators as the very lifeblood of imperialism. The philosopher Hannah Arendt has gone so far as to argue that it was expansion itself which gave rise to the 'flag of nationalism.'[87] Michael Ignatieff has described ethnic nationalism as 'autistic,'[88] meaning that its proponents are unable to converse with those outside of their nationalist vacuum. Many late Victorian and Edwardian imperialists would have agreed with this verdict were it applied to nationalisms other than their own. Where the French Canadian, Maori, and Afrikaner communities of the Empire expressed views counter to those emanating from Whitehall,[89] for example, Britons regularly denounced them as 'nationalists', an epithet implying regression.[90] The republican model of citizenship thus denotes membership in the social and political body of the nation, a membership that is signalled by praxis, by participating in civic life.[91]

In opposition to the nationalist model of citizenship stood the cosmopolitan ideal which imperial ideologues such as John Buchan had begun to feel their way towards by the early twentieth century. Britons expressed an affinity to this model in part because of the nation's close cultural and educational ties with Germany.[92] It was the German philosopher Immanuel Kant who in the eighteenth century put forward the definitive statement of a cosmopolitan citizenship. Kant's ideas, though not read in their original by many Britons, had been transmitted to British thinkers through the mediating influence of Hegel. Hegelianism had been a central influence for the school of idealism which emerged in Britain in the 1880s, largely through the writing of T. H. Green at Oxford.[93] British idealism itself constituted a 'community of opinion' rather than a system of thought.[94] The writings of Hegel, and in turn Kant, had appeared as course readings for Oxford students by the 1870s. German metaphysics occupied an important place in the intellectual firmament of late-Victorian Britain, though it never succeeded in supplanting empiricism as orthodoxy. As such, Kant himself was 'often read as attempting to integrate experience into knowledge, as attempting to reconcile the *a priori* and the *a posteriori*.'[95]

In the essays *Idea for a Universal History with Cosmopolitan Intent* (1784) and *Eternal Peace* (1795),[96] Kant argued that only the creation of a moral and political cosmopolitanism, a 'universal citizenship,' could prevent war. He disputed the very idea of ownership of state citizenship by which later nationalists asserted their patriotism, arguing: 'A state is not a possession (*patrimonium*) like the soil on which it has a seat.'[97] He also disagreed with essentialist notions of citizenship, including those based upon race: 'The state of peace among men who live alongside each other is no state of nature (*status naturalis*).'[98] Man's purpose, according to Kant, is to produce an 'internally perfect constitution,'[99] a form of world government which binds men together with the express purpose of preventing them from gravitating apart and producing war. Such a government is preferable, Kant contends, because it allows for the full exercise of freedom, man's highest goal, defined as 'the authority (*Befugnis*) not to obey any external laws except those which [he has] consented to.'[100] Kant then famously offered 'Three Articles for Eternal Peace Among States': the creation of a republican civil constitution; the construction of a federalist international system; and the consecration of universal hospitality as the basis of cosmopolitan law.[101] Despite the metaphysical grounds of his argument, and despite the fact that Kant himself spent almost his entire life in Königsberg, his third article of cosmopolitan governance and citizenship is predicated on a decidedly material international fact – namely, that for all man's differences, real or imagined, with his fellows he is bound by circumstance to share the globe.[102] This fact necessitates *society* and individual's political engagement with others.

British theorists had addressed this global ideal through the hybrid citizenship model of *subjecthood*. Even before Britons came to acquire the equality that Marshall argued for as defining full citizenship, they had secured substantial civil liberties through a shared dependence upon a single common law, contained in the institution of the sovereign. As such, Britons were *subjects*, a distinction which survived Europe's 'republican turn' in the late eighteenth century. Flowing from this common identity of subjecthood was a sense of shared cultural citizenship, the articulation of what were perceived to be common linguistic, historical, and customary bonds, both real and imagined. Subjecthood as cultural citizenship functioned as a form of self-affirmation, the expression of a common imperial identity which could, but of course did not always, bridge ethnic or racial boundaries. Subjecthood was an ambivalent and fungible identity, allowing for both inclusion and discrimination. Politicians' and theorists' negotiations between the identities of *subject* and *citizen* produced the hybrid model of citizenship which the British came to develop, and subsequently the model which conservative imperialists attempted to apply to the Empire.

Subjects *or* citizens?

Kant's three articles were challenged by nationalist voices in the latter nineteenth century and sacrificed on the battlefields of the two world wars. Yet they were of great influence in shaping the thought of British imperialists, and not just the proponents of imperial federation. British imperial thinkers, especially those on the Right, in fact unconsciously adopted a hybrid of the earlier classical and the later Enlightenment, or Kantian, model of citizenship, a hybrid that was allowed freer rein within the gossamer polity of Empire than in the arid domain of domestic politics. The Empire proved more amenable to political experimentation because it was, as Eric Hinderaker has observed, 'a process rather than a structure,' a 'negotiated system,' and a 'site of inter-cultural relations.'[103] What were the terms of this hybrid model of citizenship developed by late-Victorian and Edwardian British imperialists?

The demarcation of subject and citizen was not lost on Britons of the pre-1920 generation, and is crucial for any discussion of imperial citizenship. The term 'citizen' was an ambiguous concept in the British Empire. All under the British flag, whether in London or Lagos, were technically subjects, all owing allegiance to the crown. The wide resonance of what we can term a weak, or soft, sense of imperial citizenship was manifested in 'loyalism', a more inclusive ideology than simple Anglo-Saxonism. It was this personal relationship to the sovereign, a sense of loyalism, which provided the Empire with stability and cohesion. Loyalism was embraced by both British and non-British subjects alike, often for very different purposes. White non-British subjects such as Jews and Irish Catholics could create an imperial identity through loyalism, 'a vertical chain of allegiance to the sovereign,' attenuating ethnic divisions which might otherwise preclude a sense of common cause with Anglo-Protestants.[104] A similar dynamic emerged in Southern Africa. African subjects expressed loyalty to the British crown in the belief that it would shield them against encroaching white settlers, while loyalism appealed to those same settlers who sought the crown's protection for their property rights.[105] Colonial subjects also held dual loyalisms. Writing about the Indian prince and England cricketer Kumar Shri Ranjitsinhji, Satadru Sen argues that loyalty to both Britain and India were 'interdependent aspects of the identity of the imperial citizen.'[106] The doctrine of loyalism was central to rhetorical notions of imperial citizenship, as allegiance to the crown was reciprocated through the protection the State provided its citizens, even while abroad: witness Lord Palmerston's famous dictum of *Civis Romanus sum* in relation to the Don Pacifico affair in 1850. The status of *citizen*, understood as the political and practical relationship between constituent polities and individuals within a state structure, was not spelled out by statute, for Britain has a *living*, rather than written, constitution. This unofficial, rhetorical, and localized nature of citizenship gave rise to great discrepancies among imperial subjects in rights, benefits, and duties.

The starkest divide in citizenship status was that between subjects of the United Kingdom and the white-settlement colonies on the one hand, as compared to the dependent Empire on the other.[107] In Britain, the principle of *jus soli*, born of the soil of the place, dictated that anyone born on British soil was a natural-born British subject, a status which extended to any children born to said British subject on foreign soil. Naturalized aliens were also classified as subjects, though they were denied the political right to vote or hold public office. The status of subjecthood was deemed to reside in the male, as attested by the fact that, following the 1870 Naturalization Act and restated in the 1914 British Nationality and Status of Aliens (BNSA) Act, women's nationality was tied directly to that of her husband.[108] Thus, a woman who married an alien *became* an alien, while an alien woman who married a British subject became a subject. This pattern followed the general principle then adhered to in Europe and the United States, and reflected the uneasiness legislators felt concerning large-scale immigration.[109]

The principle of *jus soli* was also held in the settlement colonies, with the exception that the dominions dictated their own naturalization policies. In the dependencies, all under the crown were also subjects, but enjoyed fewer rights. Individuals born in British India, those territories under the direct administration of the Raj, were classified as non-European natural-born British subjects. Individuals born in non-British India, those territories controlled but not officially administered by Britain (the allied Indian principalities) were classified as British Protected Persons (BPPs), enjoying no political rights but remaining under the protection of the crown, and were thus analogous to aliens in the United Kingdom. Individuals born throughout the remainder of the dependent Empire were either BPPs or non-European British subjects, depending on the status of the territory (e.g. mandate, crown colony, protectorate, suzerainty). The heterogeneous nature of imperial citizenship created several obstacles to imperial unity, most notably concerning immigration and naturalization.

The issue of imperial citizenship, and its attendant difficulties, exercised great debate within imperial circles in the late-Victorian and Edwardian era. One such discussion circle, the Royal Colonial Institute,[110] provides a representative portrait of the debate. In a speech delivered to the Royal Colonial Institute in April 1912, E. B. Sargant, an Institute member, clearly spelled out what he believed to be the difference between the two terms: 'citizens are to be regarded primarily in their political association with one another, subjects in their individual relation to a single person who is their ruler.'[111] Thus, citizenship denotes a complex web of interpersonal relations, while subjecthood implies the more straightforward exchange of duty for protection between subject and state, as mediated through the crown. Sargant concluded that neither *British* nor *imperial citizenship* existed except as rhetorical devices, designed to generate a feeling of equality among diverse and unequal people.[112] The only true citizen of Empire was the monarch, in whom all allegiance was invested.[113] Citizenship, he continued, is a local, municipal phenomenon, and it is elastic because constantly under negotiation. Thus, national citizenship could exist only through local negotiations. Such negotiations were impracticable and potentially destructive on a national scale, thus precluding the possibility of national citizenship until such a time as political commonalities emerged sufficient to preclude conflict. Premature adoption of a national citizenship, he warned, would lead to autocracy.[114]

The key element in British political life was thus, in Sargant's view, the monarchy. Individual national allegiance and citizenship were both invested in the monarch, and this loyalty – subjecthood – provided the leavening factor of Empire. The colonies were tied to the crown through the institution of responsible government; the dependencies through the direct rule of the monarch. The demarcation between allegiance and citizenship, though, was constantly evolving, as opposed to the static fusion of both identities in the constitution of a republic. This evolution in regard to Empire, Sargant asserted, was usually in the direction of merger rather than of separation. In order to protect liberty, the predominant goal of Empire, Sargant concluded that the key question was where to place responsibility for common imperial affairs, so as to create the 'political commonalities' requisite for imperial citizenship.[115] Sargant thus proffered an organic view of imperial citizenship, one emphasizing the centrality of the crown, responsible government as the model colonial political framework, and the encouragement of imperial political competence through tutelage.

Sargant here spoke for the majority view among imperial ideologues of the era. His arguments were received positively by his peers in the Royal Colonial Institute, the hearth of conservative imperialism.[116] Other voices offered further clarification. The writer and journalist Richard Jebb agreed that imperial citizenship at present was subservient to subjecthood, and further outlined four tenets of imperial subjecthood which combined 'civil' and 'political' functions:

- the right to invoke the protection of the crown, especially overseas;
- the right to be tried under British law where consular courts have been established under the Foreign Jurisdiction Act (1890);
- the right to marry in foreign countries under the Foreign Marriages Act (1892); and
- the right to have an owner's interest in British shipping (in other words, extra-territorial trading rights).

Subjecthood, in Jebb's view, entailed no particular political rights *per se*. As the condition was passive, it provided protection in return for allegiance to the crown.[117]

F. P. Walton, an Institute member and Dean of the Faculty of Law at McGill University, argued that the term 'British citizen' had no definite meaning, except as a synonym for 'British subject,' and that since British subjects could not transfer their franchise from one imperial jurisdiction to another, the term 'imperial citizen' also had no bearing in practice.[118] Newfoundland Governor Ralph Williams reiterated the Palmerstonian notion of subjecthood,[119] while the Canadian H. E. Egerton argued: 'I think that we are forced to the conclusion that the absence of a system of common citizenship is a necessary consequence of the formless and chaotic character of the British Empire as a whole.'[120] James Bryce reminded his peers of the Roman influence that distinguished public rights, such as voting and holding office, from private rights, such as the autonomy of family relations or commerce. British citizens enjoyed the former, he noted, while British subjects enjoyed the latter. The task of creating an imperial citizenship rested in ensuring that British subjects' private rights were assured in each jurisdiction of Empire; that is, that they were mobile.[121] He was confident that British public rights were already the world's broadest, observing for instance that Indians sat in the House of Commons.

The applicability to Empire of the emerging hybrid idea of British citizenship, incorporating both 'republican' notions of citizenship and the continuing importance of subjecthood and the sovereignty of the crown, was also a matter of official interest. The Colonial Office deliberated extensively on this matter. It recognized the distinction between subjects, 'those born within the [lineage] of the King,' and citizens, a republican identity establishing individuals' constitutional tie to the State.[122] It further spelled out the central requirement of British subjecthood, namely the principle of *jus soli* (matter of place).[123] British subjecthood, the Colonial Office explained, entailed certain benefits, most importantly equal protection under the common law both at home and abroad, but did not necessarily entail political rights. Before 1918 the franchise was by no means universal in Britain. Hence, the fact that subjects of the Empire had at best limited political rights was normative, not aberrant. Indian 'coolies' for instance, though able to claim protection under British law if they were aggrieved, could be, and were, moved unilaterally about the Empire as indentured labour. The official view of imperial citizenship, then, was essentially an extension of its definition of British subjecthood, made to conform to Palmerston's vision that the 'true ideal is, and should be, a vast co-operative league of contented and emulous Anglo-Saxon States.'[124]

Such a league, even in sentiment, proved difficult if not impossible to attain. The imperial triad – Britain, the white-settlement colonies, and the dependencies – was resistant to union for two central reasons: the growth of non-British nationalisms, and the practical difficulties presented by intra-imperial migration. Writing in McGill's *University Magazine*, Walton observed the difficulty which nationalism in particular presented for any implementation of imperial citizenship. The problem was especially evident in the field of naturalization, central to any state's definition of belonging: 'I do not see how the dominions, and Canada in particular, can have it both ways. Their people either belong to the Empire or not.'[125] Here we can see the republican model of citizenship implicitly advanced, for Walton finds fault not in the dominions' continued allegiance to the crown, but in their insistence that they dictate certain *political* rights. Some commentators, including the Canadian imperialist W. Wilfred Campbell, feared that emergent nationalism in the dominions was atavistic, and lauded Empire as a progressive world force: 'Present-day imperialism is more than a mere self-satisfied jingoism . . . it is a vital force, a sort of necessary phase of human progressiveness; that instead of being the foe to the individual national life, it is the greatest means to that end.'[126]

While imperial ideologues were quick to diagnose the threat that colonial nationalism posed to the creation of imperial citizenship, their proffered preventative cures were vague, if consistent. Andrew Thompson has divided Edwardian imperialists into two schools: *free trade* imperialists, who believed imperial unity should be pursued through private rather than public initiative; and *constructive* imperialists, who wanted to draw upon the State's power to mobilize the resources of Empire.[127] Each of these groups accepted the need to improve 'imperial sentiment' and to emphasize 'character' as a unifying tool. These currents of thought were evident in the dominions as well. On his appointment to the chair of colonial history at Queen's University[128] the Canadian academic W. L. Grant declaimed:

> The study of colonial history in general, and of Canadian history in particular, can thus do something to advance the comity of nations, and

in especial to advance that great spiritual drawing together of the Anglo-Celtic race, which, were it to come, would be strong enough to guard the peace of the world.[129]

The Canadian Reverend Father Bernard Vaughan in turn asserted that 'character,' the tenets of a 'life dominated by lofty and holy principles,' should form the basis of Empire.[130] Even opponents of imperialism, such as the contrarian Goldwin Smith, drew a distinction between 'extension without break of continuity or loss of moral unity' and imperialism, which he defined as 'extension where continuity was lost and moral unity was broken.'[131] Smith thus had no difficulty criticizing Canadian nationalism where it impeded his favoured position, union with the United States. Grant, Vaughan, and even Smith thus favoured the principle of moral union as supportive of a collective (and in the case of Grant and Vaughan, an imperial) citizenship. In turn, they viewed colonial nationalism as inimical to collective citizenship because it betrayed poor character. If there were Canadian voices to champion these views, it is not surprising that British conservative imperialists advanced these positions even more vigorously.

Thompson's typology concerns imperial ideologues' thought on the role of the State in promoting imperial unity. Much of this intellectual activity was conducted by imperial pressure groups such as the Navy League or voluntary migration societies. In contrast, while imperial pressure groups were also important in facilitating debate concerning imperial citizenship, much of the discourse on that topic was conducted among individuals. I would suggest that those individuals can also be divided into two camps: centralizing social imperialists, who included both progressives and traditionalists; and cosmopolitan 'associationists.' The former group, which counted both progressive voices like Curtis and regressive ones like White, imagined imperial citizenship to be the social and political expression of a single imperial identity. While this identity might allow for a degree of self-government and national autonomy, or seek to subsume colonial identities within an English identity of 'whiteness,' the individual's place was nonetheless firmly rooted in a single idea of imperial citizenship. Cosmopolitan associationists, in contrast, sought to create space for colonial identities. Some held that the combination of local, national, and imperial identities was itself the basis of a 'broad-church' – romantic and social – idea of imperial citizenship. Other cosmopolitan associationists favoured a more political idea of imperial citizenship, embracing a decentred and cooperative imperialism which allowed for greater individual autonomy, particularly in the dominions. This divide between 'exclusive' and 'inclusive' imperial citizenships placed the incorporation of individual identities in opposition to a compromise version of citizenship that included both imperial and national identities. In explaining how British imperialists' view of Empire evolved from one of a limited nationalist entity to a one of a more cosmopolitan and inclusive body, I seek to plot the path such ideologues travelled from W. T. Stead's grandiloquent response to the Jameson Raid –

> I shall marvel greatly if the future historian, looking back on the month of January, 1896, does not regard it as marking one of those great and fateful moments in the history of a people, when a nation become conscious of its providential mission, and recognises in the revelation of great events the attesting seal of circumstance to its deep instinctive intuition of a Divine Call[132] –

to Lionel Curtis's post-First World War assessment that the imperial vision of colonial 'self-government was . . . less a liberal constitutional formula than a moral proposition,'[133] one which presented the greatest chance for peace in a world torn apart by war.

In an effort to trace this evolution in thought on imperial citizenship, the book is divided into two distinct sections: the first part gives an exegesis of the theoretical underpinnings of various conservative arguments for the creation of an imperial citizenship; and the second offers an examination of the applicability of such abstract constructions in practice through case studies of the citizenship issues of imperial naturalization, immigration, and emigration. Given the intellectual topography of late Victorian and Edwardian Britain, the issue of imperial citizenship may be best approached through the prism of intellectual biography. Through a discussion of the ideas and careers of five representative imperialists, I argue that ideas of imperial citizenship were contested between those who developed a gradually inclusive view of Empire and those who held to a more exclusive Anglo-centric understanding of Empire. The five figures are: Lionel Curtis, co-founder of the imperial pressure group the Round Table and ubiquitous prophet of Empire in the first half of the twentieth century; John Buchan, the Scottish novelist, politician, bureaucrat, and eventual Governor-General of Canada, 1935–40; Arnold White, a pugnacious journalist for, among other papers, the *Daily Express*; Richard Jebb, a well-known contemporary imperial traveller, journalist, and author of a series of influential books on colonial nationalism and imperial organization; and Thomas Sedgwick, a social worker and associate of Toynbee Hall who assisted emigration schemes to send youths to the dominions. Their careers and writings provide a jumping-off point to address five key aspects of the debate concerning imperial citizenship:

respectively

- federalism and the difficulty of incorporating all of the Empire's subjects under one political framework;
- the romantic ideal of a cosmopolitan imperial citizenship;
- the tie between imperial citizenship and the racial ideal of 'whiteness';
- intra-imperial immigration and colonial views of race; and
- emigration from Britain to the colonies as a form of 'sentimental imperialism.'

Curtis and Buchan espoused a progressive conservative concept of imperial citizenship, the product of their similar background. Their three shared central traits shaped their imperial ideas. First, each had travelled broadly within the Empire, developing a comparative knowledge of Her Majesties's overseas realms rare among their contemporaries. South Africa made an especially important impression on both men, particularly the influence of Alfred, Lord Milner. Buchan and Curtis worked directly with the proconsul, and shared Milner's certainty that a strengthened Empire offered Britain its best future. Second, both moved beyond Milner in their shared realization that the relationship between Britain and the white dominions was changing due to the emergence of colonial nationalism. The future challenge for Empire, they argued, was to redefine this relationship to the common benefit of all. Finally, both wrote for an educated audience. Whether through the *Round Table*, the *Spectator*, or their own multitudinous publications, each man sought to influence the professional and the powerful. Each gave voice, with individual inflection, to an emerging vision of Empire as organic, increasingly inclusive, and progressive.

If Curtis and Buchan represented movement toward a graduated imperial inclusiveness, Arnold White's exclusivist definition of imperial citizenship marked out a separate position to hold the line on Empire. White was an imperial journalist, professional polemicist, and public advocate of the Royal Navy. Unlike Curtis and Buchan, White had seen little of the Empire first-hand, conceived of the Empire as static rather than as evolving, and wrote for the tabloid press, primarily the *Morning Post*. He saw Empire as a British 'possession', and articulated a vision of imperial citizenship as one of 'whiteness.' An imperial ideology based upon 'whiteness' had found much support in the settlement colonies in the nineteenth century, as historians such as Adele Perry have shown us in the case of British Columbia,[134] and it was over this question that debates over the definition of imperial citizenship, both within and among the dominions and Britain, centred.

IMPERIAL CITIZENSHIP

These competing conceptions of Empire and imperial citizenship – one progressive, one parochial – were given shape through the work and ideas of those imperialists engaged in the work of Empire. The book's second part thus examines how ideas of imperial citizenship were manifested in practical terms, how they were received by subjects in the colonies, and, ultimately, why these ideas failed to take root. This conflict between inclusivist and exclusivist conceptions of imperial citizenship is illustrated in the contrast between the careers and ideas of Richard Jebb and Thomas Sedgwick.

Jebb, like Buchan and Curtis, wrote for an educated audience. His writings, however, the most important of which was *Studies in Colonial Nationalism* (1905), were of a more practical bent. Drawing on Jebb's ideas, I argue that the issue of immigration, and the attendant conflict between a liberal – though somewhat ambivalent – understanding of racial issues in Britain and the dominions' desire to dictate their own policies on race, demonstrated the practical failings of imperial citizenship. Advocates of imperial citizenship also put much faith in assisted emigration as a means of buttressing imperial unity. The efforts of one such advocate, the social imperialist Thomas Sedgwick, are examined to show the practical consequences of conceiving of Empire and imperial citizenship in English nationalist terms. Like White, Sedgwick saw individual citizens as imperial capital: he perceived imperial issues to be extensions of domestic issues, a perception borne out by the distinction he made between migration as movement *within* the Empire and emigration as movement *outside* the Empire. The difficulties his schemes encountered in New Zealand and Ontario help illustrate how competing ideas of what it meant to be a citizen of Empire ultimately precluded a single, all-embracing, imperial identity.

These five men present the historian with case studies of individuals who devoted their careers to British imperialism, and who conceptualized the Empire in terms of unity and preservation. While each held a vision of citizenship which purported to be inclusive, these visions proved impractical when given shape, particularly in reference to intra-imperial immigration. The ideal of a common imperial citizenship ultimately foundered on the shoals of colonial nationalism and the unwillingness of most Britons to concede decision-making influence to colonial voices. Indeed, its failure is directly attributable to the Empire's democratic impulses. If centralizing social imperialists failed to adequately account for colonial nationalism in their thinking on citizenship, so did the incorporation of colonial nationalism undermine the broad-church citizenship favoured by cosmopolitan associationists such as Buchan and Jebb. Nowhere was this more important than concerning the question of race and immigration, where a double-bind emerged. The dominions wished to limit non-white immigration, but could not use openly exclusionary language for fear of incurring the opprobrium of Britain; Britain could not prevent the passage of legislation which effectively sundered the concept of a shared imperial citizenship because the dominions were democratic self-governing polities, but exercised its moral suasion to perpetuate an increasingly fictive idea of such a shared imperial citizenship. Though the British Nationality and Status of Aliens Act (1914) and, later and in a much more comprehensive manner, the British Nationality Act (1948) were legislative attempts to define 'imperial citizen,' the sense of shared social identity which was a necessary ideational precursor to any formal political identity was then too faint. It was during the late Victorian and Edwardian periods when contemporaries perceived these political and social identities to have converged, which is why the discourse of imperial citizenship was at its strongest at that point. Even then, however, the very democratic ideals of the wider 'British' world ensured that a common 'British' imperial citizenship would be exceedingly difficult to attain.

This is not to say that the concept was historically insignificant. As the concluding chapter suggests, the very absence of a concrete concept of imperial citizenship ironically allowed the British to maintain imperial power into the interwar period by shifting the imperial debate toward the concept of informal Empire.[135] The debate over imperial citizenship also, paradoxically, helped establish a language which colonial nationalists later used to make their case for independence. As Kathryn Tidrick has observed, men such as Curtis helped 'give away the empire in the belief that they were acting to preserve it.'[136] The end of empire seemed far off in the early twentieth century, though, and imperial ideologues discussed imperial citizenship with the fervour of those secure both in their convictions and in their place in the world. It is to the shape and content of those discussions that I now turn.

Notes

1 For an introduction to these themes, see Pat Thane, 'The British Imperial State and National Identities,' in Billie Melman (ed.) *Borderlines: Genders and Identities in War and Peace, 1870–1930* (New York, 1998), esp pp. 30–5.
2 See Nicholas Owen, 'Critics of Empire in Britain,' in Judith M. Brown and W. Roger Louis (eds) *Oxford History of the British Empire*, vol. 4 (Oxford, 1999), pp. 188–211; Bernard Porter, *Critics of Empire* (London, 1968); and Stephen Howe, *Anti-Colonialism in British Politics* (Oxford, 1993).
3 See Iain Smith, 'Milner, the "Kindergarten", and South Africa,' in Andrea Bosco and Alex May (eds) *The Round Table and British Foreign Policy* (London, 1997), pp. 40–1, 43.

4 The conceptual notion of the 'long nineteenth century' covers the period from 1789 (or 1793, depending on the predilection of the historian) to 1914 and the beginning of the the First World War. The case for the 'official mind' of Empire and the geopolitical impulses which gave it shape is set out most famously in Ronald Robinson and John Gallagher, with Alice Denny, *Africa and the Victorians* (New York, 1961).
5 David Cannadine portrays much of the intellectual and material form of this nexus in *Ornamentalism* (Oxford, 2001).
6 See Peter Weiler, 'Forming Responsible Trade Unions: The Colonial Office, Colonial Labor, and the Trades Union Congress,' *Radical History Review*, 28–30 (1984), pp. 367–92.
7 On the Fabians' imperial views, see *Fabianism and the Empire: A Manifesto by the Fabian Society* (London, 1900); on the Liberal imperialists, see the Liberal Imperialist Manifesto and Colin Matthew, *The Liberal Imperialists* (Oxford, 1973).
8 Of the many works on Empire, national identity, and politics, see F. Coetzee, *For Party or Country: Nationalism and the Dilemmas of Popular Conservatism in Edwardian England* (Oxford, 1990).
9 On the public celebration of Empire in this era, see the essays in Eric Hobsbawm and Terence Ranger (eds) *The Invention of Tradition* (Oxford, 1983).
10 Andrew Thompson, 'Imperial Ideology in Edwardian Britain,' *The Round Table and British Foreign Policy*, pp. 1–19.
11 David Cannadine, *The Rise and Fall of Class in Britain* (New York, 1999), pp. 116–18, 138–9.
12 On tariff reform and Conservative politics in the pre-war period, see Richard Rempel, *Unionists Divided: Arthur Balfour, Joseph Chamberlain, and the Unionist Free Traders* (Hamden, CT, 1972), and Alan Sykes, *Tariff Reform in British Politics, 1903–1913* (Oxford, 1979).
13 Biographical information for individuals mentioned by name in the text can be found in Appendix 1.
14 Quoted in Peter Clarke, *A Question of Leadership* 2nd edition (London, 1999), p. 59.
15 This is not to say that the Conservatives faced no imperial challenges: see for instance the 1913 Imperial Preference Crisis or the 1909–10 debate regarding the creation of an imperial navy. Nevertheless, such events did not prove immediately compromising to the unity of the Empire.
16 See Max Beloff, *Imperial Sunset*, vol. 1: *Britain's Liberal Empire, 1897–1921*; vol. 2: *Dream of Commonwealth, 1921–1942* (London, 1969; 1989).
17 E. H. H. Green, *The Crisis of Conservatism* (London and New York, 1995), p. 159.
18 Ibid., esp. pp. 176–83.
19 Andrew S. Thompson, *Imperial Britain: The Empire in British Politics, c. 1880–1932* (Harlow, Essex, 2000), details the salience of imperialism in extraparliamentary politics.
20 See Hugh Cunningham, 'The Language of Patriotism, 1750–1914,' *History Workshop Journal*, 12 (1981), pp. 8–33. Paul Reading argues that the Liberals also had purchase on imperial patriotism during the Edwardian era. While he does demonstrate that the Liberal Party had a national consciousness and a national platform, this does not *ex ante* make it 'patriotic' – that is, the Liberals did not make 'love of country' an electoral issue. Such a position would have antagonized the Liberals' Irish Nationalist allies and, as indeed happened after 1910, compromise the Liberals' majority in the House: P. Reading, 'The Liberal Party and Patriotism in Early Twentieth Century Britain,' *20th Century British History*, 12, 3 (2001), pp. 269–302. On patriotism and the British Left, see Paul Ward, *Red Flag and Union Jack: Englishness, Patriotism and the British Left, 1881–1924* (London, 1998).
21 See A. L. Friedberg, *Britain and the Weary Titan: Britain and the Experience of Relative Decline, 1895–1914* (Princeton, NJ, 1988). A fear of decline, and conservatives' efforts to reverse this perceived trend through economies of scale

(political, financial, and otherwise), were noted features of conservatives in many turn of the century Western states. Conservatives also shared a common difficulty in adapting to the new mass politics: see Green, *Crisis of Conservatism*, pp. 319–33.

22 The best recent work on Salisbury is Andrew Roberts, *Salisbury* (London, 1999).
23 The phrase was born with Lord Rosebery's Chesterfield speech of 15 December 1901, marking Rosebery's definitive split with Sir Henry Campbell-Bannerman, then leader of the Liberal Party. On 'national efficiency,' see G. R. Searle, *The Quest for 'National Efficiency': A Study in British Politics and Political Thought, 1899–1914* (Berkeley, CA, 1971).
24 Peter Marsh, *Joseph Chamberlain: Entrepreneur in Politics* (London and New Haven, CT: 1994), is the best recent work on the Colonial Secretary.
25 While the 1900 election was fought on the issue of Empire, it is important to note that the Tories and the Liberal Unionists actually won 4 fewer seats in 1900 (399) than they had in 1895 (403): see Elizabeth York Enstam, 'The "Khaki" Election of 1900 in the United Kingdom,' unpublished PhD thesis, Duke University, 1967, p. iii.
26 Lionel Curtis contributed directly to this process with the 1916 publication of *The Commonwealth of Nations*, where he outlined the principle of a Commonwealth which later imperial thinkers were to take up.
27 The historiography on imperial pressure groups is extensive and instructive: among many examples, see Thompson, *Imperial Britain*.
28 Stefan Collini, Richard Whatmore, and Brian Young (eds) *Economy, Polity, and Society: British Intellectual History 1750–1950* (Cambridge, 2000), pp. 2, 3. Intellectual history as practised in this manner consciously navigates between a 'master narrative' account of ideas and their progression through time, and a post-structuralist intellectual history, which seeks to illuminate 'the irrationalities which shadow reason, the unconscious desires which run through habits of rational calculation, alerting us to the illusory, *impossible* quality of a transcendent, hypostatized reason': Bill Schwarz, 'Conquerors of Truth: Reflections on Postcolonial Theory,' in Schwarz (ed.) *The Expansion of England: Race, Ethnicity, and Cultural History*, (New York, 1996), p. 11.
29 The theoretical underpinnings of this position are derived from John Lukacs, *The Hitler of History* (New York, 1998), pp. 187–8. For an overview of how scholars have studied the relationship between ideas and the details of a subject's life, see Danny Postle, 'The Life and the Mind,' *Chronicle of Higher Education*, 6 (July 2002).
30 This argument is forwarded by Charlotte Gray, 'creative biographer' of Isabel Mackenzie King and of Susanna Moodie and Catherine Parr Traill. See Gray, 'The New Biography,' *Queen's Quarterly*, 108, 2 (Summer 2001), p. 256. I fail to appreciate the difference when she declaims (p. 257): 'I imagine ... but I don't invent.'
31 See for instance Julia Bush, *Edwardian Ladies and Imperial Power* (London, 1999); and Paula Krebs, *Gender, Race and the Writing of Empire: Public Discourse and the Boer War* (Cambridge, 1999).
32 See John Kendle, *Ireland and the Federal Solution: The Debate over the United Kingdom Constitution, 1870–1922* (Kingston, 1989); and Keith Jeffrey (ed.) *An Irish Empire? Aspects of Ireland and the British Empire* (Manchester, 1996).
33 See Stephen Heathorn, *For Home, Country and Race: Constructing Gender, Class and Englishness in the Elementary School, 1880–1914* (Toronto, 2000); James A. Mangan, *Benefits Bestowed? Education and British Imperialism* (Manchester, 1987).
34 The literature on the expansion of the franchise in Britain, and its impact on imperial affairs, is voluminous. Richard Price argues in *An Imperial War and the British Working Class* (Toronto, 1972) that the masses were not overcome by jingoistic fervour, remaining largely uninterested in matters of Empire.
35 See Curzon's famous indictment of Chamberlain's imperial tariff scheme: 'What would have become of him [Chamberlain] and us if he had ever visited India ... The

Colonies would have been dwarfed and forgotten, and the pivot of the Empire would have been Calcutta.': Enoch Powell, 'The Myth of Empire,' *Round Table*, 60 (1970), p. 440.

36 Frederick Cooper and Ann Stoler, 'Between Metropole and Colony: Rethinking a Research Agenda,' in Cooper and Stoler (eds) *Tensions of Empire: Colonial Cultures in a Bourgeois World* (Berkeley, CA, 1997), pp. 1–56; Simon J. Potter, 'The Imperial Significance of the Canadian–American Reciprocity Proposals of 1911,' *Historical Journal*, 47, 1 (2004), pp. 82–3.

37 Benedict Anderson, *Imagined Communities* (New York, 1983), p. 93.

38 Douglas Lorimer, 'Race, Science and Culture,' in Shearer West (ed.) *The Victorians and Race* (Aldershot, 1996), pp. 15–9, 32–3.

39 The literature on race and Empire in the late nineteenth and early twentieth centuries is vast. A representative introduction can be found in Christine Bolt, *Victorian Attitudes to Race* (London: 1971); Douglas Lorimer, *Colour, Class, and the Victorians* (New York, 1978), and 'Theoretical Racism in Late-Victorian Anthropology, 1870–1900,' *Victorian Studies*, 31, 3 (1988), pp. 405–30; Shearer West (ed.) *The Victorians and Race* (Aldershot: 1996); and Paul Rich, *Race and Empire in British Politics* (Cambridge, 1986), and 'The Long Victorian Sunset: Anthropology, Eugenics and Race in Britain, 1900–1948,' *Patterns of Prejudice*, 18, 3 (1984), pp. 3–17.

40 Charles Lamb, *The Two Races of Men*, quoted in Cynthia Ozick, *Quarrel & Quandary: Essays* (New York, 2000), p. 180.

41 Gilbert Murray, 'The Exploitation of Inferior Races in Ancient and Modern Times,' in *Liberalism and Empire* (London, 1900), p. 156.

42 Imperial racial attitudes conform to the first two, but not the third, of Peter Firchow's three-tiered model of racial discrimination: (1) *weak racism*, the belief that races/ethnicities do exist and help cause social events/phenomenon; (2) *medium racism* adds the idea that some races are superior, others not; and (3) *strong racism* asserts that action should be taken on account of such superiority: P. Firchow, *Envisioning Africa: Racism and Imperialism in Conrad's* Heart of Darkness (Lexington, 2000), p. 11.

43 For an examination of this theme, see Paul Rich, *Race and Empire in British Politics* (Cambridge, MA, 1986); Rich, 'The Long Victorian Sunset: Anthropology, Eugenics and Race in Britain, 1900–1948,' *Patterns of Prejudice*, 18, 3 (1984), pp. 3–17; and the essays in Catherine Hall (ed.) *Cultures of Empire: Colonizers in Britain and the Empire in the Nineteenth and Twentieth Centuries: A Reader* (New York, 2000).

44 Work on citizenship and Empire has concentrated mainly on the post-Second World War era, when emigration from the Commonwealth became a contentious domestic issue: Rieko Karatani, *Defining British Citizenship* (London, 2002); Randall Hansen, *Citizenship and Immigration in Postwar Britain: The Institutional Foundations of a Multicultural Nation* (Oxford, 2000); and Kathleen Paul, *Whitewashing Britain: Race and Citizenship in the Postwar Era* (Ithaca, NY, 1997). More general studies of British citizenship include Ann Dummet and Andrew Nicol, *Subjects, Citizens, Aliens and Others* (London, 1990); Vaughn Bevan, *The Development of British Immigration Law* (London, 1986); and James Walvin, *Passage to Britain: Immigration in British History and Politics* (Harmondsworth, 1984).

45 The Whig approach has been well served by Nicholas Mansergh. Antoinette Burton has recently called for a re-examination of the primacy of the *nation* in both British and imperial history: A. Burton, 'Introduction: On the Inadequacy and Indispensability of the Nation,' in Burton (ed.) *After the Imperial Turn* (Durham, NC, 2003), pp. 1–23.

46 On the evolution of British citizenship, especially in regard to the treatment of immigrants, see Hansen, *Citizenship and Immigration in Postwar Britain*; Paul, *Whitewashing Britain*; Dummet and Nicol, *Subjects, Citizens, Aliens and Others*; Bevan, *Development of British Immigration Law* (London, 1986); Walvin,

Passage to Britain; and Bernard Gainer, *The Alien Invasion: The Origins of the Alien Act of 1905* (London, 1972). There is also an engaging historiography on the role of citizenship and imperialism in education: on citizenship indoctrination in elementary schools, see Heathorn, *For Home, Country and Race*; on similar issues in the university world, see the essays in E. T. Williams, A. F. Madden, and D. K. Fieldhouse (eds) *Oxford and the Idea of Commonwealth: Essays Presented to Sir Edgar Williams* (London, 1982).
47 Thane, 'The British Imperial State and National Identities,' p. 32.
48 Paul Kennedy, 'The Theory and Practice of Imperialism,' *Historical Journal*, 20, 3 (1977), pp. 761–9.
49 The titles in John Mackenzie's Manchester University Press 'Studies in Imperialism' series are indicative of the wide domestic impact of imperialism. See also Andrew Thompson, *The Empire Strikes Back: The Impact of Imperialism on Britain from the Mid-Nineteenth Century* (Harlow, Essex, 2005); Bernard Porter presents a dissenting view in *The Absent-Minded Imperialists* (Oxford, 2004).
50 See particularly Catherine Hall, *Civilizing Subjects: Metropole and Colony in the English Imagination, 1830–1867* (London, 2002), and 'Narratives of Empire: A Reply to Critics,' *Small Axe*, 7, 2 (2003), esp. pp. 171–3.
51 See Schwarz, 'Conquerors of Truth, pp. 9–31; for varying perspectives on this approach, see E. W. Said, *Orientalism* (New York, 1979) – though Said subsequently retreated somewhat: see his '*Orientalism* Reconsidered,' *Race and Class*, 27, 2 (1985), pp. 1–15; Francis Baker, Peter Hulme, and Margaret Iverson (eds) *Colonial Discourse, Postcolonial Theory* (Manchester, 1994); Antoinette Burton, *Burdens of History: British Feminists, Indian Women, and Imperial Culture, 1865–1915* (Chapel Hill, NC, 1994); and Mrinalini Sinha, *Colonial Masculinity: The 'Manly' Englishman and the 'Effeminate' Bengali in the Late Nineteenth Century* (Manchester, 1995).
52 Rhonda Cobham, 'Fishers of Men: Catherine Hall's *Narrative and the Framing of History*,' *Small Axe*, 7, 2 (2003), pp. 156–7.
53 A. G. Hopkins has argued that 'postcolonialism' has become 'a metaphysical collective protected from criticism by inverted commas and used, often by recent converts to history, to create a gross stereotype – [a stereotype which asserts] that historical research during the past thirty years has been dedicated to destroying': *The Future of the Imperial Past*, Inaugural Lecture (Cambridge, 1997), p. 14. D. A. Washbrook presents a similar argument in a more spirited tone in 'Orients and Occidents: Colonial Discourse Theory and the Historiography of the British Empire,' in R. W. Winks (ed.) *The Oxford History of the British Empire*, vol. 5: *Historiography* (Oxford, 1999), pp. 596–611.
54 Two examples of empirical works which argue the centrality of race in imperial politics are Rich, *Race and Empire in British Politics*, and the essays in Hall (ed.) *Cultures of Empire*.
55 I draw here on Wyndam Lewis's critique of Joyce's *Ulysses*, as assessed in Luke Gibbins, 'Race Against Time: Racial Discourse and Irish History,' in Hall (ed.) *Cultures of Empire*, p. 218.
56 Sinha, *Colonial Masculinity*; Stuart Ward, 'Transcending the Nation,' in Burton (ed.) *After the Imperial Turn*, p. 50.
57 While much of the polemic over *Empire* is overdone, Ferguson invites some of it by consciously adopting a cost-benefit analysis and claiming public policy application for his argument: N. Ferguson, *Empire: The Rise and Demise of the British World Order and the Lessons for Global Power* (London, 2002), pp. 358–70. Among the many, mostly critical, reviews of Ferguson's book (and the television series from which it was drawn) from all sides, see especially Douglas Peers, 'Reading Empire, Chasing Tikka Masala: The Contested State of Imperial History,' *Canadian Journal of History*, 39, 1 (April 2004), pp. 87–104; Jon Wilson, 'Niall Ferguson's Imperial Passion,' *History Workshop Journal*, 56 (2003), pp. 175–83; Gary Peatling, 'Globalism, Hegemonism and British Power,' *History*, 89, 295 (July 2004), pp. 382–5; and Andrew Porter, 'Review: *Empire*,'

Institute of Historical Research, April 2003, available online: www.history.ca.uk/reviews/paper/porterA.html (accessed 15 October 2005). The case in favour of Ferguson's argument is summarized by Keith Windschuttle, 'The Burdens of Empire,' *New Criterion*, 22, 1 (2003), pp. 8–9.

58 See Hall, 'Histories, Empires and the Post-Colonial Moment,' *The Post-Colonial Question* (London, 1996), pp. 66–7.
59 See, for example, Ronald Hyam, 'The Study of Imperial and Commonwealth History at Cambridge, 1881–1981: Founding Fathers and Pioneer Research Students,' *Journal of Imperial and Commonwealth History*, 29, 3 (2001), pp. 75–103.
60 See for instance P. J. Cain and A. G. Hopkins, *British Imperialism: Innovation and Expansion, 1688–1914* (London, 1993) and *British Imperialism: Crisis and Deconstruction, 1914–1990* (London, 1993).
61 Robinson, Gallagher, and Denny, *Africa and the Victorians*; D. K. Fieldhouse, *Economics and Empire, 1880–1914* (Ithaca, NY, 1973).
62 Carl Berger, *The Sense of Power* (Toronto, 1970).
63 The best recent studies of British–Canadian relations covering the era from confederation to the Second World War are Norman Hillmer and J. L. Granatstein, *Empire to Umpire: Canada and the World to the 1990s* (Toronto, 1994), and R. F. Holland, *Britain and the Commonwealth Alliance, 1918–1939* (London, 1981).
64 Representative examples of such new work include C. Bridge and Kent Fedorowich (eds) *The British World: Diaspora, Culture and Identity* (London, 2003), and, for the post-1945 period, Philip Buckner (ed.) *Canada and the End of Empire* (Vancouver, 2004).
65 See Derek Heater, *Citizenship: The Civic Ideal in World History, Politics and Education* (London, 1990), p. 3.
66 Greek citizenship was particularly attractive to late nineteenth-century positivists, including T. H. Green's coterie at Oxford who advocated the creation of a 'social solidarity' through the search for the good and a consequent valuation of ethical behaviour: see Frank Turner, *The Greek Heritage in Victorian Britain* (New Haven, CT, 1981), pp. 358–68.
67 See Norman Vance, *The Victorians and Ancient Rome* (Cambridge, MA, 1997).
68 See C. P. Lucas, *Greater Rome and Greater Britain* (Oxford, 1912); and James Bryce, *The Ancient Roman Empire and the British Empire in India; The Diffusion of Roman and English Law Throughout the World: Two Historical Studies* (London, 1914). Bryce, one of the leading legal scholars of his era, also wrote copiously on citizenship: see for instance his *The Hindrances to Good Citizenship* (New Haven, CT, 1909).
69 Acts 23: 25–9. In declaring the principle of *civis Romanus sum* in the House as the climax of his defence of Britain's intervention in the Don Pacifico affair, Palmerston spoke to the global currency of British citizenship. (He also earned the reprimand of Gladstone, whose command of Latin was far superior to that of the Prime Minister.) Don Pacifico, a Portuguese Jew who was a British subject because he was born in Gibraltar, sought redress from the British Government after his house in Athens had been sacked during an Easter riot. When the Greek Government hesitated to act on the British Government's demand for restitution, Palmerston sent a British fleet to blockade the port of Athens. He then fended off parliamentary opposition to such perceived heavy-handedness by invoking St Paul, arguing that, 'as the Roman in the days of old held himself free from indignity when he could say *"civis Romanus sum"*, so also, a British subject, in whatever land he may be, shall feel confident that the watchful eye and strong arm of England will protect him against injustice and wrong.'
70 See Raymond F. Betts, 'The Allusion to Rome in British Imperialist Thought of the Late Nineteenth and Early Twentieth Centuries,' *Victorian Studies*, 15, 2 (December 1971), pp. 149–59.
71 Vance, *The Victorians and Ancient Rome*, p. 242.
72 Dummet and Nicol, *Subjects, Citizens, Aliens and Others*, pp. 32, 36.
73 See Heater, *Citizenship*, pp. 21–2, 24.

74 Thus, Edmund Burke was an influential figure for conservative imperialists of the latter era.
75 See T. H. Marshall, 'Citizenship and Social Class' (1950), reprinted in *Citizenship and Social Class*, ed. Tom Bottomore (Concord, MA, 1992), pp. 7-15.
76 Ibid., p. 18.
77 Ibid., p. 19.
78 The notion that political ideas and theories are 'images,' creations of the 'imagination,' has held the attention of numerous recent historians: see for instance Benedict Anderson, *Imagined Communities* (London: 1982), on the matrix of nationalism, imperialism, and abstract projection, or Dror Wahrman, *Imagining the Middle Class: The Political Representation of Class in Britain, c. 1780–1840* (Cambridge, 1995), on the intellectual *creation* of the middles class in late Georgian Britain.
79 Charles Tilly, 'Citizenship, Identity, and Social History,' in Tilly (ed.) *Citizenship, Identity and Social History* (Cambridge, 1996), p. 8.
80 The use of this term is significant, as Tilly defines citizenship in conscious opposition to the postmodern sensibility which he sees as increasingly hegemonic in the social sciences. This sensibility encourages skepticism regarding the possibility of verifiable social knowledge, challenges claims of systematic social change, and asserts that only language represents *reality*. Tilly argues that each of these notions is inimical to the concept of citizenship, as the latter represents a collective will/purpose/action: see ibid., pp. 2, 3.
81 Ibid., pp. 8, 9.
82 Ibid., pp. 9-11.
83 On the rise of nationalism in the late Victorian era, see Eric Hobsbawm, *Nations and Nationalism since 1780: Programme, Myth, Reality* (London, 1991), pp. 101-30.
84 The classification of class consciousness as a horizontal category and of nationalism as a vertical category is drawn from Daniel Patrick Moyniham, *Pandaemonium: Ethnicity in International Politics* (Oxford, 1993), p. 125. This terminology has a long pedigree.
85 In Britain, under the pervasive influence of liberal ideals and values, minority groups usually opted for assimilation. Britain, for instance, provided a home for countless exiles from nationalist continental conflagrations.
86 For the argument that 'the informed citizen' is central to the republican model of citizenship, see Michael Schudson, *The Good Citizen: A History of American Civil Life* (New York, 1998).
87 Expansion, Arendt has argued, was the result of the confluence of mob and capital, and gave a new life to nationalism; only outside the body politic did national, rather than local, identity become important: H. Arendt, *The Origins of Totalitarianism* (New York, 1958), pp. 154-5.
88 As Michael Ignatieff acknowledges, the term 'autistic', as a political adjective, was used by Hans Magnus Enzensburger: *The Warrior's Honour* (Toronto, 1999 [1998]), pp. 60-7.
89 The terms 'London,' 'imperial government,' and 'Whitehall' are used interchangeably to denote the British Parliament and its constituent decision-making bodies. This is to acknowledge that although the British Parliament was the nexus of imperial decision-making, different individuals and bodies were responsible for different measures.
90 Imperial historians into the 1960s largely agreed with this verdict. In A. L. Burt's comprehensive and influential textbook *The Evolution of the British Empire and Commonwealth* (Boston, MA, 1956), for instance, 'nationalism' is mainly reserved for descriptions of the Irish, the Boers (Afrikaners), and Quebeçois: see pp. 133-4, 271, 549-50. The emergence of colonial nationalism (i.e. a nationalism whose core loyalty was directed to the emerging dominion state, not the imperial State) was of course remarked upon in the dominions long before it was taken into

account by Britons: see for instance George Wrong, 'The Growth of Nationalism in the British Empire,' *American Historical Review,* 22 (1916–17), pp. 45–57.
91 Jürgen Habermas, 'Citizenship and National Identity: Some Reflections of the Future of Europe,' *Praxis International,* 12, 1 (1992), p. 3.
92 Stuart Wallace argues in *War and the Image of Germany: British Academics 1914–1918* (Edinburgh, 1988), that British Germanophilia was in the decline from the 1880s on. His study is concerned with academics, however, and their concerns in the decades before the First World War were largely with German educational organization and practice, not necessarily German thought or culture *per se.* It was the war experience itself which caused the rejection of German ideas. Thus, 'doubts were expressed before 1914 about the German model of university development, but it was the war which raised questions about the uses to which German scholarship were put': ibid., p. 5.
93 See Kurt Willis, 'The Introduction and Critical Reception of Hegelian Thought in Britain, 1830–1900,' *Victorian Studies,* 32, 1 (1988), pp. 85–111; and Sandra den Otter, *British Idealism and Social Explanation: A Study in Late-Victorian Thought* (Oxford, 1996), pp. 23–4, 41, 43–4.
94 Den Otter, *British Idealism and Social Explanation,* pp. 6–7.
95 Ibid., p. 23. The influence of Kant on British philosophers and Victorian thought in general has most often been located within liberal traditions, and furthermore is usually seen as indirect. Stefan Collini, for instance, notes the 'unreflective Kantianism of Victorian moral commonplaces,' and argues that Victorians' attention to the importance of 'feeling in moral action' represents a divergence from Kantian thought: *Public Moralists* (Oxford, 1991), pp. 63–4. In this sense, the moral cosmopolitanism expressed by Buchan and Curtis, two 'liberal' or 'progressive' conservatives, is consistent with a general late-Victorian affinity for a 'broad' Kantianism, expressing the spirit if not the detail of Kant's political ideas.
96 Sometimes translated as *Perpetual Peace* or *On Perpetual Peace;* on Kant's arguments on cosmopolitan citizenship, see also Katrin Flikschuh, *Kant and Modern Political Philosophy* (Cambridge, 2000), esp. pp. 144–206; Pauline Kleingeld, 'Six Varieties of Cosmopolitanism in Late Eighteenth-Century Germany,' *Journal of the History of Ideas,* 60, 3 (July 1999), pp. 505–24; and Howard Williams, *Kant's Political Philosophy* (Oxford, 1983).
97 Immanuel Kant, *Eternal Peace,* trans. Carl J. Friedrich, in *The Philosophy of Kant: Immanuel's Kant's Moral and Political Writings,* ed. Carl J. Friedrich (New York, 1949), p. 431.
98 Ibid., p. 436.
98 Immanuel Kant, *Idea for a Universal History with a Cosmopolitan Intent,* trans. Carl J. Friedrich, in ibid., p. 127.
100 Kant, *Eternal Peace,* p. 437, n. 4.
101 Ibid., pp. 437–48.
102 'But it is a right to visit (*Besuchsrecht*) which belongs to all men – the right belonging to all men to offer their society on account of the common possession of the surface of the earth. Since it is a globe, they cannot disperse infinitely, but must tolerate each other. *No man has a greater fundamental right to occupy a particular spot than any other*': ibid., p. 446, emphasis added.
103 As quoted in Fred Anderson, *Crucible of War: the Seven Years' War and the Fate of Empire in British North America, 1754–1766* (New York, 2000), p. xix.
104 Donal Lowry, 'The Crown, Empire Loyalism and the Assimilation of Non-British White Subjects in the British World: An Argument against "Ethnic Determinism",' *Journal of Imperial and Commonwealth History (JICH),* 21, 2 (May 2003), p. 99.
105 Andrew Thompson, 'The Language of Loyalism in Southern Africa, c. 1870–1939,' *English Historical Review,* 118, 477 (June 2003), pp. 635–40; John Weaver, *The Great Land Rush and the Making of the Modern World, 1650–1900* (Montreal and Kingston, 2003), pp. 72, 160–6.

106 Satadru Sen, *Migrant Races: Empire, Identity and K. S. Ranjitsinhji* (Manchester, 2004), p. 128.
107 Britain had secured the settlement colonies, as their collective title indicates, largely through the emigration of Britons; the dependent Empire, meanwhile, had been acquired through either force or indirect influence. As such, the ties between Britain and the settlement colonies were much stronger than those between Britain and the dependencies.
108 British Nationality and Status of Aliens Act, 1914, 4 & 5 Geo. V, c. 17, s. 10 (1); Naturalization Act, 1870, 33 & 34 Vict., c. 14, s. 10 (1). The latter Act marked a departure from previous common law precedent, which held that allegiance to the crown was indelible, by stating that 'a woman shall be deemed to be the subject of the state of which her husband is for the time being a subject.' On the evolution of married women's nationality status in Great Britain, see M. Page Baldwin, 'Subject to Empire: Married Women and the British Nationality and Status of Aliens Act,' *Journal of British Studies*, 40 (October 2001), pp. 522–56.
109 On naturalization and marriage in the United States, see Nancy Cott, *Public Vows: A History of Marriage and the Nation* (Cambridge, MA, 2000), esp. pp. 132–55; and Candice Lewis Bredbenner, *A Nationality of Her Own: Women, Marriage and the Law of Citizenship* (Berkeley and Los Angles, 1998).
110 The *Proceedings of the Royal Colonial Institute (PRCI)* were published after 1911 as *United Empire*. On the Royal Colonial Institute, renamed the Royal Empire Society in 1928 and later the Royal Commonwealth Society, see James Greenlee, *Education and Imperial Unity, 1901–1926* (New York, 1987), and Trevor Reese, *The History of the Royal Commonwealth Society 1868–1968* (London, 1968).
111 E. B. Sargant, 'British Citizenship', *United Empire*, 3, 5 (1912), p. 367.
112 A separate rhetorical reason for the increased use of 'citizen,' especially to denote 'subject,' was the increasingly pejorative understanding of the latter term. For similar reasons, Britons began to refer to 'Serbia' as opposed to 'Servia': see Walter Hely-Hutchinson's discussion in *United Empire*, 3, 1 (January 1912), p. 68.
113 Ibid., pp. 368–9.
114 Ibid., pp. 369–70.
115 Ibid., p. 373.
116 See the letters in nos 7, 8, and 9 of *United Empire*, vol. 3 (1912).
117 Richard Jebb, 'The Imperial Naturalization Bill,' *Quarterly Review*, 220, 438 (January 1914), pp. 3–4.
118 F. P. Walton, *United Empire*, 3, 1 (January 1912), pp. 65–6.
119 Ralph Williams, in ibid., p. 70.
120 H. E. Egerton, in ibid., pp. 66–7.
121 James Bryce, *United Empire*, 3, 2 (February 1912), pp. 124–5.
122 'British Nationality and Citizenship,' *Colonial Office Journal*, 6, 2 (1912), pp. 106, 107, 109; the journal, though not an official publication, was disseminated with the approval of the Secretary of State for the Colonies for the purpose of popularizing the Office's work.
123 Ibid., p. 107. Edward III expanded the definition of *jus soli* to include also the principle of *jus sanguinis* (matter of family), allowing children of British subjects born abroad to be subjects.
124 Ibid., p. 111.
125 Walton, 'Nationality and Citizenship,' *University Magazine*, 11, 1 (February 1912), pp. 24–5.
126 W. Wilfred Campbell, 'Imperialism in Canada,' speech to the Empire Club, 23 November 1904, in *The Empire Club of Canada Speeches, 1904–1905*, ed. J. Castell Hopkins (Toronto, 1906), p. 31.
127 Thompson, 'Imperial Ideology in Edwardian Britain,' pp. 9–10.
128 The second such chair in the Empire after the Beit at Oxford.
129 W. L. Grant, 'The Teaching of Colonial History,' *Queen's Quarterly*, 18 (1911), p. 186.

130 Reverend Father Bernard Vaughan, 'Imperial Citizenship,' speech to the Empire Club, 15 September 1911, in *Empire Club Speeches* (Toronto, 1911), pp. 20-1.
131 Craig Brown, 'Goldwin Smith and Anti-Imperialism,' in Ramsay Cook et al. (eds) *Imperial Relations in the Age of Laurier* (Toronto, 1969), p. 21.
132 W. T. Stead, *Review of Reviews*, 13 (February 1896), p. 102.
133 Deborah Lavin, 'Lionel Curtis and the Idea of the Commonwealth,' in Madden et al. (eds) *Oxford and the Idea of the Commonwealth*, p. 101.
134 Adele Perry, *On the Edge of Empire: Gender, Race and the Making of British Columbia, 1849-1871* (Toronto, 2001).
135 There were, to be sure, other important factors.
136 Kathryn Tidrick, *Empire and the English Character* (London, 1990), p. 223.

PART I

Theories of imperial citizenship

CHAPTER TWO

Lionel Curtis: imperial citizenship as a prelude to world government

One of the most persistent voices of Empire in the early decades of the twentieth century belonged not to a sitting politician, nor to a Tory grandee, but to a man who operated outside of official circles. Lionel Curtis, if one was forced to attribute to him a career, could best be described as an imperial spokesman and organizer. Through his writings, travels, and eclectic and exhaustive proselytizing, Curtis helped maintain imperialism as a subject of importance for the public and Whitehall alike. Imperial leaders from Cecil Rhodes and Sir Alfred Milner to Jan Smuts, New Zealand Prime Minister Sir Joseph Ward, and Winston Churchill looked to Curtis as a spokesman and consultant whenever Empire–commonwealth came to the fore as a political issue.[1] He was a figure of single-minded purpose, his outlook illustrated in a letter he sent in 1911 to the young Canadian Vincent Massey, then a Rhodes Scholar at Oxford:

> My deepest conviction is that in politics as in other matters there is a truth which can be discovered by earnest and dispassionate enquiry and that those who have the patience to reach it and abide in it will find that they meet on common ground which will give them the basis for concerted action.[2]

Through his work with the imperial pressure group the Round Table, and more broadly in his advocacy of imperial federation, Curtis played a leading role in imperial affairs through much of the first half of the twentieth century. In his interests, then, he differed little from the scores of other Oxbridge graduates who looked to Empire, rather than the Bar, politics, or the City, for their professional niche. What set Curtis apart from his peers, indeed what characterized his career in its entirety, was an industriousness of almost monastic intensity[3] and a proselytizing spirit which did not recognize defeat. He developed a reputation in imperial circles as a man above politics, a conciliator who could mediate between competing camps with fairness and equanimity.[4] His biographer, Deborah Lavin, has written that he was in the business of public relations before that 'calling' had crystallized into a profession.[5]

Curtis saw Empire as mankind's best hope of fostering and preserving peace, a goal he believed could be pursued through the means of imperial citizenship. Though this position strikes modern ears as naive, and not a little pretentious, it was consistent with the normative view of politics and the belief that political service should be devoted to a search for a common good that characterized much political debate, domestic as well as imperial, during this era. While Curtis has certainly attracted the notice of historians, his influence has been attenuated by two factors. First, he has often been studied in tandem with his Round Table peers, purveyors of the ultimately lost cause of imperial union, and thus unintentionally can appear as 'merely another clubman.'[6] Second, his political and intellectual activities have not fitted within the purview of much recent imperial historiography, in which attention has shifted from political themes to those of identity. A figure such as Curtis appears in that literature as an opponent of equality. While such works have much to tell us about the shape and scope of the Empire, attempts to dislodge older 'master narratives' of Empire have also tended to portray the dependencies as the most prominent feature of British imperialism. Such a focus would have struck contemporary imperialists as odd, for their primary interest was the settlement colonies.[7] In focusing on constructing bonds of citizenship and greater equality between the Empire's white subjects, Curtis represented a liberal, though culturally myopic, imperialism, one central to contemporaries' debates about the Empire's future. While it has become commonplace among historians to conceive of the Empire as an 'imagined community,'[8] it is less clear how contemporaries themselves 'imagined' this 'community.'[9] Curtis's ideas concerning imperial citizenship point to one of the central strands of the imperial thought web – the idea of union consecrated in an imperial citizenship.

For this fervent devotion to his cause, and his unwavering belief in its efficacy and justness, Curtis's friends referred to him as 'the prophet.'[10] A true believer, whether religious or secular, is marked above all by faith – faith that what one believes in is true, just, and of paramount importance. This is especially true in matters of the mind. Of the many and varied individuals identified closely with Empire in the early twentieth century, Lionel Curtis can be counted among its most dedicated devotees, and he carried its gospel widely.

An imperial upbringing

Curtis was born on 7 March 1872 and was raised in an evangelical environment.[11] Though he moved away from the Church of England while at Oxford, Curtis nonetheless derived from his upbringing a sense of divine mission, of service. As he recalled in 1935, 'I myself was brought up as what in America they call a fundamentalist.'[12] He transferred the biblical literalism of his childhood to the study of the Empire, which he came to see as a 'New Jerusalem.' Commenting in 1910 on South African Union, a process in which he was a leading figure, Curtis noted: 'It is indeed impossible not to feel it is the Lord's and that it is wondrous in our eyes.'[13] In the course of a speech in Johannesburg in 1906 advocating union, he invoked the Parable of the Talents, stating: 'He that is faithful in little is faithful in much.'[14] Such biblical allusions were not uncommon in pre-war British culture, despite the mounting secular assault on traditional religious life. The 'new evangelicalism' of the 1860s and 1870s had stressed an engagement with worldly affairs over personal salvation, with the Empire in particular seen increasingly as a providential field for reformism.[15] In holding such beliefs, Curtis showed a greater affinity to Gladstonian moral politics than to the *realpolitik* outlook then generally in ascendence among British politicians such as Lord Salisbury and A. J. Balfour. He evinced what one historian has termed a 'Christian–progressivist' sense of 'evolutionary salvationism.'[16] But Curtis should not be mistaken for a religious imperial crusader in the vein of David Livingstone. The real significance of his faith is that it shaped his conception of imperial governance, and the concomitant role of the individual in the imperium. Indeed, Curtis's notion of imperial citizenship much resembles the Parable of Talents, with each individual tending to his given task in service to the whole. This is the significance of Curtis's organic view of Empire.

Here Curtis's religious impulses intermingled with the Idealism of T. H. Green, a central influence on Curtis's Oxford education.[17] Green advanced a moral theory of politics which necessitated man's active pursuit of what he called 'the common good.' His ideas concerning social reform greatly influenced the New Liberals, but also resonated with liberal conservatives, such as Curtis, who found in Idealism inspiration for holistic solutions to issues of peace and Empire. British idealism itself constituted a 'community of opinion,'[18] rather than a system of thought, a distinction characterized by the ambiguity of Curtis's ideas on imperial citizenship. He epitomized the broader trend among many early twentieth-century imperialists to seek systemic rather than empirical interpretations of political and imperial problems, leaving the details for others to carry out. Indeed, Curtis achieved only a third-class degree, a record which he tried in later life to overcome through sheer industry: 'I'm only a third in greats and I spend my life panting to keep up with firsts.'[19] The combination of Curtis's evangelicalism, particularly his sense of religion as reverence, and his Idealism led him to find in imperialism a secular religion.

Despite his fervent devotion to his creed, Curtis was not attracted to partisan politics. In an age of mass democracy, his aristocratic bearing left him unsuitable for the hustings. He was much more comfortable in the smoking room, a milieu he made his own. Devoting his life instead to Empire, he produced a prodigious, if not entirely original, corpus of work on his chosen subject, securing a reputation as a mediator and man 'above politics.' Curtis's formative practical experience came in Southern Africa, where his views on imperial government and citizenship were cast in the crucible of post-South African War reconstruction. Following service as secretary to the Liberal Unionist MP Leonard Courtney, then as private secretary to Lord Welby, the Vice-Chairman of the London County Council, Curtis moved to Southern Africa in 1900 to serve his country as a cyclist in the City Imperial Volunteers. He served only a few months in that capacity before returning to England on a personal matter. South Africa, however, had cast a hold on him, and he returned to the Cape on 2 October 1900, quickly securing a post under Milner. He served under the Pro-Consul in a number of official capacities from 1901 to 1906, holding a post in the Johannesburg City Council and, later, as an assistant colonial secretary responsible for urban affairs. His status as an imperial expert was firmly established through his participation in the drafting of the Selborne Memorandum (1907),[20] the document which helped shape the new Union of South Africa's constitution two years later.[21]

Curtis shared his contemporaries' unshakeable belief in the supremacy of British political culture. His was not, however, a myopic view of imperial citizenship. The young Curtis was not unfavourably disposed towards the Boers, even during the war: 'My little experience has been that the Boer like the Englishman is not a model of all the virtues but neither is he beyond other races a villain; and just because the stupidity of our rulers has set us to shoot each other should we say that he is?'[22] Contact with Milner would temper Curtis's disdain for his 'rulers,' and indeed, he came to idolize the Proconsul under whom he worked in South Africa. Curtis's devotion to Milner was perhaps the strongest of all the members of the 'Kindergarten,' the term which came to identify the small group of young Oxford men who came out to the Cape to aid in post-war reconstruction.[23] Like many of his fellow Milnerites, he was devoted not to the great

Pro-Consul's policies or imperialism *per se*, but rather to the determined manner in which Milner pursued his convictions. In response to public criticism of Milner's anti-Germanism in the wake of the Naval Crisis of 1909, Curtis expressed his admiration for his mentor by recourse to his classical background: *Justum et tenacem propositi virum non civium ardor prava jubentium non voltus instantis tyranni mente quatit solida, neque Auster*.[24] Though Curtis was later to move away from Milner's race-based notion of imperial citizenship, the two men maintained a close working and personal relationship until 1925, when Milner died. It was Milner, more than any other person, who preached the importance of Empire, the mission to which Curtis would devote his career and indeed his life.

Towards an imperial citizenship

Curtis developed three core ideas regarding imperial citizenship, none of which he would fully articulate until the end of the Edwardian period. Of primary importance was his growing conviction that imperial federation held the key to world peace, and provided the buttress of *civilization*. Curtis understood civilization in terms of a British-led European civilization, drawn in equal parts from the Greco-Roman tradition and the legacy of liberty bequeathed by the twin revolutions of the late eighteenth century in America and France. Second, Curtis came to believe, through his constitutional work in South Africa, that imperial governance must be centralized. He had initially been intrigued by the ideas of journalist and imperial traveller Richard Jebb on colonial nationalism and the importance to Empire of allowing the (white) colonies a greater degree of autonomy.[25] However, in embracing centralization, Curtis came to argue that the imperial citizen must be intrinsically tied to the State of Empire, not to the local state. Third, in an age where the intellectual divide between the *elite* and the *masses* was widening on every front,[26] Curtis tried to reconcile his latent conviction that those most able to rule should govern with the ever-emerging political reality that democracy necessitates a role for the elector. He tried to square this circle by arguing that while all citizens of Empire are entitled to its benefits, some citizens were more equal than others. Thus his adherence to the Victorian notion of tutelage, what Thomas Metcalfe has in a less euphemistic manner termed 'authoritative liberalism.'[27] Curtis's idea of imperial citizenship was a paradox of equality in theory and inequality in practice.

These three convictions could be realized, in Curtis's view, through the creation of a federal imperial union, a political structure uniting Britain and her English-speaking of settlement, encouraging them to act in concert in pursuit of their common goals. Such an 'Anglosphere,' however, would prove to be stillborn.[28] After all, the idea of a federal imperial system was not new. Indeed, the Imperial Federation League had brought the idea to the forefront of imperial debate in the 1880s.[29] In the wake of Confederation in Canada, and increased inter-colonial cooperation in Australia, intellectuals and public figures such as the Canadian George R. Parkin had urged that London adopt the federal system for the Empire as a whole. The federalists failed the first time, for a variety of reasons.[30] Despite Joseph Chamberlain's efforts at the Diamond Jubilee in 1897, the idea of federation lost momentum until the aftermath of the South African War. While historians of the Edwardian period have drawn attention to concerns over 'national efficiency,'[31] widespread after Britain's victory in Southern Africa, there also emerged from the cauldron of war a renewed debate over the federal idea. It was seen, not only by Milner and his Kindergarten but also more widely in imperial circles, as both a means to prevent future imperial conflicts and as a template for the long-conceived idea of a union of South Africa, the prelude to imperial federation itself. It was as a participant in this public discussion that Curtis began to formulate his idea of imperial citizenship.

In a federal imperial union Curtis saw a guarantor of world peace, an idea he had derived from his earlier constitutional work in South Africa. South Africa consisted of linked but competing components, each of which pursued its own self-interest ('national interest' except that they were only colonies). This relationship made it inevitable that local conflicts would necessarily explode into regional ones, pulling all interested parties into war. This, according to Curtis, was precisely what had happened in the case of the South African War. Apart from neglecting his patron's decisive role in precipitating the contest,[32] Curtis here also ignored the decisive role of economics, especially competition over mineral resources. Cumbersome governmental machinery had not created war. Curtis's frustration, much as was Milner's, was that the lack of unhindered British regional sovereignty, owing to the existence of autonomous or semi-autonomous regional entities such as the Transvaal and the Orange Free State,[33] made it impossible for Britain to act as it wished. Thus, the Government at the Cape was unsuccessful in securing what it deemed fair economic and political rights for the *üitlander* (non-Boer prospectors) population in the Transvaal. Curtis thus phrased his analysis of the conflict and its legacy in the language of peace. He argued that a federal union, formed in the likeness of the Westminster model, was not only the best, but the only guarantee of peace: there was 'no halfway house between open conflict and union.'[34]

Curtis also drew a number of lessons from his time in municipal government. Upon leaving the Johannesburg Town Council in 1903, where he had served as town clerk since 1901, Curtis delivered a speech to his fellow-councilors in which he outlined the views he would later develop though his work with the Round Table. Government, in Curtis's mind, functioned most effectively when representative traditions were enhanced by 'study groups,' experts who would reflect on problems and advise their elected counterparts.[35] The absence of such groups led to 'government of platitude and panacea.'[36] The Round Table was the period's most successful such group.

Curtis and the Round Table
The Round Table arose from the debate over imperial defence which captured the attention of colonial and British officials alike in 1909. The immediate trigger of this debate was the alarming expansion of the German Navy. Britain believed that the dominions should contribute to the cost of their own defence. Sentiment on this issue was mixed in the dominions themselves. The issue provoked the most discussion in Canada, where the naval debate dominated the Parliamentary Sessions of 1910–11. Curtis viewed with dismay the acrimony which characterized British–dominions negotiations over this issue. In informal meetings held in South Africa throughout the summer of 1909, Curtis, along with several other members of Milner's Kindergarten, agreed that a well-defined imperial union, not dissimilar to that envisioned by Joseph Chamberlain during the tariff debate earlier in the decade, was the best method of preventing imperial cleavages. Out of these meetings was formed the Round Table. Besides Curtis, founding members included the political publicist Phillip Kerr (later Lord Lothian), the banker R. H. Brand, the writer F. S. Oliver, William Morris, George Craik, Martin Holland, and Lords Anglesey, Howick, Lovat, and Wolmer. Other members in the 1910s included Geoffrey Dawson, editor of *The Times* (1912–19), the politicians Leopold Amery and Milner, both future Colonial Secretaries, and the Oxford scholar Reginald Coupland.[37]

Though they acknowledged that the dominions cherished their independence in matters of self-government, the Round Table argued that their dependence on Britain for defence funding made formal union a necessity. The imperial union they envisioned would be governed by a new bicameral imperial parliament, consisting of two houses, an elected lower house and an upper house of peers.[38] The imperial parliament would deliberate on issues of imperial importance, most notably defence and foreign policy. It would also have the ability to impose imperial taxes and mint currency. In exchange for participating by proportionate representation in the imperial parliament, the dominions would enjoy a broad-based autonomy in domestic issues.[39] The most important domestic jurisdiction was the ability to set local tariffs, illustrating Curtis's position, at least implicitly, on the most pressing imperial issue of the early twentieth century.

To bring about such a union, the Round Table decided that cells should be developed in each dominion, under the guidance of men 'of character and capacity,' for the purpose of bringing the issue of union before the public until such a time as a formal plan could be constructed.[40] Curtis later clarified the nature of such work in a letter to Asian specialist and civil servant Valentine Chirol. He explained that the Round Table would function like a royal commission, gathering information but not advocating a position until it had completed its work.[41] Finances for this endeavour were raised from the members themselves, from wealthy benefactors, and from the Rhodes Trust.

The Round Table was from the beginning an elitist enterprise, and it never claimed otherwise. It held regular 'moots,' where members would gather to discuss pertinent imperial issues. It also founded an eponymous journal,[42] The *Round Table*, in which anonymous articles pressed the cause for imperial union. The original impetus for anonymity was to reflect a group consensus on issues and minimize allegations of personal bias.[43] The principle of anonymity was also applied to the creation of the group's plan for union, dubbed the *Green Memorandum*. Curtis, however, came to be the guiding force, writing the final copy and indeed almost the entirety of earlier drafts. When the document was finally offered to the public for perusal as *The Problem of the Commonwealth* (1916), with an initial press run of 5,000,[44] Curtis felt compelled to state in the Preface that 'the writer himself has, of necessity, had to decide what to reject and what to accept. He has no authority for stating, therefore, that the report represents any opinion but his own.'[45] This statement represents not the pro-forma introductory apologia of writers, but rather the divisions which had sprung up between Curtis and his Round Table fellow-members.[46] While these divisions produced no decisive ideological rift among the group's members, they led Curtis to assume a more independent public voice, and from that point on his ideas on imperial citizenship are more easily distinguishable from those of the Round Table as a whole.

It is difficult to adjudge the influence of the Round Table in the 1910s. The subscription rate for the journal was never large, with a maximum of 400 in Australia and a peak of 698 (of which only 372 were paid) in Canada in 1916.[47] None of the principal members, including Curtis, ever held high office, and their scheme of imperial federation was never realized. That said, the Round Table did exert informal influence. Its moots and dinners attracted leading politicians, such as Austen Chamberlain, and it benefited from broad social connections, enjoying the patronage of well-placed individuals such as Nancy Astor and Lady Selborne.[48] Curtis, meanwhile, built up a wide 'anglophone network' through his extensive travels in the Empire and continuous campaign of correspondence. Through these avenues, the Round Table on occasion gained the ear of policy-makers. Examples include Curtis and Brand converting Churchill to the idea of federation as a solution to the Home Rule crisis at social events at Cliveden in 1912, and Curtis providing a partial template for Montagu's 1917 reforms with his writing on self-rule.[49] As the decade wore on, some Round Table members ascended to positions of more direct power, particularly Kerr, who was a member of Lloyd George's 'Garden Suburb' and served as the Prime Minister's private secretary at Versailles.[50] The group's primary significance was probably in keeping imperial issues in the political consciousness, even if its prescriptions were rarely implemented. The *Round Table*, for instance, was the only journal addressing international and public affairs in Australia before 1929,[51] and the group can be given some credit for Britain's decision to create an Imperial War Cabinet in 1917, invite Indian observers to the 1917 Imperial Conference, and to invite dominion representatives to Versailles.

Curtis, particularly, also focused the public's attention on the relationship between Britain and the dominions. He argued that self-government, the goal toward which Britain's colonies were progressing, was effective only when people undertook a greater involvement in public affairs than simply exercising the vote. By 'greater involvement' Curtis did not mean increased autonomy, 'colonial nationalism' in the parlance of the period. Indeed, Curtis viewed the drift towards colonial self-reliance with concern, believing that incipient nationalist thought in the dominions served only to attenuate the common bond of Empire, not strengthen it. He did not reject colonial nationalism; nor was he ignorant of it. The principle of colonial nationalism was in fact at the heart of his idea of Empire, the goal to which imperial people were progressing. In *The Problem of the Commonwealth* he explained how this process had taken shape among the dominions:

> Each has asserted the right to decide for itself who shall inhabit its territories and how they shall live; and the people of each Dominion have constructed for themselves national governments competent to interpret public opinion on these matters, to formulate policies, and to

raise from the particular public to which they are responsible the taxation required to make them effective. And in equipping themselves to think and act as nations the peoples of the dominions like those of the United States, have severally acquired a national consciousness of their own. Canadians, Australians, and South Africans each think of themselves as nations distinct from the people of the British Isles, just as the British think of themselves as a nation distinct from the citizens of the United States.[52]

Further reflecting on Lord Durham's imperial legacy of responsible government, Curtis noted that '*in the last analysis* the colonists were free to decide all things for themselves, even the nature of their citizenship, was accepted as *articulus stantis aut cadentis imperii*, the cardinal principle of imperial policy.'[53] He thus recognized, and approved of as central to any working definition of imperial citizenship, the significance of colonial self-definition. His concern lay in the fear that the dominions would use this self-definition in a manner counter to the imperial 'common good,' by which he meant imperial unity. Specifically, he was concerned that colonial desires to conduct independent foreign relations would be counterproductive for the imperial enterprise, especially because the dominions were not able to contribute adequately to their own defence. As early as 1905, he put forth his conviction that the colonies must be reintegrated into the Empire rather than given greater autonomy: 'Colony is not a territory, a code of laws and a scheme of institutions, but a society of people, and nothing which touches the manner in which those people are to live can in the end affect them so profoundly as the ultimate and fundamental question as to who the people are themselves to be.'[54]

To prevent imperial dissolution, Curtis suggested that the dominions would enjoy proportional representation in the proposed imperial parliament, and would thus have some say in the conduct of foreign policy relating to their territory. Each constituent of Empire would send representatives based upon its taxable capacity, and according to its current distribution of the franchise. Such a structure would show respect for the colonies' varied conceptions of the franchise (women, for instance, could vote in New Zealand by 1893; indigenous peoples in South Africa could not). This idea, however, proved unacceptable both to dominion leaders and the British Government. The Liberal H. H. Asquith, British Prime Minister, was not sympathetic to the proposal of an imperial parliament when this idea was floated, apparently without the Round Table's blessing, by New Zealand Premier Sir Joseph Ward at the 1911 Imperial Conference: referring to foreign policy and defence, he stated: 'that authority cannot be shared, and the co-existence side by side with the cabinet of the United Kingdom of this proposed body ... would, in our judgement, be absolutely fatal to our present system of responsible government.'[55]

The problem of creating *citizens*

Asquith's comments illustrate the broader problem Curtis faced in formulating his ideas on imperial citizenship, and explains why those ideas remained fissiparous. Namely, Curtis struggled to reconcile the existence of multiple loyalties within the Empire with the formation of a unified imperial state. This struggle manifested itself in his thought on the nettlesome question of race; in his misreading of the American federal example as articulated by its most vocal proponent, Alexander Hamilton; in his attempt to confront such divisions in the immediate future through the principle of tutelage; and in the principle of *dyarchy* he suggested for India. Curtis's difficulty in outlining how multiple loyalties could be subordinated to a loyalty to the imperial State explains why he was unable to offer a coherent definition of imperial citizenship.

As we have seen, Curtis's ideas drew heavily on the campaigns of the imperial federationists of the 1880s and early 1890s. Curtis shared their conviction that union was a matter of politics, not *a priori* a matter of race. He pursued this line of thought in South Africa, where he and his Kindergarten peers promoted 'an anglophone form of south Africanism.' This new identity would unite white South Africans through a non-ethnic loyalism based on a shared commitment to regional progress and development.[56] While he did not share the more stridently expressed views of British racialists such as the eugenicist Francis Galton, the philosopher Karl Pearson, and the civil servant and writer Benjamin Kidd, neither was Curtis a progressive on the issue. He was particularly ambivalent concerning what was then called the 'coloured vote' in South Africa. His desire to construct an inclusive white nationalism led him to reach agreement with Jan Christian Smuts, in conversation in South Africa in 1909, that the expansion of the franchise to black South Africans was not then politically advisable.[57]

Early twentieth-century Britons often confused *race* and *culture*.[58] This muddied thought allowed men such as Curtis to hold two seemingly incongruent positions: first, that the British race was the world's most advanced; and, second, that non-Britons could become members of the British race if properly 'educated'. In accepting this position Curtis was developing the ideas of federationists such as Joseph Chamberlain and Canadian Archbishop McGoun. McGoun rejected an imperial union based upon the superiority of one race, writing that 'the people of the Anglo-Saxon race have no more right to assume sovereignty over the other races of the world, than the Greeks did to class the rest of mankind as barbarians.' Rather, imperial union was to be a political one: 'The political idea we desire to keep... is the extension of the reign of individual and local liberty... for the preservation of political rights, and for resisting injustice and oppression whether of individuals, provinces, nations or races.'[59] Even more strident voices at home, such as the outspoken radical right-wing MP Henry Page Croft, argued for an imperial citizenship based on the primacy of Empire over the local.[60]

Curtis specifically used the notion of race in his interpretation of imperial citizenship in much the same manner as the later British socialist literary critic Raymond Williams used the term 'culture.'[61] Williams, in drawing on Matthew Arnold's explication of 'culture' as denoting that which unites a civilization, appropriated the term to denote an organic society where work was creative and cooperative. While Curtis shared neither Arnold's creative impulses nor the later Williams's socialist convictions, he too held that culture conveyed the idea of union and affinity, which served to improve the intellectual life of all members of society (hence the juxtaposition in the title of Arnold's *Culture and Anarchy*). Curtis's conception of federation and its attendant imperial citizenship of local autonomy subordinate to a shared loyalty to the imperial crown were predicated upon a view of political culture as creative and cooperative.

This helps explain why Curtis was concerned fundamentally with an imperial citizenship which occluded non-white subjects. The dependent, or 'coloured', Empire provided a paradox of citizenship which he was unable to resolve. This paradox was especially apparent in the case of India. Curtis's estimate of India's population was 312,632,537, a figure which he had extrapolated from the 1911 census and published in *The Problem of the Commonwealth*. As the total population of the British Empire at this time was 433,574,001,[62] India thus made up almost three-quarters (72.1%) of the entire Empire. Any proposed imperial government must therefore address the question of Indian representation. Curtis understood this fact. The sheer size of the collected Indian provinces, however, dictated that Indian representatives would overwhelm those from the rest of the Empire if given proportional representation. A young Curtis put this problem quite baldly to Kerr in 1907. Commenting on the 'crisis' of Indian labour in the Transvaal,[63] Curtis wrote that the granting of equal rights for all imperial subjects was a dangerous proposition, for the result would be that 'in the coming centuries the great reservoir of Indian races will be opened and allowed to deluge the whole of the Imperial Dominions and submerge the white community.'[64] Curtis's views on race when he was in South Africa were similarly driven by pragmatic political goals. When he attacked *racialism*, he meant divisions between whites in South Africa. He did not argue that indigenous peoples were *unfit* for citizenship; rather, he believed that their inclusion would create cleavages between whites, thus threatening the project of union. Along with his Kindergarten peers, he thus believed that a solution to 'the native question' was necessary to create the white colonial nationalism which would lead to union. This solution was segregation, though Curtis was notably, and perhaps intentionally, vague on the specific place of indigenous peoples in the new union. Segregation was thus a means to secure other goals, rather than a goal in itself, in Curtis's thinking on citizenship and South Africa.[65] For the future of indigenous peoples in the region, this amounted to a distinction without difference.

Local patriotism was also a transitional stage for Curtis,[66] an aspirational identity which pointed toward full imperial union, not as an end in itself. An imperial citizenship which recognized all imperial subjects as equal was not in his immediate view, and indeed was impractical given the racialist attitudes of early twentieth-century Britons and the gross economic and social disjunction between white and non-white subjects. Like McGoun, Curtis believed that the common identity fostered by a shared British culture enabled the Empire to function as an institution of peace, a belief confirmed by the Empire's participation in the First World War. As he wrote in one of the draft versions of the *Green Memorandum*: 'To commonwealths war is a visitation to be faced, like famine or pestilence, only with the purpose of preventing its recurrence and protecting the liberty for which they stand.'[67] This is a variant on the central tenet of liberal international theory, which holds that liberal states, representing morally autonomous citizens holding rights to liberty, do not war with each other.[68] Curtis contrasted the benevolent imperialism of the British ideal with what he saw as a malevolent German variant that sought to spread 'its own culture over all the world, blind to the truth that for each individual and race the only culture is their own.'[69] Curtis was fully aware of the charge that the British Empire was really no different, attempting to achieve by legislation what he accused the Germans of seeking by the sword – namely, imperium. The difference which put the British in the right, he contended, was an adherence to *freedom*, a principle he contrasted to Central European *autocracy*.

Comparisons to foreign nations were, however, rare in Curtis's early work. Though he was a liberal internationalist, and came to favour the construction of international organizations, he always believed in Anglo-Saxon leadership.[70] As for how non Anglo-Saxon nations would fit within his proposed world structure, his writing on this point is largely silent. His, after all, was an insular project, reflecting a parochial (some might say chauvinistic) streak strong among imperial thinkers of the day. A notable exception was his view of the United States, and particularly the political legacy of Alexander Hamilton. The United States was seen by many imperialists as the prodigal son of the imperial world, a wayward familial relation.[71] The connection between Hamilton's federalism and the British Empire had been popularized in a biographical study of Hamilton by F. S. Oliver, a Round Table 'fellow traveller' and an influence on Curtis.[72] While Hamilton was perhaps the least insular of the founding fathers, in drawing on his legacy Curtis wanted 'to have his cake and eat it too.' On the one hand, Curtis saw in Hamilton's staunch Federalist position the ideal template for commonwealth. On the other, he elsewhere pursued the argument that the United States, in adopting an isolationist stance in world affairs for almost the entirety of its history, had reneged on its rightful duty to further the parliamentary tradition around the world. Stripped of its jingo shrillness, Kipling's famous 'white man's burden' line, delivered in verse to the United States during the latter's war with Spain, was here echoed by Curtis.[73]

Curtis further misread Hamilton in failing to see the real compromises the latter accepted in pursuing the collective goal of a united nation, most notably that concerning slavery. Curtis also did not understand that Hamilton sometimes engaged in rhetoric to make his point.[74] While Hamilton disagreed with the anti-Federalists over their view that the state government should be more powerful than the national Government, he shared with his foes a firm belief in private property as a political sacrament. It was this notion of property and ownership (Locke's legacy) which led to the awkward and somewhat disingenuous compromise over slavery. The founding fathers claimed by implication that non-white Americans would be excluded from full citizenship not because of their colour, but because they did not own property. Curtis, as we will see, shied away from any definition of imperial citizenship which recognized property as the determinant principle. Down this road lay a decreased role for Britain and the potential dominance of India if the sheer weight of the latter's demographics was translated into property ownership. A Hamiltonian federation might have been a useful model for small-scale union, as in South Africa, but it proved to be no more than rhetoric when applied to the Empire *in toto*. Furthermore, Curtis maintained an elitist disregard for mass politics with which Hamilton and his fellow-founding fathers, though they shared in spirit, had been forced to come to terms.

Here we move toward the paradox central to Curtis's notion of imperial citizenship. Commenting on the pacificist nature of true Empire, he stated:

> Empires must hold together, and that they can do only in so far as the peoples they include find that they answer to the needs not of one, but of all. The British Empire has held together in so far as Britain has discovered principles and evolved a system which are not British but human, and can only endure in so far as it grows more human still.[75]

The 'principles' which Britain had 'discovered' were those of liberty and freedom. The latter was the goal towards which the entire development of Empire was moving. This is why Curtis employed the teleological 'Project of a Commonwealth' as the working title of *Round Table Studies, Second Series* – the very endeavour of Empire was a process of spreading freedom:

> Freedom, like the principle of life in the physical world, is inseparable from growth. Commonwealths are the corporeal frame in which it is incarnate, and they cease to flourish when they cease to extend the principle that inspires them in an increasing degree to an ever-widening circle of men.[76]

This was not to say, however, that all those under the British crown were entitled to play an equal role in this process, nor even that the British themselves had set out as their goal the political education of other peoples. Rather, by assuming the imperial mantle, Britain had contracted the moral responsibility to promote improvement, much as, according to Curtis, an industrialist has a moral responsibility to ensure the welfare of his workers. The act of political education was the *telos* of Empire: 'In truth, this world-wide state is not, as some historians have vainly taught, an outcome of blunders, accidents, and crimes, but of the deepest necessities of human life. It is the project of a system designed on the only scale which is capable of meeting those needs.'[77]

If the Empire was the only means by which to meet the needs of freedom and liberty, some imperial subjects enjoyed a greater role in this process. By 1915, Curtis increasingly used the term 'the commonwealth.'[78] 'The commonwealth,' he recorded, existed to enlarge that class of citizens capable of participating in its public life: 'To endure ... a commonwealth must contain a sufficient proportion of citizens competent to share in the tasks of government, and, in fact, sharing them.' Put clearly, Curtis argued that a commonwealth, his vision for the future form of Empire, 'is a state in which government rests on the shoulders of *all its citizens who are fit for government*';[79] its success rested in the ability to 'realize its character as a commonwealth in time.'[80] The ambiguity in this last passage is unintentionally revealing of Curtis's Whiggish notion of imperial citizenship. If, instead of his intended meaning of urgency in understanding the nature of commonwealth as such, we parse this sentence to place the emphasis on the last three words, Curtis unintentionally reveals his conviction that it is important to understand Empire as a 'commonwealth in time,' a living process where citizenship gradually widens to encompass all under the British sovereign. These humanistic ideas were tempered by Curtis's separate and more conservative conviction that some men were more fit to govern than others. Thus the paradoxical nature of Curtis's thought on imperial citizenship.

Writing to Lady Selborne in 1915, Curtis expressed this conviction that in British society, and by extrapolation in the Empire, some were more fit to govern than others: 'I, belonging to the lower middle class, believe more and more firmly every day in aristocracy as understood by Aristotle. In plain words I believe in trusting political power to all who are fit to exercise it, plus as many more as can be given the vote without endangering the state too much.'[81] From this view naturally followed the conviction that the franchise should be extended only where it could be *properly* employed. Curtis's caveat that he came from humble origins – the 'lower middle class' – is intended to convey that his notion of citizenship was not one of *noblesse oblige*. Though he recoiled from such crude demarcations of social stratification, it should be noted that, like many of his contemporaries, Curtis took a marked liking to the social and material benefits of clubland and the country manor. Indeed, in June 1909 – soon before his work in pursuit of union in South Africa bore fruit, in 1910 – Curtis returned to the comforts of London and Oxford. In 1912, sponsored by his patron Milner, he obtained the position of Beit Lecturer of Colonial History at Oxford.[82]

Curtis's affinity for an aristocracy of political merit leads us to ask how such imperial tutors were selected. Here his service with Milner was decisive. The issue of leadership dominated their conversations long after both men had taken leave of Southern Africa. Milner was openly dismissive of party politics. Writing early on in the First World War, he argued that the quality of public men had declined since the nineteenth century, both because of the 'machine' nature of parliamentary government and because imperial and domestic issues, which he held to be separate, were perforce dealt with by the same men. Milner's vision was a government composed of men with a common cause (Green's influence was ever present), each with his separate task, working within the framework of an imperial constitution.[83] It is no coincidence that Milner's only cabinet service, indeed his only period of service in the House at all, was in Lloyd George's national

Government. Curtis agreed with Milner's tone, but complained to him in private that he offered no real alternative to the party system.[84]

By late 1915, Curtis was still struggling with the details of his federal system, unsure of how the dominions would relate with each other, and how the dependencies, specifically India, would be represented. The question of leadership continued to vex him. He had earlier looked with hope to Balfour, whom Lady Selborne described as a 'hero above politics,' and whom Curtis admired for his intellectual bearing. The search also briefly pointed to Lord Grey of Fallodon and Bonar Law, though in the case of the latter for reasons no grander than that he was by birth a colonial.[85] Nowhere, however, did Curtis find a figure capable of propagating the 'common cause.' He thus came to favour a form of British *influence*, rather than leadership, as the tool to best achieve a federal Empire. Besides the Round Table, whose role has been discussed, Curtis advanced this position through his network at Oxford. In his Beit seminars, he discussed a wide range of imperial issues and introduced to his students leading imperial figures of the day, from MPs to Foreign Office and Admiralty mandarins.[86] He also belonged to the Ralegh Club, a private discussion forum whose members included sitting politicians, journalists, and other merchants of opinion, and which thus had a broad impact.[87]

Curtis helped set the Ralegh's agenda, especially in bringing discussion of colonial nationalism to the fore. Some members, such as Lord Compton, disparaged the existence of cleavages in the dominions created by party politics, pointing to issues such as the then current naval debate in Canada as examples of dominion leaders being unable to see the forest for the trees.[88] A federal system, Compton argued, would rectify such difficulties by separating local and imperial affairs.[89] Edward Grigg, journalist, civil servant, honourary Ralegh Club member, and, from 1913–14, joint-editor of the *Round Table*, countered in a later gathering that colonial nationalism was not necessarily anathema to imperial union. Grigg argued that democracy, whose direction 'was all towards the formation of large states,' would act as a check to the authoritarian potential of union.[90] The academic J. G. Lockhart was less sanguine on the issue, arguing that the strength of Empire lay not in its adherence to democracy, but rather in its moral basis. Colonial nationalism, he stated, was important, but was clearly secondary to imperial loyalty.[91] The Indian J. B. Raju, speaking to the Ralegh soon after Lockhart, also saw the Empire as a universal institution. In the 'exposed fiction of a United India,' the Empire's greatest merits were the unifying forces of the English language and culture. Raju contradicted Lockhart, however, in contending that Indians were attracted not to the Empire's moral message, but rather its material richness.[92] It was this often myopic attention to ideology that led Ralegh Club members, including Curtis, to overestimate the potential of imperial citizenship and underestimate the strength and growth of colonial nationalism. Richard Jebb addressed the Club on just this issue in early 1913, arguing that a federal imperial government 'would destroy the sense of responsibility in the Dominions.' He urged that an alliance or cooperative structure, based upon mutual interest rather than force, would better achieve the stated goal of imperial unity.[93]

Curtis was particularly attentive to the question of multiple loyalties. In correspondence with Keith Feiling, the New Zealand-born Oxford historian, Curtis argued that because the nature of states is organic, the state perforce claims unlimited authority over its citizens. This occasioned the problem of dual loyalties, as a citizen of a dominion would owe complete allegiance to both his or her home land and to the Empire.[94] The potential for conflict, he believed, was obvious. Though not quite as fearful of the negative consequences of such a conflict as Hamilton had been,[95] Curtis nonetheless advanced the federal idea as the solution to this quandary. Just as the American settlement had achieved a balance between the citizen's loyalty to his local, state, and national governments, so would a commonwealth create a balance between the dominion citizen's domestic and imperial loyalties.[96] In an effort to solve the issue of multiple loyalties, Curtis took his message direct to the putative citizens of Empire themselves.

The prophet spreads the word

In an effort to influence colonial decision-makers direct through personal persuasion, Curtis organized discussion groups, formed interest groups, and travelled tirelessly throughout the Empire. Soon after his return to England in 1909, Curtis decided to travel to each of the dominions to ascertain its degree of imperial sentiment and then present the case for a federal imperial union. This decision was the direct result of the creation of the Round Table. The group had formed in September 1909, born out of a weekend moot, or discussion meeting, led by Milner at Plas Newydd, the country estate of Lord Anglesey.[97] Most of those present were Kindergarten members. Between cricket and golf, they shared their common conviction in the importance of Empire and their belief that some form of federal union was the best means for its perpetuation. One of the outcomes of the weekend meeting was the decision to send to Canada Curtis and Phillip Kerr, the Castor and Pollux of the imperial firmament, along with William Marris, a London member of the moot. Their task was to assess the receptiveness in that dominion to imperial federation. Kerr was circumspect concerning the potential success of a federal union, attentive to the possibility that the dominions would not willingly stall their evolution toward national autonomy solely out of a sense of imperial duty.[98] By contrast, Curtis was optimistic. He came away from their brief tour convinced that imperial union could be achieved. He discounted the nationalist stance of Laurier, and was so inspired by what he believed was Canada's pan-imperial sentiment that he rushed to draft the first Round Table document, the so-called *Green Memorandum*. It was this document which set forth the Round Table's vision of a federal commonwealth.

Curtis argued with his fellow Round Table members over the best means to propagate the message of federal union and to create the necessary sense of citizenship. Here force of personality carried his case. His Round Table peers were converted – some, like Kerr, more slowly than others – to the cause of union. On Curtis's return from Canada, the group decided to make the campaign public, but publish anonymously. This suited Curtis, who had no ambitions to personal glory. His missionary drive, however, demanded a more active role. As he noted later on in his trip, in a letter to his mother, 'surely God's will must work for Good not for evil.'[99] Imbued with this faith, Curtis set sail in the spring of 1910 for South Africa, Australia, and New Zealand, returning to England via Canada in early 1911.[100] His circumnavigation of the colonial globe brought Curtis into contact with politicians, business leaders, and 'ordinary' subjects.[101]

Curtis's voyages to the Antipodean dominions confirmed his belief in the over-riding importance of a common imperial citizenship. Curtis had left for the dominions eager to test Milner's argument that imperial citizenship should be built on a foundation of race–culture, a 'strong and enduring British leaven' of white men.[102] Curtis saw himself as a catalyst for such unity, and met initially with much success. Moots were formed in each of the dominions, though none achieved anything near the influence of the British organization. He found much interest in federalism in New Zealand, where he landed at the end of June 1910.[103] Touring the dominion in July, he was impressed with the 'Britishness' of the people, and approved especially of what he saw as their strong 'character.'[104] He conversed with farmers who were eager to contribute their fair share to the defence of the Empire, as well as 'ordinary' New Zealanders who expressed the dominion's reticence in accepting 'foreign' labour.[105] Curtis found the most support for his ideas among the conservative establishment, his converts including the son of John Seddon, the Prime Minister, and Professor J. Hight, political scientist at Canterbury College.[106] On the evening of 16 August, Curtis convened a group of his converts at the Wellington

Royal Oak Hotel.[107] The assembled agreed that the Empire needed change, that colonial independence was not as yet a realistic option, that the dominions should contribute to their own defence, and that dominion parliaments were not yet receptive to arguments for union. Curtis pointed to the case of South Africa, where the individual colonies could not cooperate except in formal union. As would be the case in each of the dominions where moots were formed, the group believed propaganda work must precede the release of the *Green Memorandum* to the general public. New Zealand was a 'test tube' case for Curtis, a dominion both modern and small enough to conduct 'experiments' which, if successful, could be replicated throughout the Empire. Buoyed by his perceived successes, he left Auckland for Sydney, Australia on 12 September 1910.

Despite his optimism, Curtis also noted a parochial streak in the dominions, an outlook which reinforced his argument against colonial autonomy. This nationalism he found most pronounced in Australia. Indeed, the topic dominated his discussion with Andrew Fischer, the Australian Prime Minister, in which the latter impressed upon Curtis his dominion's wish for a 'white Australia.'[108] Curtis also observed the reluctance of Australian education authorities to use non-Australian texts in schools. It was the strength of such nationalistic impulses which reinforced for Curtis the need to create strong federal powers to maintain imperial unity.[109]

Curtis also found antipodean life less serious and more philistine in tone than that of Britain. He was particularly disgruntled by what he saw as the intently parochial nature of dominion party politics. Australians, he complained in his diary, placed material gain above the cultivation of ethical and spiritual improvement: the 'real criterion of national value is character and conscience, not wealth.'[110] Fervently industrious himself, Curtis found Australian culture lax and distracted. Australians reserved their greatest energy not for political life, he lamented, but leisure:

> Sport was the curse of modern civilization and of Australia in particular. 43,000 people attended a football match in the last week. The playing fields of Eaton [sic] were all right as a national school so long as people played; but not when they looked on... People who devoted all this time to sport had no time to think. It was just a revival of the phase under the Roman Empire when the population herded in the arenas.[111]

'The root of the problem,' he observed in a letter to his mother, 'is that they [Australians] look upon work as a means to leisure instead of looking on leisure as an aid to work.'[112] The base nature of dominion politics, he noted elsewhere, was due directly to dominion subjects' sense of estrangement from the imperial decision-making process: 'The absence of responsibility in external affairs was really one of the factors contributing to the deterioration in the moral outlook of the Dominions.'[113] Curtis believed Australia's 'convict' history accounted for the dominion's nationalism,[114] betraying sympathy with the common early twentieth-century notion that behaviour was hereditary.

Such selective understanding was particularly apparent in his position on dominion immigration policy, an issue of imperial contention in the Edwardian era.[115] While he observed accurately that immigration was one of the first issues upon which the dominions, especially those south of the equator, had taken an autonomous position, he failed to understand fully the implications of this fact for the evolution of imperial citizenship. In *The Problem of the Commonwealth*, Curtis stated that the dominions did not comprehend the imperial ramifications of enacting race-based immigration measures because they felt no responsibility for or duty to the peoples of the dependencies. Specifically, the dominion governments 'failed to realize the gravity of the offense offered to racial susceptibilities throughout the Indian Empire, and the hardships often inflicted unnecessarily – and even necessarily – on individuals or whole classes of immigrants.'[116] Dominion governments articulated race-based immigration policies for purely domestic reasons. While it is accurate to argue that not all dominion citizens sought to inflict offense, the policies were nonetheless discriminatory. Curtis recognized the racial component of colonial nationalism, but did not see it as central to the dominions' identities. He interpreted such policies instead as a temporary stage in the development of responsible government, one which would be eclipsed when the dominions achieved maturity. Problems of intra-imperial immigration, which should have concerned one putatively interested in conceptions of imperial citizenship, were instead subsumed in his writing under the benign term 'experience.'[117]

The position Curtis thus implicitly proffered was the encouragement of imperial homogeneity in word, but the acceptance of colonial autonomy in practice on issues where it was shown to be a *fait accompli*. Thus, 'A colony consists not of a country represented by a certain area on the map but of the people who inhabit that area, and clearly they cannot control their own social development unless they can decide whom to admit to their community and whom to exclude.'[118] Curtis tried to square the circle by simply assigning jurisdiction over intra-imperial issues to whichever government – imperial or dominion – expressed the greater concern over them. Such a view of federalism might have worked well in the seminar room, but proved stillborn upon conception.

Curtis further argued, somewhat curiously, that the principle of free movement of imperial citizens within the Empire was only a narrowly conceived right. Noting the centrality of private property as recognized in English common law, he asserted that 'the only part of England which is legally open to an Englishman [or citizen of the British Empire] is that portion of its surface covered by the public roads, the commons, and such landed property as he himself may chance to possess.'[119] Curtis thus implied that imperial citizenship was not at its heart concerned with issues of race, though in practice it often manifested itself thus. What he failed to understand was that such a race-blind citizenship could not be imposed simply by changes in government structure or the lobbying of pressure groups. Thus an important flaw in his conception of imperial citizenship was that it did not adequately recognize the strength of colonial nationalism. This shortcoming was borne out quite starkly in Canada, where the Round Table movement stagnated. Curtis failed to appreciate Canada's linguistic and geographical divisions. Sir Robert Borden summarized Canadian frustration with a Britain-centred imperial citizenship when he complained at the 1917 Imperial Conference that his countrymen were being treated like 'toy automata.'[120]

Curtis, India, and the disjoint between theory and practice

If Curtis's understanding of nationalism in relation to the dominions was flawed, it proved especially misguided when he turned his mind to India, the lynchpin of the Empire. The case of India proved especially troublesome for Curtis, as indeed it did for all of the Round Table. It occupied a half-way house between the settlement colonies, which enjoyed responsible government, and the dependencies, governed by British fiat, and deemed by London unlikely to progress towards autonomy in the near or distant future. Unlike the other dependencies, whose cultures the British regarded as either backward or childish, Indian culture had long established roots. In the early decades of the Raj, the British had conceived of India as an unchanging or feudal land, home to Oriental 'despotism'. This view was undercut by the early nineteenth century as British scholars 'discovered' Indian traditions of self-government and aristocracy. Corresponding with the age of reform at home, late-Georgian and early-Victorian British officials, most notably James Mill, promulgated a series of reforms in India consistent with the principles of utilitarian liberalism.

The Indian Mutiny of 1857 put an end to British efforts at fostering a shared identity among British and Indians in India. The East India

Company lost its right to govern in 1858, and was completely dissolved by 1874. The British Government assumed direct control of the region, and increasingly the British came to view the societies of the subcontinent as defined by race and caste.[121] The notion that India was marked above all by its difference from Britain reached its peak during Lord Curzon's tenure as Viceroy (1898–1905). Curzon's idealized 'genteel Raj,'[122] on display at the 1903 *durbar*, in the architectural splendour of Government House in Calcutta, and at the summer retreat at Simla, contrasted sharply with the squalor in which most Indians lived, and gave expression to the growing cultural divide.[123] Curtis shared Curzon's view of India as a land of difference and saw as his main task the integration of Indian society into the imperial citizenship his federal scheme dictated. This proved an insurmountable challenge.

Curtis's attention to the question of Indians' participation as imperial citizens set him apart from many imperial thinkers who, like Joseph Chamberlain during his 1903 tariff reform campaign, conspicuously ignored India. Despite their preoccupation with the dominions, the 'Indian question' had also exercised the minds of the members of the Round Table since the group's inception. The Round Table had convened a symposium on Indian issues on 30 June 1912, the same month Kerr contributed anonymously an article on India to *The Round Table*.[124] The Indian scholar J. B. Raju by 1913 had attempted to form a Round Table moot in India.[125] In 1915, in association with two of Lord Selborne's sons then on military service in India, Raju succeeded in establishing a Round Table study group in Agra.[126] The Agra group was to remain the only Round Table institution outside of Britain and the dominions. In the United Kingdom, the Round Table moot, as the British core of the movement was unofficially known, convened a special Indian moot in the fall of 1915 to discuss measures to bring India into the federal model. The *Round Table* gave India greater coverage after the First World War began, though even the articles of the progressive L. F. Rushbrook-Williams were edited to conform to the Round Table's generally conservative position on India.[127] Here Curtis was ahead of his peers. He had studied the Indian situation as early as 1910 during his tour of Australia and New Zealand, and he attempted to 'guide' opinion in both Britain and India through his own publications and his extensive press contacts, most notably Chirol at *The Times*.[128] He cautiously supported India's eventual evolution to responsible government, and advocated Britain's role as trustee in helping to bring about this transition.

During his tenure in South Africa, Curtis had been influenced by Milner's notion of a British Empire founded on ties of blood – of race conceived of in narrow terms. The young Curtis argued: 'If the system [colonial integration] is to be a reality the place of birth must be treated as irrelevant and race and blood must be treated as the essential factor.'[129] His labours in pursuit of South African unification had attuned him to the importance of fostering a sense of shared community, however. In confronting the problem of India, Curtis realized that Milner's race patriotism and his idea of 'maintenance' were no longer practicable considerations. It was simply impossible for enough white settlers to emigrate to India to alter the demographic odds in Britain's favour, and no longer was it an acceptable option to enforce subjugation by the sword. Though undeniably brutal and a gross example of overreaction, General R. E. H. Dyer's actions at Amritsar in 1919 proved the last gasp of autocratic rule in India, despite continual low-intensity conflicts and constitutional wrangling in the subsequent three decades leading to Independence.

British rule in India had always been rule by the sword, though tempered by attempts at fostering acquiescence among the indigenous population.[130] By the end of the Edwardian era, however, reform was in the offing. The Morley–Minto reforms[131] of 1909 increased the number of Indians eligible to serve on the Raj's provincial and central legislative councils, and through the war years British officials debated the wisdom of agreeing to further constitutional concessions designed to increase Indian participation in self-government. Indeed, the Montagu–Chelmsford reforms of 1919 can be viewed as progressive in this respect, as after that date a full 10% of India's male population, numbering in real terms almost 16 million people, was enfranchised.[132] A less charitable view of British actions in India during the 1910s is that they were desperate measures designed to maintain the Raj in the face of an increasingly bellicose Congress and the *satyagraha* campaign of Gandhi and his sympathizers.[133]

Curtis began to think seriously about India in 1916. He voyaged to the sub-continent,[134] arriving in late September of that year,[135] just as the debate over responsible government for the region turned hot. Curtis was immediately struck by the divide in India over Indian self-rule. On the one hand, he met with British officials who, though often sympathetic to Indian ambitions for responsible government and equal citizenship, believed that Indian representation in any imperial parliament would not be feasible until Indians were prepared to govern themselves. In the words of Sir Reginald Craddock, whom Curtis interviewed in November 1916, self-government for India was 'like a distant peak with the light on it.'[136] Britain's official position was 'responsible government in the future; trusteeship in the present.' On the other hand, Curtis conversed with Indian nationalists who asserted India's own tradition of self-rule. At a conference of Indian princes in Delhi in October 1916, Curtis himself was lectured on the divine nature of Indian princely rule.[137] Curtis believed that imperial citizens, however defined, must also remain subjects of the British crown, the repository of imperial loyalty. As such, he was unmoved by arguments for Indian self-government predicated on the separate sovereignty of Indian rulers. He did respect the educated upper tiers of Indian society,[138] however, and envisioned a half-way house which he believed might be amenable to both sides. This house he termed 'dyarchy,'[139] a concept which was to influence the Montagu–Chelmsford reforms settled upon in 1919.

Curtis envisioned dyarchy as a system of parallel jurisdictions designed to gradually incorporate Indians into the ruling class. Britain's task was not to educate Indians for self-government in a formal manner, but rather to bring Indians into the current decision-making structure: 'It is in the workshop of actual experience alone that electorates will acquire the art of self-government, however highly educated they may be.'[140] In advancing this position in his conversations with Indian and British officials, Curtis was recommending a limited citizenship for India. He explicitly differentiated this status from self-government, however: 'while self-government involves election, election does not involve self-government.'[141] Thus, while he believed that educated Indians were capable of exercising responsibly the franchise and participating in local government, he did not believe that they were as yet capable of doing so except under the watchful eye of the Raj.

Neither, in Curtis's view, were Indians as yet ready to participate as equals in his proposed imperial parliament. Consistent with the philosophy of gradualism implicit in dyarchy, Curtis suggested that India's current position in such a body be an advisory one. Such a measure, he argued, would provide India with a voice in the Imperial Legislature, while ensuring that quarrels between Hindu and Muslim voices would not cause trouble.[142] He had some Indian support for this position. Babu Surendranatti Banerjee, editor of the Indian newspaper *Bengalie*, agreed with Curtis on the need to educate Indians in governing before responsible government could be instituted. He urged Curtis to lobby British officials to include property and education qualifications in any expansion of the Indian electorate, thereby ensuring highly qualified Indian elected representatives.[143]

Curtis's adherence to principles of tutelage was accompanied by a conviction that force was still the ultimate basis of British authority: 'to maintain order you must legislate against disorder.'[144] Writing on Indian nationalism in his travel diary, he even accepts the use of military force in the event of uprisings.[145] Still, he was hopeful a pan-imperial patriotism would result from the gradual inclusion of Indians in local and, later, national government. He was less concerned with fostering in Indians a personal devotion to the monarch, such as existed in the dominions, but rather hoped to generate local patriotism, a self-pride in the institutions which the Empire had allowed to flourish. Patriotism, in Curtis's view, was an allegiance to the higher ideals which made one's country (or, in this case, Empire–commonwealth) worth preserving. He reached back to his earlier invocation of Hamilton's federalism, noting that the local patriotisms of the old Thirteen Colonies continued to flourish under the aegis of the new American Republic. Political experience, Curtis continued, would precede the necessary social reform through which true equality would emerge: the 'creation of electorates involves an experience of responsibility.'[146]

Curtis's presence in India was not without controversy. Consistent with the Round Table *modus operandi* of anonymous publication and informal lobbying, Curtis worked behind the curtain while informally polling the public on its potential receptivity to a federal imperial system. This approach attracted criticism. The 'Indian Letter Controversy' erupted on 28 December 1916, when a private letter Curtis had intended for Kerr was leaked and published in the *Bombay Chronicle*.[147] The letter was marked 'private' and was destined for circulation to Round Table members and subscribers. In it, Curtis summarized his early conversations with Indians, and elaborated on India's place in the proposed Imperial Parliament. The *Chronicle* recounted what in its view were the letter's more pernicious points: the nefarious working methods of the Round Table; Curtis's desultory and offensive linking of India with Central Africa as imperial societies not yet ready for the mantle of responsible government; and the Round Table's goal of responsible government as the purpose of Empire in India. The response was swift and severe. *New India* wrote that Curtis's views on India were 'a tissue of misrepresentations and half-truths more diabolical than lies,' and chided the prophet for lecturing Indians on government 'in the land where village self-government existed, when England was unborn.'[148] The *Beharee* lamented that the letter was just the sort of thing to be expected from Englishmen who know nothing of India.[149]

Curtis's reputation as an honest broker in imperial affairs was preserved by the intervention of Sir James Meston, Governor of the United Provinces and an India delegate at the 1917 Imperial Conference in London, who spoke well of Curtis, calling him impetuous but loyal to the Empire.[150] Affairs in India were more combustible. His position in jeopardy of being compromised, Curtis responded to the allegations of perfidy and authoritarianism not with direct rebuttals, but by offering to the public the full context of his views.[151] In March of 1917 Curtis used the Indian press to outline his position, in which he made a virtue out of necessity by publicly endorsing the idea of responsible government as Britain's vision for India. He published his response in full as *A Letter to the People of India on Responsible Government* in May 1917. The Indian press now became more conciliatory, expressing hope that here was a voice which spoke with understanding on Indian nationalism. In extolling the virtue of gradualism as the path to responsible government, Curtis effectively sidestepped his private comparison of Indians and Africans as peoples as yet beyond the pale, too immature to partake equally in the imperial citizenship he envisioned for the dominions.

It is tempting to view Curtis's response to the letter controversy as a partial *mea culpa*, a recognition on his part that India was in fact more like Britain than he had previously thought, and that it therefore should not be patronized with 'tutelage' but instead brought into the imperial fold as a full partner.[152] Such a view is to argue, however, that Curtis's ideas on imperial citizenship were motivated by expediency. This jars with the evidence. The desire to foster a 'wider patriotism' was part of his notion of imperial citizenship as early as the later years of his service in South Africa, and he was always conscious of the need to lobby the British public on Indian affairs, for it was the British electorate that ultimately dictated Indian policy.[153] The notion of an imperial citizenship which incorporated Indians was not mere rhetoric. Had Curtis wanted to placate white subjects uncomfortable with any proposal to include 'coloured' subjects within an imperial citizenship, he could simply have avoided the issue, as he in fact did concerning Africa. Curtis certainly was not an enlightened voice on matters of race – no plan for equal citizenship ever passed his lips. That said, no one else of Curtis's generation proffered such a plan either.

On this point it is revealing that Curtis left India in 1918 a frustrated man. The Montagu–Chelmsford reforms, which in retrospect clearly laid the foundation for Indian Independence, and on which his ideas were directly influential, did not at the time satisfy Curtis. He found them too cautious, maintaining the provincial organization and devolving to Indians only limited self-government concerning 'nation-building' departments.[154] At the same time, Curtis was never able to grasp the sophistication and deep roots of Indian nationalism, and thus failed to understand why some nationalists viewed dyarchy as simply a perpetuation, by alternative means, of the status quo. His attempts to incorporate Indians within his federal concept of imperial citizenship were progressive – he explained to Kerr in 1917 that 'what you have got to do is to foster political aspirations in India instead of repressing them'[155] – but they were overtaken by the nationalist upsurge sparked by Amritsar. As was his pattern when confronted with political setback, instead of re-evaluating his message or his political strategy, Curtis moved his campaign to a different imperial front – Ireland. He served as the Colonial Office's advisor on Irish affairs, and was the second secretary to the British delegation which signed the 1921 Anglo-Irish Treaty which created the Irish Free State.[156] The Treaty drew in part on his conviction that shared authority and citizenship would subsume internecine rivalries (i.e. secure peace) within a federal structure. As with India, Curtis's ideas on imperial citizenship when applied to Ireland proved, at best, a mixed result.

Despite his various difficulties, Lionel Curtis was particularly well-suited to his chosen role as imperial spokesman. His early experiences at Oxford and in South Africa impressed upon him the importance of Empire as an instrument of peace through unity. A strong work ethic, broad social connections, lengthy publicity campaigns in each of the dominions, and an insatiable curiosity about his fellow-imperial subjects contributed to his influence. Drawing upon the Union he had helped bring about in South Africa, as well as the Hamiltonian model, Curtis argued that imperial federation would lead to unity. He saw in a federal Empire the potential template for a world state, the first step in bringing nations together within a single political framework. Curtis's co-creation, the Round Table, set about raising support for such an institution in both Britain and the dominions. Curtis believed that an imperial federation would encourage the political participation of all members of the Empire, eventually bringing about an egalitarian imperial citizenship. The midwife for this process was to be an 'authoritarian liberalism,' whereby Britain instructed the Empire's non-white members in British political culture.

Curtis's imperial reach proved longer than his grasp. In advancing an idealistic view of empire, he overlooked many of the elements which pointed instead to imperial devolution and growing nationalism. Most importantly, he failed to recognize the nascent feelings of national identity at play in both the settlement colonies and the dependent Empire, and overestimated the degree to which political tutelage could persuade colonial peoples to see the benefits of the British imperium. Here Curtis was consistent with the liberal imperialist conviction that the experience of colonial peoples, especially in the dependent colonies, was provisional, and therefore intervention was permissible.[157] In attempting to theorize the imperial state and colonial peoples's place within it, he overlooked the elements of nationhood present, especially in India, and ignored the conditions through which Britain had historically maintained imperial control. While he was open to the notion of a more inclusive Empire, and saw as one of Britain's foremost tasks the creation of such an entity, his proposals offered little immediate solace for the Empire's non-white subjects. He had convinced himself of the need for change, but not the necessity. The concept of imperial citizenship which Curtis advocated could be created only once an imperial state itself had come into being. Because Curtis and his Round Table peers were unable to help bring about such a transition,[158] the imperial citizenship he envisioned also failed to materialize.

Nonetheless, his ideas were influential in framing the political evolution of Empire in the mid-twentieth century. Perhaps of greatest significance was his concept of dyarchy, which epitomized the British style of informal Empire, and ironically, given Curtis's support for imperial federation, proved an essential stepping-stone in India's progress toward independence. Britain increasingly clung to the Empire in the interwar era as a potential counterweight to its international rivals. Curtis's ideas thus found resonance just as the Empire re-emerged as a political priority. Ideas of imperial citizenship were eclipsed in the 1930s, however, as the spectre of fascism drew attention elsewhere. Though a member of Chatham House, a collection of foreign-policy advisors that included several his Kindergarten peers, Curtis's priority remained imperial union even as events made the proposition increasingly untenable.[159] If his work for imperial citizenship became dated within his lifetime, the 'prophet' nonetheless illustrates the paradoxes at the heart of the early twentieth-century Empire: liberty and oppression, opportunity and inequality. If Curtis's structural approach to the question of imperial citizenship proved compromised, what of an imperial citizenship built upon shared cultural bonds and a sense of imperial cosmopolitanism. It is to those ideas, as evinced particularly by John Buchan, that I now turn.

Notes

1 On Curtis's early work with Milner and Smuts in South Africa, see Walter Nimocks, *Milner's Young Men: The 'Kindergarten' in Edwardian Imperial Affairs* (Durham, NC, 1968). Ward was converted to the Round Table cause when Curtis visited New Zealand in 1911, and put forward a scheme for imperial federation, widely believed to have been influenced by Curtis, at the 1911 Imperial Conference: see *Minutes of the Proceedings of the Imperial Conference of 1911*, Cd. 5745, p. 71. Curtis advised Churchill on Ireland, impressing upon the Colonial Secretary a federal solution to the Home Rule issue: see John McColgan, 'Implementing the 1921 Treaty: Lionel Curtis and Constitutional Procedure, *Irish Historical Studies*, 20, 79 (1977), pp. 312–33.

2   Lionel Curtis–Vincent Massey, 20 June 1911, Round Table Papers of Lionel Curtis (hereafter RTPLC), MSS English History, 793/5, Bodleian Library, Oxford University. The bulk of Curtis's papers for the period 1895–1919 were lost in a fire at Curtis's house at Kidlington in 1933. All that remains is a small selection of letters from his early service in South Africa, covering the years 1900–2. Beyond this material, there exist miscellaneous letters from the three decades following, mostly copies secured from other sources, and material relating to his work with the Round Table. Students of Curtis are fortunate to have a guide to his life in Deborah Lavin's biography, *From Empire to International Commonwealth: A Biography of Lionel Curtis* (Oxford, 1995).

3   Curtis's industry was legendary, his peers remarking with a mixture of bemusement and wonder on both his tenacity – Kerr remarked: 'I know of no other man with so big a furnace in his belly' – and his work habits (while labouring on the 'Egg' in 1911, Curtis wrote to Duncan that he had cut his working day back to ten hours to avoid strain). Kerr's statement appears in every substantial work on Curtis: see, for instance, Norman Rose, *The Cliveden Set* (London, 2000), p. 64, and Kathryn Seygal Patterson, 'The Decline of Dominance: India and the Careers of Lionel Curtis, Philip Kerr, and Reginald Coupland,' unpublished PhD thesis, Bryn Mawr College, 1989, p. 53. On Curtis's work habits, see Curtis–Patrick Duncan, 8 August 1911, MSS Curtis, 2/82, Curtis Papers, Bodleian Library, Oxford University.

4   The impact of a subject's personality is often difficult for historians to assess. A sense of Curtis's dynamic presence is conveyed in a recent elegy to the Round Table by the late Henry Hodson, who knew Curtis: see Harry Hodson, 'The Round Table: Until the Early 1930s,' *Round Table*, 352 (1999), pp. 677–94.

5   Lavin, *From Empire to International Commonwealth*, p. x.

6   In addition to *From Empire to International Commonwealth*, see Lavin, 'Lionel Curtis and the Idea of Commonwealth', in Frederick Madden and D. K. Fieldhouse (eds) *Oxford and the Idea of Commonwealth* (London, 1982); the essays in Andrea Bosco and Alex May (eds) *The Round Table: The Empire/Commonwealth and British Foreign Policy* (London, 1997); John Kendle, *The Round Table Movement and Imperial Union* (Toronto, 1975); and Dewitt Clinton Ellinwood Jr, 'The Round Table Movement and India,' *Journal of Commonwealth Political Studies*, 9, 1 (1971), pp. 183–209.

7   This important historical point has been raised by Andrew Thompson, *Imperial Britain: The Empire in British Politics, c. 1880–1932* (Harlow, Essex, 2000) and Phillip Buckner, 'Whatever Happened to the British Empire?,' *Journal of the Canadian Historical Association (JCHA)/Revue de la SHC*, 4 (1993), pp. 3–32. The renewed interest in Britain's ties to the settlement colonies has been given tangible form in the recently convened British World Conferences: see P. Buckner, 'Reinventing the British World,' *Round Table*, 93, 368 (2003), pp. 77–88.

8   The phrase is drawn from Benedict Anderson's seminal work *Imagined Communities* (London, 1982).

9   Historians of education are among the few to study this topic: see Stephen Heathorn, *For Home, Country and Race: Constructing Gender, Class and Englishness in the Elementary School, 1880–1914* (Toronto, 2000); and James A. Mangan, *Benefits Bestowed? Education and British Imperialism* (Manchester, 1987).

10 *The Dictionary of National Biography (DNB)* can do no better than term Curtis a 'civil servant,' a designation based on his work as a peripatetic advisor to various governments between 1920 and his death in 1955: *DNB, 1951–1960*, pp. 279. Alex May, who has updated Curtis's entry for the new *Oxford Dictionary of National Biography*, is more perceptive in terming Curtis 'the éminence grise of imperial politics': May, 'Empire Loyalists and "Commonwealth Men",' in Stuart Ward (ed.) *British Culture and the End of Empire* (Manchester, 2001), pp. 39–40.

11 *The Times*, 25 November 1955. On the influence of Curtis's evangelical roots on his later political ideas, see Gerald Studdert-Kennedy, 'Christianity, Statecraft

and Chatham House: Lionel Curtis and World Order,' *Diplomacy and Statecraft*, 6, 2 (1995), pp. 470-89, and 'Lionel Curtis: Federalism and India,' *JICH*, 24, 2 (1996), pp. 200-7.
12 Curtis (undelivered) address to the Rotary Club of Cape Town, 26 March 1935. Cited in Lavin, *From Empire to Commonwealth*, p. 18.
13 Curtis to his mother, Mrs G. J. Curtis, 1 June 1910, Curtis Papers, MSS Curtis, 2/1.
14 'Report of Curtis's speech at Carlton Hotel before his return from the Transvaal,' 30 October 1906, Curtis Papers, MSS 126/6 (Speeches); the Parable of the Talents is recounted in Matthew 25: 14-30.
15 John Wolffe, *God and Greater Britain* (London, 1994), pp. 166, 215-25 and generally.
16 Gerald Studdert-Kennedy, 'Curtis, Intense Beliefs Of,' in Bosco and May (eds) *The Round Table*, p. 257.
17 Green's central works are *Lectures on the Principles of Political Obligation* and *Prolegomena to Ethics*. German metaphysics also occupied an important place in the intellectual firmament of late Victorian Britain, though it did not supplant empiricism as orthodoxy, and J. S. Mill's *Principles of Political Economy* remained the curriculum's basis: see Kurt Willis, 'The Introduction and Critical Reception of Hegelian Thought in Britain, 1830-1900,' *Victorian Studies*, 32, 1 (1988), pp. 85-111; and Sandra den Otter, *British Idealism and Social Explanation: A Study in Late-Victorian Thought* (Oxford, 1996), pp. 23-4, 41, 43-4.
18 den Otter, *British Idealism and Social Explanation*, pp. 6-7; see also Andrew Vincent and Raymond Plant, *Philosophy, Politics and Citizenship: The Life and Thought of the British Idealists* (Oxford, 1984).
19 Curtis to Herbert Baker, 1925, cited in Lavin, *From Empire to Commonwealth*, p. 13.
20 Curtis and his Kindergarten associates referred colloquially to the Selborne Memorandum as 'The Egg,' the shell from which union would eventually hatch.
21 The details of Curtis's work in pursuing Milner's goal of a *British* South Africa, and then in framing the 'Egg,' have been well-covered elsewhere: see Lavin, *From Empire to Commonwealth*, pp. 63-80, and Kendle, *The Round Table Movement and Imperial Union*, pp. 27-30, 170-80.
22 Curtis-Leonard Courtney, 24 April 1900, MSS Curtis, 1/208. Curtis worked as Courtney's secretary with the London County Council before the latter recommended him for service with Milner.
23 Nimocks is the most complete work on this topic. The sobriquet was bestowed on the group by their South African critics, led by the lawyer Sir William Marriot and the politician and Premier John X. Merriman, who found objectionable the aristocratic cocksureness of men they deemed carpetbaggers. Lavin suggests that Curtis himself (in *With Milner in South Africa*, p. 344) brought the phrase into common usage: see Lavin, *From Empire to Commonwealth*, 36 n.
24 Curtis, 'Note on Milner Interview,' MSS Curtis, 142/190 (diaries); translation: 'Not the fury of hectoring citizens, not the tyrant's lowering frown, not the tempers of the south can touch the unshakeable mind of one who is just and faithful to his proposal.' The Milner interview was published in the *Evening Standard*, 17 October 1910.
25 On Jebb's concept of colonial nationalism, see Richard Jebb, *Studies in Colonial Nationalism* (London, 1905) and Deryck Schreuder, 'Richard Jebb 1898-1905,' in John Eddy and Deryck Schreuder (eds) *The Rise of Colonial Nationalism* (Sydney, 1988), esp. pp. 71-87.
26 As an example, witness the explosion of the popular press in the first decade of the twentieth century: see John Carey, *The Intellectuals and the Masses* (London, 1992).
27 Thomas Metcalfe, *Ideologies of the Raj* (Cambridge, 1997), p. 59. Metcalfe argues that authoritative liberalism was the ideological consequence of the Indian Mutiny of 1857, an event which scuppered the certainties of an earlier imperial

liberalism, voiced by India men such as the senior and the junior Mill: Metcalfe, ibid., pp. 44–5. He asserts that the second half of the nineteenth century was marked by a new emphasis on race, and the consequent ordering of a typology of difference.

28 The phrase is used by Owen Harries in his 'The Anglosphere Illusion,' *The National Interest*, 63 (spring 2001), pp. 130–1.
29 See Guy Robertson MacLean, 'The Imperial Federation Movement in Canada, 1884-1902' unpublished Ph.D thesis, Duke University, 1958.
30 The Imperial Federation League existed from 1884 to 1893, headquartered in London with branches in the settlement colonies. The federal idea faced competition from advocates of a military or customs, rather than political, union, and was overshadowed by the contentious Home Rule debates of the 1880s. Imperial federation was eclipsed by the imperial conference system by century's end: see John Kendle, *Federal Britain: A History* (London, 1997), pp. 48, 53, 81.
31 See, for instance, G. R. Searle, *The Quest for National Efficiency: A Study in British Politics and Political Thought, 1899–1914* (Oxford, 1971).
32 The literature on the causes of the South African war, and Milner's role therein, is vast. For an introduction to the topic, see A. N. Porter, *The Origins of the South African War: Joseph Chamberlain and the Diplomacy of Imperialism, 1895–1899* (London, 1980). The essays in Peter Warwick (ed.) *The South African War: the Anglo-Boer War, 1899–1902* (Harlow, 1980) are also still instructive. The leading contemporary account of the conflict's origins, emphasizing the negative role of capital as the foremost causal factor, is J. A. Hobson, *The War in South Africa, its Causes and Effects* (London, 1900).
33 The Orange Free State and the Transvaal were Afrikaner provinces which had resisted British rule in the late 1870s and early 1880s. After the First South African War (1880–81), they maintained domestic autonomy by agreeing to British suzerainty over foreign affairs. Britain's frustrations over its inability to influence internal affairs in the provinces brought about the Second South African War (1899–1902), whereby the Orange Free State and the Transvaal were annexed by the British in 1900 and 1902, respectively, each then becoming a crown colony. The new Liberal Government of Sir Henry Campbell-Bannerman gave the colonies self-government upon taking office in 1906.
34 Curtis diary, 16 August 1910, MSS Curtis, 142/101.
35 In holding to this view, Curtis shared much with his Fabian counterparts and their philosophy of achieving political change through the 'permeation' of their ideas into official minds.
36 Curtis, 'Copy of Speech on Leaving Johannesburg Council,' 27 November 1903, MSS Curtis, 1/222.
37 Leonie Foster, *High Hopes: The Men and Motives of the Australian Round Table*. (Melbourne, 1986), p. 12; Andrea Bosco and Alex May, 'Introduction,' in Bosco and May (eds) *Round Table*, pp. iii–iv.
38 See (Curtis) *Green Memorandum* (1910), p. 254; the *Green Memorandum* was also known as 'the annotated memorandum' and '*Round Table Studies, First Series.*'
39 Bosco and May, 'Introduction,' *The Round Table*, p. xiv.
40 'Memorandum of Conversations Which Took Place between a Few English and South African Friends at Intervals during the Summer of 1909,' MSS Curtis, 156/1/1–8.
41 Curtis–Valentine Chirol, 22 March 1912, RTPLC, MSS English History, 823/19.
42 The journal is still published by the Institute of Commonwealth Studies at the University of London.
43 Curtis–Chirol, 27 March 1912. RTPLC, MSS English History, 823/32; Curtis to Robert Seton-Watson, 4 September 1912, MSS English History, 823/82.
44 Curtis–Kerr, 16 September 1915, MSS English History, 838/27.
45 (Curtis), *The Problem of the Commonwealth* (London, 1916), p. vi.
46 See Amery–Brand, 25 May 1914, Round Table Papers, Leopold Amery, MSS English History, 812/36.

47 On Australian subscriptions, see Foster, *High Hopes*, p. 4; on Canadian subscriptions, see Reginald Coupland–R. H. Brand, 9 July 1917, Round Table Papers, MSS English History, 794/119.
48 Kendle, *The Round Table Movement*, pp. 157–9; Lavin, *From Empire to Commonwealth*, pp. 117, 132.
49 Lavin, *From Empire to Commonwealth*, pp. 120–1.
50 On the British Empire delegation to Versailles, see Margaret Macmillan, *Paris 1919* (New York, 2002), pp. 36–49.
51 Foster, *High Hopes*, p. 58.
52 *The Problem of the Commonwealth*, p. 68; New Zealand is apparently to be understood as an appendage of Australia.
53 Ibid., p. 46, emphasis in original. For an excellent account of the influence of Lord Durham's report on subsequent imperial thought, see Janet Ajzenstat, *The Political Thought of Lord Durham* (Kingston, ON, 1988), pp. 42–51 and generally.
54 Lavin, *From Empire to Commonwealth*, p. 61.
55 Quoted in *The Problem of the Commonwealth* (London, 1916), p. 101.
56 Saul Dubow, 'Imagining the New South Africa in the Era of Reconstruction,' in David Omissi and Andrew Thompson (eds) *The Impact of the South African War* (New York, 2002), pp. 79–83.
57 Curtis diary, 4 April 1909, MSS Curtis, 142/14. More strident critics have drawn a tenuous link between the Kindergarten's ambivalent position on race and the creation of apartheid in South Africa in 1948: see Bernard Magubane, *The Making of a Racist State* (Asmara, Eritrea, 1996), p. 281. Milder critics note the fundamental disagreements between the British and Afrikaner views of a future South Africa, and attribute the eventual cleavage between the two sides in part to the hauteur of Milner and his disciples: see O. Geyser, 'Jan Smuts and Alfred Milner,' *Round Table*, 360 (2001), pp. 415–32.
58 While there is not the space here for a full discussion on the topic, such usage was relatively consistent throughout Europe in the late-nineteenth century. 'Pedigree' and 'lineage' are alternate meanings. 'Race' did not take on its current pejorative meaning until the mid-twentieth century. See Andrew Wheatcroft, *The Habsburgs* (London, 1995), pp. 286–87.
59 Archbishop McGoun, *A Federal Parliament of the British People* (Toronto, 1890), pp. 2, 3–4.
60 Henry Page Croft, *The Path of Empire* (London, 1912); see also Larry L. Witherell, *Rebel on the Right: Henry Page Croft and the Crisis of British Conservatism, 1903–1914* (Newark, 1997).
61 See Raymond Williams, *Culture and Society* (New York, 1958).
62 *The Problem of the Commonwealth*, plate 2, 'Population of the World Divided According to States,' facing p. 69.
63 Milner had encouraged the import of Indian and Chinese 'coolie' labourers, a measure designed both to develop the gold-mining industry and undercut the negotiating position of African labourers. The goal in both cases was to attract large numbers of white settlers to South Africa, a dream which went unfulfilled.
64 Patterson, 'The Decline of Dominance,' p. 60.
65 Saul Dubow, 'Colonial Nationalism, the Milner Kindergarten and the Rise of "South Africanism," 1902–1910,' *History Workshop Journal*, 43 (1997), pp. 70–1, 75–8.
66 Alex May, 'The London "Moot", Dominions' Nationalism, and Imperial Federation,' in Bosco and May (eds) *The Round Table*, p. 229.
67 (Curtis) *Round Table Studies, Second Series*, Installment E (London, 1915), p. 681.
68 Michael W. Doyle, 'Kant, Liberal Legacies, and Foreign Affairs, Part I,' *Philosophy and Public Affairs*, 3, 12 (1983), p. 213.
69 Ibid., p. 683.
70 Inderjeet Parmar, 'Anglo-American Elites in the Interwar Years: Idealism and Power in the Intellectual Roots of Chatham House and the Council on Foreign

Relations,' *International Relations*, 16, 1 (2002), pp. 74–5. Curtis in 1949 engaged more directly with questions of international cooperation in the decade after the outbreak of war, advocating a world government modelled on the Commonwealth example: see *The Way to Peace* (London, 1944), *World War, its Cause and Cure: The Problem Reconsidered in View of the Release of Atomic Energy* (London, 1945), *World Revolution in the Cause of Peace* (Oxford, 1949), and *The Open Road to Freedom* (Oxford, 1950).

71 Cecil Rhodes made Rhodes scholarships available to Americans in his famous will in the hopes of strengthening cross-Atlantic ties of sentiment.

72 See Frederick Scott Oliver, *Alexander Hamilton: An Essay on American Union* (London, 1906). On Oliver's influence on imperial reconstruction, see John D. Fair, 'F. S. Oliver and Britain's Constitutional Crisis,' *Twentieth-Century British History*, 10, 1 (1999), pp. 1–26; and D. G. Boyce and J. O. Stubbs, 'F. S. Oliver, Lord Selborne and Federalism,' *JICH*, 5, 1 (1976), pp. 53–81.

73 *The White's Man's Burden* appeared in *McClure's Magazine*, 12 February 1899. The first stanza, usually quoted (rightly) to indicate Kipling's jingoism, reads as follows: 'Take up the White Man's burden/ Send forth the best ye breed –/ Go bind your sons to exile/ To serve your captive's need;/ To wait in heavy harness/ On fluttered folk and wild –/ Your new-caught, sullen peoples,/ Half devil and half child.' 'Burden' here should be read not as something necessarily unpleasant, a base means to an end (though many of course saw it as such), but rather as 'responsibility.' It is patronizing in the precise sense that Kipling is extolling the role of the Anglo-American as patron over his wards. Indeed, in the third stanza Kipling urges Americans to 'Fill full the mouth of Famine,/ And bid the sickness cease.'

74 See for example Hamilton writing in Federalist Paper 85, Concluding Remarks: Whether the Constitution Has Not Been Shown Worthy of the Public Approbation (28 May 1788): 'It is not impossible that these circumstances may have occasionally betrayed me into intemperances of expression which I did not intend; it is certain that I have frequently felt a struggle between sensibility and moderation; and if the former has in some instances prevailed, it must be my excuse that it has been neither often nor much': *Selected Federalist Papers*, Dover edition (Mineola, NY, 2001), pp. 204–5.

75 *Round Table Studies, Second Series*, Installment E, p. 683.

76 Ibid., p. 688.

77 Ibid., p. 689.

78 Rosebery had earlier used the term in reference to Australia, but Curtis and the Round Table popularized it, beginning with the 1911 *Round Table* article 'The Sprit of the Coronation': Bosco and May (eds), 'Introduction,' *The Round Table*, pp. xviii, lxvii, n. 46.

79 Emphasis added.

80 Ibid., pp. 695, 699, 700.

81 Curtis–Lady Selborne, 8 December 1915, MSS Curtis, 2/202.

82 Anon., 'Lionel Curtis: The Prophet of Organic Union,' *Round Table* (1955), p. 106. The Beit Chair in Colonial History was then held by the Canadian H. E. Egerton; the Chair, under whose auspices Beit lecturers worked, was an endowment of Alfred Beit, the South African mining magnate and a fervent imperialist.

83 Milner–Curtis, 27 November 1915, MSS Curtis, 2/188; see also A. Milner, *The Nation and the Empire: Being a Collection of Speeches and Addresses* (London, 1913), pp. xxiv–v, xxxiii.

84 Curtis to Milner, 29 November 1915. MSS Curtis, 2/199–200.

85 Lady Selborne–Curtis, 10 November 1911; 15 November 1911; 16 January 1913, MSS Curtis, 2/96, 98, 129. Andrew Bonar Law was born in rural New Brunswick in 1858; he moved to Scotland as a child.

86 RTPLC, MSS English History, 793/82–84, 202.

87 Minutes of the Ralegh Club, 6 December 1912, 2 February 1913, Rhodes House, Oxford. The ubiquitous Milner joined the group in April 1913. The club spelled

its name 'Ralegh' because that is how its namesake, the explorer Sir Walter Raleigh, spelled his own name. Curtis belonged also to the Colonial Club, a largely academic forum encompassing many Rhodes Scholars and other colonials then living in Britain.

88   The 1911 election in Canada turned on the issue of Laurier's support for a Canadian Navy. Conservative leader Robert Borden attacked Laurier for not showing sufficient imperial patriotism, while Henri Bourassa castigated the Prime Minister for neglecting Quebec.
89   Minutes of the Ralegh Club, 25 May 1913.
90   Ibid., 8 June 1913.
91   Ibid., 19 October 1913; Lockhart was also the Club's founder.
92   Ibid., 26 October 1913.
93   Ibid., 11 May 1913. On Jebb's scheme for a Britannic alliance, see Jebb, *The Britannic Question: A Survey of Alternatives* (London, 1913); see also chapter 5 of this book.
94   Curtis–Keith Feiling. 20 February 1912, RTPLC, MSS English History, 793/31.
95   'The passions of men will not conform to the dictates of reason and justice without constraint': Hamilton, Federalist Paper 15, 1 December 1787, in *Selected Federalist Papers*, p. 45.
96   *The Problem of the Commonwealth*, p. 201.
97   (Curtis) 'Memorandum of Conversations', MSS English History, c. 1007; see also Rose, *The Cliveden Set*, pp. 66, 54 and Kendle, *The Round Table Movement*, pp. 46–72.
98   Kerr was more interested in fostering relations with the United States: see Priscilla Roberts, 'Lord Lothian and the Atlantic World,' *Historian*, 66, 1 (spring 2004), pp. 105–9.
99   Curtis–his mother, 6 December 1910, MSS Curtis, 2/37.
100 See Lady Selborne–Curtis, 17 November (undated, but 1910), MSS Curtis, 2/25; Curtis–his mother, 7 July 1910, MSS Curtis, 2/10; and Curtis–his mother, 20 September 1910, MSS Curtis, 2/14. His travel itinerary is also pieced together from the remaining portions of his travel diary, found in MSS Curtis, 142.
101 For details on Curtis's voyage to Australasia, and the establishment of the Round Table moots in those colonies, see Leonie Foster, *High Hopes*, pp. 17–36.
102 Milner–Curtis, 1 December 1908, MSS Curtis, 1/231.
103 Curtis, travel diary, 29 June 1910, MSS Curtis, 142/20.
104 He noted, for instance, the large number of New Zealand youths who made their way to Britain for their education: see ibid., 7 July 1910. MSS Curtis, 142/27.
105 Curtis, diary, 29 July 1910; 30 June 1910. MSS Curtis, 142/73, 22.
106 Ibid., 12 July 1910; 2 August 1910, MSS Curtis, 142/57, 77.
107 Ibid., 16 August 1910, MSS Curtis, 142/99.
108 Ibid., 23 September 1910, MSS Curtis, 142/147.
109 Ibid., 25 September 1910; 27 October 1910, MSS Curtis, 142/152, 190. One such federal power was taxation. In 1911, Curtis wrote to Duncan, who was still in South Africa, advising the latter to implement tax collection throughout the new union. Curtis believed that a strong, unified tax policy would engender equality of purpose between Boer and Briton, thereby strengthening a sense of shared citizenship. He held a similar conviction regarding the empire as a whole. See also Curtis–Duncan, 8 August 1911, MSS Curtis, 2/82. The issue is also considered in *The Problem of the Commonwealth*, pp. 187–99.
110 Ibid., discussion with 'a farmer, McGregor,' 9 August 1910, MSS Curtis, 142/86.
111 Ibid., 26 September 1910, MSS Curtis, 142/158.
112 Curtis–his mother, 2 November 1910, MSS Curtis, 2/16.
113 Curtis, diary, 9 August 1910, MSS Curtis, 142/87.
114 Ibid., 1 July 1910, MSS Curtis, 142/27. Curtis found New Zealand a more 'moral' dominion, owing its religion-based settlement pattern.
115 See chapter 5 of this book for a more detailed discussion of imperial immigration policy and its implications for imperial citizenship.
116 *The Problem of the Commonwealth*, pp. 62–3.

117 Ibid., p. 64.
118 Ibid., p. 63.
119 *The Problem of the Commonwealth*, p. 59.
120 Christopher Richard, 'Canada, the Round Table and Imperial Federation,' in Bosco and May (eds), *The Round Table*, pp. 200, 210.
121 Metcalfe, *Ideologies of the Raj*, pp. 6–11, 25–31.
122 Julie F. Codell, 'Gentlemen Connoisseurs and Capitalists: Modern British Imperial Identity in the 1903 Delhi Durbar's Exhibition of Indian Art,' in Dana Arnold (ed.) *Cultural Identities and the Aesthetics of Britishness* (Manchester, 2004), p. 155.
123 On Simla and Government House, see David Gilmour, *Curzon* (London, 1994), pp. 204–7.
124 Curtis–Graeme Patterson, 4 June 1912, MSS English History, 823/61; Kerr–Curtis, 17 April 1912, MSS English History, 823/36; see also (Phillip Kerr) 'India and the Empire,' *Round Table*, 2 (1912), pp. 587–626.
125 Hon. Louis Palmer–Lady Selborne (undated), letter, MSS Curtis, 2/170; a date of 1913 is probable as the letter is filed with other materials from that year. The Round Table also curtailed its proselytizing work during the war years, when Curtis was preoccupied with writing *The Problem of the Commonwealth* and *Commonwealth of Nations*. Raju had worked for some time on that project – Raju was an Oxford-educated Indian, and, as noted above, a participant in Ralegh Club functions.
126 See Dewitt Clinton Ellinwood Jr, 'The Round Table Movement and India,' *Journal of Commonwealth Political Studies*, 9 (1971), p. 190.
127 Chandrika Kaul, '*The Round Table*, the British Press, and India, 1910–1922,' in Bosco and May (eds) *The Round Table*, pp. 346–9. The *Round Table* featured thirty-one articles on India between 1910 and 1922: C. Kaul, *Reporting the Raj: The British Press and India, c.1880–1922* (Manchester, 2003), p. 83.
128 Kerr–H. A. L. Fischer, 8 November 1910, MSS English History, 823/5; Kerr records that he sent Curtis Sir W. Hunter's *The Indian Empire*, which provided Curtis with much of his historical knowledge of India: Kaul, '*The Round Table*, the British Press, and India,' pp. 354–5, 358, 359–60.
129 Lavin, *From Empire to Commonwealth*, p. 60.
130 Examples of attempts to foster acquiescence include the Municipal Councils Act of 1882 (which gave local bodies jurisdiction over education, sanitation, and public health), and the Indian Councils Act of 1892 (which introduced limited elections for legislative councils): Barbara Metcalf and Thomas Metcalf, *A Concise History of India* (Cambridge, 2002), p. 135.
131 The official title of the Act to extend the franchise in India was the Indian Councils Act (1909), the most significant of the Morley–Minto reforms.
132 See J. M. Brown, 'India,' in J. M. Brown and W. R. Louis (eds) *Oxford History of the British Empire* (*OHBE*), vol. 4: *The Twentieth Century* (Oxford, 1999), p. 432 n. 8.
133 On Indian nationalism and British reform in this era, see Judith Brown's *Gandhi: Prisoner of Hope* (New Haven, CT 1989) and *Modern India: The Origins of an Asian Democracy*, 2nd edn (Oxford, 1994).
134 India was of intermittent concern before this date: see Curtis–Graeme Patterson, 4 June 1912, MSS English History, 823/61; Kerr–Curtis, 17 April 1912, MSS English History, 823/36; Kerr–H. A. L. Fischer, 8 November 1910, MSS English History, 823/5. The Round Table tentatively addressed the Indian issue in (Phillip Kerr), 'India and the Empire,' *Round Table*, 2 (1912), pp. 587–626.
135 Curtis, diary, 25 September 1916, MSS Curtis, 143/5. Curtis elsewhere records that he arrived in India in October of 1916: see Curtis, *Letters to the People of India on Responsible Government*. The date is here given as September, as that is consistent with his diary entry, though it is conceivable that either the diary date is incorrect, or that he met with the Bombay government official to whom he refers in the diary while still at sea.
136 Curtis, diary, 11 November 1911, MSS Curtis, 143/12.

137 Ibid., 31 October 1911, MSS Curtis, 143/8.
138 See David Cannadine, *Ornamentalism* (Oxford, 2001), for the argument that British imperial actors viewed the Empire in terms of class, and thus accorded respect to fellow elites in the colonies.
139 Curtis spelled out his thoughts on dyarchy and Indian citizenship in his three works on India: *A Letter to the People of India* (Bombay, 1917), reprinted in *Dyarchy*, pp. 38–95; *Letters to the People of India on Responsible Government* (London, 1918), reprinted in *Dyarchy*, pp. 357–466; and especially *Dyarchy: Papers Relating to the Application of the Principle of Dyarchy to the Government of India, to which are Appended the Report of the Joint Select Committee and the Government of India Act, 1919* (Oxford, 1920).
140 Curtis, *Letters to the People of India on Responsible Government*, p. 159.
141 Curtis, diary, 26 November 1916, MSS Curtis, 143/26.
142 Ibid., 13 October 1916 and 7 November 1916, MSS Curtis, 143/17, 32.
143 Ibid., 12 December 1916, MSS Curtis, 143/ 38.
144 (Curtis) 'Notes on India' (n.d.), MSS Curtis, 143/116.
145 Referring to potential 'rebels' he wrote that 'England could wipe them out with big guns': Curtis, diary, 14 December 1916, MSS Curtis, 143/41.
146 'Notes on India,' MSS Curtis, 143/174.
147 *Bombay Chronicle*, 28 December 1916. Patterson notes that Gandhi soon after took credit for the leak, and indeed Henry Polak, a Gandhi associate, reminded Congress the day after the letter appeared in the *Chronicle* that Curtis had supported anti-Asian legislation when he was in South Africa: Patterson, 'The Decline of Dominance: India and the Careers of Lionel Curtis, Philip Kerr, and Reginald Coupland,' p. 127. The 'letter controversy' is briefly recounted in Lavin (pp. 140–41), though she does not mention Gandhi's alleged involvement.
148 *New India*, 29 December 1916. Round Table Cuttings, MSS English History, 851/6.
149 *Beharee*, 4 January 1917, Round Table Cuttings, MSS English History, 851/13–14, 8.
150 Meston, Governor of the United Provinces, also had a less altruistic motive for defending Curtis. Meston himself had been implicated in the Curtis letter by virtue of Curtis having added (disingenuously) Meston's name as a co-writer to add weight to his impressions. Meston had also extended the invitation that brought Curtis to India in the first place, and thus saw himself partially responsible for the latter's activities.
151 *Indian Social Reformer*, 7 January 1917.
152 Patterson, 'The Decline of Dominance,' pp. 128–30. Patterson rightly observes that Curtis served Montagu in an advisory position, but it is incorrect to assume that the 1917 reforms, while representing a change of opinion for Montagu, also represented a change in position for Curtis. This is to erroneously contend that Curtis held an inflexible position regarding India before 1917, a view which is at odds with his record both at Oxford and in South Africa.
153 Kaul, *Reporting the Raj*, p. 143.
154 Philip Woods, 'The Round Table and the Montagu–Chelmsford Reforms,' in Bosco and May (eds) *The Round Table*, p. 374.
155 Ibid., p. 373.
156 McColgan, 'Implementing the 1921 Treaty,' p. 313.
157 I draw here on Uday Singh Mehta, *Liberalism and Empire* (Chicago, IL, 1999), pp. 187–90, 192.
158 See May, 'Empire Loyalists and "Commonwealth Men",' pp. 41–4.
159 Curtis developed his ideas of international cooperation and union in the three volumes of *Civitas Dei* (London, 1934–37). He continued to point to imperial federation as a model for peace until his death: see 'Address by Lionel Curtis – Prevention of War,' 14 September 1949, in *The Changing Commonwealth: Proceedings of the Fourth Unofficial Commonwealth Relations Conference, Ottawa* (Toronto, 1950), pp. 256–64.

CHAPTER THREE

John Buchan, romantic imperialism, and the question of who belongs

> Every subject's duty is the king's, but every subject's soul is his own.
> (*Henry V*, IV, i, 176–7)

In the course of inter-election campaigning for the constituency of Peebles and Selkirk in the immediate pre-war years, John Buchan's Liberal opponent, Donald MacLean, accused the Conservative Buchan of vacillating on the issue of tariffs. Buchan's response, 'consistency is not much of a virtue,'[1] was indicative of his mental outlook and political temperament, and characterized his attitude to Empire. This is not to say that Buchan lacked a focused intellect or was merely self-serving, desirous of the trappings and honours of political postings, but devoid of substance, as some critics have charged.[2] John Buchan was a practical man, whether as novelist, barrister, civil servant, historian, or, finally in 1935, as Lord Tweedsmuir of Elsfield, Governor-General of Canada. His personality was forged by the twin and often competing forces of a latent Calvinism, befitting the son of the manse that he was, and a strong Scottish romanticism, culled from, amongst other sources, a life-long devotion to Sir Walter Scott. Buchan's public life was imbued with these influences. His imperial outlook was that of a progressive conservative with a cosmopolitan sympathy held back, but only just, by his respect for tradition and stability. As Buchan himself asserted, he was 'a Conservative with a move on.'[3]

Buchan devoted the greater part of his career to the propagation and preservation of his concept of Empire, a concept he came to form during the first decades of the twentieth century. His vision was of a broad-minded notion of Empire based upon morality, values, and an understated fatalism. Part of this vision was an understanding of imperial citizenship in cosmopolitan and cooperative terms. While Buchan shared the organic impetus of Curtis's thought, he did not share his peer's desire to locate imperial citizenship within broader debates concerning imperial organization. Buchan was more interested in fostering the shared Britannic identity he believed must necessarily underpin any firm imperial citizenship. This chapter assesses the contours of what was a social understanding of citizenship and Empire.

Imperial beginnings

Discussions of John Buchan's imperialism unfailingly begin with his 1906 symposium *A Lodge in the Wilderness*. All too often, however, they fail to move much beyond this work. Buchan wrote the book, his second full-length work of fiction,[4] in the wake of his time in South Africa as a not yet 30-year-old aide to Alfred, Lord Milner. The book is a thinly veiled treatise on the nature of Empire, and while critics have rightly noted *A Lodge*'s literary failings, they have been too quick to attribute to Buchan himself the main character's views on Empire. Hence, the ubiquitous reference made by commentators to the claim of Francis Carey, the Cecil Rhodes character, that Empire is 'a spirit, an attitude of mind, an unconquerable hope ... It is the wider patriotism which conceives our people as a race and not as a chance community.'[5] On this basis, even temperate critics such as Juanita Kruse have portrayed Buchan as paternalistic, while other less measured pens have termed him 'racist,' 'misogynous,' and a mouthpiece for 'white supremacy.'[6] Such misreadings of Buchan's imperialism are the result of examining his fiction without considering his broader career. While his novels are certainly significant in understanding his views on Empire, it is important to note that before 1920 Buchan did not regard himself primarily as a novelist. Indeed, the novel upon which his fame continues to rest, *The Thirty-Nine Steps* (1915), was written as a diversion while Buchan endured a duodenal ulcer and was confined to bed in Broadstairs. In order to properly consider Buchan's imperialism, and the light it can shed on the development of imperial citizenship in the pre-1920 era, it is necessary to examine the full scope of his undertakings.

Buchan's fiction, though, is still an important key to his imperial outlook. Instead of considering his more well-known works such as *A Lodge*, *Prester John* (1910), or *Greenmantle* (1916), it is an overlooked 1910 short story in the *Atlantic Monthly* that brings Buchan's views most clearly to the fore. 'God's Providence' is an examination of the relationship between imperialism and domestic politics which characterized Buchan's own career. Anticipating Buchan's rejoinder to accusations of hypocrisy on the Scottish campaign trail, one character notes: 'Whoever makes a fetich [sic] of consistency is a trumpery body, and little use to God or man.'[7] The story is about the folly of slavish devotion to creeds. It gently mocks the impassioned calls of the imperial ideologues and displays a sympathy for a balance between tradition and change. Indeed, what most commentators on *A Lodge* have failed to recognize is that Buchan was trying to sort out what he saw as *true* imperialism from what he regarded as the jingoistic position of men in the type of Joseph Chamberlain. Buchan mistrusted jingoism even at that early age. This distinction framed Buchan's thinking on imperial citizenship. His beliefs were based upon firm moral convictions, but he realized that they could be realized only through practical means.

Alongside a fervent sense of morality, Buchan also maintained a life-long sense of fatalism. He recognized that life is full of failure and unfulfilled visions. From the time of the death of his close friend Cuthbert Medd in 1902 through the upheaval of the war years, when he lost his younger brother Alistair, and friends Tommy Nelson and Raymond Asquith,[8] he endured personal tragedy. However, while he dealt with personal failure by throwing himself into another challenge – taking up journalism and the law when his position with Cromer fell through, writing *The Thirty-Nine Steps* when he could not go to the Front – he dealt with tragedy and disappointments in the political sphere with perseverance. His fatalism and approach to failure ironically made him a progressive Tory. Thus, he embodied an interesting paradox: he envisioned imperial citizenship in idealized terms but sought to attain it through practical means.

Buchan was a moderate imperialist. His was not the imperialism of the technocrat, nor that of the jingo. He developed a notion of Empire as cooperation, from which evolved his concomitant understanding of imperial citizenship. To Buchan, citizenship was a lived principle. He approached the world with a Calvinist certainty rounded at the edges to account for what he saw as man's inherent frailty. Citizenship in Buchan's mind was a relationship of common community, of responsibility to the collective.

The central tenet of this view was a muted cosmopolitanism, grounded in conviction, not emotion. He never left the broad church of Scottish Presbyterianism, and thus his position on citizenship was guided by a firm morality. The responsibility and duty of individual and state were reciprocal and paramount. Buchan also viewed imperial democracy as a concept worthwhile but difficult to achieve. These rather sober characteristics, however, were tempered by an ecumenical understanding of race and a Romantic conservatism, the latter most familiar to the legions of Buchan's readers. From this palette, Buchan produced an impressionistic vision of imperial citizenship which was more far-sighted than that of most of his contemporaries. Like many successful people, he was a man of paradox. He was a practical idealist, promoting an ecumenical view of imperial citizenship in an age praising cultural homogeneity and 'national interest.' Unlike the parochial conservative view which held that Empire was a British possession to be developed and exploited as such, Buchan was interested in and concerned with issues which addressed the Empire as a whole, a totality. As Governor-General of Canada from 1935 until his death in 1940, he brought these views to an imperial post of prominence, and became a strong advocate of the country he came to love.

The genesis of Buchan's concept of imperial citizenship is to be found in his upbringing. The Reverend John Buchan was a Free Church minister; his mother was an equally devout Calvinist. Hence the younger Buchan grew up in an atmosphere of moral sobriety. Buchan attended Hutchesons's Boys Grammar School in Glasgow, after which, at the age of 17, he moved to Glasgow University. As such, he remained free of what the historian J. A. Mangan has called the public school ethos. Not for him the boyhood indoctrination of duty, cooperation, and Muscular Christianity coupled with a belief in the right to rule others. As Buchan wrote in his autobiography *Memory Hold the Door*, school was 'an incident, an inconsiderable incident; a period of enforced repression which ended daily at four in the afternoon.'[9] Buchan was always most at home by himself, a state-of-mind he most often sought in nature. Following the example of his literary idol, Sir Walter Scott, Buchan found inspiration in the Scottish countryside, especially the Borders of his youth. He shared the temperament of that region's inhabitants, 'realism coloured by poetry, a stalwart independence sweetened by courtesy, a shrewd, kindly wisdom.'[10]

When he moved to Brasenose College, Oxford, on a scholarship, much of the principled character that marked his mature life had already been formed. His Glasgow mentor, the classicist Gilbert Murray, had impressed upon Buchan the virtues of independent study, especially of the Greco-Roman past. Though Murray was primarily a Greek scholar, Buchan gravitated to the Romans, in whom he discovered a 'standard of values.'[11] He rejected as tendentious the philosophical Idealism of T. H. Green and his associates, then prevalent at Oxford. Though he was attracted to Platonism as a 'climate of opinion,' he began to cultivate a suspicion of systems of thought, especially those based upon what he perceived to be generalities. Ideals were not created through perception – *cogitavit, ergo fuit* – but rather were articulated from experience. They must have a distinguished pedigree and be possessed of a benevolent or productive purpose. In imperialism Buchan found an ideal suited to his worldview.

What Buchan developed at Oxford was an intellectual confidence in himself and a passionate respect for classical learning. He won numerous prizes, including the Stanhope and the Newdigate, though his disappointment at being denied a Fellowship at All Souls in 1898 lingered for many years.[12] He also set a standard of industry, producing numerous books of prose and poetry, debating in the Oxford Union, and cultivating relationships with a circle of peers who included Tommy Nelson, Raymond Asquith, and Arthur Steel (later Steel-Maitland), among others. Buchan's talent and productivity were such that he appeared in the 1898 edition of *Who's Who* at the slight age of 22, the youngest entry in that edition. He left Oxford with a First in Greats.

Following Oxford, Buchan briefly pursued a career in law, being called to the Bar by Middle Temple in 1901, and as a journalist, writing for St Loe Strachey's *Spectator*. Much of his writing for the *Spectator* concerned matters of Empire, a focus which caught the eye of L. S. Amery, then with *The Times*. Amery had been invited by Alfred Milner to assist in the reconstruction of post-war South Africa. *The Times* would not release Amery, so he suggested Buchan as a replacement. Milner gladly acquiesced, being familiar with Buchan's reputation.[13] Buchan spent three years in South Africa, working first on the Refugee Relief Committee, then heading up the resettlement of Boers on the land. He also served as Milner's political private secretary. Buchan left South Africa in 1903, and so was not part of Milner's Kindergarten, that group of devoted Oxonians who fell under the spell of 'religio-Milnernia' and helped generate support for federation, a process which culminated in the Union of 1910.[14]

Buchan returned from South Africa deeply marked by his experience under Milner. Writing to his brother Walter in late 1901, he remarked that Milner

> is the most tragic figure in S. Africa, and one of the greatest anywhere. You have a man of superhumanly clear intellect, and an iron will – both of which control a highly sensitive temperament... He is a kind of fatalist, going on doggedly with his work, but not caring much except for doing reform joined to a close-textured intellect which reformers rarely possess.[15]

Buchan admired Milner's practical idealism, and came to model his own imperialism along similar lines. Writing to Lady Murray in 1902, he noted: '[I] feel that my experience here is a magnificent education. I have to see that *things get done*.' In a note to Gilbert Murray that same year, he confessed: 'I detest official work, but I love this plain dealing with facts.' His admiration for the Pro-Consul was little changed nearly forty years on, when, in *Memory Hold the Door*, Buchan wrote that Milner 'had the instincts of a radical.'[16]

Buchan had come to South Africa long on ambition but short on experience. He found there a country which marked him only a shade less than had his own Scotland. Peter Henshaw has shown persuasively that the natural landscape of South Africa, which reminded Buchan of the Borders, fostered a lasting respect for the rural Afrikaner population, and towards the conviction that multiple loyalties could become closely linked through 'a shared engagement with nature.'[17] South Africa was a contradiction for Buchan, a mix of modernity and backwardness, a combination of the sophisticated and the 'heathen.'[18] It was there that Buchan began to develop his cosmopolitan view of Empire. Though not a pro-Boer, he had a less hostile opinion of the conflict than most of his colleagues, noting that the war 'seemed to me a case of competing equities, and ours was rather the better.'[19]

Most significantly, his time with Milner impressed upon Buchan the power of Empire as an idea. Buchan's imperialism took the form of a 'secular religion.' As he impressed upon Gilbert Murray, 'I am no lover of the demagogue of Empire.'[20] This distrust of, and increasingly disdain for, chauvinistic imperialism is important in understanding the development of Buchan's thought on imperial citizenship. His was not a proto-liberal conception of equality and rights-sharing, but rather a critical response to the emotional and intellectually thin 'new imperialism' voiced by Chamberlainite new imperialists. He did, though, maintain a grudging respect for the major advocates of the forward policy. Indeed, Milner was Chamberlain's hand-picked man-on-the-spot in South Africa. When Rhodes was close to death, Buchan's remark, 'I don't like him, but he is undoubtedly a great man, one of the few Napoleonic people we have had since Marlbourgh,'[21] illustrated his admiration for men of action, even if he found their creed of expansionism lacking.

It was the spirit of Empire, a spirit he believed he saw in Milner, that Buchan believed most valuable. It was this spirit that he found missing in many exponents of the forward policy. Chamberlain, whom Buchan met when the former visited the Cape in late December 1902, was 'a man whom you want to make General Manager of the British Empire, but whom you know will forever remain a General Manager and not a creator.'[22] Buchan returned to London in 1902. Milner had advised him to first pursue a career in finance – 'you must have money if you are to do any constructive political work'[23] – but Buchan had taken the imperial mission to heart, and hoped to enter the colonial service. He had, however, placed his money alongside his ideals, holding shares in the Imperial Cold Storage Supply Company Ltd.[24]

The position he most coveted was an assistantship to Lord Cromer, then Pro-Consul in Egypt. Buchan contends in his memoir, and in letters from the time, that Cromer wanted him but that the Foreign Office overturned the decision. This is not corroborated by the historical record.[25] What is clear is that Buchan did briefly correspond with Cromer, who wrote a favourable letter concerning Buchan's *The African Colony* (1903), a work on South African political reconstruction.

Such a posting would have suited his burgeoning interest in imperial matters. Cromer epitomized the pro-consular grandeur Buchan had found so attractive in Milner. Cromer also seemed to epitomize the practical idealism Buchan was coming to admire, an idealism which valued the first two of David Livingstone's three Cs – Christianity and civilization – while betraying suspicion of the third – commerce. In a 1908 essay for the *Edinburgh Review*, Cromer expressed his belief that the future of Empire rested 'on the degree to which the moralizing elements in the nation can, without injury to all that is sound and healthy in individual action, control those defects which may not improbably spring out of the egotism of the commercial spirit.'[26]

Buchan admired men such as Milner and Cromer for their devotion to public service. Much of his own career, like theirs, was fashioned within the public sphere, and even when he did not hold a public post he maintained the spirit of service. One of his more successful initiatives, for instance, was the Nelson Sevenpenny Library, which made available in reprint a wide variety of literature and non-fiction, both high and low, for a broader reading public. Apart from being good business, Buchan saw this endeavour as a contribution to building a new, more literate community. Literature was a serious concern for a man who kept with him a copy of *Pilgrim's Progress* as one of his guides to life.

He maintained this devotion to the common weal during the First World War. Buchan was deeply affected by the conflict, an event which shocked him as much as any of his contemporaries. Though his duodenal ulcer prevented him from serving at the Front, his work in non-combat roles was certainly impressive: *The Times* correspondent in France in 1915–16, a stint at the Foreign Office, a commissioned officer in the Intelligence Corps, communications work for Reuters, and finally a post in the War Cabinet as Director of Information. In the last-named position he oversaw the Government's propaganda efforts, organizing lecture series and picture displays,[27] though he was continually frustrated by the domineering tendencies of Lloyd George and Lord Beaverbrook. Historians, however, can be thankful to Buchan for providing much of the extant photographic record of the British war effort, the legacy of these propaganda exhibitions.[28] In addition to his official duties, Buchan penned in his spare time Nelson's *History of the War*, the sheer bulk of which indicates that he was fuelled in equal parts by industry and duty. As he noted to Gilbert Murray, 'it is a good thing to be very busy at a time like this, when most of one's friends are dying. It prevents brooding.'[29] His greatest disappointment was that ill-health prevented him from serving himself, a guilt driven home sharply by the death of many of his closest friends. Buchan acutely felt the void of the lost generation. He rejected, though, the turn to nihilism and decadence in the immediate post-war period as vacuous and disrespectful to those who had served, complaining that 'the interpreting class plumed themselves wearily on being hollow men living in a wasteland.'[30] Unsurprisingly, Buchan was not popular among the Bloomsbury literati.

Emerging from Milner's shadow

In the aftermath of imperial reconstruction in Southern Africa, Buchan came to see imperialism as an institution which could be put to the service of peace. He disavowed Milner's faith in imperial federation, illustrating that he was not a mere acolyte. Nonetheless, he shared Milner's conception of Empire as something that must be maintained, not expanded.[31] He also shared with Lionel Curtis an organic view of Empire. In his memoir, Buchan recalled the imperial fervour he then felt in a passage which merits quotation in full:

> I dreamed of a world-wide brotherhood in the background of a common race and creed, consecrated to the service of peace; Britain enriching the rest out of her culture and traditions, and the spirit of her Dominions like a strong wind freshening the stuffiness of the old lands. I saw in Empire a means of giving to the congested masses at home open country instead of blind alley. I saw hope for a new afflatus in art and literature and thought. *Our creed was not based on antagonism to any other people.* It was humanitarian and international; we believed that we were laying the basis of a federation of the world. As for the native races under our rule, we had a high consciousness; Milner and Rhodes had a far-sighted native policy. The 'white man's burden' is now [1940] an almost meaningless phrase; then it involved a new philosophy of politics, and an ethical standard serious and surely not ignoble.[32]

Beyond providing a wonderfully succinct template for the turn-of-the-century progressive conservative's mind, these thoughts reveal the cosmopolitan nature of Buchan's imperialism. The religious metaphor used in the first sentence indicates the ecclesiastical aspect to the notion of Empire, and the individual's role therein, to which Buchan held firmly. The remainder has the tone of an apologia, the admittance of a retired soldier that the results of the war in which he once fought have been called into question, but that the battle had been joined with motives relatively free of caprice or malice. The most instructive statement, though, attests that imperialism was not a creed of conquest. Rather, in Buchan's view, it was one which carried a moral benevolence. What were the tenets of such a belief, and how honestly were they adhered to? It is to these questions that the argument now moves.

At this early stage of his career, Buchan held that imperialism should take the form of a creed. He set about sketching such a creed in *A Lodge in the Wilderness*. He later admitted that his conclusions were naive, framed by an idealist's mind little enlightened by experience. In the Preface to the 1916 reprint of *A Lodge*, Buchan admits that the mood he had conveyed in 1904 had been proved *passé*.[33] Buchan's imperialism was much more a state of mind, and he came to argue that imperialism was an attitude, not an intellectual proposition.[34] Buchan's conservatism meant for him a proper understanding of Empire could be achieved only through the realization that contemporary problems were not new, but rather had deep historical roots. Although sentiment was necessary to fostering imperialism, it alone did not suffice. The only solid basis for imperialism lay in a sense of common history. As he wrote in his autobiography, 'if your back cast is poor your forward cast will be a mess.'[35] As such, one must honour the memory of one's forefathers. In a speech to an audience of London teachers shortly after the conclusion of the Great War, Buchan summarized this position: 'It is when men forget their history, or have never known it, that they believe, like Mr Trotsky, that a new world can be created by a few ... extractions ... that life can be forced into concreted canals.'[36] Stability and continuity were thus the most important virtues. Buchan, like conservatives of all hues, derived much of this line of thought from Edmund Burke, and was fond of noting that 'Burke does not proselytize.'[37] Indeed, Buchan's Empire bore much resemblance to Burke's doctrine of a liberal Empire.[38] Empire was a serious proposition, and must be treated as such.

Buchan also expressed in his public pronouncements support for Burke's vision of an organic society, by which Buchan did not mean that Empire was a free-standing entity which would endure if its citizens simply believed in it. In a speech given in Edinburgh in 1904 on the topic 'The Empire of South Africa,' Buchan argued that imperial ideas 'should be worked out in detail and given a practical form.' The colonies, he continued, should follow the example of the eponymous hero of Kipling's imperial novel *Kim*, who learns to become a servant of a cause greater than himself.[39] Writing in the *Scottish Review*, a journal of politics and culture which he edited in 1907–8, Buchan argued that ritual and pomp should be minimized, so as not to conflate imperialism and iconography, and thus create divisions between imperialists. He also stressed the intangible gains of an organic Empire: 'We gain alliances, we gain a field for the energy of our sons, and we gain the satisfaction which comes from all creative work.'[40] Speaking to the Personal Service Association in Edinburgh in 1913, he noted: 'Society is an organic life like the human body . . . if part is sick the other parts cannot be really well.'[41] The Empire, too, was an organism, dependent on the mutual cooperation of its varied peoples for its survival.

Buchan and jingoism

In conceiving of Empire as an organic whole, Buchan was not out of step with most of his colleagues on the British Right. Where he parted ways with many other conservatives of the period was in his rejection of jingoism. Jingoism characterized the imperialism of men as varied as Milner, W. T. Stead, the Poet Laureate Alfred Austin, and Buchan's superior at the *Spectator*, the Liberal Unionist St Loe Strachey. In order to understand why Buchan rejected jingoistic views on Empire, it is necessary first to outline the main precepts of jingoism itself.

Jingoism and imperialism are not synonymous. The term 'jingoism' had its origin in the Russo-Turkish crisis of 1877–78, when the British hawks' willingness to fight if necessary was aptly captured in G. W. Hunt's famous music hall verse and Disraeli sent the fleet to Constantinople in a show of force.[42] Jingoism came to connote aggressive nationalism, usually in support of the Empire. It also came to include broader celebrations of imperial triumphs and causes. The Silver and Diamond Jubilees of Victoria, Queen of the United Kingdom of Great Britain and Ireland and Empress of India, in 1887 and 1897 respectively, were elaborately florid examples of the latter.

While jingoes were necessarily in favour of Empire, imperialists were not, *ipso facto*, jingoes. Jingoism was a tangential phenomenon. Rather than being the wellspring of imperial fervour, jingo sentiment was instead a response to the *fait accompli*. It functioned as neither a cause nor a motive, but instead was a consequence, a response, a reaction. The liberal critic of Empire, J. A. Hobson, described jingoism as that 'inverted patriotism whereby the love of one's own nation is transformed into the hatred of another nation, and the fierce craving to destroy the individual members of that other nation.'[43] What Hobson does not address is the fact that such sentiments usually manifested themselves only after another *nation* had committed some transgression. An understanding of jingoism as a reactionary impulse can be expanded to incorporate celebrations of martial activity, most often by those who did not directly take part. This is well illustrated by an event which left its shadow over South Africa throughout Buchan's tenure there: the Jameson Raid of 1895.

The Jameson Raid was initiated by what is best termed a whim. There had been interest in the Cape community in fomenting a rebellion in the Transvaal to precipitate the formation of a South African Union. Leandar Starr Jameson, a Scottish doctor and close associate of Cecil Rhodes, was to lead a contingent of British border police across the Bechuanaland–Transvaal border when given the word by Rhodes. Instead, Jameson inexplicably cut telegraph lines, and decided to force the situation himself. The Raid turned into a fiasco, with Boer forces making short work of the poorly marshalled British. The gallant, if foolish, Jameson, upon hoisting the white flag, is said to have uttered, 'there goes my life.'[44] The Raid helped trigger the Boer War four years later, and Rhodes's dream of a united South Africa had to wait until 1910.

Britons' reaction to the Raid speaks directly to the relationship between jingoism and Empire. As with rumour and innuendo, jingoism operated best in an arena of stereotype and misinformation. Anti-Boer sentiment had flourished before the Raid, and Jameson's imprudence only inflamed matters. The *Daily Mail* opined that 'every petty annoyance that a spiteful and jealous child could play on another is resorted to by the Dutch towards the English. I expect it will always be so until the Dutch have had a decisive lesson.'[45] Such views were not restricted to self-identified imperialist papers, as the radical *Reynold's Newspaper* asserted that the Boers were 'stern, harsh, narrow and ignorant.'[46] Such prejudicial views were given free play in the aftermath of the Raid, for Britons, even among the political elite, had little concrete knowledge of the affair. The leaders of the Revolutionary Committee at the Cape had their death sentences commuted on the condition that they not speak of Transvaal politics for three years, by which time Southern Africa had entered a new crisis that was to culminate in the Boer War.

The response to the Raid was twofold. Jameson's critics castigated his actions as treasonous. Such voices were mostly liberal, supporters of Gladstone's principle of moral trusteeship, or imperial sceptics reluctant to support any forward policy. By bringing shame upon the nation, Jameson had compromised the values of prudence and stability which supported the notion of Empire. In contrast, Jameson's supporters, who were far more numerous, turned such logic on its head. They attempted to excuse his actions by claiming that Jameson was either dim-witted or unprepared, or both, neither of which alternatives was portrayed as particularly damning. Reaction in the City was largely favourable, as many brokers believed Jameson's folly would relieve political tension in South Africa, and thus provide more investment opportunities. This conjecture was born out by the fact that the price of shares in the region's major mining operations rebounded from a six-month decline shortly after the Raid.[47]

Jameson received even greater support from the public. This can best be elucidated in the reception he received when he returned to London in February, 1896, to appear at his trial. One pundit wrote of Jameson, 'if he was our idol before the disaster, what is he now? Why a greater idol than before.'[48] The boisterous greeting Jameson received can be compared, by appropriate historical coincidence, with the reception encountered by British troops returning from their triumph over the Asante. While the defeated Jameson waded through a throng of cheers at Paddington Station, Tommy Atkins's victorious return from West Africa was greeted by a thunderous indifference.[49] This paradox can perhaps be explained by the consistent British taste for imperial amateurs, the more vainglorious the better. Indeed, the *Pall Mall Gazette* wrote lovingly of 'our Quixote,' and 'credit[ed] Dr. Jameson with the best possible motives.'[50] Many of the heroes of the British Empire – Gordon at Omdurman, Livingstone in Central Africa, Roger Casement in the Congo – were men who either succeeded in spite of very human flaws or failed in spectacular fashion. Their most important trait, though, was that they showed chivalry and flair. Conversely, men such as Major-General H. H. Kitchener, who attained notable success in a most methodical and bureaucratic manner, were often viewed with suspicion.[51] As the *Pall Mall Gazette* aptly stated, in comparing Jameson with another quixotic hero of British history, Bonnie Prince Charlie, 'personal bravery and contempt for money are the two qualities which most surely win the popular heart, for the simple reason that we admire most what we lack most.'[52]

The Jameson Raid reveals three elements of jingoism:

- it was a transitory and event-driven phenomenon;
- it functioned independently of the imperial ethic; and
- it was driven by emotion, not ideology.

Jingoism was a response, a reaction, and as such existed only temporarily. While much of the nation celebrated the virtue of the Raid's quixotic hero, there was little call for retribution against the Boers. Though war broke out four years later, this was attributable more to damaged Afrikaner pride than to any British desire to 'do Jameson one better.'

The most striking proof of the transitory nature of jingoism was that imperial achievement was not necessarily a significant element in its generation. Men such as Lugard, Kitchener, and even Milner, while attaining great success in the field of imperial expansion and leadership, ostensibly the core of the jingo spirit, were instead often ignored or even criticized for their methods. Other crises, such as the contemporaneous Venezuelan border dispute with the United States, or the Asante War, garnered comparatively minor public responses. The imperial ethic was grounded in notions of duty, service, character, and trusteeship. Jingo heroes such as Jameson were caricatures of those virtues, men who were otherwise deeply flawed, but whose appeal resonated on a separate plain of exaggerated emotion. Imperialism demanded something of the adherent. One must be an active participant. This was Buchan's position. Jingoism, as a purely emotive phenomenon, demanded nothing at all of the participant. The jingo crowd were passive observers, members of what Hobson termed the 'cult of the spectator,' no different from the Manchester United supporter who wears red-and-white face-paint to Old Trafford, but turns on the local side if it records an own goal. More importantly, the jingo participant bore no responsibility for the actions others took in the name of their common country.

Imperial actors such as Jameson and Gordon, who embodied moral equivocation in their actions, garnered the laurels. Buchan, however, denounced what he termed their 'false imperialism,' finding it xenophobic, aggressively martial, and self-serving. In a speech in Glasgow in 1904, he dismissed jingoism as 'mere land hunger,' and argued that 'a desire to paint the map red from a vulgar ostentation is no Imperial idea.'[53] Buchan instructively does not use the term 'mafficking'[54] in his letters of the period. His time with Milner had impressed him with the need for a new imperial creed, a renunciation of old doctrine and a consideration of new ideas. Francis Carey articulated this hope in *A Lodge*, 'a creed beyond parties, a consuming and passionate interest in the destiny of [one's] people.'[55] Consolidation, based on an understanding that the time for growth, even if it was still desired, was over, was the new goal. This step accorded with the position of Milner himself, as well as that of his Kindergarten and, later, Round Table progeny. Buchan differed from Milner and the Round Table, though, in that he hoped this 'new idea' would not take the form of federation, but rather would be a closer association of English-speaking peoples, including Americans. In this he shared much of Rhodes' concept of Empire.[56] Buchan lacked, though, the lust for territory and power which possessed Rhodes (and the 'most superior' Curzon for that matter), instead envisioning the broader Empire as a plain upon which Britain could perform service and exert influence.[57]

THEORIES OF IMPERIAL CITIZENSHIP

Towards a cosmopolitan view of imperial citizenship

Buchan envisioned such service and influence in cosmopolitan terms. This notion of cosmopolitan imperialism combined an attachment to the local and the national with a sense of belonging to the Empire as a whole. As such, he disavowed excessive nationalism, understood as loyalty to one's nation–state. In a speech delivered in 1912 in opposition to Home Rule for Ireland, Buchan stated: 'I do not believe in any sort of Nationalism, or any government based on it.' This view held for the Empire as well. Imperial citizenship should encompass the principles of the hearth in combination with an imperial sensibility. He recorded in his memoir:

> I had regarded the Dominions patronizingly as distant settlements of our people who were making a creditable effort under difficulties to carry on the British tradition. Now I realized that Britain had at least as much to learn from them as they had from Britain... They [the Dominions] combined a passionate devotion to their own countries with the vision of a great brotherhood based on race and a common culture, a vision none the less real because they rarely tried to put it into words. I began to see that the Empire, which had hitherto been only a phrase to me, might be a potent and beneficent force in the world.[58]

In an address to the Galashiels branch of the Primrose League, Buchan noted this position as 'local patriotism': 'No one of us will be a good citizen of the British Empire unless he is first a good Scotsman... and a devout lover of his own shire.'[59] Such a view spoke to the indelible Scottishness he maintained throughout his life and the pleasure he found in the local everywhere he went. The South African veld was a constant character in his fiction his entire life. In Canada he became the first Governor-General to visit the Canadian Arctic, and he was honoured by indigenous tribes in Quebec and Carleton, Saskatchewan, with the title of Chief.[60] He consciously applied this notion of the importance of locality in his politics, arguing for the application of local loyalties to international causes. It was his South African experience, Saul Dubow contends, that inspired his belief in the importance of 'multiple, overlapping national identities and loyalties.'[61] The deleterious consequences of the First World War cemented this outlook in his mind. At a ceremony in 1919 to honour Buchan and the recently knighted Sir Donald Maclean for their service to the community of Peebles, Buchan reflected that 'the lesser patriotism does not exclude the greater; on the contrary, it is its surest foundation. But we have learned in the war, I hope and believe, another loyalty – a loyalty to civilization, to humanity.'[62] With these words Buchan echoed the ideas Curtis was also in the process of conceiving at this time. Such reasoning also led Buchan to support the nascent notion of a League of Nations, an idea spearheaded by his friend and former teacher Gilbert Murray.

Buchan propagated a cosmopolitan view of imperial citizenship as early as the century's first decade. In a set-piece discussion in *A Lodge*, various views are advanced as to the proper practice of imperialism. Mr. Wakefield, the practical minded colonial, asserts that what the colonies want is a business relationship, not some form of mysticism. Others argue over party politics and 'liberal' and 'conservative' imperialism. The Tory Lady Amysfort, distrustful of 'the saint in politics,' expostulates on practical imperialism. Lord Appin, a composite of Arthur Balfour and Lord Rosebery, exclaims that what should be avoided at all costs is dogmatism. All the group really agrees upon is the rejection of any imperialism which rests on brute force, terming it 'degenerate.'[63] It is Carey – ironically, given Buchan's reservations about Rhodes – who captures best the mood of broad-minded imperial citizenship, rather magnanimously stating that 'the truth can only be known to the man on the hill-top.'[64] This is not to say that Buchan's idea was patriarchal. Rather, the view from the eyrie allows the imperialist greater vision, acknowledging the full scope of Empire, not merely its localised ruts and gullies. The *Spectator*'s review of *A Lodge* struck just this note: 'There is in the whole book a power of vision which makes one feel as though one looked down from a great height ... [and saw] how the great game of our heritage should be played.'[65]

Buchan took the idea of cosmopolitan imperialism beyond his writing. As a public figure in the period between the Boer War and the First World War, he engaged in many imperial projects with an eye to propagating this position. The occasion of Canada's tercentenary as a British colony well illustrates this.[66] Buchan admired the evolution of responsible government in Canada, a view which contributed greatly to his subsequent success as Governor-General. Canada pointed to the efficacy of his cosmopolitan imperialism in its success in uniting two cultures without destroying local patriotism. For Buchan, as with many Edwardians, Laurier seemed a living example of this principle: a Québecois who had integrated the two solitudes. Buchan thus saw the tercentenary as a celebration of this cultural compromise. Public ceremony was an agent of cooperation. He noted in the *Scottish Review* that 'the best security for peace and friendship will always be the pride which comes from co-operation in a general task.' As his contribution to the tercentenary, Buchan organized a committee to erect a memorial of Wolfe and Moncalm,[67] and attempted to engage such luminaries as Lord Rosebery in the project. It did not meet with success, but an interesting postscript to this effort is to be found in June, 1917, when Buchan was serving as Director of Information, heading the Government's propaganda efforts. One of his initiatives was to propose a monument to Abraham Lincoln in Edinburgh for 4 July, in order to strengthen the Anglo-American alliance. This proposal likewise proved abortive, but it expressed his continued belief in the Anglo-American relationship, and further testified to his reputation as an international citizen.[68]

'The last Victorian'? Buchan and late Victorian morality

Buchan's conception of imperial citizenship was infused with a well-defined morality. His Calvinist roots helped shape a vision of Empire balanced between a high-minded idealism and a recognition of man's fallibility and the harshness of life. Like many of his generation, he esteemed notions of duty and service. He rejected the political relativism voiced by the more strident imperialists of his generation, such as the American businessman J. H. Hammond, who believed that 'the morality of an action cannot, of course, be made to depend upon the effects which flow from it; but it is precisely from these effects that we properly estimate the wisdom or folly of a political decision.'[69] Buchan saw the essence of politics not as a contest of power, but as the performance 'of a man's duty, not only to himself, but to his fellows and to the state.'[70] Morality was indeed the standard of both the individual and her or his actions. The measure of this morality was what the historian John Gibbins, in a separate context, has termed 'the good motive.'[71]

This conviction is similar to the significance of *altruism* for the Victorians. Stefan Collini has argued that altruism was the most pervasive component of the Victorian intellectual climate, an ideal binding the dominant liberal directive of individualism to a broader notion of public service.[72] Morality was conceived of as adherence to obligation. There existed a 'correct' answer to problems, and failure to grapple with these was seen as base selfishness. The ultimate goal was harmony, both between individuals and for society. This struggle to imbue Lockean liberalism with a social conscience was influenced both by the decline of orthodox Christianity and by a growing acknowledgment of social and economic cleavages in British society.

An important component of altruism was attention to proper character, both individual and collective. Abhorrence of apathy, respect for work as compared to Georgian leisure, self-restraint, and the domination of the will over baser motivations all marked the Victorians' mental terrain. This applied also to the national character, which, according to John Stuart Mill, was the force that bound together entities such as laws, customs, and wars.[73] It is from debates concerning national character that notions of citizenship are by necessity drawn.

Buchan was sympathetic to many of these values and shared the assumptions upon which they were based. For these reasons Gertrude Himmelfarb metaphorically characterizes him as 'the last Victorian.' She argues that Buchan epitomized Victorian ideals of service and respectability, and held a descriptive, not prescriptive, worldview. Buchan certainly went to great pains to be fair and true to principle. He exemplified the principle of altruism, as described by Collini, though he was sometimes dogmatic. As Hugh Summerville, the semi-autobiographical young writer in *A Lodge*, notes: 'The people who go back to first principles, as a rule make the journey only to find some defence for a prejudice which nothing will induce them to forego.' Rather, he advocated 'the religious value of free thought,' and applied the notion of religious 'faith' to his position on Empire: 'Religion should be like a strong tree, blown upon by every wind, but able to stand up against them and derive health and strength from their buffeting. If we believe, then we know that all things work for good to him that believeth.'[74] A system of thought, he believed, should be flexible and tolerant. Buchan's tolerance and sense of morality were manifest in his early experiences in South Africa. He was firmly convinced of the moral worth of reconstruction in South Africa, despite the criticism levelled at the Land Settlement Department for excessive bureaucracy.[75] What was important was to reintegrate the whole of South Africa into the imperial community.

Buchan later applied this same criterion in appealing for a broad patriotism during the early stages of the First World War, invoking Shakespeare's Henry V's call to arms at Agincourt, and in the aftermath of the war urging in a speech in Peebles that 'we must bring to the task that moral quality which puts the interests of the whole community before the interests of the individual.'[76] He believed this understanding of imperialism as moral purpose might be fulfilled through the creation of the League of Nations. Writing to Gilbert Murray, one of the League's leading advocates in late 1918, Buchan noted: 'All the enthusiasm that I have always had for my own brand of Imperialism I feel now attaches to this creed.'[77] Buchan, like many others, was soon disappointed by the League's inability to maintain peace, a failure which seemed to confirm his fatalistic view of the world.

Buchan's imperialism was one characterized by a moral cosmopolitanism. What was 'moral cosmopolitanism' and what was the place of the individual within this cosmos? Buchan saw imperial citizenship as manifested in the moral relationship between individual and state, specifically the proper behaviour of each party. The State was conceived of first as the Empire, and only second as *British, Canadian,* and so on. Local allegiances, as we have seen, were important, but they were important because they buttressed the broader entity of Empire. In other words, they were supported by a broader, more cosmopolitan, understanding of Empire. Buchan's moral cosmopolitanism thus meant a desire to incorporate the various peoples of Empire within a common citizenship based upon a shared morality, or proper 'character' in the language of the day. Such a citizenship would be free from national limitations and prejudices.

This was his message in an Edinburgh speech in 1904 in which he stated that the 'important thing is to get this country to make... [imperialism] part of... [the British] political outlook.'[78] He recognized a great paradox here. When faced with failure or *ennui,* whether personally or as a people, the 'only thing to do is to draw a larger circle with a wider radius.' However, he also recognized that 'those who do that often fail to complete it, and leave only a broken arc to show how vast their design was.'[79] As the fervour of the 'New Imperialism' began to cool in the aftermath of the Boer War, the challenge to imperial thinkers such as Buchan now seemed to be how to prevent the imperial arc from breaking. The forward policy now pursued was not territorial, as it had once been under men of the 'Scramble' like Sir Bartle Frere and Sir George Goldie. Now it took the form of a political activism. The task was to consolidate, to solidify, with the *ex post facto* rationalization that the *civilizing task,* the mission, was complete. For Milner and his Round Table protégées, the solution was in federation. Others, such as the imperial journalist Richard Jebb, believed colonial nationalism held the key to future imperial strength. Buchan remained aloof from such structured initiatives, preferring instead an imperial solidarity built from the individual out. Central to this view was an expansion of political participation throughout the Empire. The path to such a catholic imperialism, according to Buchan, was through democracy. It is through an examination of the conjunction of imperialism and democracy, and the contingent place of race in that relationship, that Buchan's ideas on imperial citizenship become clear.

Imperialism and democracy

Buchan's sense of catholic imperialism can be seen as an attempt, largely political, to create a shared culture, a shared idiom, a support system outside of which the individual would be rudderless, and which was therefore a necessity. In short, it was to encourage assimilation and prevent conflict. The question in regard to Empire was whether this was a chimera or a real possibility. Buchan advocated a broad imperial citizenship based upon shared responsibilities, with the conviction that the creation of cultural homogeneity would decrease the potential for conflict.

Buchan believed that the franchise was of paramount importance, for an individual could not fully realize his or her citizenship without voting. This was the covenant which tied him to the State. The State, in turn, was obligated to provide conscientious administration, and must therefore select the best possible civil servants in pursuit of this task. The twin charges of voting and administration, directed towards imperial ends, formed the core of Buchan's articulation of imperial citizenship. He saw democracy as a neutral force: 'democracy in itself, remember, is not a good thing; it is only good if it is well done.'[80] His cosmopolitanism meant that everyone was a potential equal, and he betrayed little of the patrician disdain for the masses which characterized conservatives such as Lord Salisbury. In his 'Democracy and Representative Government' in the *Fortnightly Review*, Buchan asserted: 'Everyman is a pretty sagacious fellow. He is not the neurotic being, living in a whirl of elementary emotions, that some would have us picture.'[81] It is thus highly ironic that when Buchan was finally elected to Parliament, it was for the cloistered seat of the Scottish Universities.

Buchan did express a hope that democracy held the potential to bring people together. It was intuitive, something all could grasp at various levels. Furthermore, he advocated an organic democracy – here anticipating civil society – rather than party politics. He shared this view with many who were on the fringes of organized politics and felt the party system hindered good government. One of the few favourable aspects of the war, in Buchan's mind, was that it showed the potential for consensus government.[82] Thus, he sympathized with H. H. Asquith's frustration at the political maneuvering which characterized much of the year 1916, sharing Asquith's conviction that such behaviour at a time of 'horror' was base, and hindered the proper functioning of the coalition government.[83] In the intellectual tradition of Burke, security remained for Buchan the preeminent objective; thus his opinion that the First World War was analogous to the American Civil War, in that both were conflicts within a civilization.[84]

He also advocated a broad democracy in the tradition of Benjamin Disraeli and the Conservative Party's great 'leap in the dark' of 1867. Buchan had early in his career considered writing a biography of the former Tory leader,[85] but his view of democracy was less opportunistic than had been Disraeli's. He outlined this view in a pamphlet on women's suffrage, a cause which he strongly supported. Buchan did not believe women should gain the vote because it was a 'right'. In fact, he opposed the language of 'rights' as an Enlightenment abstraction, arguing that 'in the last resort there is only one right – the right of every man and woman to do his or her duty.'[86] Women should be allowed to vote because citizenship, for which the exercise of the vote was the central component, is contingent upon the 'bearing of certain civic burdens, and is no friend of "irrelevant tests" such as gender.'[87] Character and intelligence were the true tests of citizenship, traits for which women had equal propensity as men. In advancing this position, Buchan set himself apart from not only most Conservatives of the period, but also most Liberals. Buchan also had no time for critics of female suffrage who employed the thin-edge-of-the-wedge argument. Buchan saw this as 'fear-mongering.' Any initiative can be perverted, he argued, and one legislates against the future at his peril. The proper performance of citizenship, especially of the franchise, was a necessary prerequisite to enjoying liberty.[88]

This position is to be seen in Buchan's view of imperial union as cooperative rather than prescriptive. A relationship, whether between people or between political entities, is successful when those involved participate of their own accord. Individuals are the best judge of their own interests, and should be free to act as they wish so long as they do not harm others. In regard to Empire, it laid the basis for the support of an imperial union based, not on the centralizing imperatives of Milner and the Round Table, but on the common-sense appeal of strength in numbers. Imperial union or, perhaps, more specifically imperial unity, a looser concept not necessarily requiring constitutional bonds, offered the best environment for furthering the interests of all who existed under it.

Buchan argued that unless Britain was prepared to fully administer a colony, she should not interfere in the colony's internal government. Imperial union should be an amalgam of states which were autonomous, regardless of size. This is the message he proselytized during his time at the *Spectator*, arguing: 'We must learn to regard colonials as . . . our fellow citizens . . . as no more a foreign country than Wales or Ireland.'[89] This would create an Empire of people, not territory. He advanced this argument in an anonymous piece in the *Spectator* in 1904, supporting the jurist Sir Frederick Pollock's proposition that colonial representatives be included in the Privy Council.[90] In a series of letters to Violet Markham, a close friend and liberal Milnerite, Buchan outlined his views on the franchise and Empire. He argued that the franchise in the colonies should be based on population, and grouped into 'districts,' on the model of Britain's electoral reforms of

1884–85. He had faith in expanding the franchise, citing the broad electorate in New Zealand as a positive example. He added, though, that electoral districts should be redistributed each election, to ensure that voters' input was balanced with the 'public good.'[91] By this, he meant the preservation of colonial unity and continued participation in the imperial mandate. Thus, in South Africa for instance, the Dutch vote must not be allowed to outnumber the British, for fear that Dutch-dominated colonies would cast their ballot for independence.

Buchan's position on indigenous citizenship was an extension of this argument regarding the settlement colonies. In regard to the indigenous peoples of South Africa, he had argued in 1904 that the franchise should be withheld for the immediate future, lest social and economic disequilibrium ruin the prospects for union. However, he also warned that if indigenous peoples, who outnumbered whites by a ratio of six to one in the territory south of the Zambezi river, were not brought into the imperial fold, disaster would also ensue. Thus, social prejudices must be overcome in the light of practical need.[92] This provided the impetus to search for a more cosmopolitan imperial citizenship.

Buchan's conception of the role of the State

If imperial citizenship, then, entailed responsibility to the collective, from which liberty ensued, what role was the State to play in such a relationship? In short, the State's role was to provide skilled administration. This was the lesson Buchan derived from serving under Milner. The administrative task in South Africa of organizing the Refugee Relief Committee and leavening the abuses of the concentration camps appealed to Buchan. He earned the Pro-Consul's admiration for this service, a compliment he repaid in his tribute to Milner in an *Edinburgh Review* piece in 1903.[93] Buchan also came to share Milner's frustration with party politics, what Milner called 'the system,' governed by people 'having no adequate appreciation of the supreme value of trained knowledge, or of the difference in *size* of the questions submitted to them, so that they are capable of the same levity with regard the biggest things as with regard to trifles.'[94] Buchan's disappointment in not receiving the post under Cromer furthered his disenchantment with political life, and helped mark him as a fatalist. He complained that 'fatted souls like Liberals can never be Imperialists,' and worried after the Unionists were swept from office in January 1906 that his party would have to 'start at the beginning and do the work of Disraeli all over again.'[95] He was particularly incensed at the censure of Milner in the aftermath of the Chinese flogging incident: 'It is the insufferable result to Lord M which makes me furious.'[96] Buchan admired Milner's practical capabilities as well as his imperialism, and chafed at what he perceived as an attack on the Pro-Consul's integrity. Like many of Milner's supporters, most of whom were conservatives, Buchan believed that Milner, a man who had devoted his career to public service, deserved more respect. He was particularly upset at the opportunistic bombast of Churchill.[97]

Nor did he always have an easy time of it in the Unionist party. This was largely due to his minority position as a Tory free-trader at a time when the party was pulling itself apart over the issue. Buchan had supped on St Loe Strachey's free-trade views while at the *Spectator*, and had come to believe that protection would be harmful to imperial unity, provoking internal disputes and stifling colonial initiatives. He opposed Joseph Chamberlain's argument that the British worker must accept higher bread prices in return for continued economic growth and job security. This was not because Buchan was opposed to what the historian Bernard Semmel has called social imperialism, the attempt to increase working-class patriotism through concessions such as old-age pensions and national insurance, but because he feared it would alienate the colonies by positioning them as economic clients of Britain. Buchan asserted that the colonies would trade with Britain regardless of tariff relief, and that free trade would allow them to pursue their own economic interests, a surer way to keep them within the imperial fold. In his adherence to Cobdenite free trade, Buchan differed little from the Liberal imperialist position, and indeed Rosebery, the nominal founder of the school of efficiency, was a personal and intellectual confidant of his. However, after the Conservatives moved more definitively toward tariff reform as party policy in the aftermath of defeat in both the January and December general elections of 1910, Buchan paid the price for his adherence to free trade, as leading party figures such as Arthur Balfour and Austen Chamberlain could not find time to stump for him as he attempted to win support for the next election.[98]

What Buchan found most troubling about Tariff Reform, for he was not given to long deliberation on economic policy, was that it undermined efforts to promote imperial unity. It ran counter to his conviction that one cannot legislate unity. Lord Launceston, the Milner character in *A Lodge*, states that 'unity must precede union,' and that a legislated federation was a poor idea.[99] While, in the spirit of Burke, legislators should be given freedom to innovate, they must not impose their ideas on others, this running counter to the spirit of democracy. This, in Buchan's eye, was Joseph Chamberlain's failing, and the basis for his opposition to tariff reform.[100]

Buchan's arguments concerning proper state administration, democracy, and the role of the individual led him to conceive of citizenship as a right shared by all subjects of Empire. The best means of coming to terms with the frictions that resulted in being both a democrat and an imperialist – a dichotomy which the geographer Halford Mackinder argued was irreconcilable, the two convictions being mutually exclusive – was Buchan's development of a notion of cosmopolitan imperial citizenship, where all under the flag of Empire were deemed equal, at least in capability. He did not advocate full legal equality, self-government, or some other method of formally recognizing this principle. What he did reject were essentialist notions of race and citizenship. Thus, there were no convincing arguments for denying equality, though there were cases when its realization would be gradual.

Mackinder, in the post-war work *Democratic Ideals and Reality* (1919), asserted that both Cobdenite idealists and tariff reformers were the self-same beast, in that both sought to organize the Empire in the name of *efficiency*. Both camps conceived of individuals as constituent parts of the State, and though both were legitimately concerned with the welfare of individuals, this concern was motivated by a concern for *national* efficiency, not individual efficiency. Thus both camps shied away from advocating assisted emigration schemes. Mackinder understood imperialism to be the desire to strengthen pan-imperial bonds between both the myriad subjects of the Empire, on the individual level, and between its territorial units, on the constitutional level. Imperialists, he argued, were 'organizers,' concerned with improving 'national efficiency' through imperial means. In this sense, he continued, imperialism proved inimical to democracy: 'While "the democrat is thinking of the rights of man", the organizer is "thinking how to use men", and has idealized the disciplined state, the "camp state".'[101] The only reason the Empire did not break apart was that democracy and imperialism, understood in Mackinder's sense as the spirit of using the Empire to improve national efficiency, had their respective separate quarters in the settlement and dependent Empires.

An ecumenical conception of imperial citizenship

The 'Two Empires' thesis, holding that Empire consisted of a *democratic* sphere, based in Britain and the settlement colonies, that profited from an *imperial* sphere, consisting of the dependent colonies and other possessions, is generally accepted by historians. The struggles of the decolonization era seem to support this view *ex post facto*. However, this is not to say that contemporaries were either ignorant or dismissive of this relationship. Indeed, Buchan went part of the way toward bridging this gap, and, being somewhat ahead of orthodox thought on this issue, was inevitably disappointed. His cosmopolitan ideas, starting with his time as an outsider in the aristocratic world of Oxford, meant that he had difficulty adhering to the hierarchical notions of race which his generation embraced. From the frank discussions of race of Karl Pearson, Francis Galton, and Benjamin Kidd in the 1880s, through to the milder paternalism of Frederick Lugard in the 1900s and 1910s, two generations of British thinkers, in working through the problem of the 'Two Empires,' inevitably invoked ideas of hierarchy. Either there were separate 'races', some superior, others inferior, an unbridgeable gap; or all people were fundamentally equal, but some were more advanced than others, and thus had a duty to help the 'less developed' advance. While Buchan's experiences led him toward an ecumenical conception of imperial citizenship, one which sought to overcome divisions of thought on the issue both in Britain and throughout the Empire, he was ultimately unable to transcend the question of difference, and thus failed to articulate in clear terms what such a citizenship would look like.

Buchan initially held to the belief that there were apparent and substantial differences among the races of Empire. He argued in *The African Colony* (1904) that the races were separated by a 'radical mental dissimilarity,' and propagated the notion of the 'lazy native,' stating that whites and blacks should not compete as labour because the latter exhibit less 'industry.' Buchan's *Prester John* (1910), in which an enterprising 19-year-old hero thwarts an indigenous uprising in South Africa, portrays indigenous peoples as intelligent, but impetuous and unsophisticated.[102] This was his first attempt at fiction in the vein of Rider Haggard, and was written for boys. The character of Laputa, the indigenous chief, presents a clue to Buchan's developing ideas on race and citizenship. He is at once noble and childlike, honourable and unpredictable. Bill Schwarz, in commenting on the influence of Southern Africa on Buchan's career, argues that Laputa is not a creole, but rather two distinct people, depending on whether he is conversing with a black man or a white man.[103] Laputa thus represents a transition in Buchan's thought from a paternal conception of non-British peoples, where difference is rigid and unbridgeable, to a more ecumenical one, where all men, in potential if not in practice, are equals. (It must be emphasized that Buchan was certainly not a proponent of equal status for all, at least in the short-term.) By the 1910s, Buchan's idea of moral cosmopolitanism had taken form, making it impossible for him to hold to the 'Two Empires' thesis. A character in his 1925 novel *The House of the Four Winds* sums up this new position: 'human nature was much the same everywhere, and that one might dig out of the unlikeliest places surprising virtues.'[104] This development is best shown in contrasting Buchan's reaction to the Chinese labour controversy in the Transvaal in 1905–6 with the more ecumenical spirit he advocated for Empire by the First World War.

The controversy over Chinese 'slavery,' the importation into the Transvaal of close to 50,000 Chinese labourers after 1904 to revive the faltering Rand gold industry, sharply divided Edwardian politics. The human abuses suffered by Chinese 'coolies,' combined with their low wages, led to criticism of the Unionists' labour policy, and contributed to the Liberals' triumph at the polls in 1906, though the controversy's role should not be overrated.[105] Peter Henshaw and Ronald Hyam further suggest that the Liberals's subsequent grant of responsible government to the Transvaal, rather than a magnanimous gesture designed to mend white relations in Southern Africa, was in fact motivated by a desire to rid Britain of responsibility for the Chinese labour system.[106] The 'coolie' question was the first true test of Buchan's imperial faith, as it set his attachment to Milner and the imperial mission against the strong moral convictions which would later lead him towards ecumenicalism. Writing in *The Times* in early 1904, Buchan expressed cautious support for the labour scheme.[107] He argued that Chinese labour might be a necessary, though temporary, step in the Transvaal's progress toward responsible government. The establishment of a strong economy would set the conditions for political reform. He put off criticism of the scheme as *mala fide*, focused on admitted humanitarian problems, when the real issue was the absorption of the Transvaal into the Empire. It should be noted that despite Buchan's concerns, the most forceful critiques of indentured labour in general were not humanitarian, though they sometimes used such language, but rather economic. Indentured labourers, after all, worked more cheaply than white labourers. The Chinese labour issue, in combination with debates concerning tariff reform and the Government's Education and Licensing Acts, helped politicize working-class Britons to vote against the Conservatives in 1906.

Buchan had become sensitive to the importance of colonial nationalism, the sense of place and history then developing at various rates in the colonies, and intuited the significance of this force in the future Empire. Thus, the Transvaal's wishes were to be respected, even if to do so strained the loyalty of Asian subjects or the comfort of British Liberals. This was the message he offered in the *Scottish Review* in 1908, urging the Liberal Government not to veto colonial legislation banning further Indian immigration into the Transvaal. Campbell-Bannerman's Government had granted the Transvaal autonomy by Letters Patent in 1906, and responsible government had led to the election in 1907 of the moderate Het Volk Party, under the leadership of Louis Botha. This development helped Buchan reconcile his tentative support for 'coolie' labour with his moral doubts, as he could assert once the crisis had passed that 'liberty . . . is liberty to act foolishly as well as to act wisely.'[108]

In this definition of liberty in the context of Empire, Buchan anticipated the position proffered by Laurier at the 1911 Imperial Conference. The Canadian Premier argued that 'the power of disallowance now vested in us [the Imperial Government, for which Laurier technically, as a colonial himself, did not speak] was one which in the interests of the Colonies it was better should not be exercised. Even although the Act sought to be disallowed, were one taking my property from me and handing it over to my political opponents, it would still be better for us not to interfere.'[109] The freedom to make bad decisions was the bulwark of imperial unity. This was consistent with Buchan's approval of Burke's notion of representative government, where the elected representative is given free rein to exercise his good judgement, rather than being a mere conduit of public opinion (or of his constituency office).[110]

There was a degree of willful naivety here, as support for the principle of responsible government, and, in the dependent territories, that of trusteeship, also meant a silent condoning of the often brutal suppression of internal dissent by such governments. Buchan, for instance, was noticeably silent regarding the violent suppression of the Zulu rebellion in 1906, when the Zulu population forcibly resisted the imposition by the Natal Government of a poll tax. This same paradox was later at the heart of the Amritsar Crisis of 1919, where Brigadier-General Dyer was punished as an individual, but the principle of the Raj was not, immediately anyway, challenged.[111] How much wrong is permissible in the service of right?

The 'right' Buchan upheld was the 'civilizing power' of Britain. He believed that Africa must become 'a land of political telepathy,' where the various races created a common community. Thus, it was equally damaging to Empire when white Transvaal labourers held back their labour for unreasonable wages, as they intermittently did, as it was when Africans resisted British governance. Both situations worked counter to the principle of unity for the common good. Therefore, just as the British people must be further schooled in the necessity of a common imperial purpose, so indigenous peoples, whether in Africa or elsewhere, must be taught civic duty. This was consistent with a notion of trusteeship, the position that indigenous peoples' lands are a protectorate, not a colony, and that the British 'must fulfill our trust in the *noble sense.*'[112] This appeal to nobility is instructive. Buchan, unlike many of his peers, was aware of the danger that such language could devolve into mere cant, a convenient show to mask economic and territorial aggrandizement.

Trust between ruler and ruled must be reciprocated, not taken advantage of; this remained a touchstone of Buchan's imperial philosophy. In this view, Buchan owed much to his early connection with Gilbert Murray. Murray too was a thinker among doers. He also feared the potential for opportunism and opposed inequality, writing to Buchan that the consciousness of belonging to a great nation entailed a sense of *noblesse oblige*, to which one was 'bound in self-respect.' Abuses can creep in when self-criticism is lacking, or when this self-respect is perverted, as when ideals are mistaken for facts. Thus, an individual English man is virtuous, if that is the case, not because he is English, but because he is virtuous. Murray was fearful that England, like the ancient Athens he knew as a scholar, had the potential to administer its Empire poorly if it came to believe that 'the Higher, because it is higher, has a right to behave worse,' an eventuality which would lead to 'fearfully underrating the intensity of the other people's feelings.'[113] Buchan applied this lesson to Empire, arguing that the British, as imperial missionaries (in a secular sense), must learn the culture of the indigenous peoples before their 'improvement' along Western lines was possible. After all, he contended, indigenous peoples' 'lands are a protectorate, not a colony.'[114] In the spirit of Victorian altruism, he concluded in a romantic manner, invoking the memory of Wellington, and asserting that it is better to be Icarus and risk failure, than to be a contented minor power.

If Buchan was not ahead of his time on issues of race, neither was he an advocate of a British supremacy based upon essentialist notions of racial hierarchy. While he was certainly more concerned with political progress than with racial platforms, his view of inequality in Empire is best termed paternalistic. He accepted that the principles of imperialism dictated that all the peoples of Empire were deserving of self-government, but this did not mean it must occur immediately. Here he shared the contemporary conviction that subject peoples must be tutored in the ways of democracy, ideally of the Westminster variety. Commenting on India, he argued: 'If we give freedom, we are bound to guard against its abuse, or we shall fail in our duty to those whom we govern.' He thus supported the gradual reforms encompassed in the 1909 Morley–Minto legislation, and in general seconded Lord Cromer's opinion that the premature grant of self-government would not be a liberal act, but rather merely a doctrinaire, and ultimately counterproductive, move.[115]

Because of such equivocating, Buchan's defence of the civilizing mission was notably hollow. His orthodox pronouncements on race became half-hearted by the 1910s, as if he was as much concerned with convincing himself of the validity of such arguments as he was in propagating the message to others. Buchan was, as Juanita Kruse has observed, careless in his language concerning race. He sometimes employed the stereotyped euphemisms of the day when referring to matters of race.[116] He also held tightly, especially early in his career, to the notion of *totem*, that men were of a 'type' determinative of their actions. This view of the world coloured his view of fellow-Britons as well as of colonial peoples. A belief that individuals have an 'essence' of some sort is perhaps an unsurprising position for a Calvinist to maintain, but Buchan began to move beyond this position by the early 1910s to develop a cosmopolitan view of race, one which highlighted commonalities between people rather than differences. This progression in Buchan's thought resulted in part from the emotional and mental struggles of the First World War, but also because of a growing conviction that borders, whether political or cultural, were porous and artificial, useful for practical matters, but not indicative of essential or even, necessarily, substantive differences between peoples.

Furthermore, his sense of morality was centred on the individual, not on *cultures* or *peoples*. Buchan thus sought to ameliorate divisions within his own hierarchical society as well as the racial divisions apparent within the Empire. This was apparent in his work as an historian, where he concentrated on biographies. He produced well-received studies of Montrose and Lord Arwell in 1913, and later in life wrote on Lord Minto, Sir Walter Scott, Caesar, Charles Gordon, Cromwell, and Augustus. Buchan's notion of imperial citizenship, like his histories, was rooted in a sense of fairness. One admirer was his fellow-historian G. M. Trevelyan. In a letter congratulating Buchan on the publication of *Montrose*, a biographical study of the seventeenth-century Scottish royalist and Covenanter, Trevelyan noted: 'That is the way to write history, to be an *advocate* for your own view, but a *judge* in impartiality in stating the facts.'[117] Wakefield, the colonial nationalist character in *A Lodge*, sees the Empire in catholic terms, stating that 'the boy who grows up in the backwoods and the boy who goes the conventional road of Eton and Oxford will become different men, though they may be sons of the same father.' This spirit of inclusion applied as well to men of action, Wakefield declaring: 'We must have our subalterns as well as our marshals, our Garibaldis as well as our Cavours and Mazzinis.'[118] There was also much of Buchan's personal philosophy guiding him towards an ecumenical position. Oxford, he reflected late in life, had been 'an excellent thing, for to mix with abler men than yourself is to learn humility.'[119]

It is evident that Buchan was struggling towards an ecumenical imperial citizenship as far back as his time in Southern Africa. Despite his reservations about granting indigenous peoples the franchise, or his faith in the paternalistic notion of tutelage, he nonetheless shied away from Milner's demographic plan to swamp the Boers through increased English settlement. He instead argued more positively that the Boers could be brought back into the imperial fold, the strength of Empire being 'that wide tolerance which does not seek a dead level of uniformity, but is content to give all creeds and sentiments free scope under its flag.'[120] Buchan tempered his support for war in South Africa, and he found much to respect in the Boers, a domestic people who resembled the people of the Scottish Borders he knew so well. This respect was repaid in 1919 when Smuts asked Buchan to chronicle South Africa's wartime service, a project which resulted in *The History of the South African Forces in France* (1920).[121]

His ecumenical outlook also bridged party divisions. Buchan always maintained that he was 'nine-tenths' a Liberal. His only issue with the party of Gladstone was a perceived moral smugness on its part which he believed resulted in complacency: 'Tories may think they are better born, but Liberals know that they are born better.'[122] Indeed, many of Buchan's pronouncements during the Great War were decidedly more liberal than those of the Liberal Party. He fumed at the deleterious effect on public morale (and on the quality of his despatches from the front) of the government's general censorship. He also expressed sympathy for those Britons who for moral reasons refused to serve, both before and after the introduction of conscription in 1916: he signed a petition in December 1918 in favour of a general amnesty for conscientious objectors. A central character in *Mr Standfast*, the third Richard Hannay novel, written in 1917–18, is a conscientious objector whose moral certainty marks him as a hero.[123]

While Buchan did not experience combat itself, he was not naive as to the horrors of the war. He spent much time at the battlefield as an official observer, and the war made an indelible impression on him. His personal losses – his brother Alistair, his friend Raymond Asquith – have been noted above. Even apart from those tragedies, the war confirmed Buchan's fatalism: 'one acquiesced in tragedy, but it was an acquiescence without hope of philosophy. There was no uplift of the spirit, such as is traditionally associated with battle.'[124] The tragedy led him to view a strong Empire as a bulwark against any future Armageddon. Buchan's 1917 Introduction to the revised edition of *A Lodge*, penned at the nadir of the war, expressed this sentiment thus: 'We understand, as we never understood before, that our Empire is a mystic whole which no enemy may part asunder, and our wisest minds are now given to the task of devising a mechanism of union adequate to this spiritual unity.'[125] As Andrew Lownie has observed, though, Buchan much preferred the 'spiritual unity' to the formal 'mechanism of union.'[126] Such a position was consistent with his ecumenicalism, which celebrated the diversity of Empire, emphasized a growing understanding that its variety was its strength, and argued that cooperation might better be achieved in spirit than in material practice. In advancing these views, Buchan was consistent with broader intellectual movements within the conservative tent which sought to provide collective responses to the problems of both imperial and domestic challenges.[127]

The cause which John Buchan had nurtured since his service in Milner's 'creche' at the turn of the century was that of Empire. A cosmopolitan imperial citizenship, equal parts duty, responsibility, morality, and cooperation, was his expressed vision. Buchan shared with Lionel Curtis, and indeed with most conservatives of the early twentieth century, an organic notion of Empire. *Sick Heart River*, Buchan's final novel, and a work which literary critics and general readers alike recognize as his most autobiographical work, encapsulates succinctly his notions of Empire and citizenship. Edward Leithen, the protagonist, notes of his work with a group of French Canadians and the Hare people in Canada's north that it was 'finer than the duty of kinship. It was a brotherhood of men.' Later, when Leithen is close to death, Buchan reflects on the rewards of service: 'Most men had their lives taken from them. It was his [Leithen's] privilege to *give* his, to offer it freely and joyfully in one last effort of manhood.'[128] In the final judgement, Buchan's imperialism, and his attendant notion of imperial citizenship, were largely spiritual. Ever the romantic conservative, connected to nature and place as much as to individuals or nations, he conceived of Empire as a belief. As the British Empire, teetering under the pressures of nationalism and the anti-colonialism of Washington, rallied its remaining strength against German and Japanese aggression in the late 1930s, Buchan reflected on the vitality of the early twentieth-century Empire in full bloom:

> Its dreams, once so bright, have been so pawed by unctuous hands that their glory has departed. But in those days things were different. It was an inspiration for youth to realize the magnitude of its material heritage, and to think how it might be turned to spiritual issues.[129]

These words serve to illustrate just how far Buchan's imperial thought had progressed from his early days in South Africa. His understanding of Empire evolved from one which, in the early years of the twentieth century, saw the differences among imperial subjects as of paramount importance to that which came, by the 1910s, to stress the possibility of a shared imperial identity. Buchan was unable, however, to systematically outline how his understanding of Empire might take form as an imperial citizenship. There were three reasons for this failure. First, Buchan's conception of imperial citizenship was compromised by the fact that the Empire was not a state *per se*. This made it difficult to define precisely what the individual's relationship to the imperial state should be. The first priority was perforce to create such a state, and Buchan's tentative thinking in regard to such a process was confined to the preliminary stage of engendering imperial unity. Second, the very breadth of Buchan's conception meant that it lacked cohesion. If the central progression in Buchan's imperial outlook was from a parochial to an ecumenical understanding of *race*, the constant was an inability to construct an imperial citizenship which reflected this evolution. Finally, Buchan's Victorian attention to *character*, the basis of his moral cosmopolitanism, meant that his ideas concerning imperial citizenship concentrated on how individuals acted, the performance of their duties, rather than on what rights such individuals might or should have. Buchan wrote widely on the value of bringing people together, and believed that the institution of Empire was the ideal means by which to realize this goal. He was less certain, however, about what form the Empire should assume once this ecumenical goal was attained.

Buchan's concept of imperial citizenship was a dialectic between the right of some to rule due to their character, and the right of the rest to rebel against that authority.[130] The tension between these two forces, one elitist, the other democratic, even radical, serves as an accurate description of the Empire's political trajectory in the mid-twentieth century. Buchan's vision of imperial citizenship was thus one of unfulfilled potential. If, as William James asserted, 'the one and the many' constitute the 'most central of all philosophical problems,'[131] John Buchan can be seen to have responded to the question of his age by working to bring together the one and the many under the banner of Empire. Empire, in his view, was a broad church which offered space for multiple loyalties. It was to be left to others to place those ideas within a practical framework.

Notes

1 Unidentified clipping, Scrapbook 1: Miscellanea 1904–1919, Buchan Papers, Queen's University Archives (hereafter QUA), Kingston, p. 87. The campaign was aborted with the outbreak of war in August 1914.

2 See the critical assessments of Buchan by Gertrude Himmelfarb in *Victorian Minds* (London, 1968) and Richard Usborne in *Clubland Heroes*, 2nd edn (London, 1974). Buchan's reputation has recently enjoyed a rather remarkable, and perhaps overly sympathetic, revitalization. See David Daniell's *The Interpreter's House* (London, 1975) on Buchan's fiction, and Andrew Lownie's *The Presbyterian Cavalier*, 2nd edn (London, 1997) on his life in general. On Buchan's imperial ideology, see Lownie, 'John Buchan, the Round Table and Empire,' pp. 55–63, and Bill Schwarz, 'The Romance of the Veld,' pp. 64–125, in Andrea Bosco and Alex May (eds) *The Round Table: The Empire/Commonwealth and British Foreign Policy* (London, 1997); and Peter Henshaw, 'John Buchan from the "Borders" to the "Berg": Nature, Empire and White South African Identity, 1901–1910,' *African Studies*, 62, 1 (2003), pp. 3–32.

Several more specific studies of Buchan focus on his historical significance: Patrick Cosgrove, 'John Buchan's Thrillers: The Ideology of Character,' *Round Table* (July 1972), pp. 375–86, considers the influence of the late Victorian cult of character in Buchan's novels; David Daniell, 'John Buchan and Blackwood's,' *Blackwood's Magazine*, 1918, 318 (August 1975), pp. 97–109, recounts Buchan's association with the eponymous journal; Keith Grieves, '*Nelson's History of the War*: John Buchan as a Contemporary Military Historian,' *Journal of Contemporary History*, 28 (1993), pp. 533–51, analyses Buchan's military writing; Christopher Harvie, 'Second Thoughts of a Scotsman on the Make: Politics, Nationalism and Myth in John Buchan,' *Scottish Historical Review*, 188, 1 (April 1991), pp. 31–54, is a comprehensive examination of Buchan as a 'cultural politician'; while Gina Mitchell, 'Hierarchy of Race', *Patterns of Prejudice* (November–December 1973), pp. 24–30, portrays Buchan in negative tones. See also Lownie's bibliography, in *Presbyterian Cavalier*, for a detailed listing of works about and by Buchan.

3 *Edinburgh Evening News*, undated clipping, Scrapbook 1, p. 69, Buchan Papers, QUA.
4 Following *The Half-Hearted* (London, 1901).
5 See Janet Adam Smith, *John Buchan* (London, 1965), p. 136, and Lownie, *Presbyterian Cavalier*, p. 90. True to form, David Daniell presents a more balanced assessment of *A Lodge*, noting: 'It is only now, when there is no Empire, that people who have not read this book accuse Buchan of a shocking imperialism': Daniell, 'John Buchan and Blackwood's.' The original passage can be found in *A Lodge in the Wilderness* (London, 1906), p. 58.
6 Juanita Kruse, *John Buchan (1875–1940) and the Idea of Empire* (Lewiston, NY, 1989). For the 'racist' claim, as well as a condemnation of Buchan as an anti-Semite, see Mordecai Richeler's polemics in the *National Post*, 3 December, 1999 – I owe this reference to Daryl Baswick. Jefferson Hunter casually labels Buchan a misogynist in *Edwardian Fiction* (Cambridge, MA, 1982), pp. 109–11. For a discussion of Buchan as a proto-white supremacist, see Bernard Magubane, *The Making of a Racist State* (Asmara, Eritrea, 1996), p. 240, a work which lends itself to refutation by *reductio ad absurdum*. Witness, for instance, Magubane's claim, in a discussion that attempts to attribute the genesis of apartheid to the creation of a South African Union, that the 'affinity of Kipling's, Milner's and Buchan's ideas with those of Hitler is striking': see ibid., p. 133.
7 'God's Providence,' *Atlantic Monthly*, 105 (February 1910), p. 185.
8 He pays tribute to these and other fallen friends in *These for Remembrance* (1919), his most personal book.
9 J. A. Mangan, *The Games Ethic and Imperialism* (Harmondsworth, 1986); J. Buchan, *Memory Hold the Door (MHTD)* (London, 1940), p. 30. The autobiography was published in the United States as *Pilgrim's Progress*. Buchan has been well served by two comprehensive biographies, Janet Adam Smith's *John Buchan* and Andrew Lownie's *Presbyterian Cavalier*.
10 Buchan, *MHTD*, p. 43.
11 Ibid., p. 34. Buchan dedicated his first book, *Sir Quixote of the Moors* (1895), to Murray. There is a substantial literature on the influence of classical civilization in Victorian society: see especially Frank Turner, *The Greek Heritage in Victorian*

Britain (New Haven, CT, 1981); and Norman Vance, *The Victorians and Ancient Rome* (Cambridge, MA, 1997).

12 A. J. Butler conveyed his sympathies with Buchan, noting in a letter in late 1899 that Oxford 'is an entangling place, and not favourable to the higher forms of mental or moral energy': A. J. Butler–Buchan, 5 November 1899, Correspondence General (CG), Buchan Papers, QUA (letters are filed in chronological order). Buchan garnered the Stanhope Prize for an essay on Raleigh, the Newdigate for his verse on the Pilgrim Fathers (see also Lownie, *Presbyterian Cavalier*, pp. 60–1) – the Stanhope was awarded annually for the best undergraduate history essay, the Newdigate annually for the best undergraduate poem. Fellowships at All Souls, of which there was usually only one per year, were granted to recent graduates to serve as junior tutors.
13 See Adam Smith, *John Buchan*, pp. 106–7.
14 Buchan later identified himself as a member of Milner's 'Creche': see Lownie, *Presbyterian Cavalier*, p. 72. The term 'religio-milnerania' was coined by Liberal leader Sir Henry Campbell-Bannerman. J. A. Spender, referring to Campbell-Bannerman, noted 'this blind belief in a Balliol hero he regarded as a psychological infirmity of the Oxford mind': see A. M. Gollin, *Proconsul in Politics* (London, 1964).
15 Buchan–Walter Buchan, 29 October 1901, CG, Buchan Papers, QUA.
16 Buchan–Lady Murray, 22 January 1902, emphasis in the original; Buchan–Gilbert Murray, 16 November 1902, CG, Buchan Papers, QUA; Buchan, *MHTD*, p. 98.
17 Henshaw, 'John Buchan from the "Borders" to the "Berg",' pp. 14, 7–11, 14–16.
18 Buchan–Anna Buchan (whom he called 'Nan'), 7 October 1901, CG, Buchan Papers, QUA.
19 Buchan–Lady Murray, 16 January 1902. CG, Buchan Papers, QUA.
20 Buchan–Gilbert Murray, 30 January 1902, CG, Buchan Papers, QUA.
21 Buchan–William Buchan, 20 March 1902, CG, Buchan Papers, QUA.
22 Buchan–Stair Gillon, 10 January 1903, quoted in Lownie, *Presbyterian Cavalier*, p. 78.
23 Buchan–Charles Dick, 16 May 1903, Charles Dick Papers, Box 13, Correspondence, Copy A–Z, Buchan Papers, QUA. Janet Adam Smith, beyond decoding much of Buchan's cryptic handwriting, compiled copies of his correspondence with select figures, which she then placed with the rest of his papers at Queen's University after finishing *John Buchan*.
24 Royal Bank of Scotland–Buchan, 14 March 1904, CG, Buchan Papers, QUA.
25 Janet Adam Smith contends that no position was available in the first place, and that the conversations may have been only of a hypothetical nature: see *John Buchan*, p. 148.
26 Evelyn Baring, First Earl of Cromer, 'The Government of Subject Races,' *Edinburgh Review* (January 1908), reprinted in E. Cromer, *Political and Literary Essays, 1908–1913* (Freeport, NY, 1969 [1913]), pp. 18–19.
27 On Buchan's creation of a public war-photo gallery, especially as a place where families could trace their sons, see *The Times*, 10 October 1918, p. 9b.
28 Reuters was operated as an arm of the British Government during the war, and much of Britain's telegraphic propaganda was conducted through the agency. Buchan returned to Reuters from 1919 to 1923: see Donald Read, *The Power of News: The History of Reuters* (Oxford, 1999), pp. 130–2, 136, 159.
29 Buchan–Gilbert Murray, 15 July 1915, CG, Buchan Papers, QUA. The *History* was well received, with individuals from Rosebery to Balfour expressing their approval: see for instance Rosebery–Buchan, 31 January 1915, CG, Buchan Papers, QUA. For more on Buchan as a military historian, see Keith Greaves, 'Nelson's *History of the War*,' *Journal of Contemporary History*, 28 (1993), pp. 533–51.
30 Buchan, *MHTD*, pp. 183–4.
31 It is instructive to note that Milner did not propose his line on 'maintenance' until after the conclusion of the South African War, which he had played a major role in precipitating.
32 Buchan, *Memoir*, pp. 124–5; emphasis added.

33 J. Buchan, *A Lodge in the Wilderness* (London, 1916), p. 1a. The message of the importance of Empire as a mystic whole, though, he believed was still essential, given the unrest generated by war.
34 Buchan advanced this 'argument' in a speech to the Political Economy Club entitled 'A Project of Empire,' delivered 6 April 1910: Speeches (a, i) (filed by date), Buchan Papers, QUA.
35 Buchan, *MHTD*, p. 143.
36 Buchan, untitled speech given to London teachers, 1 June 1918: Speeches (a, i), Buchan Papers, QUA.
37 Buchan, 'Literature and Life,' speech given in 1910 at an unidentified locale: Speeches (a, i), Buchan Papers, QUA.
38 On Burke's writing on Empire, see Uday Singh Mehta, *Liberalism and Empire: A Study in Nineteenth-Century Imperial Thought* (Chicago, IL, 1999), pp. 153–89.
39 Buchan, 'The Empire of South Africa,' speech given, in January 1904, in Edinburgh: Speeches (a, i), Buchan Papers, QUA.
40 Buchan, 'Imperial Fact and Sentiment,' *Scottish Review*, 28 May 1907; reprinted in *Comments and Characters* (Freeport, NY, 1970 [1940]), pp. 91–2.
41 Buchan, 'PSA,' speech given on 11 December 1911: Speeches (a, i), Buchan Papers, QUA.
42 See Robert Blake, *Disraeli* (New York, 1967), p. 637. The refrain of G. W. Hunt's *By Jingo* runs as follows: We don't want to fight;/ But by Jingo, if we do,/ We've got the men,/ We've got the ships,/ We've got the money too.' The song was performed during this period by G. H. Macdermott: see J. M. MacKenzie, 'Empire and Metropolitan Cultures,' in Andrew Porter (ed.) *The Oxford History of the British Empire*, vol. 3: *The Nineteenth Century* (Oxford, 1999), p. 278.
43 J. A. Hobson, *The Psychology of Jingoism* (London, 1900), p. 1.
44 C. M. Rodney, *Jameson's Ride to Johannesburg* (Pretoria, 1970 [1896]), p. 70. There is continued speculation that Joseph Chamberlain played a role, alongside Rhodes and the Revolutionary Committee in the Cape, in organizing the Raid, as a means of forcing the hand of Boer President Paul Kruger. This controversy centres around the so-called 'Missing Telegrams' – correspondence which disappeared (or never existed) when Chamberlain was called to account in early 1896: see Leonard Thompson, *A History of South Africa* (New Haven, CT, 1990); Sir Frederick Hamilton, 'Narrative of Events Relative to the Jameson Raid,' *English Historical Review* (1957), pp. 279–305; and Thomas Pakenham, *The Scramble for Africa* (New York, 1991), pp. 489–90, 498–503.
45 *Daily Mail*, 18 February 1896, p. 2.
46 *Reynold's Newspaper*, 5 January 1896, p. 1.
47 Hamilton, 'Narrative of Events Relative to the Jameson Raid,' p. 304.
48 Rodney, *Jameson's Ride to Johannesburg*, p. 23.
49 *Review of Reviews*, 13 (March 1896), p. 197.
50 *Pall Mall Gazette*, 4 January 1896, p. 1.
51 Even before the controversy over concentration camps and the razed-earth policy, 'methods of barbarism' in Liberal leader Henry Cambell-Bannerman's famous phrase, Kitchener was never a favourite of the British public. Despite Kitchener's avenging of Gordon in 1898, it was General Sir Garnet Wolsely (later Viscount Wolsely), who was a national hero, even though he had been unsuccessful in advancing up the Nile to Khartoum.
52 *Pall Mall Gazette*, 17 February 1896, p. 1.
53 Buchan, 'The Problem of Our African Possessions,' speech given in Glasgow, 1904: Speeches (a, i), Buchan Papers, QUA. Buchan could also see the light side of the jingo screed: Lady Flora Brume, when given the task of writing some jingo verse, instructs that to write 'comic imperial poetry ... [y]ou simply get all the names of places you can think of and string them together, and then put at the end something about the flag or the Crown or the Old Land': *A Lodge*, p. 63.
54 The relief of the Siege of Mafeking in April 1900 touched off wild celebrations in the streets of London. The term 'mafficking' briefly entered the English language after this event as a colloquial synonym for spontaneous public celebration.

55 Buchan, *A Lodge*, p. 13.
56 Despite his Cape–Cairo vision of British imperial expansionism, Rhodes also had a lifelong affinity for the United States. He directed that Americans be eligible for Rhodes Scholarships at Oxford, and worked closely with many expatriate Americans while in South Africa.
57 This view was consistent with two marks of Buchan's upbringing: the Scot's natural attraction to wanderlust, there being a disproportionate number of Scots in all facets of imperial activity; and his Calvinist distrust of excessive sentimentality – see 'Imperial Fact and Sentiment,' *Scottish Review*, 28 May (1907), p. 94.
58 'What the Home Rule Bill Means,' speech given in Innerleithen, 18 December 1912: Press Clippings (c), Scrapbook 1, Buchan Papers, QUA; Buchan, *MHTD*, p. 112.
59 Buchan, address to Galashiels branch of the Primrose League: undated clipping (probably 1911 or 1912), Scrapbook 1: Miscellanea 1904–1919, p. 78, Buchan Papers, QUA.
60 Smith, *John Buchan*, pp. 389–91.
61 Saul Dubow, 'Imagining the New South Africa in the Era of Reconstruction,' in David Omissi and Andrew Thompson (eds) *The Impact of the South African War* (New York, 2002), p. 88.
62 Buchan, 'Citizenship of Peebles,' January 1919, p. 3: Box 14, Speeches (a, ii), 3, Buchan Papers, QUA.
63 Buchan, *A Lodge*, pp. 34–8, 50–4, 182.
64 Ibid., p. 32.
65 *Spectator*, 15 December 1906, pp. 985–86. While at first it may seem unsurprising that Buchan might receive a favourable review from the journal for which he often wrote and in the editing of which he was involved, Buchan initially published *A Lodge* anonymously. The book did not appear under his name until its second printing, in 1907, so this review was of the anonymous edition. F. S. Oliver, Scottish draper and author of *Alexander Hamilton*, a biography of the American founding father, which was very influential among the men of Milner's Kindergarten, had urged Buchan to write under his own name for the initial edition. Oliver passed on Buchan's ideas to his friends in the Kindergarten, and even hinted at the early coalescing of the movement that would in 1910 become the Round Table: see Oliver–Buchan, 23 December 1906, CG, Buchan Papers, QUA.
66 Samuel de Champlain founded a fortified trading post in 1608 at the narrows of the St Lawrence, or the French 'Quebec' for the Algonquin word for 'straight.' Though there were earlier settlements in what is now Canada, including Champlain's at Port-Royal, the Quebec settlement proved permanent, and thus the date 1608 has been commonly used both in Buchan's era and in modern Canadian historiography to signify the settlement of Canada. See for instance Margaret R. Conrad and James Hiller, *Atlantic Canada: A Region in the Making* (Oxford, 2001), pp. 48–60.
67 Buchan, 'The Quebec Tercentenary,' *Scottish Review*, 30 June 1908, reprinted in *Comments and Characters*, p. 100; Rosebery–Buchan, 1908 (undated), Rosebery Papers, as filed in Box 13, Correspondence (d), Copy A–Z, Buchan Papers, QUA.
68 Buchan–Rosebery, 21 June 1917, Box 13, Correspondence (d), Copy A–Z, Buchan Papers, QUA. As director of information, Buchan also attempted to organize speaking tours of the United States, approaching speakers such as Gilbert Murray. Buchan's affinity for the United States came to the fore again in meetings with Franklin Delano Roosevelt in 1936–37. Buchan's reputation as an internationalist was furthered through his service as Reuters' foreign office director from 1916 to 1917, a post he had to resign from when he became director of information. See Read, *The Power of News*.
69 J. H. Hammond, *The Truth about the Jameson Raid* (Boston, MA, 1918), p. 47.
70 Buchan, 'Literature and Life,' speech (context unknown), 1910: Speeches (a, i), Buchan Papers, QUA.

71 See John Gibbins, 'Liberalism, Nationalism, and the English Idealists,' *History of European Ideas*, 15 (1992), esp. p. 492. Though Gibbins does not refer directly to imperialism, the idea of 'the good motive' is clearly applicable here.
72 Stefan Collini, *Public Moralists: Political Thought and Intellectual Life in Britain, 1850–1930* (Oxford, 1991), chapter 2, esp. p. 65. Collini argues that recognized intellectual movements ('Ethical Socialism,' 'New Liberalism,' etc.) tend to represent the final stage in the evolution of moral and cultural values into cultural consensus; in other words, the *process of becoming* is more important than the tenets of a movement, for the formation of a *movement* often signals the imminent decline of its values and mores.
73 Collini, *Public Moralists*, p. 108.
74 Gertrude Himmelfarb, 'John Buchan: The Last Victorian,' in *Victorian Minds*, pp. 249–71; *A Lodge*, p. 229; Buchan, 'Thought and Faith,' speech to Selkirk Public Service Association (PSA), December 1915: Speeches (a, i), Buchan Papers, QUA. Buchan attempted to combat the appeal of socialism during his pre-war campaign by offering voters 'the bribe of service, hope, and a wider horizon of fuller and richer citizenship': see *Scotsman*, 19 April 1911. The left-leaning *Edinburgh Evening News* (20 April 1911) was unimpressed by this position, scoffing that it was 'a grand, satisfying mouthful – of east wind.'
75 See *The Times*, 5 January 1903. Despite expressing reservations concerning the qualifications of some of the officials chosen to oversee resettlement, the paper lauded Buchan for displaying 'an aptitude for rapid decision and for taking responsibility.'
76 Buchan, unidentified clipping (probably early 1915): Scrapbook 1: Miscellanea 1904–1919, Buchan Papers, QUA. 'For he this day who sheds his blood with me/ Shall be my brother; be he ne'er so vile/ This day shall gentle his condition': *Henry V*, IV, iii, 61–3; Buchan, 'Citizenship of Peebles', p. 3.
77 Buchan–Gilbert Murray, 17 December 1918, CG, Buchan Papers, QUA.
78 'The Empire of South Africa,' p. 29.
79 Buchan, *A Lodge*, p. 69; the quotation comes from Summerville.
80 Buchan, 'Literature and Life,' p. 17.
81 Buchan, 'Democracy and Representative Government,' *The Fortnightly Review*, 94, (1913), p. 867.
82 Buchan–Stair Gillon, 12 February 1916, CG, Buchan Papers, QUA. Buchan was at this point responsible for Russian deputations visiting London.
83 Asquith–Buchan, 14 May 1916, CG, Buchan Papers, QUA. Buchan was on good terms with many of the so-called members of the 'Monday Night Cabal,' including Milner and Amery, which eventually ousted Asquith. The 'maneuvering' Asquith refers to in this letter concerns the debate over Home Rule in May of 1916, specifically the immediate political fallout from the Easter Rebellion and the execution of Casement and other Irish leaders. Ironically, Buchan quickly became frustrated with Lloyd George, the beneficiary of his comrades' maneuvering, and Asquith's replacement as Prime Minister. Lloyd George gave Buchan little freedom at the Ministry of Information and after the war refused to give him the knighthood he desired. Asquith was also the father of Buchan's close friend Raymond Asquith, though father and son were not particularly close. Both Buchan and the senior Asquith were devastated by Raymond's death at the Somme on 19 September 1916. See for instance Roy Jenkins, *Asquith* (New York, 1966), pp. 413–15.
84 Buchan, 'Some Problems of Modern Democracy,' undated speech, most likely delivered early in the war, when Buchan gave public lectures and served as a war correspondent for *The Times* and the *Daily News*; F. Britten Austin–Buchan, 30 May 1916, CG, Buchan Papers, QUA.
85 Buchan–Charles Dick, 6 January 1900, Box 13, Correspondence d) Copy A–Z, Buchan Papers, QUA.
86 See Buchan, 'Women's Suffrage: A Logical Outcome of the Conservative Faith,' leaflet for Conservative and Unionist Women's Franchise Association', undated (probably 1911).

87 Ibid.
88 Ibid.
89 Buchan, 'The Empire of South Africa,' p. 27.
90 (Buchan) 'Imperial Organization,' *Spectator*, 22 October 1904, pp. 586–87. He praised the Imperial Conference for furthering this spirit of imperial cooperation in 'The New Doctrine of Empire,' *Scottish Review*, 2 May 1907.
91 Buchan–Markham, 27 January and 29 January 1906, CG, Buchan Papers, QUA.
92 Buchan, 'The Problem of Our African Possessions,' pp. 11–14.
93 Buchan–Helen Buchan, 28 October 1901; Buchan–Anna Buchan, 9 December 1901, CG, Buchan Papers, QUA.
94 Milner, quoted in Semmel, *Imperialism and Social Reform* (London, 1960), p. 177. Emphasis in original.
95 Buchan–Violet Markham, 23 March 1906; 19 January 1906, CG, Buchan Papers, QUA.
96 Buchan–Violet Markham, 23 March 1906, CG, Buchan Papers, QUA. The Chinese labour controversy erupted during the 1906 election. Milner had encouraged the employment of indentured Chinese labourers in the Rand mines, a measure denounced by the radicals in the Liberal Party. Allegations that Milner had authorized the 'flogging' of some of these labourers led to a motion of censure in the House on 21 March 1906, where Milner was denounced by innuendo.
97 Buchan violently protested the censure motion *and* Churchill's speech in support of it in anonymous leaders in the *Spectator*, 24 March 1906, and the *Quarterly Review* (April 1906). Buchan remained ambivalent about Churchill throughout his career. He had expressed reservations to his friend C. H. Dick concerning Churchill's accession to the Colonial Office in 1905, and was livid over his role in the censure affair. He nonetheless admired the future Prime Minister's adventurous streak, which appealed to Buchan's romantic side, and told his youngest brother Alistair, who served with Churchill, that he was a man of stature despite his rash and unpredictable nature: see Buchan–C. H. Dick, 22 December 1905, Box 13, Copies A–Z, Buchan Papers, QUA; Buchan–Alistair Buchan, 10 June 1916, CG, Buchan Papers, QUA.
98 See Balfour–Buchan, 16 May 1912; Austen Chamberlain–Buchan, 16 May 1914, CG, Buchan Papers, QUA.
99 Buchan, *A Lodge*, pp. 74–5.
100 See accounts of the campaign in the *Peebleshire Advertiser* and *Glasgow Herald*.
101 Halford Mackinder, *Democratic Ideals and Realities* (London, 1919); see also Semmel, *Imperialism and Social Reform*, pp. 166–7.
102 Buchan, *The African Colony* (London, 1904). Edward Said has much to say about the myth of the 'lazy native' in British literature, and is highly critical of Buchan, though he draws only on *Prester John*, betraying little knowledge of the rest of Buchan's literary oeuvre: see Said, *Culture and Imperialism* (New York, 1994), pp. 162–8. For a recent survey of Buchan's reputation and the debate over his views on race, see Roger Kimball, *New Criterion*, 22, 1 (September 2003), pp. 16–23.
103 Schwarz, 'The Romance of the Veld,' p. 113.
104 Buchan, *The House of the Four Winds* (London, 1965 [1925]), p. 26.
105 On the Chinese Labour question and Edwardian politics, particularly the election of 1906, see Alan Russell, *Liberal Landslide: The General Election of 1906* (London, 1973); and Alfred Gollin, 'Balfour 1902–1911,' in Donald Southgate (ed.) *The Conservative Leadership, 1832–1932* (London, 1974), pp. 151–72.
106 Ronald Hyam and Peter Henshaw, *The Lion and the Springbok: Britain and South Africa since the Boer War* (Cambridge, 2003), p. 68.
107 *The Times*, 17 February 1904, p. 4e.
108 Buchan, 'The Colour Problem in the Colonies,' *Scottish Review*, 9 January 1908, reprinted in *Comments and Characters*, p. 122.
109 *Peebleshire Advertiser*, 1 April 1911. The occasion was a speech to the Peebleshire Unionist Organization. Besides Home Rule, the topic Buchan was directly

addressing, questions of imperial organization were at the fore in 1911 in light of debates over an imperial navy and Australia's racial policies.

110 Buchan, 'Democracy and Representative Government,' *Fortnightly Review*, 94 (1913), pp. 858–69.
111 See Derek Sayer, 'British Reaction to the Amritsar Massacre 1919-1920,' *Past and Present*, 131 (1991), pp. 130–64.
112 Buchan, 'The Problem of Our African Possessions,' pp. 14–16.
113 Gilbert Murray–Buchan, 25 April 1903, CG, Buchan Papers, QUA. Murray, though a liberal in politics, believed Buchan's Tory Party was better equipped to address these issues, as it held more firmly to principles of Empire, whereas the Liberals were more 'aimless.'
114 Buchan, 'The Problem of Our African Possessions,' pp. 24–5.
115 Buchan, 'Unrest in India,' *Scottish Review*, 16 May 1907; 'The Problem of India,' ibid., 9 July 1908; 'Lord Cromer and Egypt,' ibid., 11 April 1907.
116 Witness, for instance, his 1917 correspondence with Walter Hines Page, then American Ambassador to Britain, where Buchan refers to the Japanese Ambassador to Britain as 'the Jap': Buchan–Walter Hines Page, 17 January 1917: Page Letters, copy, Copies A–Z, Buchan Papers, QUA.
117 G. M. Trevelyan–Buchan, 21 September 1913, CG, Buchan Papers, QUA; emphasis in original.
118 Buchan, *A Lodge*, pp. 77, 62.
119 Buchan, *MHTD*, p. 93.
120 (Buchan), 'Mr Kruger's Funeral,' *Spectator*, 24 December 1904, p. 1045. Kruger's funeral was a lavish affair, with up to 12,000 onlookers, though it was notably muted as much of the crowd were Boers. Robert Brand, an Oxford colleague of Buchan's who also served under Milner in South Africa, observed that 'the Boers were an 'apathetic crowd,' who showed 'no signs of grief. It was a show, a variety from the monotony of the veld': Brand–Buchan, 18 December 1904, CG, Buchan Papers, QUA.
121 See the review of Buchan's *The African Colony* in *Blackwood's*, 176 (July 1904), pp. 75–84; *MHTD*, p. 115.
122 Buchan, *MHTD*, 145–6.
123 Balfour–Buchan, 13 October 1915, CG, Buchan Papers, QUA; W. H. Hamilton–Buchan, 9 May 1919, CG, Buchan Papers, QUA; John Buchan, *Mr Standfast* (Oxford, 1993 [1919]). The latter work draws heavily on Bunyan's *Pilgrim's Progress*, and is the most overtly moralistic of Buchan's 'shockers', as his adventure novels were termed by contemporaries.
124 Buchan, *MHTD*, p. 167.
125 Undated clipping, Scrapbook 1: Miscellanea 1904–1919, p. 172, Buchan Papers, QUA.
126 Lownie, 'John Buchan, The Round Table and Empire,' in Boscoe and May (eds) *The Round Table*, p. 58.
127 On conservatives' efforts to adapt to the new intellectual challenges of the twentieth century, and especially efforts to incorporate collectivist thought, see E. H. H. Green, *The Crisis of Conservatism* (London and New York, 1995), chapter 5.
128 John Buchan, *Sick Heart River* (Loanhead, Midlothian, 1981 [1940]), pp. 181, 213; *Sick Heart River* was published as *Mountain Meadow* in the United States.
129 Buchan, *MHTD*, p. 124.
130 Kimball, *New Criterion*, 22, 1 (September 2003), pp. 19–20.
131 William James, *Pragmatism* (New York, 1970 [1907]), p. 61.

CHAPTER FOUR

The imperial garden: Arnold White and the parochial view of imperial citizenship

If Lionel Curtis and John Buchan were representative of a breed of imperialist open to, though not necessarily always persuaded by, a broader interpretation of Empire and its underlying tenets, the polemical journalist Arnold White, by contrast, provides a stark example of a imperialist who believed that Empire was just fine as it was, except for those instances when it could benefit from becoming more like it had been. He epitomized imperialism at its most parochial. As 'Vanoc,'[1] the *Daily Express*'s shrill critic-at-large, White voiced the concerns of the emerging clerk culture of Northcliffe's *Daily Mail*, the suburbs, and Selfridge's department store. Whether admonishing the Admiralty over its neglect of Britain's Navy, protesting the unfit nature of British soldiers after the South African War or ferreting out imagined German influence in the British press, he was an untiring advocate of all things 'English.'

White saw the Empire, which included the Celtic fringe of the British Isles, as not just a figurative but also a literal extension of *England*. As such, his desire to improve the nation's health and efficiency – terms which frequently occur in White's editorials – and to promote patriotism and loyalty applied equally to both England and the Empire. His notion of imperial citizenship was thus the same as his notion of domestic citizenship. He gave little thought to the richly varied nature of the imperium, which is to say that he advanced a parochial notion of imperialism. White's ideas on Empire were founded on an emotional attachment to an imagined past of ethnocentric ascendancy. He advanced these positions in often exaggerated and voluble proposals on how to recapture imperial glory. While his tone was often strident, White published in both liberal and conservative organs. He was an ecumenical contrarian.

By contrasting the organic and tentatively cosmopolitan views of Empire fostered by Curtis and Buchan with the imperial parochialism of White, it is possible to develop the two main lines of contemporary conservative argument relating to imperial citizenship. These competing conceptual frameworks were not mutually exclusive, but rather were varying points on a spectrum which unquestionably placed Britain or, at the least, England at the constructive centre of the Empire. Expressed as general questions, the two core arguments can be outlined as follows: was the Empire a polity of individuals with England at its centre, the guiding but not necessarily determinate force or was it rather a 'Greater England', in the most literal conception of Seeley's famous phrase, a great estate upon which the English people were to leave their mark as was their self-assumed right? White, as will be made evident through an examination of his responses to some of the central issues of his era – notably immigration and the First World War – presented the case for the second view.

The Views of Vanoc

The Royal Society of St George (RSSG) issued a pamphlet in 1924, the year of Arnold White's death, which accurately summarized the views both of that institution and of the deceased. 'Patriotism,' the pamphlet began, 'is more than a sentiment: it is a conviction based upon a comprehension of the duties of a citizen, and a determination loyally to perform such duties. Patriotism is love of country, born of familiarity with its history, reverence for its institutions, and faith in its possibilities, and is evidenced by obedience to its laws and respect for its flag.'[2] The RSSG, whose head was the Prince of Wales, was formed in 1894 to encourage and engender patriotism in those of English birth, celebrate days of national significance, such as St George's Day and Shakespeare's birthday, and to promote the physical culture of England. The RSSG had branches throughout the colonies, with particularly strong groups in western Canada. The Society was primarily interested in promoting an ideal of citizenship based firmly on English culture.[3] Though his congenital distrust of organizations in which he did not have a leading hand kept him from being a member, White's close association with the group is hardly surprising.[4] It was to men such as White that the Society spoke most clearly. White took the idea of citizenship as based on the principle of *jus sanguinis* quite seriously: not for him the transfer of the franchise to Indians or Africans. White's journalism reveals a man who was not entirely comfortable with the idea of Canadians or Australians holding political rights, let alone people who had no cultural reason to know the significance of 23 April.

To understand Arnold White and what he has to tell us about conceptions of imperial citizenship, it is necessary to understand that he was both an eccentric and a self-styled man of the people. He was a self-made man, a son of the manse who had early on rejected religion and turned his ambition to the secular world. It comes as little surprise that Kipling's *If* was a later favourite poem.[5] The unifying theme in White's pronouncements was an insular *Englishness* and the desire to maintain England's international political position, especially by means of Empire.[6] Hence his concern over naval matters and limits on immigration into England, two factors contributing to the security of the nation. His writing was often harsh and hyperbolic, yet he spoke to a number of concerns which resonated quite strongly in late Victorian and Edwardian Britain. *The Athæneum* typified the response often accorded White in its review of his *Efficiency and Empire* (1901), applauding the spirit of this patriotic essay, but lamenting that White carried his criticisms too far, that he was 'perhaps a little too much of a Juvenal for the situation.'[7] Lord Rosebery expressed a similar opinion after reading a copy of the same book sent him by White: 'the book lacks a sense of proportion and carries some of its views to an extreme which will repel many who would agree, as I do, with the spirit of it.'[8] *The Times* perhaps put it best in White's obituary, noting that he had tried to speak for the ordinary Englishman, 'who delighted to see his own rather hazy ideas and prejudices presented in clear form and with compelling plausibility.'[9] Like W. T. Stead, a friend and fellow-maverick of the press, White carved out a career as a polemical journalist with an interest in social affairs and the Empire. His first success was *The Problems of a Great City* (1886), in which he argued that alien immigration, especially of Jews from Eastern Europe, had contributed to social problems in London. It was his most original work, as he was to draw upon the same theme of external threats leading to social dislocation and unrest in much of his subsequent writing.

It was as a Cassandra that White was best known to his contemporaries, the voice of efficiency and eugenics, inveterate critic of all governments, and fervent English patriot. He pursued such criticism through his journalism, and he was particularly vociferous when he believed either the free flow of information or the privacy of the individual was jeopardized. White wrote mainly for the general public, hence his pseudonyms 'Vanoc' and 'Vox Populi.' This was partly because his workman-like prose was best suited to the concerns of the masses and the newspapers that catered to them – he wrote first for the *Daily Express* and later the *Referee* – and partly because, other than his life-long role as political agent of the Duke of Bedford and his close relationships with Lord Charles Beresford and later Lord John Fisher, White had few connections among the nation's political elite. In fact, White was often contemptuous of authority, assuming a quixotic role as defender of the people in the face of alleged elite corruption and incompetence. However, his repeated attempts to enter Parliament,[10] his delight in lobbying on behalf of the Navy League, and his pleasure at having HMS *Vanoc* named after him for his role in improving sailor's shipboard living conditions, all suggest that his antiestablishment position was a reflection of his frustration at being unable to penetrate that same world. His position on imperial citizenship reflected those of conservatives who longed for the perceived certainties of Britain's imperial past, and resented pressures to reform or reshape imperial policies and philosophies.

Two influences marked White's early career. The first was the new journalism of the 1880s and 1890s, especially the work of his friend W. T. Stead at the *Pall Mall Gazette*. From Stead, White developed both his journalistic style and an approach to social affairs which saw them as indicators of the nation's political vitality.[11] The second major influence on White, as it was for many of his generation, was A. T. Mahan's *The Influence of Sea Power upon History, 1660–1773* (1890). Mahan's work legitimised White's belief that the navy was key to international influence, the dominant theory of international relations in the pre-war era. Support for a strengthened navy was to be one of the distinguishing marks of White's career.

What ideas did White seek to propagate? Primarily, White concerned himself with naval matters, being perhaps the most prominent 'bluewater'[12] man of the press in the two decades preceding the First World War. He also lobbied against immigration, arguing that it contributed to problems – overcrowding and lack of hygiene – in urban England. Not surprisingly, then, he was a leading voice in the national efficiency debate which followed the Anglo-Boer War. His interest in the latter led White to eugenics, and he spent time in the immediate post-war years on the council of the Eugenics Education Society. The constant which linked these various interests was the Empire. Imperialism, in White's mind, not only connoted the spread of British grandeur or the accumulation of wealth in far-away lands, but also, and more significantly, it was the embodiment and manifestation of the national culture. Empire was a monument to the grandeur and superiority of English culture, and he saw it as his duty, as an English citizen, to ensure that this culture should continue to flourish and prosper. However, the late Victorian and Edwardian eras were years of change. The emergence of Germany and the United States as world powers, the rise of Japan, and a concomitant erosion of British economic supremacy combined with the intellectual angst brought about by Darwin, the second industrial revolution, and the new democracy to create an environment of uncertainty and flux. Given these tensions, many men of White's generation turned to the Empire for reassurance. Renewed imperial vitality was to be the means to arrest and reverse Britain's relative decline.

White understood citizenship as an insular phenomenon, something one was born into, and he believed that both citizen and government should subordinate their individual interests and activities to the *national* interest. Empire was part of that interest, and therefore *imperial citizenship* was an extension of national citizenship. The English settlement colonies played a secondary, servile, role, with the dependencies a mere appendage. Because White viewed the Empire as a resource to be used by England for its own ends, he was ignorant of the existence of local identities at the periphery, and thus did not see a need to formulate a broader 'imperial' citizenship to encompass of such phenomena. Unlike Curtis and Buchan, White did not recognize the need for a broader imperial framework at either the governmental or the individual level. The absence of an imperial *state* was not seen by White, as it was by the other imperialists dealt with in this project, as an obstacle to be overcome; rather it was regarded as simply the natural state of affairs.

Efficiency and degeneracy

The one aspect of White's thought on English citizenship that did incorporate the Empire was his concern over national efficiency, specifically a fear of moral and physical degeneracy. If England's imperial hegemony was wavering, might this be due to deficiencies in the national character? Such fears were widespread in Britain in the aftermath of the pyrrhic victory in the Boer War, and marked a sense of urgency and crisis. The national efficiency movement, as the varied ideas which resulted from such fears came to be known, has been noted by historians as a key shift in Edwardian thought.[13] Most commentators, however, have chosen to focus on social policy or, more especially, on eugenics. In regard to the Empire, inquiries into the development and underlying rationalizations of citizenship have been unduly coloured by a preoccupation with the influence of pseudo-science. The little that has been written on White has not avoided this myopia. As astute an historian as Richard Soloway identifies White simply as 'an early eugenicist.'[14] This is understandable, as White used such language, corresponded with many of those active in the eugenics movement, and, above all, provides the historian with a dizzying array of pithy, quotable comments on the subject. While White certainly voiced many of the eugenicist ideas of the period, and indeed was even a member of the Eugenics Society, his attraction to the cause derived mostly from his taste for the unorthodox, and less from any scientific conviction. As G. R. Searle has observed,[15] what White found most attractive about eugenics was that it provided the *vocabulary* to better express his concern for a higher efficiency, which he expressed particularly in his naval advocacy.

The term 'national efficiency' incorporated diverse streams of thought which had as their goal improvement of the nation's human capital, and the improved operation of its institutional structure. The term was used in such a variety of ways as to be almost empty of meaning. For present purposes Bernard Semmel's understanding of the term suits well: he argues that national efficiency was an imperialist and nationalist creed with the goals of furthering the national interest, condemning laissez faire economics, and favouring social amelioration. The means to achieve these goals was efficiency, through heightened industrial production, a united Empire, a vigorous population, and a state of military and naval preparedness.[16] These aims could be achieved through administrative, military, and educational reform – witness the campaign for militia reform of White's patron, the Duke of Bedford, or the centralization of the school boards under the Education Act of 1902 – or by the improvement of the population, either through better physical conditioning or, more darkly, through the regulation of reproduction. White played a role in all of these debates, his position defying any easy categorization: he favoured military preparedness and a vigorous population, for instance, whereas he rejected the idea of social amelioration, convinced that this was simply socialism in sheep's clothing. He absorbed ideas from many different people who would never have come together at the same table – he was influenced by voices as diverse as Kipling and the Eugenics Education Society.[17] Thus, his synthetic arguments offer a panorama of the national efficiency movement and its role in the formulation of imperial citizenship.

Consistent with his notion of citizenship as a relationship of reciprocal duties and rewards between individual and state, White understood efficiency as a literal measure of the nation's success or failure: it was the nation's balance sheet. Morality was the currency in which such efficiency was measured, and it formed the basis of White's convictions. Proper citizenship was proper morality put to the service of the nation. White mourned the death of Queen Victoria by pointing to the powerful legacy she had left and the example of efficiency which her reign had been. In *Efficiency and Empire*, he wrote: 'Efficiency is the basis, and possibly the reason, of all moral law; the Queen's great reign was efficient because obedient to the moral law.'[18] National efficiency had been weakened by a number of factors, most significantly the lack of hope engendered in younger Britons by their poor, ill, and uneducated parents, the result of the breakdown of coherent family groups. The reason for this development, White believed, was the poor state of the English family. The family was the basic unit of any Great Nation, its health reflective of the health of the nation. It was important, then, for the family to display the physical ideals of efficiency, strength and beauty, because these were manifestations of the deeper virtues of temperance, discipline, and good temper, the marks of proper morality which White maintained had propelled England to a position of strength in the first place. He applied a similar logic to the governance of Empire, holding to a vision of the union of the settlement colonies, with India a subordinate. 'What is Empire?,' he asked, but a 'number of English speaking families.' The Empire was founded on home life, freedom, and justice, he asserted, with the sea a 'wide open common.'[19]

If family was the basis of Empire, it followed, according to White's logic, that parents who were not fulfilling their duty to the nation should be segregated, either within Britain or by being sent to the colonies – hence his support for assisted emigration – so as not to further harm the nation's efficiency. Physical deficiency, according to White, was caused by moral failings. White would not have viewed events such as Black Week[20] in the autumn of 1899 as the cause of fears about national efficiency, but rather as indicators of the true problem – a breakdown in citizenship. Citizenship was based in a strong morality; proper morality could be attained through physical efficiency and a strong family environment; therefore such efficiency had to be improved to strengthen the bonds of citizenship. While the premisses of this argument were debatable, it was nonetheless found persuasive by many at the time.

The citizenship bond was significant to White because he believed that it united individuals and staved off anarchy. White saw man as atomistic and independent, requiring some organic means of maintaining order and stability. In taking this view, he intuited the spirit of the arguments regarding imperial citizenship proffered by Curtis and Buchan. He also, however, drew upon the atomistic theories advanced by proponents of a Spencerian view of society, where 'to be a good animal is the first requisite to success in life, and to be a nation of good animals is the first condition to national prosperity.'[21] Bernard Hollander, a British physician and phrenologist, argued in a lecture White attended that the collective, the nation, holds priority over the individual, and therefore that weak individuals should be placed under the care of the State. The mentally unfit, for instance, were suitable for only the most primitive form of citizenship; that is, one where their personal security would be safeguarded by the State, but where they themselves would not be permitted to perform any role in choosing how the State itself should be constituted.[22] Hollander concluded by suggesting that Britain institute a national health exam when an individual reached the age of 20 to better ascertain national efficiency. This final point is instructive, for Britain, unlike France or Germany, had no mandatory military service, and so had no institutional means to monitor the physical health of the nation. This suggests both a historical reticence to exert strong governmental control and a less formal, more voluntary, form of citizenship. The lack of information on physical efficiency, and the more fluid relationship between individual and state, also perhaps suggest why in times of national self-doubt, such as in the aftermath of the Boer War, public debate over matters of citizenship or national efficiency could be so charged with rhetoric and so empty of action.

White's concern that England's national efficiency was in decline was rooted in a firmly Malthusian conception of population dynamics.[23] Believing that there was an *optimal* population level, above which, due to lack of resources and, more significantly for the British Isles, a lack of physical space, any increases would be counterproductive and in fact detrimental, White argued for a variety of measures to regulate population with a view to maximizing the nation's physical capital. When White's neo-Lamarckian beliefs are added to this position, his attraction to the language of eugenics seems obvious. Indeed, an argument that appears continually in his writing is that traits such as indolence, infirmity, and especially criminality were hereditary. This was a dangerous situation for the nation to find itself in, White wrote, for the lower classes, who most often displayed these traits, tended to produce the most children.[24]

White is purported to have coined the phrase 'sterilization of the unfit.' White's place in history is linked to this phrase, which is somewhat unfortunate as historians have usually misinterpreted what he meant. As spelt out in a public lecture in 1904, his understanding of 'sterilization' did not bear the standard meaning intended by others of his time, but had the sense rather of *segregation*. He believed this measure could serve as a corrective to social degeneracy. This is a difference in degree and not in kind, but nonetheless marks White as separate from Francis Galton and his lineage.

It is in this context that White's concern with race must be placed. White used 'race' as a synonym for the national culture which he believed had created the Empire, namely English culture. His was therefore an inward-looking notion. He did not dwell, as did others of his generation, on racial differences *per se*. Not for White the pseudo-science of phrenology or the like. Even his eugenics, upon closer inspection, was derived not so much from biology as from culture. He was interested in the *fitness* of his fellow-Englishman, and in eugenics he found the language to express this concern. White's arguments about eugenics were framed by a sense of common belonging and derived more from a shallow spirituality than from science: 'Vanoc' believed that the 'irresistible inference forced upon us is that beyond and above there is a Source of energy and guidance' which 'some call ... evolution, and others call ... God.'[25] Central to fostering this sense of common belonging, White argued, was encouraging among the public the Greek ideal of maintaining sound mind and body. His jeremiad in *Efficiency and Empire* concerning the unfit physical state of Britain's Boer War recruits is well known.[26] Elsewhere, he observed that the height requirements for Britain's army recruits had declined from 5 feet and 6 inches 1845 to 5 feet in 1900.[27] White was equally concerned, though, with England's upper class, particularly the country's leaders.

White also believed that strong national leadership was necessary to strengthen 'national efficiency,' a conviction epitomized by his years working as an anonymous publicist for Fisher and Bedford. White complained that decadence and materialism had drained the upper class of its leadership potential, leaving only ambitious men of the middle class to take up the task. Writing in *Black and White* in 1909, he declared that the only contemporary politicians of merit were the Tory Unionist Arthur Balfour and the Liberal Sir Edward Grey, neither of whom were typical members of the gentility.[28]

White had been critical of the Government's organization and efficiency long before such calls became popular in the immediate years before war. He had outlined these concerns in 1900 in the *Daily Chronicle*, then a Liberal imperialist paper, in a series of articles entitled 'Where We Fail.' The seven-part series proved immensely popular, and was reprinted as a pamphlet entitled *Society, Smart Society, and Bad Smart Society, Their Influence on Empire: Being Seven Letters Written to the Editor of the Daily Chronicle*. His argument was that England's governing elite, which otherwise provided sound leadership, had been corrupted by the influence of 'smart society,' and that national efficiency could be improved only if this influence was excised. By 'smart society' White referred to individuals, usually aristocrats but also scions of the new money, who owed their positions to their social standing or financial influence.[29] He was not, as has been stated, against privilege as such, but instead attacked the 'kakocrats' who often emerged from 'smart society.' These individuals were superfluous to a well-administered state, and in fact were often harmful as they acted in their own interest, not in service to the nation. Jews, marked with the additional stigma of being foreigners, occupied a prime place among White's kakocrat class. In expressing concern over the influence of financial speculators, White paralleled the thought of J. A. Hobson. Indeed, Hobson himself tacitly admitted as much in an anonymous review of White's *Efficiency and Empire* for the *Spectator*.[30]

White laid out five key areas for reform in the fourth installment of his *Daily Chronicle* series, advising that placement should be based on merit, officials should be properly trained, fair remuneration should be provided, duties should be thoroughly defined, and supervision should be carried out actively and regularly.[31] These proposals, all of which were eventually implemented, reflected his concern that bureaucrats were not accountable to anyone, and therefore free to pursue their own agendas independently of the Minister, or to avoid censure if they proved incompetent. White also criticized the national honours system, believing it rewarded position, not talent, and expressed admiration for men such as the former Liberal Prime Minister William Gladstone and the early-nineteenth century prison reformer John Howard who turned down titles. Indeed, the main recommendations of *Efficiency and Empire* were to restore responsibility in government and to open careers to talent.[32] He thought that efficiency in government should match the efficiency and sense of duty he observed in the military. He spoke on this topic at the International Eugenics Congress in 1912, observing that military training was the best way to build character. Other speakers at the conference presented more ill-founded arguments, though, tarring White's message by association.[33]

White's ideas on Empire and citizenship were not all pessimistic. He had no objection, in theory, to an expanded citizenship which encompassed most if not all members of the Empire, whether white or black, English or 'colonial'. Like many of his contemporaries, though, he did not consider such a proposition possible at that point in time. An open-ended view of the future also framed his sense of democracy. Take, for example, his position of female suffrage. Though White himself never betrayed a distinct understanding of women – his wife makes nary an appearance in his correspondence and he was estranged from his sisters – he approved of women's suffrage, in principle, and attended many suffrage demonstrations as an observer. He feared, however, that such an initiative could upset the political status quo, not because women were politically naive, but because such a precedent would give credibility to similar claims from other imperial groups, specifically India. Despite such broad-minded musings, however, White remained a convinced English patriot. His concern for national efficiency led him to conceive of Empire and citizenship as subordinate to the *national* interest. His interest in eugenics led him to understand citizenship in essentialist terms.

English nationalism and Empire

One of the 'Views of Vanoc' was that gardening, after Empire-building the great English pastime, could provide a model for proper imperial statecraft. He lamented the current situation, where Empire's 'head gardeners are addicted to the habit of allowing the winter season of international rest to slip away without making provision for the dog-days of war, when the earth is iron and the skies are brass, and it is too late to till the soil,' concluding that efficiency demanded the gardener's primary skill, foresight.[34] The health of the Empire reflected directly upon the health of England itself, White's primary concern.

Arnold White was a patriot. He saw the Empire as a living monument to England's past achievements and imperial citizenship as the fealty an individual owed to that tradition. Given his view, it is not surprising that White saw the Empire as an English possession, rather than an organic entity. Much like Joseph Chamberlain's metaphor of the undeveloped estate, White's Empire was an emanation of the English character. If he needed recourse to any justification for English supremacy, he found it in providence. In an essay published on Asquith's proposed 1912 Home Rule Bill, 'Vox Populi' referred to the American constitution as the ideal guide to proper citizenship and government. He concluded this piece by invoking the sanction of 'Divine Providence' as the final arbiter of national success.[35] The claim that successful nations, especially those conscious at their birth, were the natural result of their constituent peoples being *chosen* was common enough in the early twentieth century – such language was ubiquitous in the United States or Germany. All nations, especially in an era of conscious nation-building, saw themselves as unique or special.[36] What is of note about White's providentialism is how it illustrates the influence of American citizenship ideals upon Britain at this time.

Many of White's ideas on imperial citizenship were derived from the American political experience. Writing in 1919, White argued that the American Revolution was the most 'blessed' of all revolutions, carried out by loyal English men rebelling against a 'German' king and his corrupt ministers. Beyond his selective understanding of the Revolution, what he admired about the United States was its inherent sense of national mission, with individual liberty the reward for patriotism and the performance of national duty. White pointed favourably to the Declaration of Independence and its constant reference to 'our seas ... our coasts ... our people.'[37] With the United States firmly established as a world power-broker after their decisive intervention in the First World War, White called for a version of Churchill's later 'special relationship,' with the elder nation absorbing its offspring's energy and self-confidence, and in turn tutoring America in the merits of their common 'racial' tradition.[38]

His admiration of America's achievements was conditional, however, on England remaining the world's imperial power. This conditional admiration was based on several inter-related certainties. The first was that England had an imperial duty to spread civilization to other nations and peoples. This was not a vulgarized notion of spiritual uplift, such as was to be gained by shouldering the 'white man's burden.' In fact, White condemned such a view, arguing that the 'emotional intention,' especially when expressed by men in power, had historically been a great cause of trouble. White believed that England's imperial duty was to foster a sense of national self-determination which would result in the 'improvement' of the subject nation: 'The first effect of a sense of manhood and independence of thought is not to confer the right of unbridled insolence upon the emancipated soul, but to breathe into it the spirit of a gentleman.'[39] England was that gentleman, whose task it was to spread the gentlemanly spirit throughout the Empire. White looked to the writing of Ralph Waldo Emerson for support of his belief that civilization in turn bestowed its moral and intellectual advances upon those who were without them: 'the good of one country must either spread to all countries or it is not Civilization.'[40] As had Rhodes and the Canadian George Parkin, White considered the United States to be within the English imperium, if only unofficially, and thus it fell on her as well to participate in the task of spreading civilization.

Given his view that the United States shared with England an obligation to inculcate the spirit of self-determination around the world, White's appreciation of the renewed Monroe doctrine of the McKinley–Roosevelt era is understandable. James Monroe's 1823 pronouncement of hemispheric sovereignty had been revived during the 1895 Venezuela border dispute, and became an explicit public policy during the subsequent conflict with Spain over Cuba and the Philippines in 1898.[41] Some commentators set out the case that the sort of aggressive imperialism the United States had entered into was predatory and inconsistent with the spread of *gentlemanly* civilization. In particular, they took exception to the American practice of forcibly collecting its citizens' debts in South American countries.[42] For White, though, America's newfound interest in the international community was long overdue and was consistent with his belief that the *English* project of civilization could indeed take root overseas and produce a like-minded society.

As the frequent references to England attest, White left little doubt as to the culture which he saw as paramount. White's patriotism was in the service of England. His Anglocentrism led him to mistrust those he saw as outsiders, especially Jews and those he termed 'Celts.' He maintained a long-standing suspicion of Jewish influences in England. Writing in the *Daily Chronicle*, White argued that what he termed 'bad foreign Jews' – he acknowledged the existence of well-meaning patriotic Jews – menaced the best forms of national life, as they were materialistic and worked counter to patriotic goals. He described such 'bad' Jews as members of a 'Jewish imperium,' faulting them as cosmopolitans who chose to remain outside of the national family.[43] His negative use of the term 'imperial' as a close approximation to 'cosmopolitan' paints his own imperialism in an interesting light. As argued above, White's Empire was an extension of the English family, a 'greater England' in the most literal sense. He had no time for cosmopolitan initiatives, thus his opposition to multi-ethnic polities in Canada and the Cape Colony as threats to imperial unity. Jews, as stereotypical wanderers, were suspect in White's view for the very fact that they had no state, no homeland. As he wrote in *The Modern Jew* (1899):

> England, therefore, is in this dilemma: She is either compelled to abandon her secular practice of complacent acceptance of every human being choosing to settle on these shores, or to face the certainty of the Jews becoming stronger, richer, and vastly more numerous; with the corresponding certainty of the press being captured as it has been captured on the Continent, and the national life stifled by the substitution of material aims for those which, however faultily, have formed the unselfish and imperial objects of the Englishmen who have made the Empire.[44]

The Jewish 'problem' was that Jews had no citizenship, in that they had no loyalty to place and they did not assimilate with the cultures wherein they found themselves. The homeless were literally beyond the pale in a world where citizenship was tied to place. White's prescribed solutions to this 'problem,' similar to those proffered for other 'degenerate' members of society, were severe:

> There are two methods ... in which the evil results of a Jewish imperium inside the English Empire can be obviated. It can by destroyed and its members expelled ... or the Jewish community ... must revise their conduct and heartily work for instead of against the process of absorption.[45]

Writing in *The Times* in 1904, White suggested that Jews either face stricter monitoring upon entry to England or that a tract of land in Uganda be granted to Jews for a homeland.[46] His negative use of the term 'imperial' also betrays a conviction that the buttress of imperial citizenship was race, not in a biological sense of *inherent superiority*, though he certainly did not reject this 'possibility' out of hand, but rather in the sense that the moral character of England rested on history, tradition, and 'inherited' traits which could not be learned. One was *born* an English man or woman; one did not become one – hence his fears of his Celtic neighbours, of Jews, who were doubly suspect, being not only 'foreigners,' but also having no rooted home, and, in the years before the First World War, of German fifth columns. White's rhetoric got the better of him in his writing on Jewish topics, as evidenced by the addendum which the *Daily Chronicle* felt compelled to include after his article on 'bad Jewish influence': 'It must be understood that while we willingly give Mr. Arnold White the publicity of our columns for his interesting series of letters, we do not endorse all the views he expresses.'[47] White was cognizant of significant social problems – here the social dislocation and consequent difficulties created by the intermixing of cultures – but expressed himself in terms either too strident or too ambiguous to be convincing.

White also held a dismissive view of Britain's Celtic peoples. Great Britain was for him a construct, a Celtic device to grasp a portion of England's glory. He bristled at the perceived injustice that Great Britain was 'governed almost entirely by Scots, Welsh and Hebrews – the latter intellectually our betters but devoid of those distinctive qualities which have made such a South American phrase as "the word of an Englishman" imply good faith.'[48] In a submission to the *Watchman*, White found fault with the English liberal tradition of sanctuary, especially as it had been applied to Jews, who, he complained, did not join the 'English family.'[49] Like much of White's writing, this passage is exaggerated to drive home a point. In this instance he doubted the loyalty of the Scots, the Jews, or the Welsh. Such opinions unsurprisingly found little favour among White's Celtic correspondents, not the least of which was the Welsh Prime Minister, David Lloyd George. While vacationing at Balmoral in 1911, Lloyd George sent White the following mild chastisement after reading one of his articles:

> You are wrong in mistrusting the Celt. He is intensely loyal once his affections are engaged. He is tenacious of purpose beyond any other race in these islands. Most important of all he possesses the gift of imagination and when a country has gone deep into a rutted road, as England has, you need that power to lift it. At this juncture the peculiar qualities of the Celt are invaluable to these islands.[50]

John Buchan could not have put it better.

White's dismissive attitudes toward Celts and other 'outsiders' shaped his imperialism. An English estate, the Empire was furthermore to be a pan-England, encompassing and propagating the traditions, qualities, and character that made England a world power both militarily and culturally. Because White believed that England had contributed solely to the construction of Empire, he begrudged 'outsiders' claims on shared participation, especially when those groups did not pay tribute to England by fully assimilating. White forever saw England cheated of its just dues. The First World War provided only the most outrageous example of this. While at the *Referee* during the war, White corresponded sympathetically with many readers upset at the paper's use of 'Britain' in its articles and editorials rather than 'England,' arguing that it was the English who had founded the Empire. One such correspondent wondered why there was no 'English Brigade,' as there was for the Scots.[51] The Royal Society of St George sent White much material in this vein, asserting that the English war effort was unappreciated. One Society pamphlet reported spuriously that England had suffered 75–82% of imperial casualties, and should therefore be accorded the bulk of patriotic respect, and most of the 900,000 dominion troops had actually been born in England.[52] The imperial values of White and those who were like-minded reveal the cracks in any emerging notion of commonwealth or imperial unity, and explain in part why imperial federation and similar political schemes for imperial reorganization ultimately failed.

It is not only minorities who are nationalistic. As White shows, *majority* patriots can also hold aggressively national views. If proper respect for England's grand imperial tradition was the bulwark of White's imperial citizenship, how was such respect to be secured and perpetuated? To answer this question, we must look more closely at the relationship between citizen and state, and how White envisioned this relationship might work in terms of Empire. As will be made evident, White conceived of the imperial citizenship relationship as a replication of national citizenship.

Reciprocal citizenship

On 1 October 1916, over 1,500 people met at the Queen's Hall for a rally to demand votes for men on service. Soldiers on active duty did not have the right to exercise their franchise, as it was assumed that such a partisan activity, even if performed by proxy and in confidence, would harm morale. Such a prohibition was anathema to men such as White, as it struck at the very heart of his conception of citizenship. The most important component of this was defence–security.

Therefore, White counted the military in the front ranks of good imperial citizens, for soldiers put their lives in jeopardy in the defence of the Empire. Any benefits the individual might derive from citizenship were dependent on the maintenance of the community's security. Such a duty = reward equation constituted for White the proper relationship between citizen and state. It comes as little surprise, then, that White spoke at the Queen's Hall rally, commending the work of the military, particularly the navy, and urging that those serving England be allowed to participate in choosing its government. White suspected that Asquith's coalition Government was attempting to push through an election on a stale register. Other speakers at the rally included the suffragette Emily Pankhurst, the radical Unionist Henry Page Croft, and *National Review* editor Leo Maxse, the latter going so far as to claim with characteristic bombast that the Government's proposed Registration Bill sought to 'enfranchise the conscientious objector and disenfranchise the Victorian Cross.'[53]

For White, everyone had his or her place in the political order. The social contract which buttressed this order was between the State, which provided security and respected privacy, and the individual, who contributed to that security through service, thereby deriving the benefit of privacy. This relationship defined national citizenship; a similar relationship existed in the Empire, where subjects, regardless of their legal citizenship, were expected in White's view to work in the nation's interest. This social contract was thus the basic tenet of White's ideal of imperial citizenship. The monarch embodied this relationship, protecting the people while respecting the people's will as expressed in Parliament. The Government was reciprocally bound to act in good faith, otherwise the monarch would be forced to intervene to restore order or legitimacy.[54] White thus valued patriotism and honour in politicians, and could be acidic when those standards were not met. He discounted Winston Churchill on these lines, heading a review with the following epigram, 'A merciful Providence fashioned him hollow/ The better that he might his principles swallow.'[55] White was also critical of the replacement of Asquith by the Lloyd George coalition Government in December 1916.

Government should serve the people, not itself; conversely, government should not function simply as the mouthpiece of the masses. White deeply mistrusted demagoguery, which is ironic, in that much of his writing was just that. Nevertheless, he maintained an innate respect for aristocracy and the elite, so long as they used their position to the benefit of the State, rather than being self-seeking. White wanted an active and politicized citizenry, and deeply longed for a Carlyle-esque leader, capable of rousing the respect and loyalty of the people, while possessed of the better traits of traditional aristocratic rule, namely moral certainty and executive self-confidence.

White's belief in the importance of both national leadership and military service were reflected in his strong support for Trafalgar Day. He spearheaded the annual celebration at Nelson's column of the admiral's famous naval victory, in part to generate support for the navy and the Navy League's activities, but more broadly as a means of developing national pride. When Arthur Conan Doyle suggested that the holiday be dropped in an effort to improve England's relations with France, White retorted that this was just the sort of weakness of character the French had displayed at Waterloo, and that, furthermore, the event 'familiarizes the taxpayers and the electorate with the burdens of Imperial defence thrust upon them from without.'[56]

The State, furthermore, should employ business procedures, namely proper training and accountability. This was the theme of *Efficiency and Empire* (1901), White's best-known work. In this vein, he admired men such as Joseph Chamberlain, *actors* rather than speculators or rhetoricians. One of his correspondents voiced the view quite succinctly that the Empire should be run like a business, advocating an Empire run as a 'limited liability company...John Bull & Co.'[57] The Empire, in this vision, was an English estate, and should be viewed as such in clear, objective terms, not through platitudes such as 'Britannia rules the waves' or 'One Englishman can beat two foreigners.'[58]

In exchange for the governance provided by the State, the individual was required to help maintain the State's well-being. This meant above all military service, a theme White advanced through his work with the Navy Service League, founded in 1904. White often bemoaned the ineffective training of Britain's military, and devoted considerable time lobbying for improvements in the living standard of servicemen, particularly sailors. He was the public voice of the Duke of Bedford's scheme to improve England's militia.[59] He had little time for any individuals whom he believed did not perform their national duty. In a letter to the *New Age* in the fall of 1914, White castigated those of his fellow-writers who refused to enlist for family reasons, and argued they should be taxed, along with 'independent ineligibles' such as himself, to support the men in uniform.[60] He was deeply resentful that his age prevented him from serving.

After the introduction of conscription early in 1916, conscientious objectors, as was to be expected, found in White no ally. It was inconceivable to him that someone could decide not to participate in the defence of the Empire, and he dispensed much vitriol denouncing such 'traitors.' A representative example is the case of a conscientious objector named James Brightmore,[61] whose officers had been disciplined for using excessive force in their efforts to prevent him from deserting. White pestered the War Office with numerous missives in support of the officers, who he believed were upholding a sacred principle of active citizenship.[62] Any apparent tension in White's respect for individual liberty and the duty of national service quickly melted away, revealing a conviction that citizenship entailed duties and responsibilities, above all loyalty and patriotism. The pacifism and neutrality expressed by men like Brightmore scandalized White.[63] This was a dereliction of duty, rendering the objector no more a citizen than the alien. The most degraded person in White's world was not the enemy, whose loyalties and passions were at least assured, but the neutral whose rejection of the citizenship ideal placed him beyond the pale. Citizenship was a required state-of-being, not an option from which an individual could be absolved when desired.

Next to military service according to one's capabilities, individual citizens were expected to foster public discussion of the political issues of the day, thereby ensuring that the population at large was engaged in political life. Support for public discussion is to be expected from a journalist, but White saw his role in this as of *paramount* importance, and he defended the rights and obligations of the press with unusual vigour. In exchange for participating in the political life of nation and Empire, the individual secured a degree of personal autonomy. The State could not, in other words, make demands on the individual beyond those of military service. White believed the press to have a duty to protect this autonomy by holding the State to account. He drew selectively from the tradition of Hobbes and Locke in formulating these ideas, and in the equilibrium between national security and individual autonomy lay his ideal vision of citizenship.

Though he did not use this language consciously, White's notion of citizenship was in essence a political interpretation of Adam Smith's theory of the 'invisible hand.' Writing in the newly founded *National Service Journal* in 1904, White argued that the State should act as a trustee, while the individual-as-citizen should act as the businessman would, replacing *gain* with *duty* as the prime motivator. Individuals were thus, in a sense, raw material for the proper construction and maintenance of the State, and they were paid – that is, they derived their citizenship benefits – only once their labour was completed. These were the virtues, White concluded, which the Germany of Bismarck, Moltke, and Wilhelm II had stressed in its rise to international prominence, virtues that England would need to adopt in order to keep pace.[64]

ARNOLD WHITE

Emigration and citizenship

White's 'business' model was expressed in real terms through his long involvement in the issue of imperial emigration. His interest in this area was stimulated in the mid-1880s in the course of his campaign against foreign immigration. He was convinced that urbanization, combined with the arrival of Jews from Eastern Europe, had created social havoc. English cities now suffered from urban crowding, increased rents, the growth of the sweating industry, and other related problems which he blamed largely on the arrival of *non-English* immigrants. As a solution, White began to advocate emigration to the Empire. He travelled annually to South Africa from 1885 to 1890 in an attempt to convince local authorities to establish colonies of English labourers there. He also voyaged to Russia on five separate occasions in the 1890s to study the conditions from which Jews had been forced to flee. He published his appraisal of the situation in *The Destitute Alien in Great Britain* (1892). The lesson White derived from these travels was that social unrest occurs where there is a conflict of identity, and therefore of loyalty. Assimilation, which was the proper state of affairs, became impossible. In other words, White believed that identity must be tied to place. This, he believed, was the great strength of the United States, where one was absorbed into the American polity immediately upon disembarkation. Applied to the Empire, White adopted the view that Milner was soon to develop in South Africa, namely, that the maintenance of Empire depended on the settlement of greater numbers of Britons, both to increase the British presence and to aid in the assimilation of indigenous groups. Empire, in short, could function as a safety valve to regulate domestic pressures.

When this was the case, citizens truly became a raw material, redistributed in accord with the desire for a balanced ledger. The role of the imperial accountant – government – in such transactions was to facilitate the transfer of people and to ensure England always enjoyed a favourable balance. The preferred procedure was the organized emigration scheme. These numbered in the thousands during White's lifetime, though many, like that of Thomas Sedgwick (detailed in chapter 6), were unsuccessful. Thus, though individual liberty was a valued ideal, it was not as yet a *right* in the present understanding of this term. An appeal to *natural rights*, such as the individual's right to movement, would have bewildered White. This does not mean that White approved of the wholesale uprooting of communities for imperial purposes. Rather, he saw emigration as the solution to social problems, and hence advocated the emigration of those Britons deemed 'superfluous.' This was consistent with his notion that Empire existed *for* England, not, as with Buchan, *of* England.

While criminals were not appropriate emigrants, other disadvantaged groups certainly were. One such group consisted of those engaged in 'blind-alley employment' – individuals, mainly young boys, who worked at jobs of limited duration, usually a few years. After that time the worker was often cast out and left with few if any useful skills, becoming a drain on society. Blind-alley employees included van-boys, golf caddies, messenger boys, and hotel workers.[65] Richard Butler, White's editor at the *Referee*, was also a supporter of assisted emigration. He encouraged 'Vanoc' to stress how limited opportunities then were in Britain, and that emigrés could serve the Empire by becoming 'a useful asset as a food provider for the Mother Country.'[66] White echoed Butler's position after the First World War, reminding readers of *The Times* 'that if you settle outside the Empire you may be lost to it.'[67]

White argued that the State should take the lead concerning emigration and, to that end, he worked with the Emigrants' Information Office (EIO). Collaborators in this endeavour included Liberal Cabinet Minister Lewis Harcourt.[68] The EIO operated out of the Colonial Office and provided prospective emigrants with quarterly literature on the white dominions, including information on employment, weather, passage, and culture. White also sat on the 1907 Parliamentary Committee on Emigration, whose members included the young civil servant William Beveridge. The Committee reviewed the EIO's operations as part of its larger mandate to increase assisted emigration. In 1906, the EIO had received 14,646 queries from or on behalf of potential emigrants;[69] and, since 1895, 2,220–3,300 applications to migrate had been received yearly. Interest in Australia and New Zealand as destinations had increased, largely on account of the better climate, government assistance for passage, and ample employment opportunities. Australia at the turn of the century had the world's highest standard of living. Canada, despite the efforts of Minister of the Interior Clifford Sifton, saw a decline in enquiries, as only labourers were to be admitted as part of tightened immigration legislation.

Though he continued to support assisted emigration until his death, White had eventually moved away from the emigration schemes he favoured in the late nineteenth century to concentrate on promoting youth emigration. He lamented the graft and wastage state-operated plans often entailed. Moreover, he feared the emigration of society's least productive members could lead to resentment in the dominions and cracks in imperial solidarity. Furthermore, he was disappointed that successive governments showed only limited interest in administering mass emigration undertakings. The State had failed in its required role as imperial manager, leaving it to private individuals to take up the task of assisted emigration. Though he still worked to aid the broader emigration movement – including high-level engagements on the subject by figures such as the South African politician Louis Botha[70] – by the early 1910s he had begun to favour youth emigration. White argued that youths were better suited to adapt to new surroundings. Hence, he saw an increased role for enterprising private operators such as Thomas Sedgwick and Dr Thomas Barnardo, who between 1870 and 1914 sent 31,031 children overseas.[71] Free from the stigma of pauperism, such schemes were conducive to the development of mental and physical character, White's preeminent imperial efficiency concern. The concern White showed for a possible decrease in *imperial solidarity* can in part be attributed to the increases in non-British emigration to the dominions. For instance, in the 1907–8 fiscal year, the number of British immigrants to Canada was 59,832, while non-British immigrants numbered 94,007.[72]

Consistent with his citizenship model, White argued that assisted emigration should be suspended while Britain was at war, as the primary concern of both state and citizen was national security. He refused to attend EIO meetings during the war, arguing that the EIO should be closed to conserve scarce human and economic resources.[73] With the end of the conflict, White retreated into retirement at his cottage on Windmill Hill, Hampstead. Though his correspondence is silent on the issue, he was no doubt pleased with the passage of the 1918 Emigration Act. The legislation expressed many of his convictions concerning the State's proper role as a facilitator and caretaker of the individual's benefits for service rendered. In the case of the 1918 legislation, the State provided for both the Empire's maintenance and the liberty of its citizens. Its role was 'to improve the existing organization for affording information and assistance to those who wish to emigrate from the British Islands, and to provide for the establishment and powers of a Central Emigration Authority, and for the supervision and control of passage brokers and passage broker's agents, and emigration societies, and for purposes in connection therewith.'[74]

Through most of his career, however, White had been disappointed with the failure of the State and its constituents to live up to their respective citizenship roles. This disappointment was especially clear during the First World War. The conflict heightened White's Anglocentrism, and helps to illustrate how his English patriotism shaped his notion of imperial citizenship. An examination of White's wartime controversies also brings to the fore the limitations to his understanding of Empire.

The First World War

The outbreak of the war confirmed White's long-standing belief that Germany posed a mortal threat to the security of England and its Empire. Though Germanophobia was certainly not an uncommon trait in Edwardian Britain, White held a particularly antagonistic stance toward Germany and its citizens. He was one of the pre-war era's leading 'scaremongers.'[75] His interest in the navy soon directed his gaze upon Germany, which he saw as a threat to England's naval supremacy, especially in the North Sea. Britain's imperial security rested upon the strength of the Royal Navy, and thus a threat to its naval superiority represented a threat to the Empire at large. With these thoughts in mind, White travelled to Germany in 1908 to conduct an investigation of the German Navy for the *Daily Express*. Despite the reservations of Admiral Tirpitz, who viewed White with suspicion, the journalist was granted an audience with Kaiser Wilhelm II.[76] The Kaiser, nephew of Edward VII, had cultivated a reputation as an Anglophile in the early years of the twentieth century, taking delight in his appointment as an Honourary Admiral of the Fleet, a title granted him by his maternal grandmother Queen Victoria. Nonetheless, he harboured many grievances against England. The Kaiser complained to White of the unfair treatment the English press had in recent years accorded Germany.[77] White returned home impressed with German efficiency, but concerned about the mistrust of England expressed by the Kaiser, whom he depicted as unbalanced. As Anglo-German competition intensified in 1909 and 1910, White's was one of the earliest voices predicting conflict and thus the need for national preparedness. He later summarized his position on Germany, and offered an amateur assessment of the Kaiser's state of mind, in his 1915 publication *Is the Kaiser Insane? A Study of the Great Outlaw*.[78] White had long feared 'foreign' influences in the English press. Often this meant Jews, 'an island of aliens in the sea of English life,'[79] though elsewhere White expressed admiration for 'good Jews' and the fortitude of the Jewish race.[80] In the decade between his visit to the Kaiser and the start of war, 'foreign' increasingly meant German. White argued that, despite the commendable aspects of German culture, 'Germany wants that which England possesses,'[81] namely an empire to expand and exploit. This desire, given Germany's increased naval strength, White thought understandable; he had observed melodramatically years before he travelled to Berlin: 'The longing for a slice of territory in a temperate colony can only be compared to the longing of a lover for his mistress or of an injured Spaniard for revenge.'[82]

When war became a reality White saw Germans behind every tree. His attention was focused on the 'Hidden Hand,' what he perceived as the undue German influence on the English press which threatened to compromise the war effort. One of White's correspondents sent him a pamphlet entitled 'Why the London Press Favours Alien Immigration and English Emigration,' which denounced the 'Semitic' nature of *The Times*, a legacy of the paper's former manager Moberley Bell, and claimed that the *Daily Mail* was a 'noted [product] of the Irish immigrant's "noospoiper" factory,' while the *Daily Chronicle*'s 'proprietors are some money-grubbing ingrates who bear the Welsh name of Lloyd,' and the *Pall Mall Gazette*'s proprietor 'is an American millionaire of German descent.'[83] Though White did not share the stark xenophobia expressed in this pamphlet, the letter-writer's thoughts are perhaps indicative of the opinion his work courted, and explains why he was unable to capture mainstream support. White was also suspicious of advertisements in British papers during the week war was declared, which he believed had been placed, through ostensibly neutral groups, by the Germans. He was especially indignant about an entire page in the 5 August 1914 edition of the radical–liberal *Daily News* which declared: 'Englishmen, Do Your Duty and Keep Your Country Out of a Wicked and Stupid War.'[84] In 1915 and again in 1917 he called for an investigation into German proprietorship of English newspapers, bringing a motion to the Institute of Journalists to prohibit foreign-born individuals from becoming members. A. G. Gardiner, the Institute's president and editor of the *Daily News*, turned down White's request (a not uncommon occurrence). He challenged White to produce evidence of his claims, and dropped the issue when White would not comply.[85] Despite the Institute's refusal to hear his case, White refused to resign, 'because I never resign from anything if I am in a better position to attack from inside in the interests of my country.'[86]

White's suspicions of the existence of a 'Hidden Hand' illustrate his notion of citizenship as based in national patriotism, a citizenship based on the principle of *jus sanguinis*, something that one acquires by birth. On a more squalid note, it also shows his paranoia and penchant for fear-mongering, while demonstrating his need to construct straw men for his arguments. *The Times* summed up the popular response to White's jeremiad, noting in its review of *The Hidden Hand* (1917), in which White set out his fears of a German fifth column in England, that 'the hammering cocksureness of the style which may have all ephemeral effectiveness does not carry conviction.'[87]

White was concerned with the security of the Empire insofar as threats directed toward it presented a danger to England's own security.

A similar concern prompted his criticisms of Britain's policy regarding immigrants. He argued that Britain's immigration law was inadequate, describing the 1914 British Nationality and Status of Aliens Act as 'a legal fiction' because it did nothing to address the issue of Germans resident in Britain.[88] Part of this anxiety was occasioned by the passage of the Delbrück Law in Germany. In a speech to the Devonshire Club in the August of 1917, White drew attention to that Act, spearheaded by the German Secretary of State for Home Affairs, Herr Delbrück[89] (White had been made aware of this legislation through correspondence with an R. Feibelman of Amsterdam). Germany's previous naturalization legislation, passed in 1870 with subsequent amendments, stated that Germans would lose their German citizenship after ten years of domicile abroad, unless they had periodically registered at a German consulate. Many emigrés did not do so, most losing their citizenship when they went abroad, and their children also were lost as prospective German citizens. The growth of a German Empire at the end of the nineteenth century necessitated a change in this legislation, as Germany now required laws to cover its new colonies, as well as maintain a military force outside of Europe. New legislation, of which the Delbrück Law was in 1917 only the most recent manifestation, stated that German nationality would be lost only when the emigrant *voluntarily* revoked nationality. This contrasted with British law, which dictated that an emigré lost his British nationality if he acquired the nationality of another country. The Delbrück Act was an amendment to the German Bill on Naturalization, and permitted denaturalized Germans to retain their citizenship. Such individuals would have to formally apply to revoke their German citizenship, and permission was rarely granted for those of military age.

White would have welcomed similar legislation in Britain, as it would have more firmly defined British citizenship, particularly for Britons living beyond the United Kingdom. A German model, however, was nothing if not a threat. White feared the Delbrück Act, predicated on the notion of a 'greater Germany,' would help facilitate German fifth-column activities in Britain, and not only among Britain's lower classes. White alleged that there were numerous German–Britons among Britain's elite who held dual citizenship. He cited the City bankers Baron Bruno von Schrüder, Sir Ernest Cassel, and Sir Edgar Speyer, all Privy Council members, as well as convicted German spy Lincoln Trebitsch, as examples of those he suspected. The charges were by all appearances unfounded, Whitehall was not impressed, and the Chancellor of the Exchequer decided White's allegations did not warrant action under the Defence of the Realm Act.[90] What was ironic about White's vehement Germanophobia, and was perhaps a key to understanding its gestation, was that his great-great-grandfather was born 'Witt,' and only changed the family's surname to 'White' in the 1780s to avoid Germanophobe prejudice.[91]

Arnold White represented a stream of imperialism based upon race–patriotism. It harkened back to an era of imperial consensus, when England acted rather than dithered, and when imperial loyalty was maintained by the very fact that it was rarely tested. How else to account for many Britons seemingly heartfelt shock of the Indian 'Mutiny' in 1857 – could this *really* have happened to us? White's conservatism bore more resemblance to that of the mid-century 'age of equipoise' than to that of the late Victorian 'new imperialism.' Though he disavowed the liberal convictions expressed by many mid-Victorian imperialists, he expressed a Whiggish sympathy for aristocratic government and shared Lord Palmerston's Tory view of the 'national interest.'[92]

White's concern for the national interest speaks to the importance of patriotism in pre-1914 Britain, specifically its impact on ideas of citizenship. White's thought on citizenship developed firmly within the context of the national efficiency movement. He advanced an exclusive concept built around a reciprocal relationship between citizen and government, with commensurate duties and rewards, directed toward the national interest. Ultimately such a citizenship was parochial: outsiders were to be assimilated. The most important qualifications for such a citizenship were loyalty and an attachment to English tradition. Thus, the Crystal Palace of 1851 stood side-by-side Gordon's travails in the Sudan in 1884 as great events in *English* history. White viewed the Empire within this framework. His concept of imperial citizenship flowed from his conviction that *English* citizenship, by extension, also encompassed Britons living in the Empire. This conviction was based in ideas of cultural exceptionalism, drawing on a racialism derived from the national ego and parochialism. White ignored non-English imperial subjects in the simple, if arrogant, belief that their having been born outside of the English culture precluded them, on the principle of *jus sanguinis*, of ever becoming English citizens.

The responsibilities of imperial citizenship, namely service to the State in whatever manner necessary, came before rights or benefits. For English patriots such as White, citizenship was insular: his concern was for the nation and its people in and of themselves, not necessarily in contrast to others. White had little direct knowledge of or concern for the Empire as a group of societies separate from England itself. It is telling that beyond his visits to South Africa to oversee a settlement scheme, his visits to 'the Empire' were limited to brief voyages to visit

English warships abroad. The breakdown of imperial loyalty in the Edwardian era and after can in part by attributed to colonial subjects' rejection of a citizenship model which showed them so little interest.

Notes

1. The pseudonym was drawn from Arthurian legend, where 'Vanoc' was Merlin's son; see A. White, *The Views of Vanoc: An Englishman's Outlook* (London, 1910), p. v.
2. Arnold White Papers (hereafter WHI), File 57, National Maritime Museum (hereafter NMM).
3. Pamphlet, Royal Society of St George, WHI/57, NMM. The Society, founded in 1894, had three core objects: to encourage patriotism in Englishmen of birth or origin; to revive St Georges's Day and celebrate Shakespeare's date of birth and death (23 April) as national holidays; and to promote the culture of England.
4. White was a member of the Navy League, and wrote many of its public missives. In naval matters, his primary interest, he acted as the confidant of and public agitator for Admiral Charles Beresford and later, upon changing his allegiances, the reformer Admiral Sir John Fisher. Beresford and Fisher were naval policy rivals in the Edwardian period, the former opposing the latter's reforms, specifically the introduction of the Dreadnaught series of battleships and a home water fleet. White was also a largely inactive member of the Institute of Journalists, even though he spent most of his career on Fleet Street.
5. 'Miscellaneous Notes,' WHI/57, NMM.
6. In voicing these views, as well as in his advocacy of 'efficiency,' White betrayed the influence of Lord Rosebery on his political thought. Rosebery had expounded on these same themes in his Chesterfield speech of 15 December 1901: see Robert Rhodes James, *Rosebery* (London, 1963), pp. 429–33.
7. *The Athenæum*, 3829, 16 March 1901, p. 335.
8. Quoted by Searle, 'Introduction,' in A. White, *Efficiency and Empire*, ed. G. R. Searle (Brighton, 1973 [1901]), p. xv.
9. *The Times*, 6 February, 1925, p. 14n.
10. White stood as a Liberal Unionist for the constituency of Mile End in 1886, 1892, and 1895 after rejecting Gladstone's position on Home Rule, and as an Independent for Londonderry in 1906. He was unsuccessful each time.
11. Series such as Stead's 'The Maiden Tribute of Modern Babylon,' which appeared in the *Pall Mall Gazette* in July 1885, detailing the white slave trade in London, and the revelations of London poverty by Charles Booth display both the social concerns and loose treatment of the 'facts' that characterize much of White's journalism. White was never one to let the facts get in the way of his moral fervour, never mind a good story. Judith Walkowitz's *City of Dreadful Delight* (London, 1992) is particularly good on Stead's 'Maiden Tribute' and its cavalier handling of the facts.
12. Proponents of the 'blue-water' school of naval strategy argued that the key to the security of Britain and her Empire was a strong navy. Control of the world's waterways also strengthened Britain's economy by keeping trade routes open.
13. The standard work is Bernard Semmel's *Imperialism and Social Reform* (Cambridge, MA, 1960); see also G. R. Searle, *The Quest for 'National Efficiency': A Study in British Politics and Political Thought, 1899–1914* (Berkeley, CA, 1971); and H. C. G. Matthew, *The Liberal Imperialists* (Oxford, 1973).
14. Richard Soloway, *Demography and Degeneracy* (Chapel Hill, NC, 1995), p. 41.
15. Searle, *The Quest*, p. xviii.
16. Semmel, *Imperialism and Social Reform*, chapter 1, and p. 235.
17. White shared with Kipling both deep respect for the man in uniform and a frustration with establishment politics. On the eve of war in 1914, both suspected the Liberal Government of being 'crooked.' Kipling gave a speech at Tunbridge Wells on 16 May 1914, entitled 'Rudyard Kipling's Indictment of the Government,' a

copy of which White included in his clippings for the period. Kipling denounced the 'detoothing' of the House of Lords, the Marconi Scandals, and government plans to send troops to Ireland as signs of corrupt leadership: see the *Daily Express*, 18 May 1914. Alleged institutional corruption had diminished Kipling's ardour for imperialism, a change of heart further exacerbated by the death of his son at the Western Front in 1915.

18 White, *Efficiency and Empire*, p. 309.
19 White, lecture outline, 'The Family and the Empire' (n.d.), WHI/43, NMM.
20 'Black Week' was the term given to Britain's defeats at Stormberg, Magersfontein, and Colenso, 10–16 December 1899. The disaster resulted in the appointment of Field Marshall Frederick, Lord Roberts's appointment to succeed General Sir Redvers Buller as Commander-in-Chief of Britain's war effort.
21 Robert Reid Rentoul, 'Proposed Sterilization of Certain Mental and Physical Degenerates,' unpublished MSS, WHI/43, NMM.
22 Bernard Hollander, 'The Problem of Degeneration,' lecture given to the Ethnological Society, 15 March 1911.
23 Though he was not a member, White corresponded with members of the Malthusian League and read much of their literature. Copies of this literature can be found in White's Papers.
24 White, letter to the editor, *The Times*, 29 December 1896, p. 10e; White, 'The Half-Insane Degenerates in Society,' unpublished MSS (n.d.), WHI/43, NMM.
25 Arnold White, 'Race Culture,' in *The Views of Vanoc: An Englishman's Outlook* (London, 1910), p. 285.
26 White reported that in 1898 the medical department of the army rejected 23,287 out of 66,501 recruits because they were deemed physically unfit for service. Of the 11,000 men who volunteered for service in Manchester between October 1899 and July 1900, 8,000 were found to be physically unfit, while 1,200 of the remaining 3,000 were accepted, despite their failure to meet the military's standards for strength and chest diameter: see *Efficiency and Empire*, pp. 109, 102–3.
27 Public lecture by White, 'The Physical Condition of the Nation,' Douglas Hall, Hoxton, 8 June 1904, WHI/43, NMM.
28 White, 'The Writing on the Wall,' *Black and White*, 19 June 1909. Grey was most comfortable at his country estate at Falloden, watching birds and walking with his wife Dorothy. Balfour, the centre of the 'Souls' group at Oxford, was notable for his aloofness.
29 A. White, 'Society and the Work of the Empire,' *Daily Chronicle*, 30 January 1900, pp. 9ff. This article, which was published anonymously, was not titled as part of the 'Where We Fail' series. The two subsequent contributions of 5 February and 12 February were numbered as (I) and (II), but the 19 February contribution was numbered (IV), with the previous three submissions retroactively becoming numbers (I), (II), and (III). The numbering confusion accounts for the apparent lacuna of submission number (III).
30 Hobson published his ideas on financial speculation, as well as a broader indictment of imperialism, in *Imperialism: A Study* (1902). Hobson noted his agreement with the general thrust of White's argument, specifically the need for greater vigour among the middle class, the crisis of physical deterioration, and the need for a reformed administration which limited the influence of finance. However, he chastised White for being merely declamatory, brandishing efficiency as a shibboleth, and lacking depth of understanding, while observing that, in book form, White's message betrays a 'marked thinness of matter': *Spectator*, 29 June 1901, p. 951.
31 A. White, 'Where We Fail, IV', *Daily Chronicle*, 19 February 1900, p. 7.
32 A. White, 'Strangers Yet,' 1919, unpublished MSS, WHI/131, NMM; *Efficiency and Empire*, p. 312.
33 *The Times*, 30 July 1912, p. 4d. White was followed by a speaker who argued that tall, fair-haired people succeed in life over short, dark-haired ones, and that the former were found predominantly in the south of England, accounting for the greater prosperity evident there.

34 *The Views of Vanoc*, pp. 113, 116.
35 'Memo on British Constitution,' WHI/36, NMM.
36 Providentialism and nation-building in general have been well-covered by historians. Especially prevalent has been the idea of 'imagined communities' (Benedict Anderson, *Imagined Communities*, 1982) and the definition of the self as normative in relation to some *other*. Linda Colley's *Britons* (London, 1992) is of importance here in the context of Empire. Colley places much emphasis on the notion of providence as central to Britain's imperial identity. While this may serve well as an explanation of how Britons themselves thought, it tells little about how they were *different* than others who believed the same thing.
37 Vox Populi, 'Memo on British Constitution.'
38 White, 'Strangers Yet,' A similar spirit inspired Rhodes's vision of cultural and racial unity, reflected for example in the bestowal of Rhodes Scholarships on Americans and Germans.
39 A. White, 'Our Handbook: Civilization Forward or Backwards? The Embryo of Nationality,' unidentified cutting, 8 December 1912, WHI/33, NMM.
40 Ibid. White selectively quotes from Emerson to build his case in this document. He misunderstood Emerson's intent, namely, the advocacy of the spirit of self-reliance.
41 American President Grover Cleveland pressed Congress in 1895 to intervene on Venezuela's behalf in that country's border dispute with British Guiana. The issue offended British national pride, and aroused in the country mild anti-American sentiment, but was soon forgotten in the wake of the Jameson Raid in December 1895. The Spanish–American War broke out in 1898, and marked the United States' first tentative and brief foray into global imperialism: see David Traxel, *1898* (New York, 1998).
42 Hiram Bingham, 'The Monroe Doctrine: An Obsolete Shibboleth,' *Atlantic Monthly*, 111 (June 1913), pp. 721–34.
43 A. White, 'Where We Fail, VI,' *Daily Chronicle*, 7 March 1900, p. 7a.
44 A. White, *The Modern Jew* (London, 1899), p. xiii. This work, like all of White's monographs, was a compilation of smaller pieces, notably articles from *The Nineteenth Century* and the *North American Review*.
45 Ibid., p. xii.
46 *The Times*, 24 December 1904, pp. 4ff.
47 White, 'Where We Fail, VI.'
48 White, 'Strangers Yet,' p. 7.
49 White, 'England for the British Empire,' unpublished MS, WHI/131, NMM.
50 Lloyd George–White, 15 September 1911, 'Ministerial Correspondence,' WHI/134, NMM. The 'juncture' to which Lloyd George was referring was Britain's industrial unrest and the debate over the House of Lords, both political crises of 1911. White and Lloyd George corresponded occasionally during this period, mainly concerning White's opposition to 'Keir Hardieism' and what he perceived as Lloyd George's socialist leanings.
51 G. B. H. Burke–White (n.d.), WHI/52, NMM.
52 Royal Society of St George pamphlet (n.d., but probably early 1920s), addressed to White, WHI/52, NMM.
53 *The Times*, 2 October 1916, p. 5c.
54 White was a strong advocate of transparent government, and he campaigned vigorously against perceived corruption. He attended meetings of the National League for Clean Government, though it is not clear whether or not he was a member: see WHI/134, NMM.
55 Unidentified clipping, WHI/134, NMM.
56 *The Times*, 21 October 1897, p. 10d. White was being somewhat unfair here, as Arthur Conan Doyle was no dissenter when it came to patriotism. The latter wrote histories of both the Anglo-Boer War and the First World War, for which he received a knighthood. In viewing Nelson's victory as an *English* event, White neglected the contributions of other Britons who served on the *Victory* and its allied ships.
57 A. W. A. Pound–White, 28 July 1914, WHI/83, NMM.

58 White, 'The Future of Britain, Part I,' MS copy, *Black and White*, 1 May 1909, in WHI/61, NMM.
59 See Leonard Ray Teel, 'The Life and Times of Arnold Henry White, 1848–1925,' unpublished PhD thesis, Georgia State University, 1984.
60 (White), *New Age*, 10 September 1914, p. 460.
61 On Brightmore and conscientious objectors, see Thomas Kennedy, *The Hound of Conscience: A History of the Non-Conscription Fellowship, 1914–1919* (Columbia, SC, 1967).
62 B. B. Cubitt, War Office–White, 23 July 1917, WHI/35, NMM.
63 White was similarly upset by George Bernard Shaw's 1917 article for the *San Francisco Bulletin*, in which Shaw wrote: 'In both armies the soldiers should shoot their officers and go home, the agriculturalist to his land and the townsman to his painting and glazing' (*San Francisco Bulletin*, 2 November 1914). Shaw, who had once worked under White at the Edison Electric Light Company, was engaging in satire, but nonetheless appeared to White as unpatriotic. White sent a memo to several of the dailies, in which he expressed his hope that 'men of the stamp of Bernard Shaw would be wiped out as the swarms of butterflies disappear before the blast of the... monsoon,' and branded Shaw a 'parasite.' Shaw's sometimes patronizing assuredness and candour riled the patriotic and prosaic White to no end.

White chastised Shaw for ignoring the suffering of the soldiers and their families. Shaw, delighted to have found such a literal mind with which to spar, responded with characteristic wit: 'You have let the war get on your nerves. The front will jolly you up [Shaw was suggesting a visit, not active service]: after an hour of big gun fire you simply won't know that such a person as Shaw, the Terrible Traitor of the Hidden Hand, exists': see Memorandum, White, 19 March 1917; Shaw–White, 17 March 1917, WHI/178, NMM.
64 *National Service Journal*, 1, 7 (May 1904).
65 Malcolm Jones–White, 30 December 1913, WHI/9, NMM.
66 R. D. Butler–White, 23 December 1913, WHI/9, NMM.
67 *The Times*, 22 May 1919, p. 13d.
68 White–H. Lambert, 23 March 1907, WHI/80, NMM. The EIO was founded in 1886 as an arm's length branch of the Colonial Office. The Royal Colonial Institute and C. P. Lucas in the Colonial Office had been instrumental in its establishment. The EIO had a minimal budget drawn from the public purse, and served mainly as an advisory body, with no designs on an active role in administering emigration. See also Andrew Thompson, *Imperial Britain*, pp. 139, 140.
69 The largest number of enquiries came from skilled mechanics (28.5%), followed by labourers (8.3%), female domestics (6.2%), and clerks (5.5%): see *Report on the Emigrant Information Office* for 1907 and 1908, Cd. 3918.
70 Louis Botha–White, 13 August 1904, WHI/47, NMM. Botha wrote to thank White for his part in a small scheme to resettle English widows in South Africa.
71 See Marjory Harper, 'British Migration,' *Oxford History of the British Empire*, vol. 3 (Oxford, 1999), p. 82; Barnardo sent 28,689 youths to Canada and 2,342 youths to Australia.
72 White, 'The Waste of Human Material' and 'The Value of the Child Emigrant,' unpublished MSS, WHI/51, NMM.
73 White–EIO, 8 November 1915, WHI/51, NMM.
74 30, 8 & 9 George V.
75 On the 'scaremongers' in Britain before the First World War, see A. J. Morris, *'The Scaremongers': The Advocacy of War and Rearmament, 1896–1914* (London and Boston, 1984).
76 See Teel's thesis 'The Life and Times of Arnold Henry White, 1848–1925,' Part III, chapter 2. Due to White's subsequent criticisms of Germany, his certification to visit Germany on later occasions was revoked by the German Embassy.
77 See *Daily Telegraph*, 28 October 1908. Britain's reaction to the affair is conveyed in T. G. Otte, '"An Altogether Unfortunate Affair": Britain and the *Daily Telegraph*

Affair,' *Diplomacy and Statecraft*, 5 (1994), pp. 296–333. Anglo-German relations were further soured by the intensification of the naval 'scare' in 1909, when Germany intensified production of Dreadnaught-class battleships. Wilhelm's subsequent decision to grant an interview to a British paper, resulting in the so-called '*Daily Telegraph* affair,' provoked a diplomatic incident and precipitated a nervous breakdown from which he never completely recovered.

78 The Kaiser's political judgement and mental health were topics of much discussion in both Whitehall and Fleet Street. Recent evidence indicates that Wilhelm may have suffered from a brain defect now termed 'minimal cerebral dysfunction': see T. G. Otte, '"The Winston of Germany": The British Foreign Policy Elite and the Last German Emperor,' *Canadian Journal of History*, 36 (December 2001), p. 472.
79 White, *Efficiency and Empire*, p. 80.
80 White, *The Views of Vanoc*, pp. 83–5.
81 Ibid., p. 180.
82 (White) *Daily Mail*, 24 July 1902, p. 4d.
83 Joseph Bannister–White (n.d.), pamphlet dated 13 January 1913, WHI/9, NMM.
84 *Daily News*, 5 August 1914, p. 7. The advertisement was placed by the Neutrality League, an organization advocating peace. The League had temporary offices in Fleet Street and Carlise Place. Despite White's claims, it does not appear to have had any German connection.
85 Motion, White–Institute of Journalists, 16 October 1915. For Gardiner's response, and a report of the Institute's Annual Meeting for 1915, see *Daily News*, 18 October 1915, p. 5c.
86 White, MS, 'Chapter – The Hidden Hand in Fleet Street,' p. 9, WHI/117, NMM.
87 *The Times*, supplement, 22 May 1917, p. 479d.
88 Evelyn Miller–White, 8 February 1917; Miller–White, 22 February 1917, WHI/117, NMM.
89 White, notes for a lecture to the Devonshire Club, 29 August 1917, WHI/42, NMM: see *Memorandum on German Imperial and State Naturalization Law*, 22 July 1913, issued by the British Embassy in Berlin. Miscellaneous No. 3 (1914), Cd. 7277.
90 White, speech to the Institute of Journalists (n.d., but early 1917: see Evelyn Miller–White, 8 February 1917), p. 68, WHI/117, NMM. Von Schrüder and Cassel had been naturalized in Britain in 1878, Speyer in 1892. For White's brush with DORA, see *The Times*, 14 March 1917, p. 10d.
91 See Teel, 'The Life and Times of Arnold Henry White, 1848–1925,' p. 11. To add further irony, the publisher of The Views of Vanoc, Kegan Paul, Trench, Trübner & Co., had obvious German connections.
92 In defence of his foreign policy, Lord Palmerston delivered his famous definition of the 'national interest' in the House on 1 March 1848: 'We have not eternal allies, and we have no perpetual enemies. Our interests are eternal and perpetual, and those interests it is our duty to follow': *Hansard*, 1 March 1848.

PART II

Experiments in imperial citizenship

CHAPTER FIVE

Richard Jebb, intra-imperial immigration, and the practical problems of imperial citizenship

The organic imperialism of Lionel Curtis and the nascent cosmopolitan imperialism of John Buchan demonstrate two strains of early twentieth-century thought on citizenship and the Empire. Those men, however, travelled in the worlds of political philosophy and the civil service. They were, with only occasional exceptions,[1] strangers to the world of policy implementation. The task of giving practical shape to ideas of imperial citizenship was left to others. One such figure was the imperial journalist and traveller Richard Jebb. Like Curtis and Buchan, Jebb was primarily a theorist. However, Jebb had a clearer conception than they of the dominions' emerging political importance. Unlike Curtis and Buchan, both of whom, despite the differences in their thought, remained convinced that Britain must continue to be the centre of the Empire, Jebb began to envision Empire less as a federation and more as a confederation.

His *Studies in Colonial Nationalism* (1905) established the young author as an authority on the Empire, particularly the white-settlement colonies. Jebb spent the next decade refining his argument that the settlement colonies, soon to be termed 'dominions,' exhibited the traits of emerging nation–states. Any proposed schemes to maintain imperial unity must necessarily, he believed, take this new reality into account. Despite three subsequent books,[2] innumerable speeches in the lecture halls of Edwardian imperialism, and a platform at the *Morning Post*, Jebb was unable to win broad support for his ideas. A devastating loss as a Unionist candidate at the polls in the December 1910 election proved a decisive blow to his confidence. With the outbreak of the First World War, Jebb largely retired from active life, though he would live for another four decades.

Richard Jebb's work and career present an instructive case study in the practical problems of defining imperial citizenship. He articulated a vision of Empire that was at once inclusive and exclusive, one that rested on a set of shared values which proved difficult, if not impossible, to inculcate in the Empire's peoples. One arena in which this failure was particularly evident was that of intra-imperial migration. The migration issue is a particularly fruitful topic of study for historians of Empire because it reveals attitudes and conceptions of citizenship, and helps illustrate how imperialism was constituted, on whom it had an impact, and how it was perpetuated. It is the epitome of *practical imperialism*. Conflicts over intra-imperial immigration and citizenship laws were characterized by tensions between proponents of a 'wider patriotism' such as Jebb, who lobbied for a greater regard for colonial nationalism as the buttress of imperial unity, particularly through a common imperial naturalization process, and those of 'colonial autonomy'.

Jebb's vision betrays the fragility of pan-Empire ideals. However, the currency his activities carried, the prescience of his views, and the very fact that the contentious debate he spent much of his career commenting upon, imbued as it was with racial and political conflict, did not result in violent imperial cleavages speaks to the paradoxical elasticity and durability of the imperial ideal. Ironically, the impossibility of ever creating a commonly acceptable definition of imperial citizenship proved a stabilizing, rather than debilitating, factor, as the lack of a concrete notion of imperial citizenship allowed an environment of multiple jurisdictions and ideological ambiguity to develop. Thus, in the failure of Richard Jebb's vision of imperial citizenship, we can gain a clearer understanding of the relative strengths of the Empire in the early twentieth century. Britons' inability to create a consensual notion of imperial citizenship resulted in a sense of equilibrium, where the centralist imperatives of imperial decision-makers in Britain were balanced by the often independent actions of colonials.

Imperium et libertas

David Cannadine has argued that, 'the British Empire was at least as much (perhaps more?) about the replication of sameness and similarities originating from home as it was about the insistence on difference and dissimilarities originating from overseas.'[3] Positioning the Empire as 'a complex social hierarchy ... a social organism,'[4] Cannadine seeks to explain Britain's imperium through the nexus of class. His attention to the essentially Burkeian nature of the Empire is well placed and a valued corrective to a historiography whose attention to the tensions and conflicts of Empire can leave the reader curious as to how the institution actually survived for three centuries. However, Cannadine overestimates the putative bonds which held together Britain and the dominions. It was not just the dependent colonies which constituted separate and distinct polities. The dominions, too, despite cultural allegiances to Britain and despite a lack of control over their own foreign relations, were by the end of the nineteenth century largely autonomous nations. The Imperial Conferences of the early twentieth century were marked by nothing if not the dominions' stated desire *not* to stand alongside Britain in political federation, *not* to harmonize citizenship legislation.[5] Bonds of sentiment did not stand the test of politics and burgeoning sovereignty. Indeed, the absence of any notion of imperial citizenship poses a challenge to the claim that the Empire constituted a unified political *or* social whole. Ornamental ties were of undoubted significance in perpetuating British imperial ties. But they were also just that, ornaments. Colonial societies were not simply simulacra of Britain, nor, in Sir Charles Dilke's oft-cited phrase, a 'Greater Britain';[6] their very antithesis to such conceptions explains the Empire's lack of concrete political and social unity.

The perennial challenge of Empire was *imperium et libertas* – how to maintain both structure and unity while also preserving the cherished ideal of freedom. This paradigm was especially clear in contemporary debates concerning intra-imperial immigration, the various processes by which individuals were able to move from imperial territory to imperial territory, and the degree to which each benefited from being an imperial subject. First, the contemporary fear of the 'yellow peril,' the apparent threat presented by emergent Asian states, particularly Japan, intensified wider concerns about anti-colonial forces within the Empire.[7] As such, one of Whitehall's goals in negotiating with the dominions regarding their immigration policies was to circumvent any actions which might create or intensify anti-colonial nationalist activity in the dependent Empire. In this view, Britain favoured imperial unity over liberty. Second, intra-imperial immigration existed alongside other forms of imperial movement, including what Madhavi Kale terms 'imperial labour reallocation,' the migration, both coerced and voluntary, of over 430,000 Indian men and women to the British Caribbean between 1837 and 1917,[8] and the temporary travels of imperial subjects throughout the Empire.[9]

R. A. Huttenback has argued that immigration legislation throughout the white Empire was explicitly discriminatory and prejudicial, reflecting the racist attitudes of imperial societies.[10] Such discriminatory acts were a means of pursuing consensus within colonial societies, seen by many imperial actors as the buttress of imperial unity. There was irony in the situation. On the one hand imperialists in Britain envisioned an imperial citizenship built upon a 'wider patriotism', a pan-imperial sentiment emphasizing imperial connections such as military service, and indeed the ornamentalism Cannadine details. On the other hand, imperialists in the colonies believed such a citizenship could best be achieved by building homogeneous, not inclusive, local societies. In consequence, non-whites (and sometimes simply non-Britons) were to be excluded in the colonies because they represented a challenge to cultural unity. The result, as David Northrup writes, was a 'clumsy blend of idealism and racism.'[11] In an age that viewed consensus and unity as virtues, inclusion and multi-culturalism were not yet achievable notions.

Indeed, issues of imperial citizenship and immigration vexed the Empire's political leaders, and were a persistent theme at the quadrennial Imperial Conferences held in London. Imperial immigration played a central role in debate during the 1911 Imperial Conference. The crisis of Chinese labour in South Africa, racial debates in British Columbia, and the articulation of a 'White Australia policy' had pushed the issue to the forefront, and it became a focal point of any discussion of imperial citizenship.[12] The debate was fractious because what was under discussion was really the cultural framework of Empire. Writing to a colleague that same year, Jebb criticized what he called the 'Chinese experiment,' the importation of Chinese labourers to work in the gold and diamond mines of South Africa, for upsetting the racial and cultural consensus which buttressed his idea of a Britannic alliance.[13] Jebb's attitude is notable here, for his conflation of 'race' and 'culture' represented a central conceptual stumbling-block in debates over imperial citizenship, one imperial ideologues were ultimately unable to transcend.

In part, such blinkered thinking was the result of the multi-valenced recent etymology of the terms 'race' and 'imperialism' in late Victorian Britain. Both terms acquired new connotations in the middle of the nineteenth century. In the eighteenth century, European discourse on race was dictated by the debate between monogenists and polygenists. Naturalists such as Carl Linnaeus and *philosophes* such as Montesquieu concluded that climate held the key to human variety, and thus investigators debated whether environmental evidence supported the existence of one or a number of human races.[14] Early nineteenth-century Romantic ideas of an organic national *essence*, in part drawn from philology, and the decline of orthodox Christian ideals of a common humanity reintroduced 'race' into European thought as a term to denote 'ineradicable' differences among the human species.[15] With the rise of social Darwinian thought, especially Gobineau's *Essai sur l'inégalité des races humaines*, linguistic differences were transposed into physical ones, and then conflated with ideas of *stock*. 'Race' now took on an increasingly discriminatory meaning, polluting the older genealogical sense of the word.[16] Contemporaries began to use the same term to refer to both cultural and biological 'differences'. In the era preceding the First World War, Britons increasingly used 'race' as a close synonym of 'culture,' denoting the values and pedigree of a *national* people, including themselves (e.g. the British 'race').[17] It was also used to explain and justify European imperial expansion. Thus 'race' had become both a descriptive and prescriptive term.

'Imperialist' in its modern context had been introduced in the 1870s as an epithet to describe the nature of the Second French Republic under Louis Napoleon. In Britain, Disraeli appropriated the word from his critics, who had employed it against him, and cemented it as Conservative policy in a speech in1872 at Crystal Palace. Differing from the older *imperium*, Latin for 'supreme power,' 'imperialism' was now used in the context of military or economic expansion. In its core meaning of conflict, 'imperialism' was thus a historically specific term, rather than an ideology. It referred to action, not policy. However, this meaning was soon confused with pan-Empire sentiment, varying across the British Empire, but generally signifying a desire to promote the unity, cohesion, and stability of Empire.[18] Thus a citizenship built on a 'wider patriotism' was thought to be best achieved by seeking homogeneity, not inclusion. Douglas Lorimer sees two dominant racial views in this period: that of supporters of the 'civilizing mission' who believed in assimilation; and the outlook of those who used more stridently racist language to call for exclusion or separation. These views were given greater currency through the expansion of the public realm made possible by advances in technology and journalism, and late Victorian racist ideology developed, in part, out of 'the contradictions between democracy at home and imperialism abroad.'[19] To this I would add the contradictions between democracy at home and democracy in the colonies, a contradiction brought out most clearly regarding the dominions.

These were the ideas to which Richard Jebb gave broad currency in the first decades of the twentieth century.

Richard Jebb's imperial career

Jebb spent the bulk of his career writing for the *Morning Post*, the press organ of the British officer class.[20] The nephew of the great classicist Sir Richard Claverhouse Jebb, the younger Jebb struggled during the early part of his career to emerge from the shadow of his famous uncle,[21] eventually becoming a prolific opinion-maker in his own right. Inspired by his uncle's interests, Jebb studied the Roman Empire at Eton and later at New College, Oxford. His affinity for the

Roman ideal of citizenship and imperial unity was to be the defining mission of his later life.[22] Jebb's public-school education also marked him as significant in another way: he was schooled in what J. A. Mangan has termed the 'games ethic,' that particular English public-school view of the world which bestowed unwavering confidence on the student, and which generated the cult of the amateur, respect above all else for honour, virtue and fair play, and, not least of all, a great cultural elitism. Such attitudes are seen as disingenuous in the post-colonial era; that was not the case for Jebb's generation. This *mentalité*, perhaps more so than guns, steamships, and capitalism, was the foundation of the Victorian and Edwardian Empire.

Emerging from this world, Jebb took it as his task to participate in Empire. In an age when spiritual certainties were being seriously questioned, the agnostic Jebb found his spiritual solace in imperialism. His tool would be the pen. He wrote several books on Empire, the most significant of which was his first work, *Studies in Colonial Nationalism* (1905). Inspired by his initial tour of the Empire, *Studies* presented a detailed exposition of Jebb's nascent conception of colonial nationalism, and, as it presented the growth of the settlement colonies in a favourable manner, it was understandably well received in imperial circles.[23] Jebb envisioned 'Five Free Nations, who are peers among their peers,'[24] pursuing their own goals under the common aegis of imperial patriotism, uniting when necessary 'separate limbs, trained to concerted action in emergency.'[25] There was an obvious paradox at the heart of this argument – how to maintain the *purpose* of Empire while simultaneously respecting colonial autonomy.

Though widely influential, Jebb made little money from the publication of *Studies*. Only 513 of the 750 printed were sold, and Jebb made just short of £31 for his labour.[26] He followed the success of *Studies* by embarking on a three-volume history of the Imperial Conferences up to 1911, only the first two of which, detailing the Conferences up to 1907, were published.[27] *The Britannic Question*, published in 1913, can be seen in certain ways as a continuation of *Studies*, as Jebb again outlined his belief in colonial nationalism, incorporating into his argument lessons drawn from the previous decade. He also directly challenged the reinvigorated federationist school, with specific reference to the Round Table's scheme of an imperial parliament, by advocating what he termed 'alliance.' Though well received among fellow-imperialists, the book, like *Studies*, was not a commercial success.[28] He was also hired to write under Fabian Ware at the *Morning Post*, providing commentary on the Empire, and penning many of the paper's leaders. The *Morning Post* was a Unionist paper, vigorously supporting tariff reform;[29] Jebb himself was a member of the Tariff Reform League. He continued to hold to this position after Bonar Law, faced with the alternative of splitting the party, was forced in 1913 to reject protection as Unionist policy.[30] Jebb's staunch protectionism explains why he faded from the political scene soon after this time.

Jebb lost his only bid at elected office. He stood as a radical Unionist in the January 1910 election for the seat of East Marylebone. His fervent support of tariff reform was not to the electorate's liking, and Jebb was defeated by a landslide.[31] Like Lord Alfred Milner and many other contemporaries, he came to view party politics as an inadequate means of addressing problems, though acquaintances such as Lady Selborne and Lionel Curtis, probably quite accurately, believed Jebb had simply taken his defeat too personally.[32] Jebb's influence, though, remained more widespread, in particular as a publicist, than his electoral appeal. Jebb's ideas were central to debates over Empire in the pre-war period. In addition to tariff reform, he championed separate dominion navies, imperial partnership, and the establishment of the Imperial Conference as a governing body. The last-named project was consistent with the programme advanced by Joseph Chamberlain. Jebb's was a voice espousing the commonalities within Empire. Like Curtis, he believed that the Empire's potential for creating peace was its great gift to the world.

Jebb was not, however, simply another parochial commentator, thrusting upon the world ideas conceived while contemplating maps in the study of the Royal Colonial Institute. Like Seeley and Dilke before him, he used the inheritance left him upon the death of his father to begin an extensive tour of the Empire at the age of 25 'to study imperial questions at first hand.'[33] From 1899 to 1901, Jebb visited Ceylon and all the settlement colonies, save those in South Africa where war had broken out. In 1906 he visited the South African colonies, now moving toward unification, and later toured the West Indies. Jebb set out with an orthodox belief in 'Greater England,' but returned an advocate of 'alliance.' He returned from these two voyages, moreover, with extensive diaries that provide an invaluable record of the Edwardian Empire.[34] Jebb's principal concerns during these tours were farming and colonial land use, interests shaped by his younger years at the family home at Ellesmere. However, after landing in Canada in 1899 he broadened his perspective to include the prevailing attitudes toward Empire of the various colonies he visited. Jebb also found time to indulge in more leisurely pursuits, including skating in Canada, and fishing and cycling in Australia and New Zealand.[35]

Jebb's success as a writer granted him access to London's club society. He was a member of the Royal Colonial Institute and the

Compatriots (fellow-members included Buchan and F. S. Oliver).[36] His association with the Compatriots is especially illustrative of his position on Empire. Founded in 1904, the group's *raison d'être* was imperial consolidation, its members believing that Britain had a responsibility to develop the Empire.[37] As such, they supported tariff reform and assisted emigration, and believed that imperial affairs should be guided by imperial experts such as themselves. Just as significantly, members viewed their contest with *laissez-faire* free traders as not just an economic crusade, but also a *moral* one.[38] Jebb enthusiastically supported all of these views. Jebb also gave speeches to numerous other imperial groups, including Oxford's Ralegh Club. Though opposed to the Round Table's pro-federation stance, Jebb enjoyed mostly congenial relations with the group's members, though he remained somewhat jealous of Curtis's greater public standing. For his part, Curtis thought Jebb a writer of the second order, though he liked him.[39]

After the publication of *The Britannic Question* in 1913, Jebb largely retired from public life: 'I feel that I must go out of the business, to which I have given nearly twenty years, for I have come rather abruptly to the end of my tether.'[40] This had as much to do with the declining fortunes of the intellectual freelance, increasingly superceded by specialists and technocrats, as it did with Jebb's ideas' lack of receptivity. Jebb withdrew from public life in 1914, contributing to the war effort as a musketry instructor in Britain, having been deemed unfit for active service. After a brief stint as a staff captain at GHQ in France in 1919, Jebb retired to the family house at Ellesmere, where he remained until his death in 1953, contributing works periodically on imperial matters and becoming active in local politics.[41] What was distinctive about Jebb, then, and what makes his opinions all the more valuable to the historian, is that he had a rare comparative knowledge of the Empire.

Jebb and colonial nationalism

Jebb was a colonial nationalist. What he observed while visiting the settlement colonies were societies that were British in nature, but pursuing widely different social and political agendas. They had 'begun the road from the colonial to the national status.'[42] Rather than seeing this as cause for concern, Jebb believed this evolution could become the very buttress of imperial unity: 'if diversified nationalism, within workable limits, is valued as a progressive element in human civilization, then the new policy [unity based upon colonial nationalism] is desirable as well as practicable.'[43] Perhaps Jebb's key observation was that this process was inevitable. Just as it was nearly impossible to remove settlers once they had cultivated territory, Jebb saw colonial nationalism as a permanent development. Britain's response, according to Jebb, should be to encourage, not reverse, such nationalism: 'it is easier to quicken the followers than to turn back the leaders.'[44]

He differentiated between colonialism, the despotic rule over dependencies marked by sentimental ties to the mother nation and the pursuit of selfish goals, on the one hand, and nationalism, the manhood of a state, characterized by self-respect, on the other.[45] Each colony was at a separate stage of development, and should be treated accordingly. As did many of his generation, Jebb divided the Empire into two: 'the Rulers, i.e. the autonomous partner nations, and the Ruled, i.e. the peoples of the Dependencies.'[46] Jebb's main critique of imperialism was that London treated all colonies the same, as if they were simply part of a 'Greater England.' To correct this mistake, Jebb pointed to the Imperial Conferences as an alternative means of governing the Empire. The first Conference had been convened in 1887 in response to fears that the colonies might be dragged into international conflicts. The Conference was periodically reconvened by London over the subsequent two decades, and by 1911 it included representatives of all the settlement colonies in addition to observers from India. The remaining crown colonies and dependencies were represented by the Colonial Office. Central to Jebb's support of the Conference system was the notion of *consensus*. For Jebb, 'the best Empire is that in which the average state government exhibits the highest sense of Imperial responsibility with the least measure of Imperial compulsion.'[47] The Conference was to be the *via media* for expressing colonial nationalism, promoting civic spirit, but also a body flexible enough to adapt to changing imperial circumstances, as alliances are by definition fluid. Jebb favoured the creation of an 'independent secretariat' – he is vague as to how this would be organized – to oversee the Conference process.[48] However organized, the Conference would succeed as a consultative executive body because it would be binding by consensus, not by dictate. (Further detail on the structure of imperial government proposed by Jebb can be found in Appendix 2.)

Jebb's ideas found support in various circles. The Unionist and jurist Sir Frederick Pollack would not go as far as *alliance*, but did support the notion of *partnership*. Pollack believed an imperial partnership would provide for security along the lines of Burke's view that the function of the state was the maintenance of security.[49] Pollock also saw the Imperial Conferences as a better means of preserving unity than moving towards federation or preserving the status quo. Jebb's ideas were echoed in the immediate post-war years by Leopold Amery, future Colonial Secretary in Stanley Baldwin's first government, who wrote in the *Morning Post* that 'the idea of the Empire as a possession of the United Kingdom '... is obsolete. We must conceive the Empire as a chain of British nations girding the world.' Amery also predicted a British Empire at the beginning of the twenty-first century with 200 million white members.[50] Jebb had other, less abstract, reasons for favouring the Imperial Conference system over more centralist models. It would provide a more sympathetic forum for the other two planks of his imperial vision, tariff reform and cooperative defence. Jebb, as has been noted, was a protectionist, but one by necessity rather than conviction. With Britain facing growing economic competition from Germany and the United States, tariff reform was seen as necessary if the nation was to retain its economic dominance. The colonies, he argued, were especially vulnerable as they were too small to compete on their own. Jebb discussed this issue in a series of letters with Leopold Amery in 1912. He suggested that delegates to the Imperial Conference should discuss measures 'to the effect that the policy of the British Government would recognize the unity of the Empire in the event of any attempt by any foreign country to penalise any British state, individually, on account of Imperial Preference.' This would be the economic equivalent of Palmerston's *civic Romanus sum*.[51] Jebb found some support for this view in the colonies. Speaking for the Empire, the *Brockville Times*, for example, printed the following protectionist rhyme:

> We don't want to Retaliate,
> But, by jingo, if we do.
> We've got the Pine
> We've got the Spruce
> And we've got the Nickel too![52]

The Britannic alliance would allow each colony to protect its own industries in raw and semi-produced goods while still enjoying access to the large imperial market. Alliance was also Jebb's answer to the vexing imperial question of defence: he argued that alliance would allow each colony to create its own navy, if so desired, with the understanding that defence resources would be pooled in wartime.

Jebb and imperial citizenship

Much of Jebb's writing is concerned with issues of imperial state formation. How did these issues affect people on an individual level? Jebb believed a common citizenship was key to maintaining the Britannic alliance. Arguing that competent imperial governance was beneficial to both governed and governor, he wrote that most imperialists will agree in regarding British rule in those countries as a noble task, hitherto credibly performed upon the whole, and one in which it is desirable that the Britannic peoples should take an active interest and a common pride, because it would tend to elevate the type of citizenship in their own countries by fostering the sense of a high public responsibility.[53]

As has been noted, the term 'citizen,' used at the state level, is a republican term. All those under the British flag were of course 'subjects.' British subjecthood was buttressed by the doctrine of personal allegiance to the crown, with subjects in turn entitled to protection under British law, particularly in relation to foreign powers. Imperial citizenship, as an extra-legal notion, rested in the main upon shared notions of loyalty, sentiment, and culture. Where the *de facto* status of 'citizen,' understood as one's relation to one's own state, became important politically concerning the Empire was in regard to intra-imperial issues. On this level of imperial citizenship, unlike that of imperial subjecthood, all were most certainly not equal.

There were frequent difficulties with regard to determining the status of persons born in territories with an ambivalent administrative relationship with Britain – such as the Transvaal before October 1899 or the many protectorates. The debates over imperial citizenship, especially in terms of attempts to cultivate and codify mutual interests, however, mainly concerned the interests of the dominions as against those of Britain (which had constitutional hegemony over the non-dominions, i.e. colonies without self-government). As such, issues of race were pushed to the periphery, and the definition of citizenship was contested in the main with reference to whites. As imperial idealists such as George Wrong argued, imperial unity was to be based not on race, which fostered isolationism, but rather on liberty, an internationalist virtue which encouraged temperance. British citizenship, Wrong suggested, made one a citizen of the world.[54]

Jebb agreed with this view, criticizing what he termed the 'tribalism' of, for example, Henri Bourassa or Paul Kruger, whose definitions of nationalism were based on ethnicity. He saw tribalism, 'the tendency to hate your neighbour in trying to be different from him,'[55] as the greatest threat to the Empire. Hence his virulent denouncement of Ulster nationalism, which was not *true* nationalism because it pointed to independence rather than unity. Jebb's antipathy toward Ireland was based upon the common contemporary view of England's Celtic cousins as troublemakers: 'I've no use for the Irish. All agitators and no work, 'all talk and nothing else.'[56]

Jebb believed there were two key elements in fostering a strong sense of imperial citizenship, the first of which was the cultivation of *democracy* – the 'motor of imperialism.'[57] Such cultivation took the form of imperial trusteeship – Britain's duty was one of tutelage, instructing other societies in self-government until they were ready to take that mantle for themselves. The principle of imperial trusteeship was based upon the conviction that while equality may be the professed goal, it was not achievable at the present. Speaking to the Royal Colonial Institute in 1906, Jebb stated that 'the theory that all British subjects have equal political rights has long been denied by palpable facts which Imperial statesmanship cannot hope to alter, and could not alter . . . without first destroying the national principle as the basis of Imperial organization.'[58] He looked with hope to a time when common values would create a truly integrated Empire: 'Can you imagine Commissioners of the India Civil Service holding examinations in Melbourne and Cape Town to fill the Service of a ViceRoy born in Quebec?' Given this dream, he was dutifully impressed to find, when visiting Ceylon, that its Supreme Court judges were chosen in part by judges from other colonies.[59]

Unlike Joseph Chamberlain, who neglected the sub-continent in his imperial pronouncements, India was key to Jebb's imperial vision, as it was to the Empire itself. As illustrated in Appendix 2, India was to be treated like the other dependencies regarding constitutional authority. Jebb did not believe India was 'ready' for self-government at the time, but he did recognize its special nature, and believed it should be granted equal status with the settlement colonies in the realm of tariff and immigration policy. This was a somewhat empty concession, though, as the volume of trade and immigration into India was dwarfed by the volume directed from India to the rest of the Empire.

Concomitant with the development of democracy in Jebb's vision was stability. Imperial sentiment must be encouraged through education, improved knowledge of other parts of the Empire (here travel was important), and mutual support. Jebb was duly impressed with the aid quickly given by New Zealand and the Australian colonies in 1900 to famine-struck India, and to Ottawa, hit by fire.[60] Imperial loyalty, finally, should be based in national self-respect. Jebb held these views earnestly. He was not unaware of the negative connotations 'trusteeship' had even at that time. While visiting the Canadian Prairies, he acknowledged that others held a view of imperialism as parasitical when remarking that the real 'white man's burden' was the mosquito.[61]

Jebb's vision of a Britannic alliance, an organic Empire which respected the growing autonomy of the colonies while maintaining, at least for the moment, a preeminent position for the metropolitan Government in London, did not come to pass. It conflicted both with the centralist position advanced by Curtis, and other Round Table members, and with the very colonial nationalism Jebb himself sought to accommodate. The tension between British and colonial interests confounded every imperial issue of the age. The most visible such issue was that of intra-imperial immigration, to which I now turn.

Conflicts concerning intra-imperial immigration

In a letter to the Canadian nationalist J. S. Ewart, Jebb responded to Ewart's contention that 'organic community is too ambiguous' by arguing that democratic communities 'are held together, I think, not by the Reserve force of a central government but by the systems they have evolved, or are evolving, of mutual aid-in-living.'[62] What Jebb meant by this term was a collection of communities which, while they recognized each other's autonomy, also shared a common identity, a common spirit, and a responsibility to aid in the maintenance of the collective. As he argued in speech in 1913, 'the best Empire is that in which the average state government exhibits the highest sense of Imperial responsibility with the least measure of Imperial compulsion.' A Britannic alliance, Jebb continued, was 'the exemplar of a new and higher order of international combination, based upon confidence instead of upon compulsion.'[63] However, while 'mutual-aid-in-living' was the ideal, the reality was rather less congenial, as conflicts over immigration proved imperial citizenship an impractical notion.

Imperial conflicts concerning immigration were at their heart conflicts between the liberal outlook of London and the desire of various colonies to set their own policies. The imperial metropole believed itself to be a largely homogeneous society. Despite the presence of Jewish and Irish immigrants, a small but vibrant black community, and both temporary and permanent visitors from the dependent Empire, especially India, Victorian Britons developed a national identity which stressed 'Britishness'.[64] Predicated on cultural markers such as language and historical memory, and underwritten by racialized assumptions about the existence of observable differences between ethnic groups, this national identity proved resistant to 'outsiders.'[65] While it disavowed a belief that differences between ethnic groups were permanent and indelible, Britons' sense of national identity stressed a 'deterministic cultural particularism' which nonetheless replicated many of the consequences of biological racism.[66]

Given that Britons' sense of homogeneity was predicated in part on the presence at home of marginalized minorities, the countervailing prevalence of liberal *laissez-faire* ideology and the absence of the dislocation often concomitant with mass immigration nonetheless gave rise to relatively liberal views in Britain concerning immigration and the movement of people.[67] Temporary measures had been enacted to monitor the arrival of aliens during the Napoleonic Wars, but these had fallen into disuse soon after Peterloo. A Naturalization Bill of 1870 gave the Home Secretary unfettered discretion over immigration in the name of the public good. The origin of the five years' residency requirement for naturalization applicants is to be found here. However, officially until the Aliens Act of 1905 and in practice not until the outbreak of war in 1914, aliens faced no substantial barriers to entry to the United Kingdom. In fact, between 1823 and 1906, when the Home Office began extraditing Germans of 'questionable' character, there was not one person lawfully removed from Britain.[68] The British Nationality and Status of Aliens Act (1914) gave the State greater powers to restrict 'unwanted' immigration, though the greatest protests over the Act were not about questions of naturalization but about its exclusion of married women.[69] Victorian notions of tolerance and inclusion were thus strong enough to contain periodic outbursts of xenophobia.[70] The Colonial Office believed similar liberal ideals should flourish throughout the Empire. Note that this did not mean that all people were to be treated equally; non-whites generally did not enjoy the same full citizenship rights as whites. Rather, it meant that all subjects should be given the opportunity to participate in Empire, whether as 'bearers of civilization' or as pupils. Thus, policies of exclusion were officially unacceptable to London.

That was the principle. The fact was, however, that the various settlement colonies wished to exclude certain groups, whether fellow-subjects, such as Indians, or foreigners, such as Chinese, for a variety of reasons. These reasons were often economic, though there were also cultural factors at work.[71] White governments in the English-speaking world, including the United States, were also pressed by unions and newspapers to view Asian cultures as oppressive and despotic, and as promoting servility. Many Australians, particularly in Queensland, and British Columbians feared that Asian immigrants would steal jobs by undercutting wages, and complained that such immigrants saved money to send back to their home countries, rather than investing it where they worked. There were also fears of 'cultural dilution'. As Lord Carrington, the Governor of New South Wales, noted in correspondence with Colonial Secretary Lord Knutsford in 1888, 'it is uniformally [sic] considered here that if these Colonies *are to be an offshoot of Britain*, they must be kept clear of Chinese immigration.'[72] It was not so much that Asians would 'dilute' the white population through intermarriage and miscegenation, though Jebb and others did voice concern over what was crudely termed 'leakage.' The concern, especially in Australia, was over the 'yellow peril.' Put simply, this was the fear that Asian peoples would overrun the Continent, pushing out the whites and terminating a British cultural presence in the Antipodes.[73] This fear was accentuated by Japan's 1905 victory in the Russo-Japanese War, though exclusionary policies predate that epochal event. Racist assumptions thus fed upon economic and cultural fears to create an environment particularly amenable to the implementation of discriminatory policies, and particularly resistant to an idea of imperial citizenship rooted in pan-imperial equality, even if only in principle.

Colonial decision-makers faced a paradox. On the one hand, British settlers generally desired a homogeneous state, as this was seen as the best guarantee of a consensual and united society. On the other hand, because these were new societies, human capital was of the utmost importance. As David Northrup has illustrated, the abolition of slavery in the British Empire in 1833 led to a large-scale increase in the recruitment of indentured labour, an easily available replacement pool of workers.[74] It had the added benefit of being inexpensive. Chinese labour thus proved indispensable, for example, in building the Canadian Pacific Railway, while in Australia Chinese labourers often worked land ahead of whites, thus expanding productive acreage. Hundreds of thousands of Indian migrant labourers also voyaged overseas, where they laboured on plantations, farms, or in mines. Between 1831 and 1920, almost 1.13 million Indians became indentured labourers throughout the British Empire, with 429,454 travelling to the British Caribbean, 451,786 to Mauritius, 152,184 to Natal, 56,000 to Fiji, and 39,437 to East Africa.[75]

While non-white indentured labourers had thus played an important role in constructing the physical infrastructure of the settlement colonies, the completion of most of these capital projects by the late-nineteenth century, combined with the emergence of new sources of low-wage labour (such as Southern Europeans in Canada), gave rise to more racialist attitudes and policies designed to discourage non-white labourers from either remaining or arriving in the settlement colonies. The conflict between economic need and discriminatory predilections was especially stark concerning Asians from within the Empire. The 1842 Treaty of Nanking, which signalled the end of the first Opium War with Manchu China, guaranteed the British extraterritorial rights in the treaty ports in exchange for the promise of protection, of person and property, to Chinese migrants throughout all British dominions.[76] A complete ban on Chinese immigrants by any dominion would, therefore, have been impossible. Furthermore, for those Asians residing within the Empire, such as the Chinese of Hong Kong and the Straits

Settlement or the Indians of the sub-continent, exclusionary legislation would have contravened implicit notions of imperial equality. The concept of imperial subjecthood, after all, guaranteed freedom of movement throughout the Empire.

As the Victorian age came to a close, however, the white colonies became more overt in their expressed anti-immigration sentiments. The most significant example was the so-called Natal Act. Passed by the Natal Government in 1897 with the aim of preventing the importation of 'coolie' labour from India, the Act reflected white settlers' unease at the fact that there were by the turn of the century more Asians living in the colony than whites (see Appendix 3). The Act defined a 'prohibited immigrant' as one who, 'when asked to do so by an officer shall fail to himself write out and sign, in the characters of any language of Europe, an application to the Colonial Secretary in the form set out in Schedule.'[77] It was transparently a test designed to exclude Asians. The new state of South Africa adopted these exclusionary principles when it passed the Immigrants Restriction Act (1913). A similar approach was taken in Australia and New Zealand, where legislation was passed linking the number of Chinese immigrants allowable per steamer to the tonnage carried, New Zealand setting the ratio at one immigrant to every 10 tons carried.[78] Australia and New Zealand also implemented diction tests. Canada opted for a passport system to control Indian immigration and a poll tax system to minimize the extent of Chinese immigration. The passport system, into which was incorporated the requirement that immigrants arrive by a continuous journey from their port of origin (almost impossible for Indian emigrants), was particularly contentious because it seemed to restrict the free intra-imperial movement to which Indians, as British subjects, were entitled. Radhika Viyas Mongia has termed the policy 'racial exclusion without naming race.'[79] This inconsistency in one of the putative principles of imperial citizenship – equal treatment of British subjects under the law – which imperial ideologues were trying to propagate was brought into the open in 1914, when the *Komagata Maru*, carrying 376 mostly Indian passengers, was turned away at Vancouver harbour.[80] The following year, Britain passed the Defence of India Act, requiring that all Indian migrants (save, notably, soldiers) have a passport, a tacit acknowledgment on London's part that the dominions had sovereignty over their own immigration policies.

The poll tax system also discriminated among British subjects. Though employers were able to subvert the intent of the system by paying the cost to maintain their labour supply, the measure nonetheless expressed the anti-immigration sentiment then evident in British

Columbia.[81] However, as E. B. Robertson realized, at 'each increase of the head tax a falling-off in Chinese immigration occurred until such time as the Chinese were in a position to accommodate themselves to the new arrangement.'[82] By 1914, in fact, the Canadian Government proposed eliminating the poll tax and entering into a bilateral agreement with the Chinese Government similar to the Lemieux Agreement with Japan, which set immigrant quotas.

One means of resolving the conflict between Britain and the dependencies over the nature of immigration was to create a uniform imperial naturalization policy. This issue was brought to the fore at the 1911 Imperial Conference. To rectify the situation, the delegates at the Conference attempted to establish a unitary system of imperial naturalization, thereby creating a greater sense of common imperial citizenship. Sir Wilfrid Laurier, the Canadian Premier, proffered his conviction that 'a man who was a British subject *anywhere*, should be a British subject *everywhere*.'[83] F. S. Malan, the South African Minister of Education, tentatively supported this view, but added the proviso that this should be 'subject to the local laws as regards the rights of British subjects.'[84] The stumbling-point, which New Zealand's Premier Sir Joseph Ward clearly expressed, was the desire to keep the question of naturalization separate from a definition of British citizenship. In short, the dominions, with Laurier slightly out of step, wanted to maintain the right to diversity of policy, though they might support a uniform position on intent. Winston Churchill, then Home Secretary and speaking for Britain on this issue, sympathized with the dominions' attitude, and supported the principle of colonial autonomy. However, he also appealed for a uniform policy, not the least because Britain wanted to maintain its own residency requirement, and thus wished the dominions to harmonize their standards with its own.

Malan quite succinctly voiced the dominions' reservations, expressing concern that under a uniform naturalization policy an individual might be able to circumvent local law by appealing to the imperial standard, thus challenging the principle of responsible government. This was a particular point of contention in Southern Africa, as well as in other regions such as British East Africa, where large numbers of indentured labourers had come for term contracts. These labourers sometimes had the option at the end of their terms to be naturalized in their new country. In colonies such as the former Natal this was an issue of concern for white subjects, who feared becoming politically and economically marginalized unless they were permitted to determine the terms of naturalization.

The delegates to the Conference ratified a resolution calling for a uniform naturalization law.[85] The compromise declared that Empire-wide naturalization should be granted to any alien, who, in addition to any other requirements:

- has resided not less than 5 years within the Empire, or has served the crown for 5 out of the last 8 years;
- is of good character and has an adequate knowledge of the English or other official language; and
- intends to reside within the Empire or serve under the crown.

The applicant also had to live in the country of application for one year. By 1912, all the dominions had agreed to the legislation, except for Canada which objected to a perceived violation of its autonomy regarding naturalization as dictated by Section 91 of the British North America Act.[86] While the measure would have allowed for a degree of colonial autonomy in terms of procedure, it was not ratified immediately by dominion legislatures, and once the First World War began the opportunity for such an initiative had passed.

Jebb was of mixed opinion concerning the harmonizing of naturalization temporarily achieved in 1912. While it went some way to resolving the contentious issue of imperial citizenship, and promised easier intra-imperial travel, the resolution also signalled a shift in imperial affairs. Jebb, as noted, had long seen the Imperial Conference as the ideal means of incorporating colonial nationalism into imperial governance, providing a platform upon which the colonies could participate as equals. Policy harmonization, however, was a temporary victory for the centralist school of thought. Though such harmonization might incorporate the dominions' concern with monitoring the *character* of immigrants, it standardized naturalization, and thus placed limits on the dominions' decision-making autonomy.

Furthermore, the defeat of Laurier's 'uniformity of effect, diversity of method' model – and Laurier's subsequent retreat from that position – dealt a crippling blow to Jebb's imperial vision. Centralism gained further adherents during the war years, beginning with the 1914 British Nationality and Status of Aliens Act, which gave the Home Secretary strong powers to restrict immigration. Fears of German spies and a palpable need for unity of action made Jebb's decentralized position seem weak and potentially dangerous in a time of imperial need. Despite the move towards standardization, however, confusion as to imperial citizenship and its possibilities persisted. The war, and its attendant heightening of claims of national identity, made clear a potential division between a person's *legal* and *birth* nationality. The dominions' participation in the war notwithstanding, imperial unanimity existed only in the abstract: in practical matters of consequence, local sentiment and colonial nationalism carried the day.

Colonial exclusion: a local or an imperial phenomenon?

The shift toward more overtly discriminatory legislation throughout the Empire was a manifestation of developing colonial nationalism. It is important not to reason thereby, however, that the Government at Westminster advanced a uniform and liberal imperial immigration policy as a counter to this development. The liberal outlook evinced by Whitehall did not reflect a progressive position on immigration *per se*; rather, it reflected the fact that Britain herself faced no large influx of non-white immigrants, and thus could study the issue in terms of imperial unity rather than of national interest. Indeed, in a speech to the 1897 Imperial Conference, Joseph Chamberlain declared: 'What I venture to think you [the colonies] have to deal with is the character of the immigration. It is not because a man is of a different colour to ourselves that he is necessarily an undesirable immigrant, but it is because he is dirty, or immoral, or he is a pauper, or he has some other objection.'[87]

Britain's *laissez-faire* attitude to Asian immigration was furthered by the Government's freedom to act unimpeded in this field in the dependent and protected territories of Empire. The example of India illustrates that freedom. The Interpretation Act of 1899 set out the citizenship status of Indians, reasserting the demarcation between non-European British subjects and British Protected Persons (BPPs).[88] Those born in the Native States of India were aliens for the purpose of British law, even though they had claims to British protection under the Foreign Jurisdiction Act.[89] Non-British individuals born in India, whether BPPs or non-European British subjects, could become European British subjects upon application. The naturalization process in India was covered by the Indian Naturalization Act of 1852 and its subsequent amendments,[90] the principles of which pertained to the other dependencies as well. However, neither BPPs nor non-European British subjects could become fully naturalized members of the Empire, thus precluding them from political equality with white subjects. This applied in particular to the case of India, where the difference between subject status and naturalization status allowed whites to rule as a caste unto themselves.[91]

Britain exercised a similar freedom in regard to protectorates. With the Foreign Jurisdiction Act of 1890, the British Government assumed the consent of all foreigners and British subjects living in territories where Britain had jurisdiction without territory.[92] This was directed specifically at protectorates where the British operated at arm's length, either through charter companies, such as in certain territories in

Southern Africa, or through alliances with native rulers, as in many Indian provinces. While the Act did not survive the transfer of authority over such territories from the Foreign Office to the Colonial Office under Chamberlain's tenure as Colonial Secretary, the principle was maintained. An 1894 Order in Council outlining charter company rule in Matabeleland, for instance, decreed that indigenous law would be maintained 'so far as that law is not repugnant to natural justice of morality, or to any Order made by Her Majesty in Council, or to any Proclamation or Ordinance.'[93] The principle of 'jurisdiction without territory' was subsequently invoked in *Staples* v. *The Queen*, an 1899 case in Matabeleland concerning an accused thief's appeal to be tried by jury rather than by judge, in accordance with Magna Carta. The Lords of the Judicial Committee upheld the Matabeleland judge's dismissal of the appeal, on the grounds that Matabeleland was for legal purposes a 'foreign state', as it had not been acquired by the 'cession or conquest of territory.'[94] Thus, while English law was not automatically applicable to a protectorate, indigenous law could be deemed repugnant 'to a statute or order applied in some special way to British subjects in the foreign country in question.'[95] Indigenous law was certainly overridden in the case of white immigration, and subsequently whites faced no barriers to travelling to any British protectorate – hence the ease with which men such as Lionel Curtis travelled to and from British India.

When a territory became part of the British Empire, as in the case of the Transvaal and the Orange Free State at the conclusion in 1902 of the Second South African War, its residents could apply for naturalization. Those not deemed subjects were not required to obtain a certificate of naturalization, a time-consuming procedure which verified the proper character of the applicant, but had only to take an oath of allegiance.[96] That oath could be taken outside the United Kingdom, in any dominion or in other imperial possessions in the case of officers in HM Service.[97] British subjects could be naturalized in states where Britain had extraterritorial rights, but this was not encouraged, as there was usually no applicable legislation in the specific extra-British jurisdiction to provide for this, and the individual would reside outside the bounds of protection guaranteed to a British subject. The case of one J. W. Hendricks illustrates this situation. Hendricks had worked in Siam in the early twentieth century and sought to become a naturalized subject of that country. Though Siam was an independent state ruled by a monarch, then Chulalongkorn (1868–1910), it was regarded by Britain as part of its 'informal Empire.'[98] The British judge to whom the case was referred assented to Hendricks's request, but cautioned that 'in a barbarous country a mere present of oxen to a chief might be enough: but in a sovereign state we should surely ask that there should be some general law on the point before Great Britain can consent to the loss of one of her subjects.'[99]

The dominions themselves were resistant to a *general law* on imperial immigration, as we have seen. Dominion subjects, however, also evinced feelings of loyalty to Britain, and thus sought to avoid direct confrontation. To circumvent any obvious affront to imperial equality, colonial governments framed exclusionary legislation in the language of 'control' and 'expedience.' The preamble to Canada's Act to Restrict and Regulate Chinese Immigration to Canada (1885), for instance, stated in part: 'it is expedient to make provision for restricting the number of Chinese immigrants coming into the Dominion, and to regulate such immigration.'[100] The exclusionary laws passed in most of the settlement colonies shared a common concern over the 'character of the immigration.' Again, Canada provides an instructive example in the following memorandum its Government sent to the British Foreign Office:

> No person shall be permitted to land in Canada who is feeble-minded, an idiot, an epileptic, or who has had an attack of insanity during the past five years, or one who is deaf or dumb, or dumb, blind, or infirm, unless he belongs to a family either accompanying him or already in Canada, who give satisfactory security that he will not become a public charge.
>
> No person shall be permitted to enter Canada suffering from a loathsome, infectious, or contagious disease, or one who is a pauper or destitute, or a professional beggar or vagrant, or a prostitute or person living off the prostitution of others, or one who has been convicted of a crime involving moral turpitude.[101]

Canada's efforts to regulate Chinese immigration centred in part around the definition of imperial citizenship, specifically whether Chinese were or were not imperial citizens. Once again colonial nationalism was at the fore. Mackenzie King, befitting his growing stature as a Canadian nationalist, left no doubt as to his position on this matter: 'that Canada should desire to restrict immigration from the Orient is regarded as natural, that Canada should remain a white man's country is believed to be not only desirable for economic and social reasons, but highly necessary on political and national grounds.'[102] In words which could easily have been Jebb's, King went on to argue that 'in matters which so vitally affect her own welfare, Canada is the best judge of the course to be adopted.'[103] However, King did acknowledge that Canada must keep in mind the obligations of common imperial citizenship in relation to Asian members of the Empire, and thus stopped short of supporting measures which explicitly rejected Asian British subjects' right to intra-imperial travel. In practice

Canadian autonomy won out. Chinese were treated as a bloc, with no division recognized between those who were British subjects and those who were aliens: 'under our Chinese Immigration Act all persons of Chinese origins are treated alike, irrespective of citizenship.' The emergence of colonial nationalism and the subsequent increase in stringent immigration legislation manifest both a hardening of attitudes towards non-Europeans, based on racialist attitudes, and a colonial anxiety about the nature of imperial citizenship, itself the result of the dichotomy between the idea of a 'wider patriotism' and the notion of state autonomy.

Jebb had become particularly interested in immigration questions as his first tour progressed, for he saw it as a key element in the economic development of the colonies. What is immediately evident from Jebb's diaries is that antipathy to immigrants, Asians in particular, varied from region to region. For instance, while visiting Toowoomba, Victoria, in 1900, he makes mention of a prominent store sign 'reassuring him' that 'No Chinamen, Blacks, or Assyrians are among our Customers.'[104] However, later in the month, while visiting Queensland, Jebb conversed with a sugar planter who supported Chinese immigration. The planter argued that his industry depended upon 'coloured' labour, and that Chinese farmers were often pioneers, who bought land from sugar companies to plant bananas, and in turn prepared the soil for later sugar crops, at which time the company would repurchase the land.[105] What Jebb perceived was that the immigration 'problem' was really one of localized attitude, resistance to Asian immigration out of proportion to the latter's size, which was numerically quite limited.

Nonetheless, Jebb was largely sympathetic to the exclusionary practices of the settlement colonies. His support for colonial nationalism led him to advocate restricting labour migration as necessary to colonial autonomy. He defined imperial citizenship with an eye to the practical, arguing that 'the nature of Imperial citizenship must be deduced from the purpose for which the Empire is thought to exist.'[106] That purpose was the development of 'civilization' based upon British culture, a development to be pursued along lines of union: 'Under alien skies their men, with ours, shall "drive the road and bridge the ford".'[107] He believed that Asian immigrants were often desired, whether as cheap labour, because they would perform tasks whites would not, or because they were pioneers in their willingness to improve infertile land.[108]

Nonetheless, Jebb also shared the prejudices of his era. Take, for instance, his comments in a paper given to the Royal Society of Arts in 1908. He argued that Australian opposition to Asian immigration was based upon the belief that the two races could not coexist, Asians being difficult to assimilate because they came from a 'mature civilization.' They would instead remain a 'helot' class of poor labourers.[109] Jebb believed that national autonomy and sentiment were the strengths of Empire. In a letter to the journalist (and later politician) Leopold Amery, Jebb argued that 'it is in the best interests of the Empire that there should be more uniformity throughout its centres and dependencies in the law of alien immigration exclusion.'[110] In Kuranda, Australia, while noting the racial animosity the locals exhibited toward Asian migrants, he unconsciously betrayed his own patronizing view of aliens in recording that he was unable to aid two Chinese puzzling over a train schedule: 'their pidgeon [sic] English wasn't sufficient – me no save.'[111]

As this evidence shows, Jebb believed that minority cultural differences, which ran against the majority desire for consensus and homogeneity, were the determining factor in generating immigration tensions, as illustrated by diary entries. He recorded the following after witnessing a Chinese costermonger being abused by a customer: 'The Chow lost his temper ... I never saw such an absolutely demoniacal face in my life – the flat yellow features livid with passion and the little devilish eyes blinking and quivering with tears ... Save us from the yellow devil if this fiend is an example.'[112] Jebb did go on to stress that his views on immigration were part of a broader imperial thesis, that of Britannic alliance, and that his strictures allowed for exceptions in certain cases. This was a necessary caveat, as Britain in 1902 entered into an alliance with Japan, a condition of which was a mutually acceptable immigration agreement which exempted Japanese from any exclusionary policies.[113]

There was an unbridgeable division between the imperial ideal of uniformity, expressed in the sentiment of *wider patriotism*, and the goals pursued by the autonomous colonies now giving birth to their own nationalism. The dominions were young nations which presumably would have welcomed settlers and labour from any available source. But, as H. H. Stevens, a British Columbia MP, put it in a speech in 1913, 'I do not want any one to go away with the idea that the Canadian has a very violent antipathy towards the Asian races, but 'it was a question that had to be dealt with if Canada was to remain a white man's country and develop *properly*.'[114] The same language was used by supporters of the 'White Australia' policy vociferously voiced by Henry Parkes, and later to become the central issue of the Australian conscription debate of 1916–17.[115] A professed desire for a homogeneous (read Anglo-Saxon) society and the pronouncement of racial antipathy, even if expressed by different voices, proved to be two sides of the same coin.

If racial exclusion was a localized phenomenon, not a systematic characteristic, of imperialism, it nonetheless permeated discussions of citizenship throughout the Empire. Values of consensus and a concomitant belief in the virtue of homogeneity, whether pronounced as in Australia or certain parts of the other colonies, or more muted, as in Canada's national policy, signified colonial priorities, and betrayed the ties, or lack thereof, between different parts of the Empire. At its heart, the issue of non-white exclusion was a conflict between notions of liberalism (the freedom to enter into relationships, the primacy of the individual), and incipient nationalism (the desire to create a communal society, based on consensus and homogeneity). This conflict came to a head over the issue of intra-imperial immigration, a phenomenon which challenged both the social and legal ideas of imperial citizenship put forth by imperial ideologues. Intra-imperial immigration was problematic. Ostensibly, a British subject could move freely throughout the Empire. After all, the age of the passport had not yet come, and borders were more permeable than they proved to be later in the twentieth century.[116] However, the variance in naturalization laws throughout the Empire challenged the principle of imperial unity and made it difficult to frame an official or unofficial notion of shared imperial citizenship.

The central conflict defining efforts to create an imperial citizenship was whether to value centrally legislated inclusion or local responsible government as the highest imperial virtue. Exclusion, after all, was often a democratic notion, insofar as it expressed the popular will of a state's people. This was especially the case in the settlement colonies where the franchise, with the exception of South Africa, was broader than in Britain. But democracy was also supposed to be the bearer of freedom and liberty, the buttress of trusteeship. What does one do when it instead breeds intolerance, an inclusive, rather than exclusive, communalism? This paradox emerged not just in relation to non-white immigration, but also in regard to the prospective citizenship of indigenous peoples. In some cases, such as in New Zealand where the Maori were accorded citizenship, democracy facilitated inclusion. In others, such as in Canada for indigenous peoples who did not assimilate or in Australia, where Aborigines were refused the franchise, it could facilitate exclusion.[117] Thus, the social identity of *whiteness* drove the political discourse of citizenship in the settlement colonies, with varying results. However, if one values state autonomy, as did Jebb and indeed most Britons of this era, it proved difficult to place qualifiers on this ideal in the form of pan-imperial legislation, especially in an age which had not yet conceived of a theory of universal human rights. One thing was clear: it would be Ottawa and Cape

Town, Auckland and Melbourne, not London, that dictated the composition and constitution of citizenship throughout the Empire.

In advancing a definition of imperial citizenship centred on the principle of unity, Richard Jebb was a man of his age. As we have seen, a unified Empire was the common goal of Curtis, Buchan, and White, as different as their conceptions of Empire may have been. Where Jebb differed from his peers was in his notion of a Britannic alliance, which incorporated the key idea of colonial nationalism. He was one of the first Britons to recognize the new national identities which were then emerging, and he accorded these identities a central place in his idea of Empire. Jebb believed a new citizenship could be fashioned which incorporated colonial nationalism through the social bonds of mutual aid-in-living. As Andrew Thompson has illustrated in the case of South Africa, such social bonds – family ties, allegiance to the monarch, notions of shared cultural or linguistic ties, an ideological commitment either to racial or liberal values (or both) – can be described as 'loyalism,'[118] and Jebb was correct to surmise that they could persist alongside greater dominion political autonomy. For Jebb, this autonomy would be recognized through the Imperial Conference, an institution he believed ideal for mediating the various and sometimes conflicting desires of the Empire's constituent polities. Even India, Jebb forecast, would someday soon have an equal place at the Conference.

It was in regard to India, though, and more broadly in regard to the dependent Empire, that Jebb's notion of a common imperial citizenship codified in a Britannic alliance ran aground. Like many of his contemporaries, Jebb held at best ambivalent views on race, and the idea of a common imperial citizenship ran afoul of the competing views on imperial naturalization and intra-imperial immigration held by Britain and the dominions. The failure to agree upon a common imperial naturalization policy precluded the creation of the sense of 'wider patriotism,' built upon mutual aid-in-living, that Jebb believed essential in producing imperial amity.

The failure to harmonize naturalization policies, and the failure to create a unified system of citizenship in general, however, perhaps paradoxically worked to sustain the Empire, as it allowed the settlement colonies the leeway to pursue their individual goals, while keeping alive the desire for imperial unity. Thus the idea of Empire – imbued as it was with ambiguous and sentimentalized notions of service, duty, and cooperation – could persist in an idealized state without being compromised, at least fatally, by circumstance. The elites with whom David Cannadine is concerned in *Ornamentalism* continued to attend royal tours and collect imperial ribbons, while the continental drift of colonial nationalism advanced unimpeded and inexorably.

Richard Jebb sounded this note in a letter to J. L. Garvin, editor of the *Pall Mall Gazette*, in 1913:

> I have ... grown out of the notion that there is any possibility of winning the present generation of Englishmen to the conception of the Brittanic Commonwealth which I again put forward in the book [*The Britannic Question*] but I am still sanguine that the action of inaction of the Dominions may keep the door open to this ideal and eventually consummate it.[119]

The conceptual fluidity of imperial citizenship ensured that imperial bonds between individual and crown, periphery and metropole, were largely self-defined, ultimately providing colonial voices with the language to contest imperial rule, and perhaps explaining why the transition from Empire to Commonwealth was relatively more peaceful than were the decolonization processes of other European empires.

Notes

1. Curtis's dyarchy proposal was a guiding influence in the formation of the Montagu–Chelmsford reforms of 1919. Curtis himself, however, never held elected office, though he made a successful and long career as an advisor to political leaders. Buchan proved ill-suited to elected office.
2. R. Jebb, *The Imperial Conferences: A History and Study in Two Volumes* (London, 1911); *The Britannic Alliance: A Survey of Alternatives* (London, 1913); *The Empire in Eclipse* (London, 1926).
3. David Cannadine, *Ornamentalism: How the British Saw Their Empire* (Oxford, 2001), p. xix.
4. Ibid., p. 9.
5. On the Imperial Conferences, see *The Colonial and Imperial Conferences from 1887 to 1937*, ed. Maurice Olivier (Ottawa, 1954), vols 1 and 2; and John Kendle, *The Colonial and Imperial Conferences* (London, 1967).
6. Sir Charles Dilke, *Greater Britain* (London, 1868).
7. On the 'yellow peril' and the evolution of race as a political issue in the early twentieth century, see Howard Winant, *The World Is a Ghetto* (New York, 2001). On early forms of anti-colonialism and nationalism in the Empire, see for example John R. McLane, *Indian Nationalism and the Early Congress* (Princeton, NJ, 1977).
8. Madhavi Kale, *Fragments of Empire: Capital, Slavery, and Indian Indentured Labour Migration in the British Caribbean* (Philadelphia, PA, 1998), pp. 5, 1; see also Hugh Tinker, *A New System of Slavery: The Export of Indian Labour Overseas, 1830–1920* (London, 1974); and David Northrup, *Indentured Labour in the Age of Imperialism, 1834–1922* (Cambridge, 1995).
9. For an excellent study of imperial travel, see Angela Woollacott, *To Try Her Fortune in London: Australian Women, Colonialism, and Modernity* (New York, 2001).
10. See R. A. Huttenback, 'No Strangers within the Gates: Attitudes and Policies towards the Non-White Residents of the British Empire of Settlement,' *JICH*, 1 (summer 1974), pp. 271–301, and *Racism and Empire* (Ithaca, NY, 1976).

11 Northrup, *Indentured Labour*, p. 146.
12 For an introduction to these topics see Alan Jeeves, 'Control of Migratory Labour in the South African Gold Mines in the Era of Kruger and Milner,' *Journal of Southern Africa Studies*, 2 (1975), pp. 3–29; Kay Anderson, *Vancouver's Chinatown* (Montreal, 1991); Patricia Roy, *A White Man's Province: British Columbia Politicians and Chinese and Japanese Immigrants, 1858–1914* (Vancouver, 1989); Hilda Glyn-Ward, *The Writing on the Wall: Chinese-Japanese Immigration to BC, 1920* (Toronto, 1974); and Ivan Krisjansen, 'Australian Orientalism and Liberal Governance: Asian Labour in South Australia and the Northern Territory, 1890s,' *Labour History*, 80 (2001), pp. 173–90.
13 Richard Jebb–Sir Charles Bruce, 4 March 1912, Jebb Papers, Institute of Commonwealth Studies (ICS), University of London. Jebb's correspondence is filed by date in Jebb Papers, File A.
14 H. F. Augstein, 'Introduction,' in Augstein (ed.) *Race: The Origins of an Idea, 1760–1850* (Bristol, 1996), pp. xi–xxi.
15 Ibid., xxi–xxiii; and Thomas Metcalfe, *Ideologies of the Raj* (Cambridge, 1997), pp. 14–15.
16 See Raymond Williams, *Keywords* (Oxford, 1983 [1976]), pp. 248–50, for the full etymology of the term 'racial.' The word was first introduced to English in the seventeenth century from the French *race* and the Italian *razza*. It had several early meanings: '(i) offspring in the sense of a line of descent'; '(ii) a kind of species or plant'; '(iii) general classification, as in "the human race"'; and '(iv) a group of human beings in extension and projection from sense (i).' Williams stresses the ambiguity that arose when the term began to be used to describe differences within a species, specifically *homo sapiens*. On Gobineau, see Michael Biddiss, *Father of Racist Ideology: The Social and Political Thought of the Count Gobineau* (New York, 1970).
17 See Paul Rich, *Race and Empire in British Politics* (Cambridge, 1986), p. 7.
18 See Williams, *Keywords*, pp. 159–60; and R. Koebner and H. D. Schmidt, *Imperialism: The Story and Significance of a Political Word* (Cambridge, 1964). For the varied use of the term 'imperialism' for imperial unity, see for instance Carl Berger, *The Sense of Power* (Toronto, 1970).
19 Douglas Lorimer, 'Race, Science and Culture,' in Shearer West (ed.) *The Victorians and Race* (Aldershot, 1996), pp. 22–3.
20 On the history of the *Morning Post* in this era, see Keith Wilson, *A Study in the History and Politics of The Morning Post, 1905–1926* (Lewiston, 1990).
21 Even after the elder Jebb died in 1906, Richard had to write to the *Halifax Chronicle* to inform that paper that a leader of his which it had picked up from *The Morning Post* had not been written by his uncle: Jebb–*Halifax Chronicle*, December 14 1906, Jebb Papers, A, ICS.
22 On Roman citizenship, see the relevant sections of chapter 1 of this book, as well as Norman Vance, *The Victorians and Ancient Rome* (Cambridge, MA, 1997).
23 *The Times* (26 May 1905), wrote that 'Mr. Jebb's book has no small originality'; the *Spectator*, 94, 17 June 1905, p. 897, remarked that *Studies* 'is essentially a work which will be welcomed, not derided in Canada and Australasia. And that is to say no small thing of its merits, and of the successes with which its author has achieved his object'; and the *Academy*, 68, 29 April 1905, p. 469, judged that the book 'should be studied by all who wish to understand the trend of colonial aspirations, whether they agree with them or not.'
24 Ibid., p. 335.
25 Jebb–C. H. Cahan, 3 April 1912, Jebb Papers.
26 For the publication history of *Studies in Colonial Nationalism* see Deryck Schreuder, 'Richard Jebb, 1898–1905,' in Eddy and Schreuder (ed.) *The Rise of Colonial Nationalism*, p. 87. *Studies* sold for 12s 6d; Jebb Papers, introductory material, ICS.
27 Jebb, *The Imperial Conference*; a manuscript edition of the proposed third volume, detailing the conference of 1911, is located in the Jebb Papers.

28 *The Britannic Question* sold only 369 copies, out of an initial press run of 600, in its first two months, and quickly went out of print: see Longman Green–Jebb, 23 June 1913, Jebb Papers, A, ICS.
29 See Wilson and Stephen Koss, *The Rise and Fall of the Political Press in Britain* (London, 1981), vol. 1.
30 Jebb–Austen Chamberlain, 6 December, 1919 (misdated: the year should be 1910), Jebb Papers, A, ICS. On tariff reform and Bonar Law's decision, see J. H. Grainger, 'Between Balfour and Baldwin,' in Donald Southgate (ed.) *The Conservative Leadership, 1832–1932* (London, 1974), pp. 174–5.
31 The defeat was particularly galling for Jebb because East Marylebone was a staunch Conservative constituency (Lord Robert Cecil was the MP before moving to Blackburn). In the general elections spanning the period 1885 to December 1910, 63% of East Marylebone voters had supported a Conservative–Unionist candidate. In January 1910, Jebb ran as a representative of the Imperial Democratic League, a radical tariff reform branch of the Unionist Party sponsored in part by Fabian Ware, then editor or the *Morning Post* and Jebb's boss. The group sought to force Balfour's hand regarding tariff reform by electing a number of its members. They failed. In East Marylebone, Jebb took votes away from the other Unionist candidate, allowing a Liberal to win the seat with a minority poll: see Henry Pelling, *Social Geography of British Elections, 1885–1910* (London, 1967); Wilson, *A Study in the History and Politics of the Morning Post*, pp. 153–5; and the *Evening Standard*, 23 November 1910.
32 'He [Jebb] is still as charming and friendly as ever, but five years of journalism has perverted his judgement and the election fiasco [Jebb's defeat] has poisoned his mind': Lady Selborne–Richard Feetham, 27 April 1911, MSS Curtis Papers 1/68, Bodleian Library, Oxford University.
33 Deryck Schreuder, 'Richard Jebb 1898–1905,' in John Eddy and Deryck Schreuder (eds) *The Rise of Colonial Nationalism* (Sydney, 1988), p. 65.
34 The diaries are especially valuable for studying the gestation of *Studies in Colonial Nationalism*. Jebb did not keep up a substantial correspondence until 1906, when the publication of *Studies* and his position at the *Morning Post* secured his status as an imperial commentator.
35 Diary, 2 March, 1899, Jebb Papers, B/2/1, ICS. His diaries are notable for the almost complete absence of personal matters. Even his wedding – to Margaret Ethel of Settle, Yorkshire, in Yokohama, Japan – receives little mention.
36 Schreuder, 'Richard Jebb 1898–1905,' p. 79.
37 A. Milner, *Constructive Imperialism: Five Speeches* (London, 1908), pp. 42–4; Leopold Amery, *The Fundamental Fallacies of Free Trade: Four Addresses on the Logical Groundwork of the Free Trade Theory* (London, 1908), p. 40; see also the essays included in *Compatriots' Club Lectures: First Series* (London, 1905).
38 See Andrew S. Thompson, *Imperial Britain: The Empire in British Politics, 1880–1932* (Harlow, Essex, 2000), p. 87. Thompson's work is especially useful for the student of Edwardian conservative pressure groups, detailing the activities of the Tariff Reform League, the Navy League, and the Emigration Committee of the Royal Colonial Institute, in addition to the Compatriots.
39 Jebb was close to Richard Feetham, a copy of whose Witwatersand convocation speech, from 31 March 1951, is preserved in Jebb's Papers (Q/2/10), testament to a long acquaintance. Curtis invited Jebb to speak at the Ralegh Club, and often provided Jebb with copies of lecture series he gave while Beit Lecturer at Oxford (Curtis–Jebb, 14 April 1913, Jebb Papers, A, ICS). Curtis could also be condescending to Jebb, though, indicative of the former's elitist bent. Curtis admonished Jebb for accusing him of orthodoxy (Curtis–Jebb, 17 April 1913, Jebb Papers, A, ICS), and complained, both privately and directly to Jebb, that Jebb misrepresented the Round Table's scheme in public. He also termed Jebb's work 'primitive': MSS Curtis Papers, 142/101. Lady Selborne was less kind, terming Jebb 'an extraordinarily pig-headed as well as puzzle-headed man': MSS Curtis Papers 1/68.
40 Jebb–Lionel Curtis, 15 April 1913, Jebb Papers, A, ICS.

41 *The Times*, 1 July 1953; C. S. Nicholls (ed.) *Dictionary of National Biograph: Missing Persons* (Oxford, 1993), pp. 348–49.
42 R. Jebb, *Studies in Colonial Nationalism* (London, 1905), pp. ix.
43 Ibid., p. viii.
44 Ibid.
45 Jebb, 'The Imperial Ideal,' unpublished MS, pp. 11–12.
46 R. Jebb, 'Notes on Imperial Organization,' *Royal Colonial Institute, Proceedings*, 38 (1906–7), p. 18.
47 Richard Jebb, 'Britannic Alliance,' MS, p. 1, Jebb Papers, G/7, ICS.
48 Jebb–Sir Bevan Edwards, 9 July 1910, Jebb Papers, A, ICS.
49 See Sir Frederick Pollock–Royal Colonial Institute, 13 November 1906, Jebb Papers, A, ICS.
50 *Morning Post*, 12 November 1919.
51 See Jebb–Amery, 20 May 1912, Jebb Papers, A, ICS.
52 Diary, 13 March 1899, Jebb Papers, B/2/1 81, ICS.
53 R. Jebb, *The Britannic Question* (London, 1913), p. 194.
54 George Wrong, 'Growth of Nationalism in the British Empire,' *American Historical Review*, 22 (1916–17), p. 51.
55 Jebb–Lord Grey, 24 March 1910, Jebb Papers, A, ICS.
56 Diary, 10 May 1899, Jebb Papers, B/2/2, ICS.
57 Jebb, 'The Imperial Ideal,' MS, p. 1, Jebb Papers, G/23/37, ICS.
58 Jebb, 'Notes on Imperial Organization,' pp. 18–19.
59 Jebb, 'Imperial Ideal,' p. 34; Diary, 27 November 1900, Jebb Papers, B/2/28, ICS.
60 Diary, 6 May 1900, Jebb Papers, B/2/20, ICS. Jebb termed this 'Charitable Imperialism.'
61 Diary, 9 June 1899, Jebb Papers B/2/2, ICS.
62 Richard Jebb–J. S. Ewart, 6 February 1913, Jebb Papers, A, ICS.
63 Jebb, 'Britannic Alliance,' MS of speech to the G. E. Club, 25 November 1913, Jebb Papers, G/23/5, ICS.
64 William D. Rubinstein, *A History of the Jews in the English-Speaking World: Great Britain* (Basingstoke and London, 1996). On immigrant communities in Britain in the late nineteenth and early twentieth centuries, see Jeffrey Green, *Black Edwardians* (London, 1998), and Shompa Lahiri, *Indians in Britain* (London, 2000).
65 This sense of national inclusivity sometimes resulted in overt acts of intolerance, though the marginalization of ethnic groups remained a rather more covert phenomenon. On examples of 'anti-alienism' in Britain, see Panikos Panayi (ed.) *Racial Violence in Britain 1840–1950* (Leicester and London, 1993).
66 On the interrelationship between 'racialism' and 'racism,' see George Fredrickson, *Racism: A Short History* (Princeton, NJ, 2002), pp. 8, 6–7.
67 Kathleen Paul details how the interplay between an explicit belief in liberty and tolerance and an implicit belief in a 'British' national identity helped define Britain's increasingly circumscribed immigration policies in the aftermath of the 1948 British Nationality Act: see Paul, *Whitewashing Britain: Race and Citizenship in the Postwar Era* (Ithaca, NY, 1997).
68 Vaughn Bevan, *The Development of British Immigration Law* (London, 1986), p. 64.
69 Pat Thane, 'The British Imperial State and National Identities,' in Billie Melman (ed.) *Borderlines: Genders and Identities in War and Peace, 1870–1930* (New York, 1998), pp. 39–40.
70 Exceptions to this general outlook include the strained reception of Russian Jews in the 1880s and 1890s, and the growing suspicion of German immigrants in the two decades before the First World War.
71 I draw here on the work of Laura Tabili, who argues that racial conflicts in interwar Britain were derived from material factors – colonial labour and struggles over political power (influenced by domestic social relations) – and thus were not epiphenomenal, but historically contingent: Tabili, *'We Ask for British Justice': Workers and Racial Difference in Late Imperial Britain* (Ithaca, NY, 1994), p. 181.

72 *Correspondence relating to Chinese Immigration into the Australian Colonies, 1888*, file folder 63, 19 April 1888, p. 33 (italics added), National Archives of Canada (NAC), RG 25 F4, vol. 1004.
73 On Chinese emigration to Australia, see C. Y. Choi, *Chinese Migration and Settlement in Australia* (Sydney, 1975).
74 Northrup, *Indentured Labour*, pp. 17–29.
75 Ibid., Table A2, pp. 159–60. Almost 200,000 Indians also worked as indentured labourers in other European colonies.
76 Ann Dummet and Andrew Nicol, *Subjects, Citizens, Aliens and Others* (London, 1990), p. 117. The term 'dominion' was the legal term for any British territory.
77 P. E. Lewan, Appendix, *Journal of the Royal Society of Arts*, 24 (April 1908); see also *Memorandum respecting the Immigration of Persons into British Dominions, with special reference to Chinese Immigrants*, March 1907, TNA PRO FO 881/8893. This document provides a summary of relevant legislation for Consular Officers' use in reviewing Chinese applications for entry into the Empire.
78 *Memorandum respecting the Immigration of Persons into British Dominions*, p. 13.
79 Radhika Viyas Mongia, 'A History of the Passport,' in Antoinette Burton (ed.) *After the Imperial Turn: Thinking With and Through the Nation* (Durham, NC, 2003), p. 208.
80 See 'Baba Gurdit Singh's Account of the Komagata Maru Incident,' NAC, Reel K-79 (former reference: MG55/30–No.159); and Hugh Johnston, *The Voyage of the Komagata Maru: The Sikh Challenge to Canada's Colour Barrier* (New Delhi, 1979).
81 See Mackenzie King, *Report of the Royal Commission Appointed to Inquire into the Methods by which Oriental Labourers Have Been Induced to Come to Canada* (Ottawa, 1908), pp. 69–71.
82 E. B. Robertson–J. G. Mitchell, 29 June 1914, NAC, RG 76 C-4784, part 3.
83 Conference Proceedings for the 1911 Imperial Conference, *The Colonial and Imperial Conferences from 1887 to 1937*, vol. 2: *Imperial Conferences Part I*, ed. Maurice Olivier (Ottawa, 1954), p. 86.
84 Ibid.
85 See Jebb, *The Imperial Conference*, vol. 2, pp. 304–6; and Jebb, 'Naturalisation,' pp. 11–12, 18, 20–2.
86 'Naturalisation,' pp. 20–2.
87 Report of the Proceedings of the Colonial Conference, C. 5091, p. 14, quoted in R. Jebb, *The Imperial Conference*, vol. 1 (London: 1911), p. 329.
88 For definitions of the varieties of citizenship status in India, see chapter 1, this book.
89 'Nationality of K. S. Ranjitsinghi: Memo on Nationality Status of Persons Born in India, and on Question of Naturalisation of Such', TNA PRO HO 144/462/B32357.
90 Indian Naturalization Act, XXX of 1852, 16 July 1852 (amended in 1876), copy included in TNA PRO HO 144/450/B30711. The most significant sections were as follows: 1 Any person living under the government of the East India Company (or, after 1876 under the sovereignty of Queen Victoria, when she assumed the title of Empress of India) could apply for naturalization. 2 Applicants must supply vital statistics and time of residence. 7 Once approved, the memorialist was accepted as if he or she had been natural-born, with all benefits therein (this differed from the dominions, where naturalized subjects were precluded from voting or holding political office, and made it easier for the British to absorb people from the various principalities and territories they loosely controlled). 12 In India, 'government' meant whoever was commissioned to head a territory, so it could be either the British themselves, or the local Indian ruler in the principalities allied to Britain. The memorialist would finally be required to pledge an oath of allegiance.
91 This separation of subject status also buttressed the case for maintaining the principle of the 'two Empires' in regard to responsible government and

intra-imperial cooperation. Witness, for example, Lionel Curtis's argument in *The Problems of the Commonwealth* (London, 1916) for excluding India from direct representation in any imperial parliament. Also note that while an Indian delegation was invited to the 1911 Imperial Conference in London, it was as an observer, not as a full delegate.

92 See Peter Burroughs, 'Institutions of Empire,' in A. Porter (ed.) *Oxford History of the British Empire*, vol. 3: *The Nineteenth Century*, pp. 194–5; and the Foreign Jurisdiction Act, 53 & 54 Victoria.
93 'Matabeleland Order in Council, 1894,' TNA PRO HO 144/462/B32357 65588.
94 *Staples v. The Queen*, pp. 4, 3, TNA PRO HO 144/462/B32357 655888.
95 Ibid.
96 See the case of Miss Elsa Marguerite Orbanowska, 'Naturalization by Virtue of Annexation,' 3 February 1908, TNA PRO HO 144/686/103210.
97 'Re: Naturalization–C. Kristonson,' TNA PRO HO 144/462/B20366.
98 Siam preserved its independence by negotiating a series of treaties with Western governments, beginning with Great Britain. In 1855, King Mongkut agreed to reduce tariffs on British imports, allowed British subjects to buy land and open businesses in Siam, and granted Britain extra-territorial jurisdiction over its subjects. Britain, in turn, refrained from absorbing Siam into its Empire, wishing to preserve it as a buffer state between India and French Cochin China. British advisors also provided Mongkut and then Chulalongkorn with guidance, especially in financial affairs. The 1904 *entente cordiale* between Britain and France eliminated colonial tensions in the region, and in 1909 Britain signed a treaty with Siam, in which extra-territorial jurisdiction was renounced in exchange for the exclusive right to finance the building of railways in the north of the country: see A. J. Stockwell, 'Expansion in South-East Asia,' in Andrew Porter (ed.) *Oxford History of the British Empire*, vol. 3: *The Nineteenth Century* (Oxford, 2001), pp. 380–1, 387–9.
99 Memorandum, Judge Skinner Turner, 9 March 1906, TNA PRO HO 144/823/140752.
100 Act (48–49 Victoria, c. 71), 20 July 1885, NAC, RG 25, F4, vol. 1004.
101 Memorandum, pp. 6–7, TNA PRO FO 881/8893.
102 King, *Immigration to Canada from the Orient and Immigration from India in Particular*, NAC, RG 25, F4, vol. 1004, p. 7.
103 Ibid. King had corresponded with Jebb in the years before the First World War, and was sympathetic to Jebb's ideas: see R. MacGregor Dawson, *William Lyon Mackenzie King: A Political Biography* (Toronto, 1958), p. 78. Even in later life, King found *Studies in Colonial Nationalism* a useful guide to imperial politics: see Jack Granatstein, *How Britain's Weaknesses Forced Canada into the Arms of the United States* (Toronto, 1989), p. 51.
104 Diary, August 3 1900, Jebb Papers, B/2/25, ICS.
105 Ibid., August 22 1900, Jebb Papers, B/2/26, ICS.
106 Jebb, 'Problem of Asian Immigration,' *JRSA*, 56 (1908), p. 595.
107 Jebb, *Studies in Colonial Nationalism*, p. 336.
108 Jebb gathered such opinions in places as remote as Thursday Island in the East Indies and as central as Vancouver: see for instance Diary, 2 May 1899, Jebb Papers, B/2/1, and 10 September 1900, Jebb Papers, B/2/27.
109 Jebb, 'Problem of Asian Immigration,' pp. 587–8.
110 Jebb–Amery, 13 May 1912, Jebb Papers, A, ICS.
111 Diary, 24 August 1900, Jebb Papers, B/2/26, ICS.
112 Ibid., August 24 1900, Jebb Papers, B/2/26. It should be noted that Jebb was only 26 years old at the time, and his views matured as he gained more experience. Whether he genuinely moderated his view on racial differences or simply came to express himself in a more sophisticated manner is difficult to ascertain.
113 The 1902 alliance had been preceded in 1894 by an Anglo-Japanese Commercial Treaty, which granted nationals of each country freedom of entry and movement in the other's territory. In an often overlooked aspect of the agreement, Britain

offered to negotiate a special exemption for any colony that had reservations about Asian immigration but still wished to adhere to the Treaty. Queensland was the only colony which opted for this in 1894, and only did so in light of its need for labour. Canada joined the Treaty in 1906 seeking to advance trade with Japan, provoking anti-Japanese riots in British Columbia. The Antipodean colonies (with the exception of Queensland) never became signatories, as they believed the 'yellow peril' to be real.

114 *Vernon News*, 9 October 1913; emphasis added.
115 Avner Offer, '"Pacific Rim" Societies: Asian Labour and White Nationalism,' in Eddy and Schreuder (eds) *The Rise of Colonial Nationalism*, p. 241.
116 Passport Correspondence, 9 December 1901, TNA PRO FO 613/2. The National Registry and its initiation of the ID card during the First World War proves something of an exception, though this measure applied only to the United Kingdom, and was confined to wartime: see Jon Agar, 'Modern Horrors: British Identity and Identity Cards,' in Jane Caplan and John Torpey (eds) *Documenting Individual Identity: The Development of State Practices Since the French Revolution* (Princeton, NJ, 2001). My thanks to Jon Agar for providing me with a copy of this essay.
117 Julie Evans, Patricia Grimshaw, David Philips, and Shurlee Swain, *Equal Subjects, Unequal Rights: Indigenous Peoples in British Settler Colonies, 1830s–1910* (Manchester, 2003), p. 9.
118 Andrew Thompson, 'The Languages of Loyalism,' *English Historical Review*, 138, 477 (June 2003), pp. 620–1.
119 Jebb–J. L. Garvin, May 28 1913, Jebb Papers, A, ICS.

CHAPTER SIX

'Practical imperialism': Thomas Sedgwick and imperial emigration

> The Colonies offer happy and prosperous homes to thousands who are unable to gain a livelihood within the narrow limits of these islands, owing to the pressure of over-population and consequent over-competition. In transplanting them to our own Colonies instead of to foreign lands, they retain their privileges as citizens of this great Empire, and live under the same flag and the same Sovereign.[1]
> (Edward, Prince of Wales, 1889)

So spoke the future King Edward VII, then the Prince of Wales, in a speech delivered in 1889 to the Royal Colonial Institute (RCI) on the subject of imperial emigration. Edward expressed the conviction, shared by many of his countrymen, that the Empire was, in Sir Charles Dilke's famous phrase, a 'Greater Britain.' Its people shared British culture and heritage, common bonds which provided the basis for imperial growth and success. The future growth of the Empire, then, should come through British emigration. This would have the added benefit of relieving domestic population pressures without contributing to the economic growth of Britain's competitors on the global stage. The Prince concludes by invoking citizenship, noting that British emigrants would benefit by moving to the Empire, as opposed to foreign nations.

The idea of channelling emigration within the Empire was a common one in the late Victorian and Edwardian eras. It also illustrates the intertwined notions of imperialism and citizenship. Emigration was a case of imperial citizenship at work, or, as the social worker and emigration advocate Thomas Sedgwick put it, 'Practical Imperialism.'[2] As we have seen, the creation of a true imperial citizenship was hampered by cleavages between London and the dominions over immigration policy, mainly concerning non-white immigrants. Those imperial ideologues involved in the national efficiency movement believed such differences could be alleviated if emigration to the Empire were managed, either by the State or by voluntary organizations. This had been Milner's hope for maintaining British hegemony in Southern Africa, and social imperialists like Sedgwick applied the same logic to the other settlement colonies. Social imperialists favoured a centralized model of imperial citizenship, predicated on the conviction that Empire was a structured relationship which offered greater benefits than did national autonomy or devolution. However, as an analysis of Sedgwick's assisted emigration work will demonstrate, the social imperialist programme of fostering a common imperial citizenship based upon a social ideal of 'Britishness' proved no more successful than did the broad church approach of Jebb or Buchan, the ethnic 'whiteness' of White, or the centralist political approach of Curtis. The dominions were as resistant to the centrifugal idea of citizenship professed by social imperialists like Sedgwick as Britain was opposed to the dominions' more exclusionary citizenships.

Assisted emigration

Thomas Sedgwick was convinced that emigration was central to the future of Empire because it would consolidate a common identity. His conception of imperial citizenship was thus primarily social. In his words, 'Understanding means unity – unity means strength – strength and solidarity for the British Empire mean Security and Progress for Civilization.'[3] The view that emigration served to strengthen the sinews of Empire had long been part of the imperial landscape. What had not been decided was the nature of imperial emigration. State-assisted emigration plans were common during the eighteenth and early nineteenth centuries, when mercantilist concerns over limited world resources dictated that the Government play a prominent role in directing the flow of emigrants. Edward Gibbon Wakefield's emigration interests in South Australia during the 1830s are perhaps the best known of this period, and the British Government formed the Colonial Land and Emigration Office in 1840 to promote emigration to the colonies. Such activist measures began to wane, however, by mid-century.[4] This shift in policy occurred for two significant reasons: first, the colonies began to assert their independence, with the supervision of immigration one of the earliest concerns to fall under their assumed jurisdiction; second, the Corn Law debates of 1841–46 led to the primacy of the ideas of the Manchester School in political economy. Central to the thought of Cobden and his followers was a free exchange of labour, and the State consequently surrendered control of emigration to private operations. Market forces would henceforth dictate the flow of emigration.

Consistent with W. E. Gladstone's ambivalence in regard to Empire, British governments maintained a *laissez-faire* approach to emigration for much of the Victorian period. The Tory governments of Lord Derby and Benjamin Disraeli,[5] though more active in imperial affairs, nonetheless adhered to their political rival's policy on the matter of emigration. Britain eventually established the Emigrant Information Office (EIO) in 1886,[6] a government agency which provided prospective migrants with information concerning opportunities in the colonies.[7] The State also maintained a minimal role in directing imperial emigration through three separate government branches: the Board of Trade collected statistics on passenger traffic on British ships; the Home Office engaged in a limited business in sending reformatory boys to the colonies; and the Local Government Board also helped despatch a small number of poor children under the auspices of the Poor Relief Acts of 1848–49, and after the passage of the Unemployed Workmen's Act of 1905, it had the authority to transport unemployed workers and their families.[8] In general, though, the large-scale emigration of the nineteenth century, one of the largest mass movements of people in European history, unfolded without the direct involvement of the Government. An astonishing total of 22.6 million individuals left Britain between 1815 and 1914.[9] Only about 10% of these emigrants received government assistance; 25% were funded by family or friends,[10] and the rest relied on either private associations or their own means.

The individualized nature of imperial emigration continued unabated into the early years of the twentieth century. Emigration became more organized in the 1880s, when it emerged as one of the preferred solutions to the social problems identified by reformers such as Charles Booth of the Salvation Army.[11] Thomas Barnardo's child emigration scheme and the East End Emigration Fund were the most successful, or at least most visible, of such endeavours.[12] It was the rupture of the South African War, though, especially the controversy it engendered concerning the physical and moral unpreparedness of the British people, which led to the re-emergence of assisted emigration. Fears of declining national efficiency were manifest in the social imperialism expressed by individuals as varied as Joseph Chamberlain, Milner,[13] the 'protectionist' economist William Cunningham, and others who advocated instilling imperial patriotism in the working classes through social welfare measures.[14] Assisted emigration sponsors joined the ranks of tariff reformers, army reformers, and supporters of national insurance, in order to convince British workers that Empire, rather than socialism, was the system that offered them the greatest rewards.

The 1907 Imperial Conference resolved that greater efforts should be undertaken to direct British settlers to the dominions. This message was taken up by semi-official voices such as Sir H. Rider Haggard, a member of the Royal Dominions Commission in 1913, who believed that assisted emigration would strengthen personal pan-imperial ties. The assisted emigration movement reached a symbolic peak in 1910 when forty-nine emigration organizations convened for the RCI's conference on emigration.[15] The majority of assisted emigration schemes of the pre-1919 era were privately organized. The British Government still preferred to stay out of the emigration business. John Burns, the President of the Local Government Board, explained to the 1907 Imperial Conference that direct state involvement in emigration would necessitate choosing between colonies as preferred destinations, a measure counterproductive to imperial harmony. The Government furthermore believed that charitable organizations could better administer such schemes. The rate of emigration remained satisfactory in London's eyes.[16] Indeed, the annual flow of outward passengers reached a historic apex in 1910–12, averaging 440,014 emigrants per year for this three-year period. This number can be compared to a total of 405,230 assisted emigrants under the Empire Settlement Act (1922) from 1922 to 1936.[17]

Yet there was growing concern among advocates that the official neglect of imperial emigration could compromise the strength and efficiency of the British Empire. This was a particularly compelling argument in the heightened environment of pre-1914 international and imperial competition. One aspect of this comparative decline was the increasing number of British emigrants who were choosing the United States, rather than the British Empire, as their new home. Social imperialists like Sedgwick thus believed it imperative to direct more emigrants to the settlement colonies, lest the Empire's *British* character abate. The imperial citizenship that Sedgwick articulated was thus a defensive rather than a progressive one, designed to build upon existing bonds of cultural attachment rather than create new ones. His task was complicated by the dominions' paradoxical attitudes toward immigration.

Assisted immigration

Two paradoxes characterized imperial emigration in the decades preceding the Great War, and at the centre of each was the nature of imperial citizenship as understood by the participating parties. These paradoxes were: a colonial desire for autonomy tempered by a lingering sense of imperial dependence; and colonial cultural allegiance to the

United Kingdom challenged by burgeoning colonial nationalism. It was within this framework of British–colonial tension that Sedgwick and other advocates of assisted emigration operated. Though this tension manifested itself in a different manner in each settlement colonies, it had similar causes. First, there was a colonial desire to dictate immigration policy, and specifically the type of acceptable immigrant.[18] In the Antipodes, and to a lesser degree in Canada, the desire to attract the proper type of immigrant meant Anglo-Saxons, while non-British immigrants, largely Asians, were to be rejected. The theme of colonial selectivity in immigration policy was a topic of constant analysis in both the metropolitan and colonial press,[19] and one which I have examined in relation to the ideas of Richard Jebb. The colonies also demanded an active role in the screening of applicants and in the administration of the emigration schemes.[20] Many colonial jurisdictions had moved aggressively into immigration issues, drafting policies on acceptable immigrants, and placing demands on agents such as Sedgwick who proposed to assist Britons to their shores. In South Australia, for example, the Government passed the following regulations regarding prospective immigrants:

- the immigrants must be nominated by a current citizen;
- they must be rural or agricultural workers;
- they must not move to 'congested' areas;
- the nominees must help contribute to the price of their passage;
- they must settle on the land; and
- they must be under 50 years of age.[21]

The Government of Victoria was even more specific in its desires, advertising only for male artisans and female textile machinists, brush-makers, tie-and-scarf makers, and shirt- and pyjama-makers. Victoria also offered assisted emigration for this limited pool of prospective emigrants, which is more than 'closed' territories such as Queensland did.[22]

While the settlement colonies demanded immigrants of an acceptable professional and social nature, they were hampered in their selection by practical needs and the sometimes countervailing interests of the imperial Government. The most glaring practical need was, of course, demographic. The colonies may have preferred certain types of immigrant, but as developing economies and democracies what they needed above all were simply bodies. Only Canada had, nearby, in the United States, a viable alternative source to Britain from which to attract potential immigrants. Population density in the colonies was strikingly low, and natural growth did not come close to meeting the need for increased population, a situation only exasperated by the depression of the 1890s. Thus, while public rhetoric and public policy might bring one to see the settlement colonies as restrictive and even closed, they were in fact out of necessity open to immigration, Asian immigration included. Representative of this dichotomy was the British Immigration League of Australia. Its Sydney branch advised its subscribers that while Australia was a prosperous nation, it was also a small nation among large ones, with a scant population of only 4.5 million people occupying 3 million square miles. In advocating increased emigration to Australia, the League employed the citizenship argument that 'Territories must belong to those who can fill them up.'[23] The League adhered to the notion of 'democratic imperialism', and framed its mission of attracting immigrants of British background in terms both patriotic (and thus national) and imperial (and thus extra-national):

> The need for population in Australia is universally admitted, but the number of people who will personally exert themselves on behalf of the immigrant is, to put it mildly, insignificant. This is undoubtedly our greatest weakness, as compared to Canada and the United States, where it is hardly too much to say that every citizen recognizes a direct and personal duty in helping the newcomer to establish himself in his adopted country. This is a spirit of patriotism which it must be admitted we have not got, and any organization that endeavours to encourage it is well worth sympathy and support.[24]

Citizenship is here conceived of as a duty, a responsibility, to the collective, the nation. Though citizenship is imbued with patriotism, drawing upon sentiment and emotion, it is at its base a practical matter – here concerned with the growth of the nation through immigration. The colonies desired to organize their own immigration affairs, vigorously pursuing policies of autonomy, yet they remained dependent on Great Britain to supply the actual immigrants out of an expressed preference for Anglo-Saxon stock.

In Australia there were many colonial citizens sympathetic to this message, with innumerable organizations, formal and informal, engaged in attracting immigrants to that country. Some, such as MP Richard Arthur, endorsed Sedgwick's ideas concerning emigration of urban youth from England.[25] Other voices, such as the operators of the Dreadnought Trust, worked directly with agents in London to bring young settlers to Australia.[26] Many of these groups, though, encountered the same problems which hampered Sedgwick, especially the inability of many boys to raise enough money to acquire even the documentation (such as a birth certificate) necessary to establish them as acceptable emigrants. The cost of assisted passage to the Antipodes, while decreasing rapidly, also posed a stumbling-block for both the potential emigrant and the colonial Government's Treasury. The rates for a third-class passage from Britain to South Australia in 1911, for instance, were £15–21 via the Suez Canal (a quicker but largely commercial route), and £16–30 via the Cape of Good Hope (which remained in this period the preferred passenger route).[27] Additionally, though the journey time from Britain to Southern Australia had declined from approximately three months in 1852 to just under one month by 1904, many emigrants were still daunted, both physically and mentally, by the distance.[28]

Lower cost and shorter distance were the primary reasons why Canada remained a popular destination for emigrants in this era. In 1910, a third-class fare from England to Toronto cost £7 8s 9d, while the same fare from England to Victoria was £14 5s 3d. The passage from England to eastern Canada took only about a week, the Empress of the Atlantic line advertising that its Liverpool–Quebec City run spent only four days on the open sea.[29] Britain's North American outpost was viewed at home as the most developed of the settlement colonies. Laurier's boast – 'I think we can claim that it is Canada that shall fill the twentieth century' – epitomized the confidence and sense of opportunity invoked by 'Canada.'[30] At the same time, the colony's reputation as a barren wasteland was in the process of being altered by Canadian Minister of the Interior Clifford Sifton's vigorous expansion of the western territories. Canada, like Australia and New Zealand, was also actively recruiting new citizens from the mother country. This combined sense of expansionist idealism and practical necessity was captured in a letter in 1912 to the *Standard of Empire* by Arthur Hawkes, a Canadian immigration advocate. Hawkes wrote that immigration was 'the living epistle of the only political religion that can preserve British unity throughout the world.' Warming to his topic, he commented on the interconnectedness of imperial immigration: 'Rachel said, "Give me children or I die." The Canadian state says, "Give me people so that I may meet my obligations." The British state says, "Give my people room, or they perish from overcrowding"'[31] – expressing a sense of religious purpose shared by Sedgwick. Sedgwick's ventures illustrate both the hopes and, more significantly, the practical problems of the assisted emigration 'solution,' and it is to these ventures that I now turn.

Sedgwick's assisted emigration schemes

Thomas Sedgwick is recorded by the pre-eminent historian of imperial migration Stephen Constantine as a 'minor philanthropist,' and elsewhere is referred to as simply a 'youth worker.'[32] While his emigration work was not as prodigious as that of the Dreadnought Trust or Dr Barnardo's Homes, the fact that he ran his schemes almost entirely on his own renders him a particularly appropriate representative of the sizable brigade of men and women who sought to give Empire its practical form. He attempted to apply, intuitively, the principles, thoughts, and sentiments of imperialism voiced by writers and intellectuals such as Curtis and White, Buchan and Jebb. His assisted emigration schemes are thus a case study in applied imperial citizenship, and their fortunes illustrate some of the strengths and weaknesses of that idea.

Sedgwick, born in 1874,[33] was a social worker, one of the many progressive men and women who devoted themselves to alleviating, as best they could, social and economic inequities. He served briefly in London as an official of the Cape Colony, which may be how his interest in imperial emigration began. Sedgwick lived and laboured for most of his life in the borough of Poplar, in the East End of London. The experience of working with the poor seems to have affected those involved in two distinct ways. There were those who became advocates of social reform, convinced that the route to a more just society lay through economic redistribution and the improvement of the physical and mental environment of the poor. The Bosanquets, the Salvation Army, the Fabians, and later the New Liberals and the Labour Party all believed that social engineering was both possible and desirable.[34] Collective effort would produce collective gain. And there were others, notably the members of the Charitable Organisation Society, who held to the mid-Victorian creed of self-help.[35] The spirit of Samuel Smiles and Thomas Arnold had bequeathed a lingering faith in character and self-reliance. Self-improvement was best attained through inner improvement, which had the added benefit of discharging society of further relief responsibilities. The reduction of the Poor Law roles was of particular interest to advocates of national efficiency. Sedgwick was one such advocate, and he brought to his work in assisted emigration the mission of improving the nation's moral and physical ardour.

In a speech delivered at Hawkes Bay, New Zealand, he told his audience that he considered himself a proponent of imperial 'migration,' rather than imperial 'emigration,'[36] arguing that to move from Britain to New Zealand was no different from moving from Cornwall to Cumberland. It was a form of resettlement. *Migration* thus constituted movement within the Empire, while *emigration* denoted movement to regions outside of the Empire.[37] While Sedgwick himself used 'emigration' when referring to his plans, he understood this term to mean movement within the Empire. In advocating the emigration of the poor and the destitute,[38] he hoped to create a broader Anglo-Saxon imperial citizenship, by which he meant a greater sense of sentimental attachment between Britain and its settlement colonies. Here Sedgwick found common cause with his contemporary Kingsley Fairbridge, whose Child Emigration Scheme also relocated youths to agricultural settings in the colonies, and who believed assisted emigration 'would create imperial citizenship – "patriotic, capable and self-reliable citizens".'[39]

Sedgwick was one of many social imperialists who looked particularly to child and juvenile emigration as the ideal means to reinforce imperial solidarity. Between 1870 and 1930, almost 98,000 child emigrants were sent to Canada alone, where they were known as 'Home Children.'[40] Assisted youth emigration was part of a broader movement in the early twentieth century to improve children's living conditions, highlighted by the Children's Act of 1908. Emigration advocates referred to such youths as the 'bricks of Empire building,'[41] an investment in the imperial future. Most were children, coming in the main from reformatory and industrial schools.[42] Sedgwick saw in assisted youth emigration the answer to two contemporary concerns. First, it would help relieve Britain's socio-economic stresses, particularly overcrowding and poor health.[43] Indeed, London grew by an average of almost a million people per decade between 1861 and 1911; and by the latter date as many people lived in the imperial capital as lived in Canada.[44] The youths he hoped to assist in emigrating were not currently contributors to the British economy, and would find better opportunities in the colonies. Emigration thus represented the redistribution of a common population.[45] Second, Sedgwick believed assisted emigration would invigorate the Empire: it would strengthen the cultural bonds he believed were the core of imperial citizenship, provide much needed labour to growing colonial economies, and create an ever larger market for Britain's finished products. Emigration to the colonies was especially attractive to those Britons who felt that the class system denied them opportunity at home, a frustration not confined to the poor. The petty bourgeoisie, particularly the newly emergent class of clerks, were particularly attracted by the prospects of emigration. The protagonist in Shan F. Bullocks' *Robert Thorne: The Story of a London Clerk* (1907) articulates that dream by emigrating to New Zealand in the hope of creating a life where his children have 'a chance of being something better than typists and clerks.'[46]

Sedgwick hoped to provide such opportunity. He was interested specifically in aiding those youths on relief who represented a cost to Britain's economy. As such, he aimed to attract young boys engaged in the sort of 'blind-alley' jobs which Arnold White bemoaned, such as van-boys, or those who had no vocation at all. Emigration would transform those boys into productive imperial citizens. Echoing the popular contemporary slogan 'idle hands for idle lands,'[47] Sedgwick's plan embodied a sense of rural idealism, for liberating blind-alley boys from a stultifying urban life and exposing them to the fresh air and honest labour of rural life would improve their physical and moral character, necessary preconditions for imperial citizenship. Consistent with the evangelicalism central to social imperialism, Sedgwick thus believed his scheme would improve both the lives of the boys themselves and the imperial collective.

Previous emigration schemes had mainly confined themselves either to paupers and the unemployed or to individuals who had sufficient capital to pay their own expenses. The novelty of Sedgwick's plan was that it provided passage for a heretofore largely ignored stratum of society. He began preparations in 1910 for his first emigration project, the Scheme for the Emigration of Town Lads to Colonial Farms, of which he named himself honourary secretary. The Scheme's committee worked out of Toynbee Hall in the East End of London. Sedgwick settled upon New Zealand as the Scheme's destination because he believed it was progressive, had a mild climate, and most closely resembled Britain in the temperament of its people.[48] It also had an acute shortage of young labourers. Sedgwick calculated that New Zealand would require up to 1,000 boys per year as labour. He argued that the boys would become 'centres of immigration for their friends and families,' as well as future producers and defenders of Empire.[49] Sedgwick had voyaged to Wellington earlier in the year and secured a promise from the New Zealand Government that it would supervise the boys once they arrived. He also negotiated a £10 passage for each boy, though he had to raise the money himself. He recruited fifty boys, twenty-five each from London and Liverpool, to participate in the inaugural project.[50] The boys ranged in age from 16 to 19, each having to pass a physical exam, and provide two character and fitness references.[51] The cost of the project would be £600, covering 50 steamer fares plus £4 per boy for expenses. Upon returning to London, Sedgwick, in association with the Central Emigration Board, secured most of the necessary funds through private donations. New Zealand farmers and friendly societies also contributed a small amount to the project. Sedgwick had no pecuniary interest in the Scheme itself.

The New Zealand Labour Department selected 50 farms, out of the 200 which showed interest, to take in the boys. The young immigrants were offered the choice of labouring on sheep, cattle, or fruit farms. New Zealand's Secretary of Labour was authorized the boys' guardian and he administered the plan once they arrived from Britain.

Each boy would be apprenticed for 3 years, or until he turned 21. Sedgwick had negotiated a 5s' weekly wage, as well as room and board, though most farmers paid their new charges 8–10s per week, the higher wage indicative of the country's desperate need for labour. Each youth kept a wage book, checked periodically by a Department of Labour inspector, and interest was paid on deposits. The first £10 the boys earned was garnished to reimburse the original sponsors, and, after the initial sponsorship had been paid, Sedgwick estimated that each boy would have between £70 and £90 after three years. The Secretary of Labour would hold this money in trust until each boy reached the age of 19. The Secretary could cancel the indenture within fourteen days if any boy was found 'guilty of such misconduct as would entitle an employer to dismiss a servant.'[52]

Preparation was key to the Scheme's fortunes. Sedgwick impressed upon his recruits the importance of hard work and the necessity of honouring their pledge. Sedgwick and the first group of fifty boys left Britain together aboard a Shaw Savill and Albion Ltd steamer, travelling third class. After a brief stopover at Cape Town they arrived in Wellington on 24 January 1911. The boys passed the time en route playing deck sports and, it appears, eating: each boy gained an average of ten pounds' weight during the voyage. Soon after landing in Wellington, Sedgwick told the *New Zealand Times* that the very act of emigration was liberating for the youth emigrants: 'it is a unique opportunity for them to steady, shake off old associations and habits and develop in anticipation of the new life in the Britain of the South.'[53] The boys left immediately for their respective farms, 22 going to farms on the South Island, 28 to the North Island. Only 3 of the 50 were deemed by doctors to be in poor health.[54]

Sedgwick recorded the impressions of several boys from the original scheme in an effort to raise funds for follow-up ventures. Some appreciated the common bonds which made New Zealand feel like home:

> I am in as good a situation as a fellow could wish for. We have good food, and the people are all good Britishers.[55]

Some were simply thankful for change:

> I would much rather be out here than in the Old Country.[56]

Others expressed their appreciation for new opportunities and material comforts:

> The last five months I have been out here has seemed to be no longer than a Saturday night in the butcher's shop I used to work in in the Old Country. As to food, why a man that is worth one thousand pounds cannot have any better than I got.[57]

The scheme seemed a success from the boys' perspective, and only one of the fifty youths fled his farm to strike out on his own in the first month of the Scheme's operation. Most of the boys's hosts also had favourable reviews of the project. One farmer told Sedgwick that his 'boy is acquitting himself well ... his manner and obligingness are a perfect eye-opener to us colonials.' Another explained that his boy 'is very intelligent and in every way promises to make a good citizen.'[58] There were some criticisms of the Scheme, largely concerning the utility of city youths as farm labourers. One farmer complained, in a letter to the periodical *Truth*, that farm-owners deserved better quality labour, given that they had contributed a portion of the project's budget.[59]

Some outside critics complained that 'the boys were the failures of the large cities in the Old Land,'[60] and would perform no useful service in the new country. The New Zealand press, however, was largely supportive of the Scheme. The *Graphic* chastised local critics as 'parochial,' while the *New Zealand Mail* supported Sedgwick's Scheme as 'scientific,' and concluded that it would be successful because 'youth is plastic, and can mould itself to its environment.'[61] The *New Zealand Times* reported that the boys had settled in without incident.[62] Sedgwick also spoke with local leaders in an effort to generate support for follow-up ventures. Arguing that the 'immigration business' benefited everyone, he hoped either to persuade the shipping lines to offer reduced passages to future emigrants or to gain a pledge from the New Zealand Government to fund a portion of the passage. He delivered the same message to various branches of the New Zealand Farmers's Union, investing the money he received for these appearances into the Scheme.

After he had completed his travels in New Zealand, Sedgwick drew six conclusions for the future success of youth emigration:

1. the attractions of life abroad should be downplayed to avoid attracting lazy emigrants;
2. supervision of the boys is essential;
3. government officials should perform supervisory roles;
4. the apprenticeship system is the ideal labour arrangement;
5. youths of 15–16 are the ideal age, as older boys find it harder to adapt to a new environment and were more independent; and
6. friends should be separated to avoid problems.[63]

Sedgwick returned to England on the steamer *Ionic* in June of 1911 to begin preparations for the next group of migrants. Despite the fact that he had failed to secure a promise of future funding from the New Zealand Government,[64] he was in high spirits, even promising to pay for the first triple wedding among Sedgwick settlers. In a farewell letter to the original group of boys, he imparted his personal creeds: 'Live cleanly in thought, word and deed: purity and contentment are the sources of happiness.' 'Read all you can, especially the Bible, the handbook of life.' and 'Always buck-up – like the runner who dug pins into himself to keep up.'[65] Here was a mind shaped by the mid-Victorian evangelical spirit of industry, doggedness, and honour – in short, 'character.'[66] He believed that a broader common imperial citizenship could be fostered through social engineering. His programme, however, soon ran aground. The New Zealand Scheme turned out to be the high-water mark of Sedgwick's work, after which his programme lost momentum.

Before sailing for England, Sedgwick stopped briefly in Australia to survey the state of emigration in that colony, but was similarly unable to secure any state funding there. Once back in Britain, Sedgwick set about canvassing for a follow-up group of boys to send to New Zealand. He also began to contemplate a Canadian initiative. He toured church and municipal halls in both London's East End and the country at large, exhibiting slides and lecturing on living conditions in the colonies in an effort to sell his emigrant programmes.[67] One meeting, at Stepney Central Hall, attracted an estimated crowd of 1,500,[68] in part due to the presence of several '*Titanic* orphans' – Sedgwick made much use of the *Titanic* metaphor to illustrate the tragic nature of life in the East End. The meetings were also designed to advertise to the colonies the great reserve of available labour ready for export.

Given that the New Zealand Government refused to fund a second project, Sedgwick looked to the Canadian province of Ontario for his second major emigration project. Canada had long been the favoured destination for British emigrants: passage there was comparatively affordable; land was readily available; and the country's proximity to the United States offered markets and opportunities not present in Australasia. Perhaps because of these advantages, however, Canada had devoted few resources to attract new immigrants, while the more hospitable climates of coastal Australia and New Zealand helped those colonies draw increasing numbers of new arrivals. Shorter and more affordable steamship travel by the early twentieth century also helped. Sedgwick thus believed Canada should adopt a more active role in emigration. He suggested that Canadian Government harmonize federal and provincial immigration policies and methods, and introduce greater flexibility in regard to the types of immigrant granted entry.[69] Sedgwick, though, like Richard Jebb before him, failed to understand the Canadian federal system. His Ontario project failed in part because he tried to negotiate the specifics of the scheme with local authorities, but lobbied the Canadian Government for institutional aid.

His discussions with the Canadian Government centred on the suitability of reformatory children as immigrants. The Emigration Branch of the Canadian Department of the Interior informed him that Canada accepted such cases only on an exceptional basis, usually refusing reformatory children on moral grounds.[70] His solicitors in England had informed him that he could emigrate boys under two conditions: first, where there were no parents, and a guardian had not been appointed by the State; and, second, where the parents were 'no good,' and no longer retained custody under the Custody of Children Act.[71] Canadian farmers needed labourers, though, and Sedgwick found Ontario provincial authorities receptive to his idea.[72] With the aid of a minor provincial official named John Farrell, he organized his second major emigration endeavour.[73] Sedgwick accompanied a group of fifty boys to Ontario, arriving in Canadian waters on Dominion Day 1912.[74] Upon arrival in Toronto, the boys separated to venture to their final destinations, the project being organized in a manner similar to the New Zealand plan. Funds had been raised during Sedgwick's lecturing tour, with the Canadian Department of Colonisation to reimburse sponsors. The boys had to repay their first £10 10s for their passage. The average age of the Canadian group of boys was below those of the two New Zealand groups, and most came from London.

The Ontario project soon encountered difficulties. Most problematical was the fact that the Canadian Department of Colonisation had been slow to return Sedgwick's investment, citing ambivalent reports on the quality of the boys' labour.[75] This compromised continued fund-raising efforts in England, and jeopardized the possibility of future initiatives. Sedgwick was also forced to take a harder stance with the boys, assuming a less fatherly and more stern demeanour. As an inducement to hard work, he told them he would publish a list of their successes and failures. The heavy-handed message probably reflected his concern over criticism that youths made poor immigrants. Indeed, in February 1912 he had received reports from the New Zealand Department of Labour that 10 of the 50 boys had left their original farms.[76] Most of those who fled were over 19, and Sedgwick began to consider sending younger boys, on the premiss that they were more impressionable and easier to discipline. He was also sensitive to humanitarian criticisms of youth emigration. Several cases of neglect of child emigrants had been reported in Canada in the year preceding Sedgwick's arrival,[77] and despite the relative success of Dr Barnardo's houses, public opinion was not on Sedgwick's side. Indeed, public pressure against the poor conditions and treatment encountered by child migrants, combined with a growing view that the migrants represented a moral and social contagion, brought the practice to a virtual end in Canada by the late 1920s.[78]

As the Canadian initiative was running aground, Sedgwick received word from New Zealand that the Government would not help finance future schemes.[79] In its report on the first year of Sedgwick's Scheme, the Department of Labour cited an attrition rate of 20% as evidence of the Scheme's failure.[80] Sedgwick suggested that 80% was still an acceptable success rate, but was unable to offer productive suggestions for future improvement, instead resorting to stereotype to explain the absconders' actions: most of them, he observed, were Irish Liverpudlians.[81]

A lack of funds and the lukewarm reception of Canadian authorities led to the collapse of the Ontario initiative by the spring of 1913. Sedgwick lost touch with most of the boys, and was unable to secure either federal or provincial government follow-up funding. He returned to England and continued to agitate for assisted youth emigration, but his opportunity had passed. Despite frequent speeches and contributions to the periodical press extolling the merits of his schemes, Sedgwick could not find adequate funding for a third initiative. Complicating his efforts was a growing public perception that the Empire was losing its attraction for emigrants. The Colonial Office reported in May 1913, that almost 40% of British emigrants were now sailing for non-imperial ports.[82] This represented a precipitous decline even from 1911, when the *New Zealand Times* estimated that only 20% of British emigrants voyaged to non-imperial nations.[83] These statistics were in fact inflated. Only a third of emigrants went to the Empire in 1900, but this increased to 68% in 1910 and 78% in 1913.[84] This discrepancy illustrates the pervasiveness of public anxiety concerning imperial unity, and perhaps indicates that the sense of social cohesiveness which imperial citizenship was built upon was in decline even as demographic imperial ties remained strong. Sedgwick was forced to retreat to private life by late 1914, the nation's concerns now redirected to war.

A lack of direction

Assisted emigration did not create a stronger sense of imperial citizenship, in part because of its masculine focus. In 1909, 43,546 more men than women emigrated to the colonies, a difference that increased to 67,619 in 1910.[85] The gender discrepancy exacerbated the demographic imbalance in Britain. In 1913, the Committee for Junior Migration, a pro-emigration pressure group, recorded that there were 1,340,814 more women in Britain than men. This figure contrasted sharply with the dominions, where there were 759,624 more men than women.[86] The Committee recommended that widows, waitresses, orphan girls, domestics, as well as young couples, should be encouraged to emigrate to the dominions. While Sedgwick also articulated a masculine imperial citizenship, he did recognize the need for the emigration of young women.[87] This belief, however, derived from practical rather than progressive motives: 'many jobs on the farms can be neglected, but house work has to be done.'[88] He also feared that the Empire could face 'race suicide' if more women were not brought to the Antipodes. In this regard he shared much of Arnold White's view of Empire. The parochial nature of this view, though, was tempered by Sedgwick's philanthropic outlook. He supported the emigration of 'surplus' and 'unattached' urban women, a class he believed lived in conditions worse than those under which American slaves had suffered.[89] Sedgwick failed to attract much support for female emigration, however, not least because potential upper-class supporters opposed the idea of recruiting as emigrants members of the 'underclass.' Lady Selborne, for instance, did not support the Women's Emigration Society as it did not attract 'good' recruits.[90] Such differences illustrate the lack of a common ideal of imperial citizenship, and reinforces the domestic focus of most social imperialists' citizenship.

Sedgwick's efforts to create imperial citizens through emigration was further compromised by the lack of cooperation between domestic aid groups. The British Government's Labour Exchanges, the Distress Committees, and the Boards of Guardians offered little help to their charges. The Central Unemployment Body (CUB) for London, for instance, engaged in limited work migrating unemployed young people to other regions of Britain. Sedgwick believed that the CUB was unsuccessful because it could not attract charges of proper 'character,' as evidenced by the fact that only £21,012 of the £126,924 spent on assisted passage schemes (both within and outside of Britain) was recovered from the emigrants and their sponsors for the year 1912–13.[91] Furthermore, the CUB required each prospective boy migrant to obtain a guarantor, which Sedgwick argued was a prohibitive obstacle for blind-alley youths. Finally, the CUB did not work with those who, like Sedgwick, advocated emigration to the Empire. Other emigration agencies, such as the Boys' Country Work Society and the Child Emigration Society,[92] two of the larger child emigration bodies, also tended to operate as independents.

The lack of coordination between immigration organizations was in part a symptom of the concern over national efficiency: the aid agencies did not want to further contribute to the decline of Britain's moral and physical capacity. Sedgwick offered another explanation for the charitable bodies' disinterest in assisted emigration – self-perpetuation. If the problem of overcrowding were solved, Sedgwick contended, then aid agencies such as the Boards of Guardians, which had the authority to remove some of their poorest charges, would be 'improved' out of existence. He cited as evidence for this contention Earl Grey's response to a question put to him by the Dominions Royal Commission (a body which reported to the Government on emigration to the dominions):

> *Q 3,406 Chairman*: Why do they [the Guardians] exercise their powers so seldom?
> *Earl Grey*: Well, I think it is more a question of ignorance. Sometimes improper motives came in. They do not like to get rid of the little patronage it gives them in keeping children within the area of their own jurisdiction.[93]

It was not only private organizations that were ambivalent about aiding assisted emigration. Sedgwick was also unsuccessful in gaining the assistance of the imperial Government. 'The Home Government,' he wrote in a letter to the New Zealand boys in March 1913,

> has never been Imperial, except in wartime, and the English people are Imperial mouthed and not Imperial minded. Consequently we have no Imperial Department of Migration, Trade, or Communication. If we do not get more Britishers in Canada and South Africa, they will no longer be British after the next few years, but will be American and Boer–Dutch.[94]

While it is hard to imagine that the boys were particularly interested in their patron's perorations on imperial unity, most emigration advocates would have concurred with Sedgwick's view. He pushed unsuccessfully for the creation of an imperial migration department which would oversee the movement of people throughout the Empire,[95] but his lobbying came to nothing. He was also unable, as we have seen, to secure further funding from either the New Zealand or the Canadian Government. Some of these difficulties, no doubt, were born of Sedgwick's belief that personal charitable efforts were the most socially efficient means of attaining success. After all, he avoided working directly under government control, arguing that bureaucratic emigration work would be dictated by short-term concerns.[96] Independent work also offered other advantages: he could write without the hand of a government superior on his shoulder.

The only organization whose ideas approximated Sedgwick's vision of an Empire united by sentiment and open to free migration was the Over-Seas Club (OSC). It seemed to represent his ideal of imperial citizenship, and he joined many other imperialists – including Richard Jebb, the first chairman of the OSC's central committee – as a subscriber. The OSC was an ideal vehicle of imperial citizenship, its creed being in effect a synthesis of the imperial citizenship ideas voiced by the ideologues discussed in previous chapters: 'Believing the British Empire to stand for justice, freedom, order and good government, we pledge ourselves, as citizens of the British Commonwealth of Nations, to maintain the heritage handed down to us by our fathers.'[97] The OSC was founded by John Evelyn Wrench, who was inspired by Cecil Rhodes's privately disseminated idea of creating a secret imperial society. Richard Jebb was the first chairman of the OSC's central committee. Wrench wished to unite imperial interests, and bemoaned the multiplicity of imperial interest groups. The OSC was conceived during the 1909 Imperial Press Conference, a gathering of Empire press lords, and came into being in 1910. It is a telling comment on the OSC's *raison d'être* that one of the names rejected for it was 'Citizens of Empire.' The OSC had 50,000 associates (members who expressed their support in writing) in 1911, and its subscribers' list steadily increased throughout the 1910s.[98] Members disavowed the Milnernian view of a centralized, federal Empire, instead implicitly embracing Jebb's idea of association and alliance.

The OSC sought to promote the 'tremendous responsibilities incurred by citizenship of the British Commonwealth,' and supported service and community work which had as their goal the promotion of freedom.[99] Members gave shape to those lofty goals by sharing information about their communities with fellow-subjects around the Empire, and donating money to imperial causes. In 1913 the OSC absorbed the Patriotic League of Britons Overseas, a sister organization which also raised funds for the war effort, the combined entity now known as the Over-Seas League.[100] Ultimately, though, the Over-Seas League remained largely a cultural organization, exerting little influence on imperial policy. The League illustrates the currency of a social and cultural conception of imperial citizenship based upon a shared British identity. Equally, its political impetus, particularly its inability to coordinate its activities with government departments in either Britain or the colonies, shows the weakness of a political ideal of imperial citizenship. By the 1920s the League had become merely a form of imperial freemasonry, replete with lofty rhetoric but soft on concrete policy, including any involvement in imperial migration.

The failures of domestic aid agencies and the irrelevance of the OSC as an agent of assisted emigration point to the absence of the sort of imperial sentiment Sedgwick hoped to foster, and furthermore the lack of a common citizenship ideal. Colonial nationalism, in its desire for an independent immigration policy, and the preference of the imperial Government to maintain its *laissez-faire* approach to citizenship issues, conspired to doom Sedgwick's vision of mass assisted 'migration' within the imperial supra-state.

Sentimental citizenship

A key element in Sedgwick's thought on empire was the need to develop the sentiments of a shared imperial citizenship, by which he meant a shared knowledge of and concern for the other peoples of the Empire. Despite the omnipresence of immigration advocates in the British and the colonial press in the generation preceding the First World War, the social imperialist goal of solving Britain's social problems by redistributing imperial citizens had its critics in both Britain and the settlement colonies. In the words of Sedgwick's Canadian contemporary, the humourist and imperialist Stephen Leacock: 'You cannot make a nation by holding a basket at the hopper of an immigration chute.'[101] Imperial citizens, in other words, were not merely units to be shifted about on a ledger. Sedgwick himself came to place greater stress upon mutually shared imperial sentiments in response to the lukewarm success of his two youth emigration ventures. In a letter to Lord Strathcona, in March 1912, Sedgwick complained that the British schools which he had visited in the course of his speaking tours rarely displayed pictures or artifacts of the colonies; most had only imported German rural landscapes.[102] Britons, mixing together contempt, paternal aloofness, and gentle regard, held a view of colonial life as rustic yet idyllic, *déclassé* yet imbued with opportunity – in short, a place to which to send one's sons, though perhaps not the first-born. In contrast, Sedgwick believed many colonists maintained an affection for an England which had largely ceased to exist, remembering the favoured aspects of English life, forgetting the less pleasant.[103] The sentimental relationship between mother country and dominion was an unequal one.

Sedgwick shared these concerns with Jebb, who, as we saw in the previous chapter, also believed that sentimental ties were integral to any prospective imperial citizenship. Writing to Jebb, Sedgwick complained that not only were pictures of the colonies absent from British schools, but one could not find in the shops postcards or cheap books on the Empire's history and lore. British adults as well, he continued, were ignorant of the Empire. His complaint was that there existed little *reliable* information on the colonies. There was certainly no lack of mass-produced imperial ephemera at this time, though he found most of it lacking. Popular dramas on Empire were misleading, and he was particularly exercised, for instance, by scenes of Indian scalpings. Popular lectures and exhibits on imperial topics were rare; there were few books by colonial authors in public libraries, and there was a general disregard for news from the colonies in the British press. Knowledge of the Empire was, he observed, much more plentiful in the dominions. Sedgwick thus suggested that the colonies could send to Britain pictures, films, and lantern slides which showed attractive aspects of colonial life and geography.[104] His appeals produced a ready response, with offers of slides, pictures, and other visual material pouring in from almost every colony.[105]

Sedgwick's concerns were reflective of those of the intellectual and political elite, that substantive matters of Empire were largely ignored by the British people. The wild celebration of the relief of the siege of Mafeking, or strong sales of Pears' Soap wrapped in packaging emblazoned with imperial motifs, might indicate that the Empire held a popular attraction.[106] However, the quiet desperation voiced by social imperialists suggests that generating a sense of sentimental imperial citizenship at home was an uphill struggle. It is instructive that the concern for generating a sentimental attachment between Briton and colonial, in other words a sentimental citizenship, was held primarily by those imperial advocates who had travelled widely throughout the Empire. More parochial voices in both the colonies and Britain resisted such a sentimental citizenship. Some of the criticism Sedgwick received regarding his emigration schemes was predicated along inclusive and often xenophobic lines, as in the following letter:

> Sir, before you arrange for Englishmen to leave England for the Colonies, please see that Jews return to Palestine and other foreigners to their own countries; after that Irishmen to Ireland, Welshmen to Wales and Scots to Scotland. Then when much ground is cleared of undesirables, we shall find that Englishmen will be able to obtain work and their sons can be recruited for England's army and navy services.[107]

The persistence of these attitudes should not, however, be overemphasized. Indeed, the letter-writer's decision not to sign his name indicates that such attitudes were no longer commonly acceptable.

There were also voices in the colonial world which hoped to build imperial citizenship through bonds of sentiment. A representative example is the periodical the *Indian Emigrant*, an Indian bi-monthly newspaper which advocated equal citizenship rights throughout the Empire, and also lobbied for the interests of Indians living abroad. The paper implicitly endorsed the vision of Empire put forward by ideologues such as Curtis, arguing that Empire was an institution of peace, where different people have proved capable of living together. It was 'a half-way house between nationalism and cosmopolitanism.'[108] Indian imperialists applauded India's inclusion in the 1917 Imperial Conference, though as an observer rather than a voting delegation. Sir Satyendra Sinha, India's spokesman at the Conference, proposed a three-pronged revision to imperial immigration regulations. He suggested that Indians domiciled in the dominions be allowed to bring out their wives, that Indians be treated at least on equal grounds with other Asians, and that if exclusionary practices were allowed in the dominions, then India should be allowed the same right to exclude prospective immigrants.[109] Other colonial voices expressed their support for imperial citizenship as part of their campaign for greater equality. The *Jamaica Times*, for instance, registered its frustration with Canada's policy of restricting West Indian immigration, and editorialized that an imperial community based upon insular attitudes and commercial concerns was doomed to failure: 'Imperialism that confines itself to commerce and that is frigid in sentiment is one of those sordid bonds that wrecked the roseate hopes of the late Mr. Joseph Chamberlain.'[110] Not all dependent subjects, of course, voiced conditional support for Empire as long as it promised reform. Indian nationalists especially were uncomfortable with the status quo. Some argued that the solution to growing tensions between Indian nationalists and the white Empire was to grant the sub-continent self-rule and full British citizenship, so that India could negotiate as an equal over divisive issues with the dominions.[111] After Amritsar, many Indian spokesmen renounced Empire *in toto*, and agitated for independence.

In the main, these debates on race and citizenship went largely unnoticed by British emigration advocates. Like Sedgwick, most were attentive to commonalities, not differences, and thus tended to ignore those factors which differentiated the colonies and dependencies from Britain. Even those imperial actors who were attentive to issues of colonial nationalism and imperial sentiment found it difficult to see how India, in particular, could be easily incorporated into an imperial citizenship which was based upon British ideas of politics and culture. Jebb had observed this difficulty, arguing that India could not be accepted on equal terms into the imperial family proper. He hoped that through his proposed system of Britannic alliance India would enjoy the autonomy to set its own immigration policy, thus attaining equality of purpose, if not of treatment, throughout the Empire. Jebb advanced an essentialist position in regard to the Indian peoples, writing that

> with their own immemorial civilization, traditions, and indigenous ideals, all essentially non-European, and with their widely different standard of living, all of which differentiates the Indian peoples from the Britannic, a free exchange of population is not easy to contemplate.[112]

Contemporaries thus saw imperial immigration and the suitability of subject peoples for imperial citizenship as two separate, if sometimes overlapping, issues.

Thomas Sedgwick was a utopian, seeing in assisted emigration the solution to a wide variety of imperial problems. He had visions of eventually sending up to 50,000 boys to New Zealand, with their families following their paths.[113] In the line of British utopians such as Robert Owen, Sedgwick, though not himself a socialist, saw assisted emigration as the panacean solution to Britain's social-imperial problems. He even lobbied to attach the royal seal to his scheme. Informing George V by letter that 'the first party of town lads for colonial farms beg to convey to Your Majesty the expression of our most dutiful and humble devotion to your Throne and person on our departure for the Dominion of New Zealand,'[114] Sedgwick petitioned the monarch to grant the Scheme official approval to increase its momentum and legitimacy.[115] The throne was the recipient of countless petitions on such issues, most of which never came before the King, and Sedgwick's case was no exception. His request was denied.[116]

Sedgwick's ideas betray a shift away from earlier Victorian certainties of rational calculation – that problems can be understood and overcome through detached observation and scientific prescription. His thought on emigration reflected the broader late Victorian desire to engage more directly with social problems. His solution to domestic problems of overcrowding and urban malaise was to extricate those individuals or groups deemed responsible. As a fellow-advocate of assisted emigration put it, 'What is the Empire for, if not to be a contented prosperous community...Every citizen of Britain, man or woman, is entitled – from the very fact of being a British citizen – to a tangible share in the Imperial real estate.'[117] Sedgwick's imperial citizenship was based on the perceived moral benefits of a rural existence, and in that sense was rooted in the pastoral Romanticism represented best by Ruskin. That was not, however, why it failed. Instead, it was his conception of citizens as commodities, interchangeable and ultimately replaceable, that proved the stumbling-block. The social engineering inherent in Sedgwick's schemes, like that of social imperialists as a group, conceived of imperial citizenship in the aggregate but not in the particular. Thus, it could offer little resistance to burgeoning colonial nationalist identities which provided a connection between the individual and a sense of place.

Notes

1 Draft copy, RCI–King George, Sedgwick Papers (SP), 2/1/8, Library of the Royal Commonwealth Society (LRCS). The RCI presented Edward VII's speech as part of its petition to George V to grant royal assent to Sedgwick's New Zealand emigration scheme.

2   Sedgwick used the term 'practical imperialism' as the title of his New Zealand scheme: see 'Circular Letter Introducing Sedgwick's Pamphlet,' 23 May 1913, SP, Volume 1, 4/20, LRCS, Cambridge University. The SP archive was reorganized in 2001, but the file numbers used in this chapter reflect the original (pre-2001) numbering scheme. They can be cross-indexed with the current filing system through the finding guide available at the LRCS, Cambridge University.
3   Cutting, SP, 2/1/1, LRCS.
4   See Stephen Constantine, 'Introduction,' in Constantine (ed.) *Emigrants and Empire: British Settlement in the Dominions Before the War* (Manchester, 1990), pp. 1–21.
5   Derby's Government was in office for 1851–52, 1858–59 and 1866–68, Disraeli's in 1868 and for 1874–80.
6   Memorandum on the History and Functions of the Emigrants Information Office, *British Parliamentary Papers*, Cd. 3407, LXVIII, 1907.
7   The EIO's most significant initiative was the publication of circulars detailing the social and economic conditions which a prospective emigrant could expect to find in the colonies: see for instance Great Britain EIO, *Combined Circulars on Canada, Australasia, and the South African Colonies* (London, various years).
8   Keith Williams, 'A Way Out of Our Troubles: The Politics of Empire Settlement, 1900–1922,' in Constantine (ed.) *Emigrants and Empire*, pp. 24–5.
9   Marjory Harper, 'British Migration and the Peopling of the British Empire,' in Andrew Porter (ed.) *Oxford History of the British Empire* (*OHBE*), vol. 3: *The Nineteenth Century* (Oxford, 2001), p. 75.
10 David Northrup, *Indentured Labour in the Age of Imperialism, 1834–1922* (Cambridge, 1995), p. 9.
11 The Salvation Army was founded by Booth in 1878. On its assisted emigration work, see Michelle Langfield, 'Voluntarism, Salvation, and Rescue: British Juvenile Migration to Australia and Canada, 1890–1939,' *Journal of Imperial and Ccommonwealth History* (*JICH*), 32, 2 (May 2004), esp. pp. 88–95; and Marjorie Harper, 'Emigration and the Salvation Army, 1890–1930,' *Bulletin of the Scottish Institute for Missionary Studies*, 3–4 (1985–87), pp. 22–9.
12 On Barnardo's schemes, see Gail H. Corbett, *Nation Builders: Barnardo Children in Canada* (Toronto, 2002); and Gillian Wagner, *Barnardo* (London, 1979).
13 Milner, then a Liberal, worked closely with Booth and others at Toynbee Hall in the 1880s.
14 See Bernard Semmel, *Imperialism and Social Reform* (London, 1960), esp. chapter 1, on social imperialism.
15 Official Report of the Emigration Conference Held on May 30–31, 1910 (London, 1910), p. 3.
16 Williams, 'A Way Out of Our Troubles,' p. 29. John Burns addressed the Colonial Conference on 25 April 1907: see the minutes of the 1907 Conference in *The Colonial and Imperial Conferences from 1887 to 1937*, ed. Maurice Ollivier, vol. 1 (Ottawa, 1954), pp. 257–8.
17 See table 7.1 in Stephen Constantine, 'Migrants and Settlers,' in Judith M. Brown and William Roger Louis (eds) *OHBE*, vol. 4: *The Twentieth Century* (Oxford, 1999), pp. 165, 173.
18 The term 'colonial' here denotes what, after 1907, were referred to as the dominions. There were emigration schemes which sought to colonize the dependencies, but these by and large came to little. Witness for instance the British East Africa Corporation's unsuccessful scheme to settle British emigrants in Britain's East African protectorate: Major E. H. Leggett, 'Colonization on the Equator' (British East African Corporation, undated, but probably 1912–13), SP, 2/53/353, LRCS.
19 See for instance the *Morning Post*, 16 September 1911; and the *Dominion*, 9 July 1910.
20 'Proceedings of Conference on Immigration,' RCI, 30–1 May 1910.
21 'Assisted Immigration Regulations, South Australia,' SP, 1/42/123, LRCS.
22 Government of Victoria Emigration Form of Application, SP, 1/44/128, LRCS.

23 'Stop! Look! Listen!,' publication of the British Immigration League, Sydney, 1911, SP, 1/45/134, LRCS.
24 *Sydney Morning Herald*, 16 November 1911.
25 Undated clipping of letter to the *Daily Telegraph*, SP, 2/41/131, LRCS. Arthur also solicited funds for the Millions Club, which raised passage fares for child emigrants.
26 *Sydney Daily Telegraph*, 31 December 1912. The Dreadnaught Fund worked with the Central Unemployed Body in London to select and provide assisted passage to Australia to young unemployed boys.
27 'Assisted Immigration Regulations, South Australia,' SP, 1/42/123, LRCS.
28 For travel times, see Robert Kubicek, 'Empire and Technological Change,' in Brown and Louis (eds) *OHBE*, vol. 4: *The Twentieth Century*, table 12.4, pp. 254–5.
29 'Work and Wages in Canada,' Canadian Pacific pamphlet, May 1910, SP, 1/47/143, LRCS.
30 Laurier speech, 18 January 1904; on Laurier and the expansion of Canada, both economically and demographically, see O. D. Skelton, *The Life and Letters of Sir Wilfrid Laurier*, vol. 2 (Toronto, 1971 [1922]).
31 Hawkes, letter to the editor, *Standard of Empire*, 9 February 1912.
32 Constantine, *Emigrants and Empire*, 9; Geoffrey Sherington and Chris Jeffrey, *Fairbridge: Empire and Child Migration* (Perth, 1998), p. 29.
33 See Sedgwick–Canon Gibson Smith, 31 January 1911, SP, 1/11/31, LRCS.
34 See, for instance, Stefan Collini, *Liberalism and Sociology* (Cambridge, 1979); and George L. Bernstein, *Liberalism and Liberal Politics in Edwardian England* (Boston, 1986).
35 Asa Briggs's *Victorian People* (Oxford, 1954) remains a useful study of the mid-Victorian period, though K. Theodore Hoppen, *The Mid-Victorian Generation, 1846–1886* (London, 1997), has challenged the 'equipoise' thesis.
36 *Daily Telegraph* [Hawkes Bay], 8 March 1911. On this theme, see also Stephen Constantine, 'British Emigration to the Empire–Commonwealth since 1880: From Overseas Settlement to Diaspora?' *JICH*, 31, 2 (May 2003), pp. 19–25.
37 See Sedgwick, *Spectator*, 110, 7 June 1913, p. 964; and *Town Lads on New Zealand Farms* (London, 1913), p. 8.
38 See, among other sources, *Christchurch Press*, 23 March 1911.
39 Charles Fairbridge, *The Times*, 24 May 1910, p. 24, cited in Sherington and Jeffrey, p. 27.
40 Juvenile migrants were those 14–21 years old, children those 3–14 years old: A. M. C. Maddrell, 'Empire, Emigration and School Geography: Changing Discourses of Imperial Citizenship, 1880–1925,' *Journal of Historical Geography*, 22, 4 (October 1996), p. 386 n. 19; Stephen Constantine, 'Children as Ancestors: Child Migrants and Identity in Canada,' *British Journal of Canadian Studies*, 16 (2003), p. 150.
41 Philip Bean and Joy Melville, *Lost Children of the Empire* (London, 1989), p. 79. The experiences of child emigrants sent to the colonies has attracted the attention of numerous scholars. See also Gillian Wagner, *Lost Children of Empire* (London, 1982); Joy Parr, *Labouring Children: British Immigrant Apprentices to Canada, 1869–1924* (London, 1980), and Elwyn Jenkins, 'Children's Literature and British Child Emigration Schemes: A Missed Opportunity,' *Journal of Commonwealth Literature*, 35, 1 (2000), pp. 121–9.
42 Maddrell, 'Empire, Emigration and School Geography,' pp. 377, 386 n. 25.
43 Sedgwick, *New Zealand Times*, 8 February 1911.
44 London grew from a population of 3,222,270 in 1861 to a population of 7,251,358 in 1911; Canada's population in 1911 was 7,205,000: see the *Spectator*, 110, 31 May 1913, p. 912.
45 This idea gained adherents in the 1900s, and was a perennial theme of discussion in the non-government institutions of Empire, such as the RCI. See for instance William Pearson, 'Canadian Colonisation: A Suggestion,' *United Empire*, 1, 8 (August 1910), p. 561.

46 Quoted in John Carey, *The Intellectuals and the Masses* (London, 1992), p. 62.
47 Langfield, 'Voluntarism, Salvation, and Rescue,' p. 96.
48 *Wanganui Herald*, 18 March 1911, clipping in SP, 1/21/57, LRCS.
49 *Spectator*, 105, 27 August 1910, p. 310.
50 *Evening Post*, 14 January 1911; *New Zealand Times*, 10 January 1911, clipping in SP, 1/6/17, LRCS.
51 Sedgwick, MS copy of 'Notes on New Zealand Expedition, prepared for the 1911 Imperial Conference,' 3 March 1911, SP, 1/19/48, LRCS.
52 Sedgwick, 'Town Lads on New Zealand Farms,' *United Empire*, new series, 2, 12 (December 1911), pp. 872–5; see also *New Zealand Times*, 23 January 1911.
53 Sedgwick interview, *New Zealand Times*, clipping (n.d., but either late January or early February), SP, 1/7/19, LRCS.
54 *New Zealand Labour Department Journal*, 7 February 1911, SP, 1/6/17, LRCS.
55 'Opinions of Some of the Lads on their Situations,' Sedgwick MS notes, SP, 1/34/88, LRCS.
56 See Sedgwick, *Spectator*, 107, 11 November 1911, p. 792.
57 Ibid.
58 'Opinions of Farmers Employing the Boys,' Sedgwick notes, SP, 1/32/84, LRCS.
59 'A Farmer,' *Truth*, clipping (n.d.), SP, 1/10/27, LRCS.
60 *Evening Post*, 2 February 1911.
61 *Graphic*, 1 February 1911; *New Zealand Mail*, 1 February 1911.
62 *New Zealand Times*, 17 March 1911.
63 Sedgwick, 'Resumé as to Progress of the Scheme,' 6 May 1911, SP, 1/36/96, LRCS.
64 The New Zealand Government wished to revisit the scheme after twelve months to assess its merit, and reserved judgement on assisted passage until that point.
65 Sedgwick–Boys, 17 June 1911, SP, 1/41/111, LRCS.
66 See Collini, *Public Moralists* (London, 1991) and Dan Gorman, '"The Character Creed": How Character Shaped the British Imperial Endeavour,' *Australasian Victorian Studies Journal*, 4 (1998), pp. 127–40.
67 See for instance his speech at the Socialist Hall, St George Street, 22 February 1912, SP, 1/72/256, LRCS. The issue of providing emigrants with information on their prospective new homes held the attention of the press until the outbreak of war, with regular reports on initiatives such as that proposed by Sedgwick: see for example *The Times*, 30 December 1912; *Daily Mirror*, 6, January 1913; and *Morning Post*, 12 March 1913.
68 *Morning Post*, 1 March 1912.
69 Sedgwick, 'Notes for Conference on January 10, 1912,' SP, 1/54/191, LRCS.
70 Department of the Interior, Emigration Branch–Sedgwick, 31 January 1912, SP, 1/73/263, LRCS.
71 Hermann H. Myer & Co.–Sedgwick, 14 December 1911, SP, 1/72/256, LRCS.
72 H. A. MacDonnel–'Farmers of Ontario' (n.d.), SP, 2/35/242, LRCS.
73 Correspondence of the Provincial Secretary, RG 8-5, Box 14, Archives of Ontario, Toronto.
74 *United Empire*, 3, 8 (August 1912), p. 683; Superintendant of Immigration, Ottawa–Sedgwick, 1 October 1912, SP, 2/29/193, LRCS.
75 Sedgwick to an unidentified Canadian farmer who had one of the Scheme's boys (no name given, perhaps because the two had corresponded often, as was Sedgwick's custom), 4 March 1913, SP, 2/33/223, LRCS.
76 Department of Labour, New Zealand–Sedgwick, 19 February 1912, SP, 2/47/318, LRCS.
77 See for instance Saskatchewan's *Carlyle Herald*, 31 August 1911, or the *Regina Morning Leader*, 25 August 1911, on the alleged abuse suffered by one Rose Violet King.
78 Constantine, 'Children as Ancestors,' pp. 150–1.
79 See Sedgwick–W. J. Massey (New Zealand MP) – undated, but likely April 1913 – SP, 2/50/340, LRCS. Also Department of Labour, New Zealand–Sedgwick, 19 February 1913.

80 One-year report on Emigration Scheme of Thomas Sedgwick, New Zealand Department of Labour. The report is included in Department of Labour, New Zealand–Sedgwick, 22 March 1912, SP, 2/48/322, LRCS.
81 Sedgwick–Department of Labour, New Zealand, 3 May 1912, SP, 2/48/323, LRCS.
82 *Colonial Office Journal*, as noted in the *Review of Reviews*, 47 (May 1913), p. 482.
83 *New Zealand Times*, 15 June 1911.
84 Colin Newbury, 'The March of Everyman: Mobility and the Imperial Census of 1901,' *JICH*, 12, 2 (1984), p. 80. Stephen Constantine records that the number of emigrants bound for imperial destinations actually rose from 43.2% of all British national passengers in 1900–04 to 68.2% in 1915–19: see Constantine, 'Migrants and Settlers,' in Brown and Louis (eds) *OHBE*, vol. 4: *The Twentieth Century*, p. 167, table 7.4.
85 Sedgwick, 'A Chance for the Girls,' draft paper (probably 1912), p. 2, SP, 2/18/116, LRCS.
86 'Female Migration,' anonymous pamphlet, Committee for Junior Migration, SP, 2/17/107, LRCS.
87 On female emigration to the Empire, see Julia Bush, *Edwardian Ladies and Imperial Power*; '"The Right Sort of Woman": Female Emigrators and Emigration to the British Empire, 1890–1910,' *Women's History Review*, 3, 3 (1994), pp. 385–409; and Lisa Chilton, 'A New Class of Women for the Colonies: *The Imperial Colonist* and the Construction of Empire,' *JICH*, 31, 2 (May 2003), pp. 36–56.
88 Ibid.
89 'A Chance for the Girls,' 4. His rather naive assessment of American slaves was that they at least had 'ample cottages, plenty of food and general kind treatment.'
90 Lady Selborne–Lionel Curtis, 13 October 1916. Curtis Papers, MS 2/25207, Bodleian Library, Oxford University. The Women's Emigration Society was one of the larger of a sizable community of female emigration bodies; others included the Colonial Intelligence League.
91 Sedgwick, 'Employment of the Unemployed,' undated presentation notes on Central Unemployment Body for London, July–June 1912–1913, SP, 3/3/8, LRCS.
92 G. Bogue Smart, *Report on British Immigrant Children and Receiving Homes* (Ottowa, 1910, 1911), for the Canadian Department of the Interior. Kingsley Fairbridge, a Rhodes Scholar from Australia, was the honourary secretary of the Child Emigration Society, which received small yearly donations from the Rhodes Trust before the First World War.
93 Sedgwick, letter to the editor, *Spectator*, 111, 5 July 1913, 16–17.
94 Sedgwick–New Zealand Boys, 28 March 1913, SP, 2/50/341, LRCS.
95 See Sedgwick–Reverend Canon Garland Brisbane, 2 February 1911, SP, 1/8/21, LRCS.
96 *Fielding Star*, 25 February 1911, clipping, SP, 1/17/44, LRCS; *Lyttleton Times*, clipping (n.d.), SP, 1/31/80, LRCS.
97 John Evelyn Wrench, *The Story of the Over-Seas League* (London, 1926), pp. 41, 43. The extended version of the creed sheds further light on the idea of imperial citizenship as the guardianship of a trust, with overtones of Freemasonry: 'I believe in our glorious Empire of Free Peoples./ In the sacredness of our mission./ In the unselfishness of our aims./ In the ultimate triumph of our cause./ I believe in our great past./ And in a great future./ In the emptiness of riches./ And in the dignity of labour./ I believe in right thinking and pure living./ And in the inspirational power of women./ I believe in national re-birth./ In a new Empire and a new world./ I believe in the need of humbleness./ In the vision of the mountain-tops./ I believe in God's guidance in the days ahead./ I believe': ibid., p. 55.
98 Ibid., pp. 20, 26.
99 Ibid., pp. 42, 45.
100 Ibid., p. 39.
101 Stephen Leacock, quoted in the *New Zealand Times*, 15 June 1911.
102 Sedgwick–Lord Strathcona, 13 March 1912, SP, 2/5/28, LRCS.

103 Colonial subjects did not hold only favourable opinions of Britain, of course. Many rejected the overt British class structure, and were particularly leery about accepting poor children for fear of replicating some of the social ills they had left behind: see for instance Sedgwick, 'Evidence on the Migration to Colonial Farms of Boys from Reformatories and Industrial Schools, to Be Tendered to the Department Committee': SP, 1/73/261, LRCS.
104 Sedgwick–Jebb, 7 March 1912, SP, 2/6/33, LRCS. In commenting on Britons' knowledge of the Empire, Sedgwick was here anticipating one of the more popular lines of analysis in recent imperial historiography. For varying perspectives on this issue, see John Mackenzie, *Propaganda and Empire* (Manchester, 1984), the essays in John Mackenzie (ed.) *Imperialism and Popular Culture* (Manchester, 1986); and Anne McClintock, *Race, Gender and Sexuality in the Colonial Context* (London, 1995).
105 London County Council–Sedgwick, 22 February 1912, SP, 2/7/34, LRCS.
106 Advertising and commercial products can be read as manifestations of public interest in Empire, but also as manifestations of commercialism and the *attribution* by advertisers and businessmen of wants and beliefs to generate demand for a product. Jonathon Schneer argues that it 'was impossible, in turn-of-the-century London, to avoid the imperial subtext,' and points to the fact that Britons '*elected*' (emphasis in original) to partake of 'museums, exhibitions, music halls, nigger minstrelsy, the Regent's Park zoo, and the Sherlock Holmes stories' as evidence that they acquiesced in the imperial message. There is some truth to this claim, but these activities drew on many other contexts as well: see Schneer, *London 1900: The Imperial Metropolis* (New Haven, CT, 1999), pp. 93, 114, 113; and Anandi Ramamurthy, *Imperial Persuaders: Images of Africa and Asia in British Advertising* (Manchester, 2003).
107 'An Englishman'–Sedgwick, letter (n.d.), SP, 3/7/41, LRCS.
108 *The Indian Emigrant*, 111, 12 (July–August 1917), p. 205.
109 'Memorandum on Indian Emigration,' as presented by Indian representatives at the Imperial War Conference, 27 April 1917; reprinted in ibid., pp. 212–15; see also Singh's contribution to debate at the Conference, 27 April 1917, and Resolution 9, 'Note on Emigration from India to the Self-Governing Colonies,' written by the India Office, 22 March 1917: *Imperial War Conference, 1917, Extracts from Minutes of Proceedings and Papers Laid before the Conference*, Cd. 8566, pp. 117–20.
110 *Jamaica Times*, 1 August 1916.
111 See for instance K. M. Panikkar, *The Problems of Greater India* (Madras, 1916).
112 Richard Jebb, *The Britannic Question* (London: 1913), pp. 202–3.
113 *East End News*, 13 December 1911.
114 Bean and Melville, *Lost Children of the Empire*, p. 79.
115 Sedgwick–Lord Stamfordham, 12 February 1912, SP, 2/1/3, LRCS.
116 Under Secretary of State, Colonial Office–Sedgwick, 5 June 1912, SP, 2/1/6, LRCS.
117 C. Reginald Enock, 'Imperial Colonial Development,' *Journal of the Royal Society of Arts*, 58, 2987 (1910), p. 337.

CHAPTER SEVEN

The failure of imperial citizenship

If there has been a theme characterizing Britain's relationship with her overseas relations throughout the twentieth century it is ambivalence. This book has evaluated the efforts of a select group of late Victorian and Edwardian imperial ideologues to articulate a concept of citizenship which could unite Britons at home and in the Empire. Their efforts ended in frustration: the broader public was not convinced of the necessity of a clearly defined imperial citizenship. Perhaps those ideologues asked too much of their putative fellow-imperial citizens. As one of Richard Jebb's correspondents observed, 'The average man has only a certain amount of public spirit and disinterested idealism in his composition and if he exhausts it on "green hills far away" like a federal parliament [or, for that matter, a "Britannic alliance"], he will have very little left for more necessary needs at home.'[1]

Despite their varied arguments, Lionel Curtis, John Buchan, Richard Jebb, Arnold White, and Thomas Sedgwick all shared a desire for the transfer abroad of existing, though albeit sometimes unspoken, notions of British citizenship, which is why they stressed imperial loyalty, unity, service, education, and 'character'. A citizenship built upon liberalism and tolerance is at its heart consensual. Citizenship has a dual nature: it is both a political idea, setting out the rights and responsibilities of membership of a state, and a social and cultural idea, a collective coming to terms with the fact, *pace* Kant, that individuals must perforce live with other individuals. Late Victorian and Edwardian imperial ideologues saw the social idea of citizenship as the more important of the two. This helps explain the often negative view held by Britons regarding those of their peers who 'went native.' Such behaviour was seen as unnatural, not only because it transgressed social conventions or because it offended the prevalent belief in the 'superiority' of the British race, but because it was construed as a rejection of the consensual notion of identity upon which contemporary ideas of citizenship were based.

Imperial citizenship was conceived of as an extension of, rather than a replacement for, the identity of 'British subjecthood'. The concept of subjecthood was the repository for the benefits accrued by all those who lived under the crown, including the right to protection and the right to move freely about the Empire. It did not spell out any specific responsibilities to the State or the collective, however, and thus, to draw upon Charles Tilly's terminology, proved a 'thin' rather than 'thick' bond. Faced with decentralizing pressures in the late Victorian and Edwardian eras, imperial ideologues tried, either directly or indirectly, to build through the concept of imperial citizenship more concrete bonds to ensure that the Empire could resist dissolution. Imperial citizenship was to provide a social and political contract between the subjects of Empire. That their concept of imperial citizenship came close to an ideal of 'whiteness' spoke to their belief that the most important imperial bonds were those between the broader 'Anglo-Saxon' world.[2] The dependent Empire, with the partial exception of India, was largely absent from their considerations, a racism of exclusion which arose from a normative sense of British superiority, and the belief that non-white societies did not adhere to the racialist ideal of cultural homogeneity prevalent throughout the 'British world'.

As Robinson and Gallagher note,[3] Britain's 'other' Empire, the dependencies, was acquired, if not in a fit of absence of mind, then certainly for negative or contingent reasons – to protect trade routes, to make sure someone else did not gain an advantage. A desire to 'civilize' non-white societies was not a primary motive of Empire-building in the first place, a fact which helps explain why the dependent Empire figured little in contemporaries' thinking about imperial citizenship. Even the liberal reforms, both political and attitudinal, which ideologues such as Curtis and Buchan proposed to foster a greater sense of Britishness in the dependent Empire instead gave wind to nationalist sails. It was left to liberal internationalists such as those of the League of Nations Union, who drew on a more liberal imperial heritage rooted in the missionary and anti-slavery movements, to articulate a more humanitarian mission to imperialism after the First World War, by which point the idea of imperial citizenship was a dead letter.[4]

By looking at the imperial intentions and perceptions of individual Britons, the intention has been to avoid presenting Britain's imperial history as an *a priori* one of structural cultural domination. Such a structuralist approach fences in historical subjects, unintentionally obfuscating the agency of both colonizer and colonized. It also risks denouncing *all* attempts by individuals from one culture to engage with those of another.[5] This debate has marked historical discussions of the post-colonial world and clouded our understanding of why most of those societies have not progressed as quickly as their founders certainly hoped. By emphasizing either a common identity of otherness or a 'multiplicity of margins,'[6] post-colonial studies indirectly attenuate the sense of national cohesiveness, modelled on that perceived to be held by Britain, that helped colonial societies attain independence in the first place, and attributes to Britain and Britons a common imperial motive which, as is argued in this book, did not exist. There were as many disparate and autonomous ideas of Empire in the metropole, benevolent, malevolent, and otherwise, as there were identities and means of resistance on the periphery. One cannot argue for multiplicity in the one and not the other. Neither were all imperial ideas divorced from experience. If Arnold White saw little of the Empire, deriving instead his ideas on imperial citizenship from a parochial position, Curtis, Buchan, Jebb, and Sedgwick travelled widely throughout the Empire. If they nonetheless reproduced paternalist concepts of imperial citizenship, they were paternalist concepts derived from experience, not from insularity.

Of the five imperialists whose ideas have provided the content of this study, Lionel Curtis, the 'imperial prophet,' devoted the greatest energy to the project of imperial citizenship. Curtis's imperialism evolved from one of race–patriotism, developed under Milner at the century's dawn, to one extolling Empire as a 'citadel of freedom.' This citadel he termed a 'commonwealth,' built around mutual loyalty to the sovereign. Curtis saw in Empire the potential for a world state, the means of bringing nations together within a single political framework. The goal was world peace; the means of attaining this lofty ideal was imperial federation. Drawing upon Alexander Hamilton's conception of federalism, Curtis favoured a federal Empire in which Britain would be first among equals. His notion of imperial citizenship can be described as one of *authoritarian liberalism*. Though the term appears to be an oxymoron, it signifies an attempt to impose British liberal principles throughout the Empire, as opposed to allowing the nations to develop on their own. In seeing the experience of colonial peoples as provisional, Curtis denied their autonomous role in asserting self-definition. His authoritarian liberalism can be contrasted to the *democratic authoritarianism* expressed in the colonies, where policies of exclusion and homogeneity developed through democratic means. Curtis's principles were expressed most clearly in his support of political tutelage for the less 'advanced' nations of Empire. The idea of dyarchy, specifically, was designed to create a half-way house for India as it progressed toward equal standing in the imperial family.

Curtis failed, however, to accord sufficient standing to colonial nationalism within his proposed Anglosphere. He believed that colonial nationalism was simply a parochial attitude, and thus failed to foresee the evolution of the dominions as independent polities.

In contrast to Curtis's federalist notion of imperial citizenship, John Buchan offered a more tempered understanding of imperial citizenship. Buchan, the Scottish romantic, shared Curtis's sense of Empire as a 'secular religion,' but envisioned a more organic imperium. Buchan's sense of imperial citizenship was cosmopolitan and ecumenical. In the early twentieth century, these terms connoted an expanded understanding of Empire which sought to combine national and imperial identities. Buchan's inclusiveness entailed the expansion of existing identities and boundaries which he believed had stood the test of time, while also incorporating newer ideals which promised productive change. One such ideal was *democracy*. Buchan favoured an expanded democracy as the best means of fostering spiritual unity, a broad church consecrated by its shared devotion to peace. He envisioned imperial citizenship as the lived principle of such an Empire, one which required the active participation of all. Morality and 'character' were the most important requirements of such citizenship. Thus, in principle, no one was ideologically precluded from membership, though in practice Buchan did not support extending citizenship to the dependencies.

If Curtis and Buchan were each struggling towards a less stratified Empire, White represented the imperial status quo. Curtis and Buchan believed that the Empire was rooted in British values; White believed that Empire existed *for* Britain or, more specifically, England. White's English nationalism, his insular prejudices (as seen in his antipathy to Germany), and his attention to maintaining stability each point to the pervasive impact the national efficiency movement had on Edwardian imperial politics. In an effort to counter fears of national decline, White articulated a notion of imperial citizenship which identified patriotism as loyalty to country. Such a citizenship was reciprocal, in its obligations, though the citizen was clearly in a subservient role. The citizen's first priority was fealty to the State. The Empire, White argued, should be run as a business, with emphasis placed on principles of efficiency and a perpetual campaign waged against waste. In order to counter what he perceived as critical domestic socioeconomic problems, he advocated the emigration of 'surplus' population to the Empire and opposed foreign immigration to England. Finally, White displayed a latent Whiggishness: his association with the Duke of Bedford, Lord Beresford, and Lord Fisher signalled the esteem in which he held aristocratic governance.

THE FAILURE OF IMPERIAL CITIZENSHIP

Curtis and Buchan represented movement among imperial ideologues toward a graduated imperial inclusiveness, while White's exclusivist definition of imperial citizenship marked out a more conservative position to hold the line on Empire. This conflict between forward- and backward-looking ideologies was illustrated in the contrast between the careers and ideas of Richard Jebb and Thomas Sedgwick. Jebb's idea of a Britannic alliance expressed elements both of Curtis's constitution-building and of Buchan's sense of organic Empire. What set Jebb apart from Curtis and Buchan was his attention to colonial nationalism. He accorded the dominions a greater place within his definition of imperial citizenship than did either Curtis or Buchan, arguing that imperial unity was possible only through the creation of a 'wider patriotism'. Such a patriotism would evolve through the concept of 'mutual-aid-in-living,' the harmonization of centrist and peripheral interests. Jebb's putative alliance was compromised by the practical difficulties of imperial cooperation. One such difficulty was the failure to harmonize imperial naturalization legislation. Intra-imperial immigration, perhaps the most significant channel through which Jebb's envisioned wider patriotism might flow, was never opened. Though the goal of imperial citizenship was cultural consensus, local, national, and imperial identities proved at perpetual variance. The issue of immigration, and the attendant conflict between a liberal, though somewhat ambivalent, understanding of racial issues in Britain and the dominions' desire to dictate their own policies on race illustrated the practical failings of imperial citizenship.

Thomas Sedgwick also advanced a utopian view of imperial citizenship. He stayed closer to the shore, however, in conceiving of Empire and imperial citizenship in English nationalist terms. Like White, Sedgwick looked upon individual citizens as imperial capital. Sedgwick perceived imperial issues to be extensions of domestic issues, a perception borne out by the distinction he made between migration as movement *within* the Empire and emigration as movement *outside* the Empire. Drawing upon the ideas of social imperialism which developed within the national efficiency movement, he saw assisted emigration as a means of solving domestic concerns of overcrowding, economic stagnation, and cultural decline. Sedgwick's work also illustrates the divisions present within the dominions themselves, which were increasingly nationalist and autonomous, yet still tied to Britain by economic, military, and, most significantly, cultural bonds. Finally, Sedgwick's difficulties, especially in raising money for his operations, point to the lukewarm manner in which his fellow-Britons viewed any such schemes of imperial citizenship.

The early twentieth-century debate over imperial citizenship thus produced two camps: centralizing social imperialists, which included both progressives such as Curtis and traditionalists such as White and Sedgwick; and cosmopolitan 'associationists' such as Buchan and Jebb. The centralizing social imperialists sought to incorporate individual identities within a single concept of imperial citizenship, whether within the framework of an imperial federation, as Curtis proposed, or subsumed within an English identity which preserved the imperial traditions of the nineteenth century, as White advocated. Cosmopolitan associationists, conversely, favoured a compromise model of citizenship that allowed space for both imperial and national identities. As both Jebb and, belatedly, Buchan came to accept, colonial nationalism could not be reversed. If the Empire was to be preserved, it must be in a manner which respected the place of colonial nationalism. Cosmopolitan associationists believed an imperial citizenship constructed through the various intra-imperial social connections of Britishness was the best means of ensuring the Empire's future.

Both the centralists and the associationists, however, experienced defeat. They were unable to create a *hybrid* citizenship, one which incorporated elements of both the classical and the republican model of citizenship, and took cognizance of the historically specific concerns of their age.[7] Rejecting the explicit division between the terms 'centralist' and 'associationist,' each camp of conservative imperialists viewed imperial citizenship in terms of both *Gemeinschaft* (community), an ethnic conception of a nation including a common language and shared history and culture, and *Gesellschaft* (society), a mutual living arrangement interconnected by socio-political institutions. They proved unsuccessful in combining the two. Despite their differences, the imperium conceived by both centralizing social imperialists and cosmopolitan associationists was one of English culture girding the earth. Leopold Amery, a confidant of both Curtis and Buchan,[8] noted that it remained essential that imperial subjects' allegiance remain to the crown, as Empire alone was capable of keeping international peace and 'educating' Britain's subject races in political competence. These goals were to be achieved, Amery concluded, through the stimulus of British culture.[9] The dominions served as overseas extensions of this culture, and imperial citizenship meant the expansion of British cultural traditions. Indeed, this sense of shared cultural citizenship long outlasted serious discussions of imperial citizenship as a political ideal. While it is overstating the case to suggest that the dominions merely reproduced 'English life all over again,' as J. A. Froude observed of Australia,[10] many (though obviously not all) dominion subjects nurtured a sense of cultural connectedness through modes as varied as the BBC's Empire Service, celebrations of Edmund Hillary's conquest of Everest as one of their own, or devouring Buchan's fiction in part out of a proprietary interest in the (romanticized) imperial world he conjured.[11] As but one symbolic example, it is surely indicative of the lingering cultural resonance of Britishness that Canada did not replace the Red Ensign as its national flag with the Maple Leaf until 1965.[12]

Ultimately, and ironically, the idea of imperial citizenship failed because it was expressed, at least by its more progressive proponents, in democratic terms. Imperialists such as Buchan and Curtis saw liberty as a society's most important virtue, and pointed to democracy, in its Westminster form, as one of the pillars of any prospective imperial citizenship. Yet these very democratic values, a self-consciously broader acceptance of which was a point of pride for subjects in the dominions, also implied the liberty of choice. That the dominions used this liberty of choice to define their own national identities in a manner counter to the various imperial identities implied in the positions of both centralizing social imperialists and cosmopolitan associationists meant that a unified imperial citizenship was never possible. By defining their own national identities, particularly through their racially exclusive attitudes and legislative responses to immigration, the dominions remind us that democracy itself is value-free, capable of licensing both progressive and exclusionary outcomes.

Why, then, did the idea of imperial citizenship hold such promise for so many imperialists, both in Britain and in the dominions? Partly it gave voice to a shared cultural identity of Britishness that was still strong in the early twentieth century. More importantly, it helped manage intra-imperial tensions. Indeed, the very inability to craft a definitive imperial citizenship in a political sense, and more broadly, the multiple views on what a social conception of imperial citizenship might entail, was in fact fortuitous. As with the concept of loyalism, a language upon which many groups, often diametrically opposed on other issues, could agree, the idea of imperial citizenship represented a touchstone. It was a familial bond which buttressed the imperial family until the dominions were ready to go their own way. The very ambiguity of 'imperial citizenship', which bundled together the concepts of subjecthood and loyalism, and political and social ideas of citizenship, perhaps even attenuated some of the inherent tensions of the Empire's dissolution. Helen Irving's thoughts on the benefits of Australian citizenship's lack of historical precision can be applied to imperial citizenship as well: the lack of

> any definition of citizenship... has served us well. It has shielded us from the inappropriate values of the past; it has allowed the evolution

of different approaches to Australian politics; it has serve to reinforce restraint and to permit tolerance of ways of doing things that are not otherwise prohibited.[13]

The fact that the dominions did not craft racially exclusive definitions of citizenship, for instance, in part to avoid running foul of the shared social and political identity implied in the idea of imperial citizenship, has meant that later generations have not been constitutionally hamstrung by the racial attitudes of the early twentieth century (the social legacy of such attitudes is a separate matter). Ideals of civil rights, racial equality, and national self-determination, largely foreign to the mentality of the pre-1920 imperial world, have thus been incorporated into subsequent understandings of citizenship, if not always easily.

What the late Victorian and Edwardian discourses concerning imperial citizenship reveal is an ideological community in transition. Imperialists were forced to rethink their imperial convictions. What this collective rethinking revealed was a division between political and social conceptions of Empire. Citizenship was primarily a social construction, drawing more on the idea of community than on that of individual rights. Citizenship meant a sense of commitment to the community, and thus preceded, rather than being conferred by, the assumption of political rights such as the franchise.[14] This is why the imperialists studied in this book did not overtly exclude women, even though, in Britain, women did not yet have the vote. They were not particularly progressive on the issue of female suffrage (though Buchan was a supporter);[15] rather, political rights were of secondary importance. Imperial citizenship was first and foremost the expression of a sense of belonging to the *British* community, a sense women shared equally with men. This conception of citizenship as a sense of belonging, however, became untenable as the assumption of political rights became more pronounced as the twentieth century progressed. To return to the citizenship typologies of Charles Tilly and T. H. Marshall, the imperial citizenship evinced by early twentieth-century imperial ideologues was a *thin* citizenship, entailing few rights and responsibilities, and was rooted in the nineteenth-century idea of citizenship as the expression of civic belonging. It meant above all an identification with the whole, which in late Victorian and Edwardian imperial ideology meant the organic imperial state. Such a thin civic citizenship was rendered obsolete by the *thick* social citizenship, consecrated in political rights, whose origins Marshall traces to the Representation of the People Act (1918) granting women aged 30 and over the franchise.

The ideal of imperial citizenship thus did not survive the First World War. The decentralization of Empire, the process which imperial ideologues had sought to stem by strengthening citizenship ties, instead continued apace. The common-code system, expressed through the British Nationality and Status of Aliens Act 1914 (4 & 5 Geo.V., c.17), designed to define subjecthood as the signifier of imperial membership, faltered in the face of continued colonial nationalism, particularly the dominions' measures to define their own citizenship through naturalization and immigration legislation.[16] Though motivated by its wish to have a Canadian representative at the League of Nations' new Permanent Court of International Justice, rather than to challenge the definition of imperial citizenship, the Canadian Nationals Act (1921) nonetheless established a decentralizing precedent. The other dominions followed suit in the interwar era. Some made minor revisions to the common-code system, such as New Zealand's 1934 Amendment to the British Nationality and Status of Aliens Act allowing women who married aliens to retain their British subjecthood, while Ireland's Nationality and Citizenship Act (1935) renounced subjecthood altogether.[17] Britain recognized the dominions as separate political entities in the Balfour Declaration (1926), and further confused the issue of imperial citizenship through the introduction of the 'divisible crown,' making the monarch the separate sovereign of each dominion. The latter measure thus severed the connection between subjecthood and citizenship, decentring the concept of loyalty and facilitating further devolution. The *de facto* dual citizenship enjoyed by imperial subjects under the common-code system, the principle of imperial citizenship which ideologues such as Curtis and Jebb wanted to strengthen, ironically ended after the Second World War with the creation of a nominal 'commonwealth citizenship' under the British Nationality Act (1948). Commonwealth conferences in 1946 and 1947 gave birth to the Canadian Citizenship Act (1946) and the Australian Nationality and Citizenship Act (1949); similar legislation followed throughout the Commonwealth. While the British Nationality Act did facilitate large-scale colonial emigration to Britain, the Act in fact acknowledged the existence of multiple citizenships within the Commonwealth as opposed to creating a single Commonwealth (imperial) citizenship.

The mass migration to Britain of non-white subjects, a process symbolically begun when the *Empire Windrush* docked on 21 June 1948 with 492 Jamaican migrants on board, ironically further weakened the concept of imperial citizenship. The liberal discourse which, as this book has argued, dominated domestic British political conceptions of citizenship was overturned by a new discourse wherein, in Kathleen Paul's words, 'formal definitions of citizenship increasingly have had less influence than racialized images of national identity.'[18] New arrivals from the West Indies, and later Africa and South-East Asia, forced

Britons to confront an imperial past which had previously been abstract and idealized. Colonial migration thus, as C. L. R. James once said, helped to 'decolonize' Britain itself.[19] Part of this process of 'domestic decolonization' was a turn to discussions of *British* nationality and citizenship at the expense of imperial identities.

The social conception of imperial citizenship, the foundation for Jebb's 'wider patriotism' and Sedgwick's 'sentimental imperialism,' also declined after the First World War, though less precipitously. Despite the last gasps of the imperial die-hards at home, and a lingering sense of pan-imperial Britishness which can be detected in cultural and sporting events such as the Empire/Commonwealth Games (first held in Hamilton, Ontario, in 1930),[20] the increased frequency of royal tours, a sense of colonial camaraderie during the Second World War,[21] and the continued attraction for dominion students of British universities, the dominions nonetheless increasingly conceived of themselves in national terms as the twentieth century progressed.[22]

It is true that many of the large number of return migrants – Marjory Harper estimates that almost 40% of English and Welsh migrants, and a third of Scottish migrants, returned between 1870 and 1914[23] – retained aspects of their new-found colonial identities and strengthened pan-imperial familial bonds.[24] Yet, as the twentieth century unfolded, colonials in Britain attached ever greater importance to their national, rather than their imperial, identity. The construction of new buildings for dominion high commissions on prominent sites in London were expressions of such nationalism – Australia House (1918) on the Strand, and Canada House (1925) and South Africa House (1933) on Trafalgar Square.[25] Emigration from Britain to the dominions fell off after 1945, while non-British immigration increased, further attenuating British ties. The former dominions are now multi-cultural societies which, if they mirror the Edwardian Empire's ethnic diversity, have established new cultural identities of which Britishness is but one small component. There remain Empire Clubs in the former dominions today, yet those venerable organizations have become gathering places for professional elites rather than expressions of a lingering imperial citizenship. In Britain itself, the most overt signs of collective identity for visitors from the former dominions are not sites of British history or culture, but commercial establishments such as the Maple Leaf Pub in Covent Garden and tours by sporting teams such as the New Zealand All Blacks rugby team.

While the modern Commonwealth lays claim to some of the ideals of imperial citizenship, such as its self-identification as an association for promoting world peace and cultural measures such as the

Commonwealth Writers Prize,[26] few of the social and political ties upon which Edwardian imperial ideologues based their thinking remain. The British world with which those ideologues identified expired alongside Empire itself. That the current analogies drawn by scholars between globalization and the British Empire, whether positive or negative, focus on questions of military, economic, or cultural power, rather than citizenship,[27] illustrates clearly that the ideal of imperial citizenship was an idea firmly of its age.

Notes

1 J. A. Stevenson–Jebb, 13 Sept. 1914, Jebb Papers, A, ICS.
2 One expression of this direction of imperial loyalty was the erection of public monuments throughout the dominions, celebrating themes such as the United Empire Loyalists or the dominions' contributions to the South African War.
3 R. Robinson and J. Gallagher, *Africa and the Victorians* (New York, 1961).
4 *Objects and Rules of the League of Nations Union* (London, 1919), pp. 3–4, British Library of Economic and Political Science, Records of the League of Nations Union, F 1/1; see also Daniel Gorman, 'Liberal Internationalism, the League of Nations Union, and the Mandates System,' *Canadian Journal of History*, 40, 3 (2005), pp. 449–77.
5 For a study which evaluates the work of an early twentieth-century British imperialist outside of a structure of hegemony, see Rodney Koeneke, *Empires of the Mind: I. A. Richards and Basic English in China, 1929–1979* (Stanford, 2004).
6 B. R. Tomlinson, 'What Was the Third World?,' *Journal of Contemporary History*, 38, 2 (2003), pp. 316, 318.
7 Conservatives also debated these points in the field of economics. A *Methodenstreit*, or clash over methods, ensued between classical economists of the Manchester school of free trade and proponents of the new historical economics, who attacked free trade as it was then constituted, instead favouring a deductive model of economics: see E. H. H. Green, *The Crisis of Conservatism: The Politics, Economics and Ideology of the British Conservative Party, 1880–1914* (London, 1995), chapter 5.
8 Amery, who wrote widely and sagely on imperial matters, could easily be included alongside the individuals studied in this project but for the fact that he attained high office, and thus moved from the realm of the dissemination of ideas to that of the formulation of policy.
9 Leopold Amery–Robert Brand (n.d., but 25 May 1914), Round Table Papers, Leopold Amery File, MSS English History 805/38, 39, Bodleian Library, Oxford University.
10 Quoted in David Cannadine, *Ornamentalism* (Oxford, 2001), p. 34.
11 John Mackenzie, 'In Touch with the Infinite: The BBC and the Empire, 1923–1953,' in Mackenzie (ed.) *Imperialism and Popular Culture* (Manchester, 1998), p. 181; Peter Hansen, 'Coronation Everest: The Empire and Commonwealth in the "Second Elizabethan Age",' in Stuart Ward (ed.) *British Culture and the End of Empire* (Manchester, 2001), pp. 62–4; Andrew Lownie, *John Buchan: The Presbyterian Cavalier* (London, 1995), p. 294.
12 See Gregory A. Johnson, 'The Last Gasp of Empire: The 1964 Flag Debate Revisited,' in Phillip Buckner (ed.) *Canada and the End of Empire* (Vancouver, 2005), pp. 232–50; and Alistair B. Fraser, 'A Canadian Flag for Canada,' *Journal of Canadian Studies*, 25, 4 (1990–91), pp. 64–80.
13 Helen Irving, 'Citizenship Before 1949,' in Kim Rubenstein (ed.) *Individual, Community, Nation: 50 Years of Australian Citizenship* (Melbourne, 2000), p. 15.
14 The Representation of the People Bill (1918), which conferred citizenship to women 30 years of age or older, provided they or their husbands held property worth at

least £5, stemmed in part from the expressed commitment to a sense of shared community evidenced in women's patriotic war service: see Nicoletta Gullace, *'The Blood of Our Sons': Men, Women and the Renegotiation of British Citizenship during the Great War* (Basingstoke, 2002), p. 146.
15 J. Buchan, 'Women's Suffrage: A Logical Outcome of the Conservative Faith,' leaflet for the Conservative and Unionist Women's Franchise Association (n.d., but probably 1911), Scrapbook 1: Miscellaneous, 1904–1919), Buchan Papers, QUA.
16 Rieko Karatani, *Defining British Citizenship* (London, 2003), pp. 70–1, 80–3.
17 Ibid., pp. 90–3.
18 Kathleen Paul, *Whitewashing Britain: Race and Citizenship in the Postwar Era* (Ithaca, NY, 1997), pp. 111, 189.
19 Quoted in Bill Schwarz, 'Introduction: Crossing the Seas,' in Schwarz (ed.) *West Indian Intellectuals in Britain* (Manchester, 2003), p. 3.
20 See *British Empire Games, Scrapbook: Volume 1 (1929–)*, Hamilton Public Library, Hamilton, Ontario, Special Collections, R796.4 BRI v.1 CESH.
21 See Daniel Gorman, 'The Experience of Commonwealth and Colonial Soldiers in World War II,' in Timothy Dowling (ed.) *Personal Perspectives: World War II* (Santa Barbara, CA, 2005), pp. 147–74.
22 Phillip Buckner suggests that 'a huge reservoir of emotional support for the continuation of the British connection' existed in Canada at least into the 1950s, though this is something different than the perpetuation of a *British* identity: Buckner (ed.) *Canada and the End of Empire* (Vancouver, 2005), p. 6.
23 Marjory Harper, 'Introduction,' in Harper (ed.) *Emigrant Homecomings* (Manchester, 2005), p. 2.
24 Marilyn J. Barber, '"Two Homes Now": The Return Migration of the Fellowship of the Maple Leaf,' in ibid., p. 197.
25 Mackenzie King–Peter Larkin, Canadian High Commissioner, 10 July 1925, Canadian National Archives, RG 25, Series B-1-b, vol. 289, file P 9/59; on dominion–Britain relations after 1919, see Lorna Lloyd, 'Loosening the Apron Strings: The Dominions and Britain in the Interwar Years,' *Round Table*, 369 (2003), pp. 279–303.
26 The Commonwealth Writers Prize is technically awarded by the Commonwealth Foundation, an international organisation (originally a charitable trust) created by the Commonwealth Heads of Government in 1965 to promote civic and cultural ties within the Commonwealth.
27 Comparisons between late twentieth- and early twenty-first-century globalization and the British Empire are growing in number by the year: see Niall Ferguson, *Empire* (New York, 2003). For an identically titled, yet more theoretical, study of globalization, see Michael Hardt and Antonio Negri, *Empire* (Cambridge, MA, 2000). Hardt and Negri's concept of 'the multitude,' while approximating an idea of global citizenship, is rooted in resistance to modern capitalism and the biopower upon which they claim it rests, not an allegiance, whether social or political, to a broader world body.

APPENDICES

Appendix 1 Biographical information on persons referred to in the text

Biographical entries detail the respective individuals' careers during the years covered by the book (1895–1919); thus, no details are given for their careers after 1919–20, and any titles bestowed after 1919 are not noted (e.g. Winston Churchill's entry is limited to his imperial service up to the end of the First World War, and neglects his later public activities and knighthood). Individuals are listed according to the name by which they were known during this period, and by which they are referred to in the text.

Amery, Leopold Stennet (1873–1955) British statesman. The Indian-born Amery was a long-standing Conservative MP; he served as Colonial Under-Secretary and First Lord of the Admiralty, becoming Colonial Secretary in 1919.

Asquith, Herbert Henry (1852–1928) British statesman and Prime Minister (1908–1916). The Liberal Asquith also served as Home Secretary (1892–95) and Chancellor of the Exchequer (1905–08).

Balfour, Arthur James (1848–1930) British statesman and Prime Minister (1902–5); the Conservative Balfour presided over the end of the Boer War, passed the Education Act (1902), and, later, as Foreign Secretary in 1917, was responsible for the *Balfour Declaration*, indicating the British Government's support for a Jewish homeland in Palestine.

Baring, Evelyn, 1st Earl of Cromer (1841–1917) Colonial administrator and Consul-General in Egypt (1893–1907), he was responsible for the financial reform of Egypt.

Barnardo, Thomas John (1845–1905) Philanthropist and physician; Barnado was the founder of Dr Barnardo's Homes for Destitute Children.

Beresford, Charles, Baron (1846–1919) Naval Commander; Lord of the Admiralty (1886–88), Conservative MP, Commander of the Mediterranean Fleet (1905–7) and Channel Fleet (1907–9). Beresford was closely associated with the 'blue water' school of naval policy.

Bosanquet, Bernard (1848–1923) Philosopher, member, with his wife Helen, of the Charity Organization Society and a leading neo-Hegelian scholar.

Botha, Louis (1862–1919) South African soldier, statesman, and Prime Minister; attended the 1907 and 1911 Imperial Conferences in London.

Bourassa, Henri (1868–1952) Canadian politician and journalist; he opposed Canadian participation in the Boer War and the First World War, founded the

APPENDICES

newspaper *Le Devoir*, and was a proponent of French Canadian nationalism and an opponent of imperialism.

Brand, Phillip (1878–1963) Banker and public servant, member of the Kindergarten.

Campbell-Bannerman, Sir Henry (1836–1908) British statesman and Prime Minister (1905–8), Campbell-Bannerman united the Liberals under his leadership, drawing together the party's pro-Boer and Liberal Imperialist wings.

Casement, Sir Roger (1864–1916) British consular officer, Irish nationalist; he was instrumental in exposing Belgium's exploitative rule in the Congo, and later executed for treason for playing a leading role in the Sinn Féin rebellion of 1916.

Cecil, Beatrix Maud, Lady Selborne (1858–1950) A strong supporter of Empire, and early opponent of female suffrage, she was the daughter of the 3rd Marquess of Salisbury.

Cecil, Edgar Algernon Robert (1864–1958) Lord Salisbury's eldest son, member of the Ralegh Club, and was elected Tory MP in 1903.

Cecil, Robert (Arthur Talbot Gascoyne), 3rd Marquess of Salisbury (1830–1903) British statesman and Prime Minister 1885–86, 1886–92, 1895–1902), Salisbury served as his own Foreign Secretary until 1900.

Chamberlain, Joseph (1836–1914) British statesman, businessman, Mayor of Birmingham (1873–75), and Liberal and Liberal Unionist MP, he became Colonial Secretary in 1895 in the Unionist Coalition Government. He was the leading political force in promoting the Boer War, and was an ardent advocate of imperial union. He resigned in 1903 to campaign for tariff reform. He suffered a stroke in 1906 and retired from public life.

Chamberlain, Joseph Austen (1873–1937) British statesman, the son of Joseph Chamberlain; he was a Liberal Unionist and Conservative MP, Chancellor of the Exchequer (1903–6 and 1919–21).

Chesterton, Gilbert Keith (1874–1936) A literary critic, poet, novelist, and social commentator, Chesterton converted to Catholicism in 1922.

Chirol, Sir Ignatius Valentine (1852–1929) Journalist, author, civil servant.

Churchill, Winston (1874–1965) British statesman. Served in Africa in the Fourth Hussars from 1895 to 1899. His journalism on the Boer War made him famous. Was a Conservative MP (1900–4), a Liberal MP (1904–15), an independent MP (1915–24). He held numerous cabinet positions during this era, including Colonial Under-Secretary (1905), President of the Board of Trade (1908–10), Home Secretary (1910–11), the Admiralty (1911–15), Minister of Munitions (1917), and Secretary of State for War (1919–21).

Coupland, Reginald (1884–1952) Historian of the British Empire and Commonwealth; an early admirer of Curtis, he was Beit Lecturer in Colonial History at Oxford in 1913.

[218]

APPENDICES

Courtney, Leonard (1832–1918) Journalist and statesman; Liberal Unionist MP, a leading pro-Boer, and forceful advocate of proportional representation.

Croft, Sir Henry Page (1881–1947) British politician who supported imperial preference, and in 1917 helped found the 'Nationalist Party', which advocated a xenophobic imperialism.

Cunningham, William (1849–1919) Economic historian at the University of Birmingham, an advocate of tariff reform, and Archdeacon of Ely.

Curzon, George Nathaniel, Marquess of Kedleston (1859–1925) British statesman and Viceroy of India (1898–1905); he introduced political and social reform to India, created the North West Frontier Province, and partitioned Bengal.

Dilke, Sir Charles Wentworth (1843–1911) British politician, author, and advocate of Empire. A Liberal radical, his career came to an end in 1885 over his alleged involvement with a fellow-MP's wife.

Dyer, Reginald (1864–1927) British Brigadier General responsible for the Amritsar massacre in 1919.

Ewart, John Skirving (1849–1933) Canadian lawyer and publicist, and an advocate of Canadian constitutional independence.

Feetham, Richard (1874–1965) Judge; he was a member of the Kindergarten, an intellectual leader in the drafting of the Selborne Memorandum, and an MLA in the South African Legislature.

Feiling, Keith Grahame (1884–1977) Historian; he served in India during the First World War as a commissioned officer.

Fischer, Andrew (1862–1928) Australian statesman and Prime Minister; born in Scotland, he became leader of the Australian Labour Party in 1907, served as Prime Minister on three occasions, supported Australia's entry into the First World War, and was Australia's High Commissioner in London (1916–21).

Fisher, John A., Baron of Kilverstone (1841–1920) British Naval Commander, Lord of the Admiralty (1892–97), First Sea Lord (1904–15); in 1906 he introduced the Dreadnought series, and improved naval training and living conditions.

Frere, Sir Bartle (1815–1884) Governor and High Commissioner of the Cape Colony (1877–80); an advocate of British expansion in Southern Africa.

Galton, Sir Francis (1822–1911) Explorer and scientist, he was the founder of the study of eugenics, drawing on the thought of his cousin Charles Darwin.

Gandhi, Mohandas K. (1869–1948) Indian nationalist leader; he studied law in London, protested the discriminatory treatment of Indians in South Africa, especially Natal, and raised an ambulance corps of Indians during the Boer War. He returned to India in 1914, and though he supported the British war effort, became a leading figure in the Indian Congress Movement; he pioneered the use of *satyagraha*, and, after protesting the Amritsar massacre, was jailed for two years for treason.

APPENDICES

Gardiner, Alfred George (1865–1946) Journalist and editor of the radical *Daily News*, he was a strong supporter of liberal politics, who favoured war against Germany in 1914.

Gladstone, William Ewart (1809–1898) British statesman and Prime Minister (1868–74, 1880–85, 1886, 1892–94). Though not a little Englander, Gladstone was ambivalent towards Empire, though it should be noted that much of the Empire's late nineteenth-century expansion occurred under his administrations. Gladstone himself was particularly supportive of national self-determination, particularly in the Balkans.

Goldie, Sir George (1840–1925) West African trader, eccentric, director of the United Africa Company, and founder of Nigeria.

Gordon, Charles George (1833–1885) General in the British Army, 'Chinese Gordon' helped suppress the Taiping Rebellion, was Governor of the Sudan (1877–80), and in 1884 was besieged at Khartoum by the Mahdi's troops and killed before relief was sent. He became an imperial hero.

Grant, George (1835–1902) Principal of Queen's University, Kingston, Grant was a Canadian supporter of imperial federation.

Grey, Edward, Viscount of Fallodon (1862–1933) British statesman and Liberal Foreign Secretary (1905–1916), Grey was a Liberal Imperialist.

Grigg, Sir Edward (1879–1955) Civil servant and politician; he was *The Times'* leading foreign correspondent for much of the 1900s and 1910s, and the first editor of *The Round Table*.

Harmsworth, Alfred, 1st Viscount Northcliffe (1865–1922) Journalist and newspaper proprietor who revolutionized British journalism with his *Daily Mail*, launched in 1896, and was a leading advocate of the 'new journalism'; he became the proprietor of *The Times* in 1908.

Hichens, William Lionel (1875–1940) Businessman; a member of the Kindergarten, he was Treasurer of the Transvaal and the Orange Free State (1903–07), and was a leading industrialist.

Hobson, John Atkinson (1858–1940) British economist and publicist; he formulated the economic theory of under-consumption, and in his most famous work, *Imperialism: A Study* (1902), he critiqued imperialism as a system driven by excess capital in the domestic market to seek new markets abroad.

Howard, Mary, Lady Murray (1865–1956) An accomplished classicist and collaborator in the public life of her husband Gilbert Murray.

Jameson, Sir Leander Starr (1853–1917) British colonial statesman; he led the infamous Jameson Raid into the Transvaal in December 1895, and was subsequently sentenced to 15 months in prison, of which he served 6. He went on to become Prime Minister of the Cape Colony (1904–8) and supported the South African Union.

APPENDICES

Kerr, Phillip, Marquess of Lothian (1882–1940) Publicist and diplomat; Kerr was a member of Milner's Kindergarten, a founding member of the Round Table, an imperial journalist, and a member of Lloyd George's 'garden suburb' after 1916.

Kidd, Benjamin (1858–1916) Civil servant; Kidd's *Social Evolution* (1894) advocated a social-Darwinian approach to foreign affairs.

King, William Lyon Mackenzie (1874–1950) Liberal MP, Minister of Labour (1909–11), Liberal leader (1919); King was a colonial nationalist who strongly championed a greater role for the colonies within the Empire.

Kipling, Rudyard (1865–1936) His journalism, poetry, and prose made him the preeminent imperial writer of the era; he won the Nobel Prize for Literature in 1907.

Kitchener, Herbert Horatio, 1st Earl of Khartoum and of Broome (1850–1916) British Field Marshall who won back the Sudan for Britain in 1898, led the war effort in south Africa (1900–2), was Commander-in-Chief in India (1902–9), Consul-General in Egypt (1911), and Secretary of State for War (1914).

Kruger, Paul (1825–1904) President of the Transvaal (1883–1902); held the Afrikaner side in the Boer War, opposing the integration of the Orange Free State and the Transvaal into the Empire.

Laurier, Sir Wilfrid (1841–1919) Canadian statesman and Prime Minister (1896–1911); as Liberal Party leader he advocated self-government for Canada, and opposed imperial federation.

Livingstone, David (1813–73) Missionary and African explorer.

Lloyd George, David (1863–1945) Statesman and Prime Minister (1916–22), the Welsh Liberal served as President of the Board of Trade (1905–8) and Chancellor of the Exchequer (1908–15); he was a political supporter of home rule.

Lucas, Sir Charles Prestwood (1853–1931) Civil servant and imperial historian; he was the first head of the Dominions Department (1907), the forerunner of the Dominions Office.

Lugard, Frederick (1858–1945) British soldier and colonial administrator who served the crown in Uganda and Nigeria, and became a leading proponent of the concept of indirect rule.

Mackinder, Sir Halford (1861–1947) Founder of modern geography, Liberal imperialist, and, after a political conversion, advocate of protection and a neo-mercantile vision of Empire.

Markham, Violet Rosa (1872–1959) Public servant. The host of influential political and social discussions at her Gower Street home, she opposed female suffrage until 1918, the same year she lost her only contest for a seat in Parliament.

Massey, Charles Vincent (1887–1969) Rhodes Scholar and lecturer in modern history at the University of Toronto, he was an Anglophile Canadian and an admirer of Curtis.

APPENDICES

Maxse, Leopold James (1864–1932) Journalist and editor of the *National Review*; a strident Germanophobe.

Milner, Alfred, 1st Viscount (1854–1925) British statesman and High Commissioner for South Africa (1897–1905), Milner devoted his life to Empire, was a leading figure in precipitating and prosecuting the Boer War, presided over post-war reconstruction, and later served in the War Cabinet from 1916 to 1921, holding the post of Colonial Secretary (1919–21); he was the spiritual head of the Round Table and a leading social imperialist.

Morel, Edmund Dene (1873–1924) Journalist and campaigner for a democratic foreign policy; he was a co-founder of the Congo Reform Association, which helped expose King Leopold II's brutalities in the Belgium Congo.

Murray, Gilbert (1866–1957) Classical scholar, Professor of Greek at Glasgow (1889) and Oxford (1908), he was also a Liberal throughout his life; a supporter and eventual President of the League of Nations.

Naoroji, Dadabhai (1825–1917) Indian politician, the first Indian elected to the House of Commons (1892, for Central Finsbury) – despite Lord Salisbury's belief that the voters would never elect a 'black man' – and a founder of the Indian National Congress.

Oliver, Frederick Scott (1864–1934) Retailer and imperial publicist, his *Alexander Hamilton* (1906) was influential in shaping the thought of Round Table advocates of imperial federation.

Palmer, William Waldegrave, 2nd Earl of Selborne (1859–1942) British statesman, High Commissioner for South Africa and Governor of Transvaal and the Orange Free State (1905–9); he was the political force behind South African Union, and lent his name to the Selborne Memorandum, the constitutional plan which the members of the Kindergarten were influential in framing.

Pankhurst, Emmeline (*née* Goulden) (1857–1928) Suffragette, founder of both the Women's Franchise League (1899), and, with her daughter Christabel, the Women's Social and Political Union (1903); her other daughter, Sylvia, promoted pacifism and internationalism.

Parkes, Sir Henry (1815–1896) Australian statesman, he was the Premier of New South Wales five times, and helped draft the Australian constitution.

Parkin, Sir George Robert (1846–1922) Canadian educator; the self-titled 'wandering evangelist of Empire,' he was the leader of the Imperial Federation Movement in the 1880s, and from 1902 until his death the secretary of the Rhodes Trust at Oxford; knighted in 1920.

Pearson, Karl (1857–1936) Scientist and Professor of Eugenics at University College, London, a pioneer of the study of human evolution and heredity, he favoured a social-Darwinian view of Empire.

Pollock, Sir Frederick (1854–1937) British jurist and Liberal Unionist politician.

APPENDICES

Primrose, Archibald Philip, 5th Earl of Rosebery (1847–1929) British statesman and politician, he served as Gladstone's Foreign Secretary (1886, 1892–4), was briefly Prime Minister (1894–95), and was a leading Liberal imperialist in the 1890s and the early twentieth century.

Rhodes, Cecil (1853–1902) British colonial statesman; Rhodes spearheaded British expansion south of the Zambezi, was behind the Jameson Raid, and promoted the Cape–Cairo line. His will provided for scholarships at Oxford for colonials, Americans, and Germans; the Rhodes Trust, another of his bequests, has been a guiding force in imperial studies since his death.

Russell, Herbrand Arthur, 11th Duke of Bedford (1858–1940) Military advocate, patron of zoological and scientific research, Lord-Lieutenant of Middlesex (1898–1926)

Shaughnessy, Thomas George, 1st Baron Shaughnessy (1853–1923) Canadian railway executive who helped secure financing for the Canadian Pacific Railway, and served as its president from 1899 to 1918.

Smuts, Jan Christian (1870–1950) South African statesman; he fought in the Boer War, held several cabinet posts in the Cape House of Assembly, fought on the side of Britain in the First World War, and became Prime Minister of South Africa in 1919; he was an advocate of colonial nationalism, and favoured the League of Nations.

Stead, William Thomas (1849–1912) Journalist, editor of the *Pall Mall Gazette* and later of the *Review of Reviews*, he was a leading figure in the 'new journalism' and a strident opponent of the Boer War; he was lost with the *Titanic* when it sank in 1912.

Steel-Maitland, Sir Arthur (1876–1935) Politician and economist, Conservative MP (1910–29, 1930–35) and Political Under-Secretary for the Colonies (1915–19).

Strachey, John St Loe (1860–1927) Journalist, editor of the *Spectator* (1898–1925), and Liberal Unionist advocate of Empire.

Trevelyan, George Macaulay (1876–1962) Historian; the son of the politician Sir George Trevelyan, he studied at Cambridge and served in the First World War.

Walpole, Hugh (1884–1941) Novelist, born in New Zealand, whose earliest commercial success was *The Secret City* (1919).

Ward, Sir Joseph (1856–1930) New Zealand statesman and Prime Minister, a Labour politician who was most noted for his social reform measures, including the world's first Ministry of Public Health, and the provision of pensions for widows; knighted in 1901.

Ware, Sir Fabian (1869–1949) Journalist, editor of the *Morning Post* (1905–11), and director of the Imperial War Graves Commission.

Wrench, John Evelyn (1882–1966) Founder of the Over-Seas Club, later the Over-Seas League.

Appendix 2 Representation of Richard Jebb's Britannic alliance

FIG. I.
COLONIAL DEPENDENCE:
"OUR COLONIES."

⊙ - Parliament
▢ - Imperial Conference

FIG. II.
BRITANNIC ALLIANCE:
"FIVE FREE NATIONS."

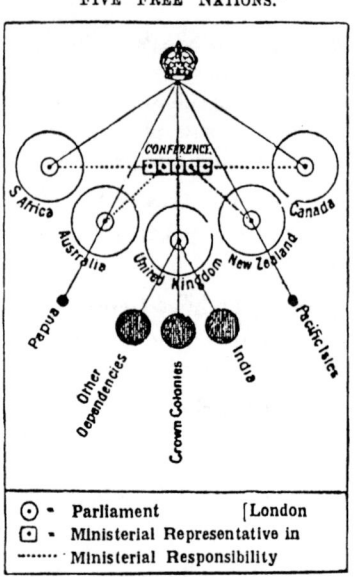

⊙ - Parliament   [London
▢ - Ministerial Representative in
······ Ministerial Responsibility

FIG. III.
IMPERIAL FEDERATION:
WITH SUBJECT DEPENDENCIES.

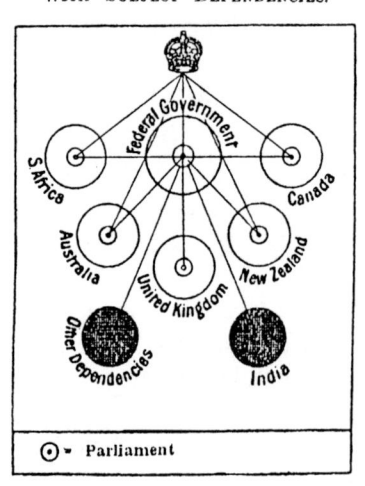

⊙ - Parliament

FIG. IV.
IMPERIAL FEDERATION:
WITH RACIAL EQUALITY.

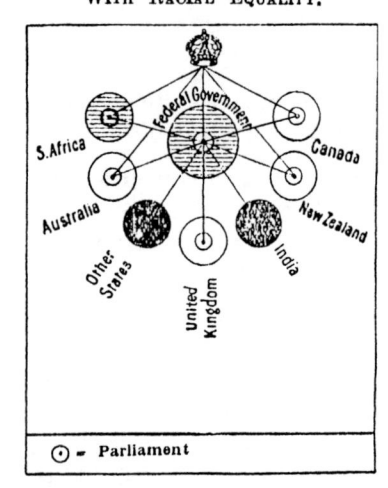

⊙ - Parliament

Source: Richard Jebb, *The Britannic Question: A Survey of Alternatives* (London: Longmans, Green 1913), endpiece facing p. 262.

APPENDICES

Appendix 3 Ratio of Asians to whites throughout the British Empire

Colony location	Year	Chinese	Japanese	British Indians	Other Asians	Total Asians	Whites	Asian to white %
Australia	1901	29,837[a]	3,571	9,184	2,886	45,478	3,731,428	1.2
New Zealand	1901	2,836	17	24	152	3,029	769,690	0.3
Natal	1904	171[a]	–	100,727	20	100,918	97,109	103.9
Cape	1904	1,346	–	8,866	619	10,831	579,741	1.7
Transvaal	1904	874	–	8,928	546	10,348	298,167	3.4
Orange River	1904	7	–	458	58	523	142,679	0.4
South Africa: total British	1904	2,398	–	118,779	1,243	122,420	1,117,696	10.9
British Columbia	1901	14,576	4,515	–[b]	–	–	159,566	11.9
Rest of Canada	1901	2,467	159	–[b]	–	–	–	–
Canada: total	1901	17,045	4,674	–[b]	–	21,717	5,349,598	0.4

Notes: – indicates no recorded Asians living in these territories, or a lack of data; [a] includes Japanese estimate; [b] Canadian totals do not include British Indians.

Source: P. E. Lewin, Appendix, *Journal of the Royal Society of Arts* LAI (24 April) 1908, p. 604; the dates given represent the closest available year for which data are available to 1901, a census year.

BIBLIOGRAPHY

Manuscript sources

Bodleian Library, Oxford University
British Conservative Party Papers
Lionel Curtis Papers
The *Round Table* Papers
Alfred, 1st Viscount Milner, Papers

Rhodes House, Oxford University
Ralegh Club Papers
Richard Feetham Papers
Cecil Rhodes Collection
W. T. Stead Correspondence

National Maritime Museum, Greenwich
Arnold White Papers

National Archives of Canada, Ottawa
Sir Robert Borden Papers
W. L. Mackenzie King Papers
Sir Wilfrid Laurier Papers

Queen's University Archives, Kingston, Ontario
John Buchan Papers

Library of the Royal Commonwealth Society, Cambridge University
Colonial Office, *Census of the British Empire*, 1901 (1906)
Thomas Sedgwick, 'Migration Scrapbooks, 1910–1914'

Institute of Commonwealth Studies, University of London
Richard Jebb Papers

Official Sources

For individual document citations within these files, see the appropriate footnote in the text.

The Colonial and Imperial Conferences from 1887 to 1937, ed. Maurice Ollivier, vols 1 and 2 (Ottawa: 1954).

BIBLIOGRAPHY

Combined Circulars on Canada, Australasia, and the South African Colonies, (EIO) (London: Emigrants' Information Office, selected years, 1895–1914).
The Declaration of Commonwealth Principles, Singapore, 22 January 1971.
Hansard: Parliamentary Debates (Britain, Canada, and New Zealand: selected years 1895–1914).

National Archives, Kew

HO 144
FO 613, 881
CO 212, 214

National Archives of Canada, Ottawa

RG 13, 25, 74, 76

Newspapers and periodicals

Blackwood's
Daily Express
Daily Mail
Daily Mirror
Daily News
Daily Telegraph
Dominion
Edinburgh Evening News
Empire Club of Canada Speeches
Evening Post
Fortnightly Review
Journal of the Royal Society of Arts
Indian Emigrant
Manchester Guardian
Morning Post
National Service Journal
New Statesman
New Zealand Times
Nineteenth Century [and After]
North American Review
Pall Mall Gazette
Proceedings of the Royal Colonial Institute
Queen's Quarterly
Rand Daily Mail
Review of Reviews
Reynold's Newspaper
Round Table
Scottish Review
Spectator

BIBLIOGRAPHY

Standard of Empire
Sunday Times
Sydney Daily Telegraph
The Times
United Empire

Reference sources and series

Dictionary of Canadian Biography (Toronto: University of Toronto Press, c. 2000).
Dictionary of National Biography (Oxford: Oxford University Press, 1882–1961).
Dictionary of South African Biography (Pretoria: HSRC Publishers, 1995).
Oxford Dictionary of National Biography (Oxford: Oxford University Press, 2003–).

Primary sources

Baring, Evelyn, 1st Earl of Cromer. *Political and Literary Essays, 1908–1913* (Freeport, NY: Books for Libraries Press, 1969 [1913]).
Bourassa, Henri. *Independence or Imperial Partnership? A Study of the Problem of the Commonwealth by Mr Lionel Curtis* (Montreal: Le Devoir, 1916).
Buchan, John. *The Half-Hearted* (London: T. Nelson, 1900).
—— *The African Colony: Studies in Reconstruction* (London: T. Nelson, 1903).
—— *A Lodge in the Wilderness* (London: T. Nelson, 1906).
—— *Some Eighteenth Century Byways* (London: T. Nelson, 1908).
—— *Prester John* (London: Houghton Mifflin, 1910).
—— *Nelson's History of the War* (London: T. Nelson, 1915–19).
—— *The Thirty-Nine Steps* (London: T. Nelson, 1915).
—— *These for Remembrance* (London: T. Nelson, 1919).
—— *The History of the South African Forces in France* (London: T. Nelson, 1920).
—— *Homilies and Recreations* (London: Books for Libraries Press, 1969 [1926]).
—— *Comments and Characters* (London: T. Nelson, 1940).
—— *Memory Hold the Door* (Toronto: Musson, 1940).
—— *Sick Heart River* (London: Hodder & Stoughton, 1940).
Cramb, J. A. *The Origins and Destiny of Imperial Britain* (London: E. P. Dutton, 1915).
Croft, Henry Page. *Path of Empire* (London: J. Murray, 1910).
Curtis, Lionel. *The Form of an Organic Union of the Empire* (London: Macmillan, 1908).
—— *A Practical Inquiry into the Nature of Citizenship in the British Empire and into the Relation of its Various Communities with Each Other* (London: Macmillan, 1914).
—— *The Commonwealth of Nations* (London: 1916); also appeared as *Project of a Commonwealth* (Round Table Studies, Second Series) (London: Macmillan, 1915).

BIBLIOGRAPHY

—— *Letter to the People of India on Responsible Government* (London: Macmillan, 1918).
—— *Dyarchy: Papers Relating to the Application of the Principle of Dyarchy to the Government of India* (Oxford: Clarendon, 1920).
—— *The Government of South Africa*, 2 vols (Cape Town: 1908).
—— *Green Memorandum* (London: Ballantyne, 1910); also appeared as the 'Annotated Memorandum' and 'Round Table Studies, First Series.'
—— *A Practical Inquiry into the Nature of Citizenship* (London: Macmillan, 1914).
—— *With Milner in South Africa* (London: Blackwell, 1953).
Egerton, G. W. *Federations and Unions within the British Empire* (Oxford: Clarendon, 1911).
Hammond, J. H. *The Truth About the Jameson Raid* (Boston, MA: 1918).
Hayward, Charles. *The Abolition of War: The British Empire's Terrible Responsibility and Glorious Opportunity* (London: C. W. Daniel, 1916).
Hobson, J. A. *The Psychology of Jingoism* (London: G. Richards, 1900).
—— *The War in South Africa, Its Causes and Effects* (London: Garland Publications, 1972 [1900]).
—— *Imperialism* (London: G. Allen Unwin, 1972 [1902]).
Jebb, Richard. *Studies in Colonial Nationalism* (London: E. Arnold, 1905).
—— *The Imperial Conferences: A History and Study in Two Volumes* (London: Longmans, Green, 1911).
—— *The Britannic Question: A Survey of Alternatives* (London: Longmans, Green, 1913).
—— *The Empire in Eclipse* (London: Chapman, 1926).
Johnson, Stanley C. *A History of Emigration from the United Kingdom to North America, 1763–1912* (London: Frank Cass & Co., 1966 [1913]).
Hunt, John D. *The Dawn of a New Patriotism: A Training Course in Citizenship* (Toronto: Macmillan, 1918).
King, Mackenzie. *Report of the Royal Commission Appointed to Inquire into the Methods by Which Oriental Labourers Have Been Induced to Come to Canada* (Ottawa: 1908).
Mackinder, Halford. *Democratic Ideals and Realities* (New York: H. Holt, 1942 [1919]).
McGoun, Archbishop. *A Federal Parliament of the British People* (Toronto: C. Blackett Robinson, 1890).
Milner, Alfred, 1st Viscount. *The Nation and the Empire: Being a Collection of Speeches and Addresses* (London: Constable, 1913).
—— *The Milner Papers*, ed. C. Headlam, vol. 2 (London: Cassell, 1933).
Muir, Ramsay. *The Character of the British Empire* (London: Constable, 1917).
Oliver, F. S. *Alexander Hamilton: An Essay on American Union* (London: Macmillan, 1906).
Panikkar, K. M. *The Problems of Greater India* (Madras: 1916).
Rodney, C. M. *Jameson's Ride to Johannesburg* (Pretoria: State Library, 1970 [1896]).
Sedgwick, Thomas. *Town Lads on New Zealand Farms* (London: P. S. King & Sons, 1913).

—— *Lads for the Empire: Imperial Migration* (London: self-published, 1914).
White, Arnold. *Efficiency and Empire*, ed. Geoffrey Searle (Brighton: Harvester Press, 1973 [1901]).
—— *The Problems of a Great City* (New York: Garland Press, 1985 [1886]).
—— *The Modern Jew* (London: 1899).
—— *Society, Smart Society, and Bad Smart Society, Their Influence on Empire: Being Seven Letters Written to the Editor of the Daily Chronicle* (London: Daily Chronicle, 1900).
—— *The Views of Vanoc: An Englishman's Outlook* (London: 1910).
—— *The Hidden Hand* (London: 1917).
Wrench, John Evelyn. *The Story of the Over-Seas League* (London: 1926).

Secondary sources

Abernathy, David B. *The Dynamics of Global Dominance: European Overseas Empires, 1415–1980* (New Haven, CT: Yale University Press, 2000).
Achebe, Chinua. 'An Image of Africa,' *Massachusetts Review*, 18, 1977, pp. 782–94.
Adam Smith, Janet. *John Buchan* (London: Rupert Hart-Davis, 1965).
Anon. 'Lionel Curtis: The Prophet of Organic Union,' *Round Table*, 46, 182, March 1956, pp. 102–9.
Amery, L. S. *Thoughts on the Constitution* (London: Oxford University Press, 1947).
Anderson, Benedict. *Imagined Communities* (London: Verso, 1982).
Anderson, Kay. *Vancouver's Chinatown* (Montreal: McGill–Queen's University Press, 1991).
Arnold, Dana (ed.) *Cultural Identities and the Aesthetics of Britishness* (Manchester: Manchester University Press, 2004).
Ashcroft, Bill, Griffiths, Gareth, and Tiffin, Helen. *The Empire Writes Back*, 2nd edn (London: Routledge, 2003).
Augstein, H. F. (ed.) *Race: The Origins of an Idea, 1760–1850* (Bristol: Thoemmes Press, 1996).
Backhouse, Constance. *Colour-Coded: A Legal History of Racism in Canada, 1900–1950* (Toronto: University of Toronto Press, 1999).
Bean, Philip and Melville, Joy. *Lost Children of the Empire* (London: Unwin Hyman, 1989).
Berger, Carl. *The Sense of Power* (Toronto: University of Toronto Press, 1970).
Betts, Raymond F. 'The Allusion to Rome in British Imperialist Thought of the late Nineteenth and Early Twentieth Centuries,' *Victorian Studies*, 15, 2, December 1971, pp. 149–59.
Bevan, Vaughn. *The Development of British Immigration Law* (London and Dover, NH: Croom Helm, 1986).
Bosco, Andrea and May, Alex (eds) *The Round Table: The Empire/Commonwealth and British Foreign Policy* (London: Lothian Press, 1997).
Bothwell, Robert, 'Something of Value? Subjects and Citizens in Canadian History,' in William Kaplan (ed.) *Belonging: The Meaning and Future*

BIBLIOGRAPHY

of Canadian Citizenship (Montreal: McGill–Queen's University Press, 1993), pp. 25–35.

Bridge, C. and Fedorowich, K. (eds) *The British World: Diaspora, Culture and Identity* (London: Frank Cass, 2003).

Brown, J. M. and Louis, W. R. (eds) *Oxford History of the British Empire (OHBE)*, vol. 4: *The Twentieth Century* (Oxford: Oxford University Press, 1999).

Buchan, William. *John Buchan: A Memoir* (London: Buchan & Enright, 1982).

Buckner, Philip. 'Whatever Happened to the British Empire?' *Journal of the Canadian Historical Association (JCHA)/Revue de la SHC*, 4, 1993, pp. 3–32.

Bush, Julia. *Edwardian Ladies and Imperial Power* (London: Leicester University Press, 2000).

Burroughs, Peter. 'Institutions of Empire,' in Andrew Porter (ed.) *OHBE*, vol. 3: *The Nineteenth Century* (Oxford: 1999), pp. 170–97.

Burton, Antoinette (ed.) *After the Imperial Turn* (Durham, NC: Duke University Press, 2003).

Bush, Julia. '"The Right Sort of Woman": Female Emigrators and Emigration to the British Empire, 1890–1910,' *Women's History Review*, 3, 3, 1994, pp. 385–409.

Butler, J. R. M. *Lord Lothian (Philip Kerr) 1882–1940* (London: Macmillan, 1960).

Cain, P. J. and Hopkins, A. G. *British Imperialism: Innovation and Expansion, 1688–1914* (London: Longman, 1993).

Cannadine, David. *Ornamentalism* (Oxford: Oxford University Press, 2001).

Cesarini, David and Fulbrook, Mary (eds) *Citizenship, Nationality and Migration in Europe* (London: Routledge, 1996).

Chilton, Lisa. 'A New Class of Women for the Colonies: *The Imperial Colonist* and the Construction of Empire,' *Journal of Imperial and Commonwealth History (JICH)*, 31, 2, May 2003, pp. 36–56.

Choi, C. Y. *Chinese Migration and Settlement in Australia* (Sydney: Sydney University Press, 1975).

Cole, D., 'The Problem of "Nationalism" and "Imperialism" in British Settlement Colonies,' *Journal of British Studies*, 10, 1971, pp. 160–82.

Collini, Stefan. *Public Moralists: Political Thought and Intellectual Life in Britain, 1850–1930* (Oxford: Oxford University Press, 1991).

Constantine, Stephen (ed.) *Emigrants and Empire* (Oxford: Manchester University Press, 1990).

—— 'British Emigration to the Empire–Commonwealth since 1880: From Overseas Settlement to Diaspora?' *JICH*, 31, 2, May 2003, pp. 16–35.

—— 'Children as Ancestors: Child Migrants and Identity in Canada,' *British Journal of Canadian Studies*, 16, 2003, pp. 150–9.

Cook, Ramsay G., Brown, Craig, and Berger, Carl (eds) *Imperial Relations in the Age of Laurier* (Toronto: University of Toronto Press, 1969).

Cooper, Frederick and Stoler, Ann. 'Between Metropole and Colony: Rethinking a Research Agenda,' in Cooper and Stoler (eds) *Tensions of Empire: Colonial Cultures in a Bourgeois World* (Berkeley: University of California Press, 1997), pp. 1–56.

BIBLIOGRAPHY

Cunningham, Hugh. 'The Language of Patriotism,' *History Workshop Journal*, 12, 1981, pp. 8–33.

Daniell, David. *The Interpreter's House* (London: Nelson, 1975).

Dubow, Saul. 'Colonial Nationalism, the Milner Kindergarten and the Rise of "South Africanism," 1902–10,' *History Workshop Journal*, 43, 1997, pp. 53–85.

—— 'Imagining the New South Africa in the Era of Reconstruction,' in David Omissi and Andrew Thompson (eds) *The Impact of the South African War*. (New York: Palgrave, 2002), pp. 76–95.

Dummet, Ann and Nicol, Andrew. *Subjects, Citizens, Aliens and Others* (London: Weidenfeld & Nicolson, 1990).

Eddy, John and Schreuder, Deryck (eds) *The Rise of Colonial Nationalism* (Sydney: Allen & Unwin, 1988).

Ellinwood Jr., Dewitt Clinton. 'The Round Table Movement and India,' *Journal of Commonwealth Political Studies*, 9, 2, 1971, pp. 183–209.

Evans, Julie, Grimshaw, Patricia, Philips, David, and Swain, Shurlee. *Equal Subjects, Unequal Rights: Indigenous Peoples in British Settler Colonies, 1830s–1910* (Manchester: Manchester University Press, 2003).

Ferguson, Niall. *Empire* (New York: Basic Books, 2003).

Field, H. John. *Toward a Programme of Imperial Life: The British Empire at the Turn of the Century* (Westport, CT: Greenwood Press, 1982).

Firchow, Peter. *Envisioning Africa: Racism and Imperialism in Conrad's* Heart of Darkness (Lexington: University of Kentucky Press, 2000).

Fletcher, Ian Christopher, Nym Mayhall, Laura E., and Levine, Philippa (eds) *Women's Suffrage in the British Empire: Citizenship, Nation, and Race* (New York: Routledge, 2000).

Foster, Leonie, *High Hopes: The Men and Motives of the Australian Round Table* (Melbourne: Melbourne University Press, 1986).

Fredrickson, George M. *Racism: A Short History* (Princeton, NJ: Princeton University Press, 2002).

Füredi, Frank. *The Silent War: Imperialism and the Changing Perception of Race* (London: Pluto Press, 1998).

Gellner, Ernest. *Conditions of Liberty: Civil Society and its Rivals* (London: Penguin, 1994).

Gibbins, John. 'Liberalism, Nationalism, and the English Idealists,' *History of European Ideas*, 15, 1992, pp. 491–8.

Goldberg, David Theo (ed.) *Anatomy of Racism* (Minneapolis: University of Minnesota Press, 1990).

Gollin, A. M. *Proconsul in Politics* (London: A. Blond, 1964).

Green, E. H. H. *The Crisis of Conservatism: The Politics, Economics and Ideology of the British Conservative Party, 1880–1914* (London: Routledge, 1995).

Greenlee, James. *Education and Imperial Unity, 1900–1926* (New York: Garland Press, 1987).

Gregory, Robert. *India and East Africa: A History of Race Relations within the British Empire, 1890–1939* (Oxford: Clarendon Press, 1971).

BIBLIOGRAPHY

Hall, Catherine (ed.) *Cultures of Empire: A Reader* (New York: Routledge, 2000).

—— 'Histories, Empires and the Post-Colonial Moment,' in Iain Chambers and Lidia Curti (eds) *The Post-Colonial Question* (London: Routledge, 1996), pp. 65–77.

Hall, Stuart. 'When Was the "Post-Colonial"? Thinking at the Limit,' in Iain Chambers and Lidia Curti (eds) *The Post-Colonial Question* (London: Routledge, 1996), pp. 242–60.

Hardt, Michael and Negri, Antonio. *Empire* (Cambridge, MA: Harvard University Press, 2000).

Harper, Marjorie, 'Emigration and the Salvation Army, 1890–1930,' *Bulletin of the Scottish Institute for Missionary Studies*, 3–4, 1985–87, pp. 22–9.

—— *Emigration from Scotland between the Wars: Opportunity or Exile?* (Manchester: Manchester University Press, 1998).

—— (ed.) *Emigrant Homecomings* (Manchester: Manchester University Press, 2005).

Heater, Derek. *Citizenship: The Civic Ideal in World History, Politics, and Education* (London: Longman, 1990).

Heathorn, Stephen. *For Home, Country, and Race: Constructing Gender, Class, and Englishness in the Elementary School, 1880–1914* (Toronto: University of Toronto Press, 2000).

—— '"Let us Remember that We, Too, Are English": Constructions of Citizenship and National Identity in English Elementary School Reading Books, 1880–1914,' *Victorian Studies*, 37, spring 1995, pp. 395–427.

Hendley, Matthew, 'Constructing the Citizen: The Primrose League and the Definition of Citizenship in the Age of Mass Democracy, 1918–1928,' *JCHA*, 7, 1996, pp. 125–51.

Henshaw, Peter, 'John Buchan from the "Borders" to the "Berg": Nature, Empire and White South African Identity, 1901–1910,' *African Studies*, 62, 1, July 2003, pp. 3–32.

Himmelfarb, Gertrude. *Victorian Minds* (New York: Knopf, 1968).

Howard, Michael. 'Empire, Race and War in Pre-1914 Britain,' in Hugh Lloyd-Jones, Valerie Pearl, and Blair Worden (eds) *History and Imagination: Essays in Honour of Hugh Trevor-Roper* (London: Gerald Duckworth & Co., 1981), pp. 340–55.

Hutcheson, J. A. *Leopold Maxse and the National Review, 1893–1914: Right-Wing Politics and Journalism in the Edwardian Age* (London: Garland, 1989).

Huttenback, Robert. *Racism and Empire* (Ithaca, NY: Cornell University Press, 1976).

—— 'No Strangers within the Gates: Attitudes and Policies toward the Non-White Residents of the British Empire of Settlement,' *JICH*, 1, 1973, 271–302.

Hyam, Ronald. *Britain's Imperial Century, 1814–1914* (London: Barnes & Noble, 1993).

BIBLIOGRAPHY

Ignatieff, Michael. *The Warrior's Honour* (Toronto: Penguin, 1999; second edition).
Irving, Helen. 'Citizenship before 1949,' *Individual, Community, Nation: 50 Years of Australian Citizenship*, Kim Rubenstein (ed.) (Melbourne: Australian Scholarly Publishing, 2000), pp. 9–20.
Jenkins, Roy. *Asquith* (New York: E. P. Dutton & Co., 1966).
Judd, Denis. *Empire* (New York: HarperCollins, 1996).
Kale, Madhavi. *Fragments of Empire: Capital, Slavery, and Indian Indentured Migration in the British Caribbean* (Philadelphia: University of Pennsylvania Press, 1998).
Karatani, Rieko. *Defining British Citizenship: Empire, Commonwealth, and Modern Britain* (London: Frank Cass, 2003).
Kaul, Chandrika. *Reporting the Raj: The British Press and India, c. 1880–1922* (Manchester: Manchester University Press, 2003).
Kendle, John. *The Colonial and Imperial Conferences* (London: Longman, 1967).
—— *The Round Table Movement and Imperial Union* (Toronto: University of Toronto Press, 1975).
—— *Federal Britain* (New York: Routledge, 1997).
Kirkby, Diane and Coleborne, Catharine (eds) *Law, History, Colonialism: The Reach of Empire* (Manchester: Manchester University Press, 2001).
Kleingeld, Pauline. 'Six Varieties of Cosmopolitanism in Late Eighteenth Century Germany,' *Journal of the History of Ideas*, 60, 3, July 1999, pp. 505–24.
Kumar, Krishan. 'Civil Society: An Inquiry into the Usefulness of a Historical Term,' *British Journal of Sociology*, 44, 3, September 1993, pp. 375–95.
Koebner, Richard and Schmidt, Helmut Dan. *Imperialism: The Story and Significance of a Political Word, 1840–1866* (Cambridge: Cambridge University Press, 1964).
Koeneke, Rodney. *Empires of the Mind* (Stanford, CA: Stanford University Press, 2004).
Kruse, Juanita. *John Buchan (1875–1940) and the Idea of Empire* (Lewiston, NY: Edwin Mellen Press, 1989).
Lahiri, Shompa. *Indians in Britain* (London: Frank Cass, 2000).
Langfield, Michelle. 'Voluntarism, Salvation, and Rescue: British Juvenile Migration to Australia and Canada, 1890–1939,' *JICH*, 32, 2, May 2004, pp. 86–114.
Laquine, Eleanor (ed.) *The Silent Debate: Asian Immigration and Racism in Canada* (Vancouver: Institute of Asian Research, UBC, 1998).
Lavin, Deborah, *From Empire to International Commonwealth: A Biography of Lionel Curtis* (Oxford: Oxford University Press, 1995).
Lester, Alan. *Imperial Networks: Creating Identities in Nineteenth-Century South Africa and Britain* (New York: Routledge, 2001).
Lorimer, Douglas. *Colour, Class and the Victorians* (New York: Leicester University Press, 1978).
—— 'Theoretical Racism in Late-Victorian Anthropology, 1870–1900,' *Victorian Studies*, 1988, 31, 3, pp. 405–30.

BIBLIOGRAPHY

Lownie, Andrew. *John Buchan, The Presbyterian Cavalier* (London: Canongate, 1995).

Lowry, Donal. 'The Crown, Empire Loyalism and the Assimilation of Non-British White Subjects in the British World: An Argument against "Ethnic Determinism",' *JICH*, 31, 2, May 2003, pp. 96–120.

MacKenzie, John. *Propaganda and Empire* (Manchester: Manchester University Press, 1984).

——— *Imperialism and Popular Culture* (Manchester: Manchester University Press, 1986).

Madden, Frederick and Fieldhouse, D. K. (eds) *Oxford and the Idea of Commonwealth: Essays Presented to Sir Edgar Williams* (London: Croom Helm, 1982).

Maddrell, A. M. C. 'Empire, Emigration and School Geography: Changing Discourses of Imperial Citizenship, 1880–1925,' *Journal of Historical Geography*, 22, 4, October 1996, pp. 373–87.

Magubane, Bernard. *The Making of a Racist State* (Asmara, Eritrea: Africa World Press, 1996).

Magubane, Zine. *Bringing the Empire Home* (Chicago: University of Chicago Press, 2004).

Mangan, J. A. *The Games Ethic and Imperialism* (Hammondsworth: Viking, 1986).

Markus, Andrew. *Australian Race Relations, 1788–1993* (St Leonards, NSW: Allen & Unwin, 1994).

Marshall, T. H. 'Citizenship and Social Class,' reprinted in T. H. Marshall and Tom Bottomore (eds) *Citizenship and Social Class* (Concord, MA: Pluto Press, 1992).

Marzorati, Gerald et al. 'The Origins of Duty,' *Harper's Magazine*, February 1991, pp. 44–54.

Matthew, H. C. G. *The Liberal Imperialists* (Oxford: Oxford University Press, 1973).

McClintock, Anne. *Imperial Leather: Race, Gender and Sexuality in the Colonial Context* (London: Routledge, 1995).

Mehta, Uday Singh. *Liberalism and Empire* (Chicago, IL: University of Chicago Press, 1999).

Metcalfe, Thomas. *The Ideology of the Raj* (Cambridge: Cambridge University Press, 1995).

Midgley, Clare. *Gender and Imperialism* (Manchester: Manchester University Press, 1998).

Miller, J. D. B. *Richard Jebb and the Problem of Empire* (London: Institute of Commonwealth Studies, 1956).

National Archives of Australia. 'The Meaning of Citizenship,' *Citizenship in Australia*, available: www.naa.gov.au/Publications/research_guides/guides/ctznship/frames/intro.htm.

Newbury, Colin. 'The March of Everyman: Mobility and the Imperial Census of 1901,' *JICH*, 12, 2, 1984, pp. 80–101.

Nimocks, Walter. *Milner's Young Men: The 'Kindergarten' in Edwardian Imperial Affairs* (Durham, NC: Duke University Press, 1968).

Northrup, David. *Indentured Labour in the Age of Imperialism, 1834–1922* (Cambridge: Cambridge University Press, 1995).

BIBLIOGRAPHY

Page, Robert J. D. *Imperialism and Canada, 1895–1903* (Toronto: University of Toronto Press, 1972).

Pakenham, Thomas. *The Scramble for Africa* (New York: Avon, 1991).

Paul, Kathleen. *Whitewashing Britain: Race and Citizenship in the Postwar Era* (Ithaca, NY: Cornell University Press, 1997).

Peatling, G. K. 'Globalism, Hegemonism and British Power: J. A. Hobson and Alfred Zimmern Reconsidered,' *History*, 89, 295, July 2004, pp. 381–98.

Peers, Douglas M., 'Reading Empire, Chasing Tikka Masala: The Contested State of Imperial History,' *Canadian Journal of History*, 39, 1, April 2004, pp. 87–104.

Plant, G. F. *Oversea Settlement* (London: Oxford University Press, 1951).

Porter, Andrew (ed.) *OHBE*, vol. 3: *The Nineteenth Century* (Oxford: Oxford University Press, 1999).

Porter, Bernard. *The Absent-Minded Imperialists: Empire, Society and Culture in Britain* (Oxford: Oxford University Press, 2004).

Potter, Simon, 'The Imperial Significance of the Canadian-American Reciprocity Proposals of 1911,' *The Historical Journal*, 47, 1, 2004, pp. 81–100.

Price, C. A. *The Great White Walls Are Built: Restrictive Immigration to North America and Australia, 1836–1888* (Canberra: Australian Institute of International Affairs–Australian National University Press, 1974).

Ramamurthy, Anandi. *Imperial Persuaders: Images of Africa and Asia in British Advertising* (Manchester: Manchester University Press, 2003).

Read, Donald. *The Power of News: The History of Reuters* (Oxford: Oxford University Press, 1999).

Reynolds, David. *Britannia Overruled: British Policy and World Power in the Twentieth Century* (London: Longman, 2000).

Rich, Paul. *Race and Empire in British Politics* (Cambridge: Cambridge University Press, 1986).

—— ' "Milnerism and a Ripping Yarn": Transvaal Land Settlement and John Buchan's Novel 'Prester John',' in Belinda Bossoli (ed.) *Town and Countryside in the Transvaal* (Johannesburg: Ravan Press, 1983).

Roberts, Priscilla, 'Lord Lothian and the Atlantic World,' *Historian*, 66, 1, spring 2004, pp. 97–129.

Rose, Norman. *The Cliveden Set* (London: Jonathan Cape, 2000).

Said, Edward. *Culture and Imperialism* (New York: Vintage, 1994).

—— *Orientalism* (New York: Vintage, 1978).

—— 'Orientalism Reconsidered,' *Race and Class*, 27, 2, 1985, pp. 1–15.

Samuels, Raphael (ed.) *Patriotism: The Making and Unmaking of British National Identity* (London: Routledge, 1989).

Sayer, Derek, 'British Reaction to the Amritsar Massacre 1919–1920,' *Past and Present*, 131, 1991, pp. 130–64.

Schneer, Jonathan. *London 1900: The Imperial Metropolis* (New Haven, CT: Yale University Press, 1999).

Schudson, Michael. *The Informed Citizen: A History of American Civil Life* (New York: Martin Kessler, 1998).

Schwarz, Bill (ed.) *The Expansion of England: Race, Ethnicity and Cultural History* (London: Routledge, 1996).

BIBLIOGRAPHY

—— (ed.) *West Indian Intellectuals in Britain* (Manchester: Manchester University Press, 2003).
Searle, G. R. *The Quest for National Efficiency: A Study in British Politics and Political Thought, 1899–1914* (Oxford: Blackwell, 1971).
Semmel, Bernard. *Imperialism and Social Reform* (London: George Allen & Unwin, 1960).
Sen, Satadru. *Migrant Races: Empire, Identity and K. S. Ranjitsinhji* (Manchester: Manchester University Press, 2004).
Sherington, Geoffrey. '"A Better Class of Boy": The Big Brother Movement, Youth Migration and Citizenship in Empire,' *Australian Historical Studies*, 33, 120, October 2002, pp. 267–85.
Sherington, Geoffrey and Jeffrey, Chris. *Fairbridge: Empire and Child Migration* (Perth: Woburn Press, 1998).
Sinclair, Keith. *Imperial Federation: New Zealand Attitudes, 1880–1914* (London: Athlone Press, 1955).
Sinha, Mrinalini. *Colonial Masculinity: The 'Manly Englishman' and the 'Effeminate Bengali'* (Manchester: Manchester University Press, 1995).
Skinner, Quentin, 'Some Problems in the Analysis of Political Thought and Action,' *Political Theory*, 2, 1974, 277–303.
—— 'Meaning and Theory in the History of Ideas,' *History and Theory*, 8, 1969, pp. 3–53.
Soloway, Richard. *Demography and Degeneracy* (Chapel Hill: University of North Carolina Press, 1995).
Stokes, Eric. *The English Utilitarians and India* (Oxford: Oxford University Press, 1959).
Stokes, E. 'Milnerism,' *Historical Journal*, 1, 1962, pp. 47–60.
Swinfen, D. B. *Imperial Control of Colonial Legislation, 1813–1865* (Oxford: Oxford University Press, 1970).
Symonds, R. 'The Early Search for a Role for Rhodes House,' *Round Table*, 1983, pp. 484–9.
Tabili, Laura. *'We Ask for British Justice': Workers and Racial Differentiation in Late Imperial Britain* (Ithaca, NY: Cornell University Press, 1994).
Tidrick, Kathyryn. *Empire and the English Character* (London: I. B. Tauris, 1990).
Tilly, Charles (ed.) *Citizenship, Identity and Social History* (Cambridge: Cambridge University Press, 1996).
Tinker, Hugh. *A New System of Slavery: The Export of Indian Labour Overseas, 1830–1920* (London: Oxford University Press, 1974).
Thane, Pat. 'The British Imperial State and the Construction of National Identities,' in Billie Melman (ed.) *Borderlines: Genders and Identities in War and Peace, 1870–1930* (New York: Routledge, 1998), pp. 29–45.
Thompson, Leonard. *A History of South Africa* (New Haven, CT: Yale University Press, 1990).
Thompson, Andrew. 'The Language of Imperialism and the Meanings of Empire: Imperial Discourse in British Politics, 1895–1914,' *Journal of British Studies*, 36, April 1997, pp. 147–77.

—— *Imperial Britain: The Empire in British Politics, c. 1880–1932* (Harlow: Longman, 2000).
—— 'The Languages of Loyalism in Southern Africa, c. 1870–1939,' *English Historical Review*, 118, 477, June 2003, pp. 617–50.
—— *The Empire Strikes Back? The Impact of Imperialism on Britain from the Mid-Nineteenth Century* (Harlow, Essex: Longman, 2005).
Thornton, A. P. *The Imperial Idea and its Enemies* (New York: Anchor Books, 1968).
Tinker, Hugh. *A New System of Slavery: The Export of Indian Labour Overseas, 1830–1920* (London: Oxford University Press, 1974).
Turner, Frank. *The Greek Heritage in Victorian Britain* (New Haven, CT: Yale University Press, 1981).
Usborne, Richard. *Clubland Heroes*, 2nd edn (London: Barrie & Jenkins, 1974).
Vance, Norman. *The Victorians and Ancient Rome* (Cambridge, MA: Harvard University Press, 1997).
Ward, Stuart (ed.) *British Culture and the End of Empire* (Manchester: Manchester University Press, 2001).
Weaver, John. *The Great Land Rush and the Making of the Modern World, 1650–1900* (Montreal and Kingston: McGill-Queen's University Press, 2003).
West, Shearer (ed.) *The Victorians and Race* (Aldershot: Scolar Press, 1996).
Winant, Howard. *The World Is a Ghetto* (New York: Basic Books, 2001).
Winks, Robin W. (ed.) *OHBE*, vol. 5: *Historiography* (Oxford: Oxford University Press, 1999).
Witherell, Larry L. *Rebel on the Right: Henry Page Croft and the Crisis of British Conservatism, 1903–1914* (Newark: University of Delaware Press, 1997).
Woollacott, Angela. *To Try Her Fortune in London* (New York: Oxford University Press, 2001).
Wrench, John Evelyn. *The Story of the Over-Seas League* (London: Whitefriars Press, 1926).
Young, Robert C. *Colonial Desire: Hybridity in Theory, Culture and Race* (London: Routledge, 1995).

Unpublished works

Agar, Jon. 'Modern Horrors: British Identity and Identity Cards,' unpublished paper.
May, Alex. 'The Round Table, 1910–1966,' D.Phil thesis, University of Oxford, 1995.
Patterson, Kathleen. 'The Decline of Dominance,' Ph.D thesis, Bryn Mawr College, 1989.
Paul, Elaine. 'Lionel Curtis and the Unification of South Africa, 1901–1909,' Ph.D thesis, University of South Carolina, 1978.
Teel, Leonard. 'The Life and Times of Arnold Henry White, 1848–1925,' Ph.D thesis, Georgia State University, 1984.

INDEX

Aliens Act (1905) 159
Amery, Leopold 46, 81, 154–5, 168, 210
Amritsar 63, 67, 102
Arnold, Matthew 50
Asante War, Fourth (1895–6) 88, 89
Asquith, H. H. 49, 95
Asquith, Raymond 79, 81
assisted emigration 209
  of children and juveniles 186
  cost of 183–4
  nineteenth century history of 179–80
  state's limited role in 180–1, 193
  and voluntary agencies 180, 186, 193
  see also White, Arnold; Sedgwick, Thomas; Immigration
Astor, Nancy 48
Australia
  anti-Asian sentiment in 159, 160
  attraction of for British emigrants 134
  Australia House 214
  immigration policy of 161, 183
  see also Jebb, Richard
  White Australia policy 149, 168
Australian Nationality and Citizenship Act (1949) 213

Balfour, A. J. 42, 123
Balfour Declaration (1926) 213
Banerjee, Babu Surendranatti 64
Barnardo, Thomas 135, 180, 185, 191
Beaverbrook, Max Aitken, Lord 83
Bedford, Herbrand Arthur Russell, Duke of 120, 131
Beresford, Charles 117
Bodin, Jean 14
Borden, Sir Robert 61

Bourassa, Henri 156
Brand, R. H. 46, 48
British Immigration League of Australia 183
  see also Australia, immigration policy of
British Nationality Act (1948) 28, 213
British Nationality and Status of Aliens Acts (1914) 20, 28, 138, 159, 163, 213
British Protected Persons (BPPs) 20, 164
Buchan, John 17, 25–6, 121, 146, 153, 208, 210
  African Colony, The 83, 100
  and Canada 90, 91
  conservatism of 77, 79, 85–6, 106
  cosmopolitan views of 90–2
  democracy, views on 94–7
  and First World War 83–4, 104, 105
  as historian 104
  History of the South African forces in France, The 105
  and imperial state 97–9
  and jingoism 79, 86–9
  see also jingoism
  Lodge in the Wilderness, A 78, 85, 89, 91, 104, 105–6
  Memory Hold the Door 80
  Milner's influence on 81–2, 84, 97
  and morality 92–4
  Prester John 100
  racial views of 100–4
  Sick Heart River 106
  in South Africa 81–2, 93, 97, 105
  see also South Africa
  upbringing 80–1
Burke, Edmund 85, 95, 98, 102

INDEX

Burns, John 181
Bryce, James 13, 22

Campbell, W. Wilfred 23
Canada
  anti-Asian sentiment in 159, 160, 168
  and assisted emigration 190-2
  Canada House 214
  immigration policy of 134, 161-2, 166-7, 182-3, 184
    see also Jebb, Richard; Sedgwick, Thomas
Canadian Citizenship Act (1946) 213
Canadian Nationals Act (1921) 213
Cannadine, David 147-8
Carrington, Charles Robert, Lord 159
Casement, Roger 88
Chamberlain, Joseph 62, 82, 98, 125, 164, 180
Charitable Organisation Society 185
Child Emigration Scheme 186, 193
Chirol, Valentine 47, 62
Churchill, Winston 98, 162
citizenship, concept of 1-2
  classical concepts of 13-14
  dual nature of 205-6, 212
  and imperial history 9-10
  and post-colonialism 10-12
  republican concepts of 15-16
  and subjecthood 9, 18-23, 210, 213
    see also subjecthood, concept of
colonial nationalism 23-4, 48-9, 56-7, 59-60, 101-2, 153-5, 163, 168, 170-1, 195, 209-10
  see also Jebb, Richard
Colonial Office
  and emigration 134, 192
  and imperial conferences 154
  position on imperial citizenship 22-3, 159
Compatriots Club 153
Conan Doyle, Arthur 131
Conrad, Joseph 3
conscientious objectors 105, 131-2

Coupland, Reginald 46
Craddock, Sir Reginald 63
Croft, Henry Page 51, 130
Cromer, Evelyn Baring, Lord 83, 103
Curtis, Lionel 25-6, 84, 90, 121, 146, 207-8, 210
  concept of commonwealth 54
  and dominion immigration policy 60
  and federalism 45, 56-7
  Green Memorandum 58, 59
  and Idealism 42-3
  and India 62-7
  influence of Alexander Hamilton on 53, 65
  influence of Milner on 43-4
  and Ireland 67
  Letter to the People of India on Responsible Government, A 66
  opinion of Richard Jebb 152, 15
  The Problem of the Commonwealth 47, 48, 51, 60
  racial views of 50-2, 66
  and the Round Table 46-50
    see also Round Table
  travels to the colonies 57-61
  upbringing 42
Curzon, George Nathaniel, Lord 62

Defence of India Act (1915) 161
  see also India
Dilke, Sir Charles 148
Disraeli, Benjamin 95, 150
Don Pacifico affair 14, 19
Dreadnought Fund 183, 185
  see also Australia, immigration policy of
Durham, John George Lambton, Lord 49
dyarchy 64-5, 68, 207
  see also Curtis, Lionel and India

East End Emigration Fund 180
Edward VII, King 4, 178

[240]

INDEX

Egerton, H. E. 22
Emerson, Ralph Waldo 126
Emigration Act (1918) 135
Emigrants' Information Office (EIO) 134, 135, 180
Empire/Commonwealth Games 214
Empire Windrush 213
eugenics 118
Eugenics Education Society 118, 120
Ewart, J. S. 158

Fairbridge, Kingsley 186
  see also Child Emigration Scheme
Feiling, Keith 57
Fischer, Andrew 59
Fisher, Admiral John 117
Foreign Jurisdiction Act (1890) 22, 164
Froude, J. A. 210

Galton, Sir Francis 100, 122
Gardiner, A. G. 137
George V., King 4, 199
Gladstone, William 42, 87
Gobineau, Joseph 149
Gordon, Charles 88
Grant, W. L. 23–4
Green, T. H. 17, 42, 55, 80
Grey, Sir Edward 56, 123
Grigg, Edward 56

Haggard, Sir H. Rider 181
Henshaw, Peter 82
Himmelfarb, Gertrude 93
Hobson, J. A. 2, 86, 89, 124

Immigration
  contrast between British and colonial views of 158–60, 169, 182
  parallels to labour migration 148, 160
  see also Curtis, Lionel; White, Arnold; Jebb, Richard; Sedgwick, Thomas; assisted emigration; race

Imperial Conference (1911) 49–50, 102, 149
  debate on naturalization at 162–3
Imperial Federation League 45
India
  citizenship rights of inhabitants 20, 23, 164
  claims to greater citizenship rights 197–8
  demographics of 51
  nationalism in 64–6
  see also Curtis, Lionel; dyarchy
Indian Naturalization Act (1852) 164
indigenous citizenship rights 97, 169

James, William 107
Jameson Raid 87–8
Jebb, Sir Richard Claverhouse (uncle) 150
Jebb, Richard 25–7, 44, 57, 94, 196, 209, 210, 214
  Britannic Question, The 151
  and colonial nationalism 156, 209
    see also colonial nationalism
  democracy, views on 157
  idea of Britannic alliance 153–5, 158, 209
  imperial subjecthood, views on 21–2
  India, views on 157, 198
  and intra-imperial immigration 167–8, 209
  and Over-Seas Club 194–5
  racial views of 159, 167–8, 170
  Studies in Colonial Nationalism 27, 146, 151
  and tariff reform 152, 153
  travels to the colonies 152
  upbringing 150–1
jingoism 86–9
  see also Buchan, John
jus sanguinis 16, 116, 139
  see also citizenship, concept of
jus soli 16, 20, 22
  see also citizenship, concept of

INDEX

Kant, Immanuel 17–18, 19
Kerr, Phillip 46, 48, 51, 57–8, 62
King, Mackenzie 166
Kipling, Rudyard 53, 85, 120
Kitchener, H. H. 88
Komagata Maru incident 161
Kruger, Paul 156

Lamb, Charles 8
Laurier, Sir Wilfrid 58, 102, 162, 163, 184
Leacock, Stephen 196
League of Nations 91, 93, 213
Lloyd George, David 128
Livingstone, David 83, 88
loyalism 19, 170, 210
Lucas, C. P. 13

Mackinder, Halford 99
Mahan, A. T. 118
Malan, F. S. 162
Markham, Violet 96
Marshall, T. H. 15–16, 212
Massey, Vincent 40
Matabeleland
  as example of 'jurisdiction without territory' 165
Maxse, Leo 130
Milner, Alfred 3, 26, 40, 46, 55–6, 78, 94, 180
  and Chinese labour in South Africa 97–8, 101
  and the 'Kindergarten' 43–4, 57, 81
  see also Curtis, Lionel; Buchan, John
Morel, E. D. 2
Montagu-Chelmsford reforms (1919) 63, 64, 66
Morley-Minto reforms (1909) 63, 103
Murray, Gilbert 8, 80, 91, 103

Natal
  Natal Act (1897) 161
  and naturalization policy 162
  Zulu Rebellion 102

national efficiency 6, 14, 99, 178–9, 208
  see also White, Arnold
naturalization 209
Naturalization Act (1870, Britain) 20, 159
  in dependent territories 165–6
  proposed common imperial policy on 162–3
Navy League 5
Nelson, Tommy 79, 81
'new imperialism' 82, 94
New South Wales 159
New Zealand
  immigration policy of 161
  need for labour 187
  see also Sedgwick, Thomas

Oliver, F. S. 46, 53, 153
Over-Seas Club 194–5

Pankhurst, Emily 130
Parkes, Henry 168
Parkin, George R. 45, 126
Pollock, Sir Frederick 96, 154

Queensland 159, 167

race
  concept of 8–9, 149–50
  and culture 50–1
  and immigration legislation 164–9
  see also Curtis, Lionel; Buchan, John; Jebb, Richard; White, Arnold; Immigration
Raju, J. B. 56–7, 62
Ralegh Club 56–7, 153
Ranjitsinhji, Kumar Shri 19
Representation of the People Act (1918) 212
republican ideas of citizenship 15–18
Rhodes, Cecil 40, 82, 87, 89
Round Table 46–50, 57–8, 89, 151
Royal Colonial Institute 5, 20–2, 152
  and imperial immigration 181

INDEX

Royal Society of St. George 116, 129

Sargant, E. B. 21
Scott, Sir Walter 80
Sedgwick, Thomas 25, 27, 133, 135, 209, 210
  ambivalent relationship with imperial Government 194
  imperial immigration, views on 181, 199
  New Zealand immigration scheme 187–90, 191
  Ontario immigration scheme 190–2
  and 'practical imperialism' 178
  role as imperial publicist 190, 197
  and 'sentimental citizenship' 196–8, 214
  social imperialism of 185–6, 199
  subscribes to Over-Seas Club 194
  see also Over-Seas Club
  upbringing 184–5
Selborne, Beatrix Maud Cecil, Lady 48, 152, 193
Selborne Memorandum (1907) 43
Shaw, George Bernard 4
Siam
  example of subjecthood and extraterritoriality 165
Sifton, Clifford 134, 184
Smith, Goldwin 24
Smuts, Jan Christian 50, 105
South Africa
  Chinese labour in 97–8, 101, 149
  immigration policy of 161
  South Africa House 214
  see also Curtis, Lionel; Buchan, John
South African War (1899–1902) 6, 45, 87, 165

Stead, W. T. 117, 118
Strachey, St Loe 81, 86, 98
subjecthood, concept of 18, 19–22, 156, 161, 206
  see also citizenship, concept of

tariff reform 6, 98, 151–2, 155
Tariff Reform League 5
Tilly, Charles 15–16, 206, 212
Trevelyan, G. M. 104
trusteeship 102–3

Wakefield, Edward Gibbon 179
Walton, F. P. 22–3
Ward, Sir Joseph 40, 49, 162
Ware, Fabian 151
women's suffrage 96
White, Arnold 25–6, 193, 208, 210
  anti-Semitism of 127–8, 136
  and assisted emigration 133–5
  Efficiency and Empire 117, 124, 131
  and eugenics 122–3
  and First World War 129, 136–8
  and immigration law 138
  influence of American history on 125–6
  minorities, views on 127–9, 133
  and national efficiency 119–25
  and the navy 117, 118
  political leadership, ideas on 123–4
  race, views on 122–3
  relationship between individual and the state, views on 129–32
  women's suffrage, views on 124
Wilhelm II, Kaiser 136
Wrench, John Evelyn 195
Wrong, George 156

Lightning Source UK Ltd.
Milton Keynes UK
23 September 2010

160290UK00001B/21/P

9 780719 082146